FOUNDATIONS
OF
CHRISTIANITY

FOUNDATIONS
OF
CHRISTIANITY

A Study in Christian Origins

KARL KAUTSKY

Authorized Translation from the
Thirteenth German Edition

Monthly Review Press
New York

Originally published by International Publishers Co., Inc.
copyright © 1925 by International Publishers Co., Inc.

Library of Congress Catalog Card Number: 72-81774

ISBN: 0-85345-262-8

Monthly Review Press
155 West 23rd Street
New York, N.Y. 10011

Manufactured in the United States of America

10 9 8 7 6 5 4 3

CONTENTS

CONTENTS

PART THREE

THE JEWS

PART FOUR

THE BEGINNINGS OF CHRISTIANITY

INTRODUCTION

I HAVE long been interested in Christianity and Biblical criticism. Fully twenty-five years ago I contributed an article to *Kosmos*, on the origin of prehistoric bible history, and two years later I wrote another for the *Neue Zeit* on the origin of Christianity. It is therefore an old hobby to which I am now returning. The occasion for this return was the necessity of preparing the second edition of my *Forerunners of Socialism*.

The criticisms of the latter book—those that I had the opportunity to read—had found fault particularly with the Introduction, in which I had given a short outline of the communism of primitive Christianity. It was declared that my view was one that would not bear the light of the knowledge resulting from the latest investigations.

Soon after these criticisms appeared, Göhre and others proclaimed that this view—namely, that nothing definite could be said about the personality of Jesus, and that Christianity could be explained without reference to this personality—first advocated by Bruno Bauer and later accepted in its essential points by Franz Mehring and myself, and formulated by me as early as 1885, was now out of date.

I therefore did not wish to publish a new edition of my book, which had appeared thirteen years before, without first carefully revising, on the basis of the latest literature on the subject, the notions of Christianity which I had obtained from earlier studies.

As a result I came to the gratifying conclusion that nothing needed to be changed, but the later investigations did open up to me a multitude of new points of view and new suggestions, which expanded the revision of my Introduction to the *Forerunners* into a whole book.

Of course, I make no claim that I am exhausting the subject, which is far too gigantic to be exhausted. I shall be satisfied if

I have succeeded in contributing to an understanding of those phases of Christianity which strike me as the most essential from the standpoint of the materialistic conception of history.

Nor can I venture to compare myself in learning, as to matters of religious history, with the theologians who have made this study their life task, whereas I have had to write the present volume in the few hours of leisure that my editorial and political activities have allowed me, in a period when the present moment was quite sufficient to monopolize the attention of any person participating in the class struggles of our times, to such an extent that little time was available for the past: I am referring to the time between the opening of the Russian Revolution of 1905 and the outbreak of the Turkish Revolution of 1908.

But possibly my intensive share in the class struggles of the proletariat has afforded me precisely such glimpses of the essence of primitive Christianity as may remain inaccessible to the professors of Theology and Religious History.

Jean Jacques Rousseau has the following passage in his *Julie, ou la Nouvelle Héloise*:

"It seems ridiculous to me to attempt to study society (*le monde*) as a mere observer. He who wishes only to observe will observe nothing, for as he is useless in actual work and a nuisance in recreations, he is admitted to neither. We observe the actions of others only to the extent to which we ourselves act. In the school of the World as in that of Love, we must begin with the practical exercise of that which we wish to learn." (Part II, Letter 17.)

This principle, here limited to the study of man, may be extended to apply to the investigation of all things. Nowhere will much be gained by mere observation without practical participation. This is true even of the investigation of such remote objects as the stars. Where would astronomy be today if it should be limited to mere observation, if it should not be combined with practice, with the use of the telescope, spectral analysis, photography! But this principle holds true even more when applied to the things of this earth, with which our practice has a habit of forcing us into a much closer contact than that of mere observation. What we learn from the mere observation of things is mighty little when compared with that which our practical work on these things and with these things gives us. Let the reader merely recall the immense importance which the experimental method has attained in the natural sciences.

Experiments cannot be made, as a means of investigating human society, but the practical activity of the investigator is nevertheless by no means of secondary importance; however, the conditions for his success are similar to the conditions for a fruitful experiment. These conditions are a knowledge of the most important results obtained by other investigators, and a familiarity with a scientific method that will sharpen the appreciation for the essential point of each phenomenon, enabling the investigator to distinguish the essential from the non-essential, and revealing the common element in varying experiences.

The thinker equipped with these faculties, and studying a field in which he is engaged in active work, will have no trouble in arriving at conclusions to which he would have had no access had he remained a mere observer.

This holds true particularly of history. A practical politician, if equipped with sufficient scientific training, will more easily understand the history of politics, and more swiftly find his bearings in its study than a closet-philosopher who has never had the slightest practical acquaintance with the motive forces of politics. And the investigator will find his practical experience to be of particular value, if he is engaged in studying a movement of the class of society in which he himself has been active, and with whose peculiar character he is therefore best acquainted.

This familiarity with the facts was hitherto almost exclusively within the reach of the possessing classes, who monopolized learning. The movements of the lower classes of society have as yet found few appreciative students.

Christianity in its beginnings was without doubt a movement of impoverished classes of the most varied kinds, which may be named by the common term "proletarians", provided this expression be understood as meaning not only wage-workers. A man who has become familiar with the modern proletarian movement,

and who understands the common element of its phases in the
various countries by having worked actively in it; a man who has
learnt to live in the feelings and aspirations of the proletariat,
fighting by their side, may lay claim to an ability to understand
many things about the beginnings of Christianity more easily
than scholars who have always viewed the proletariat only from
afar.

But while the scientifically trained practical politician has the
advantage of the mere book scholar in many ways in writing
his history, this advantage is often effectively counterbalanced
by the stronger temptation to which the practical politician is
exposed, to permit his detachment to be disturbed. Two dangers
particularly threaten the historical productions of practical politicians more than those of other investigators: in the first place,
they may attempt to mold the past entirely after the image of
the present, and, in the second place, they may seek to behold
the past in the light of the needs of their present-day policy.

But we Socialists, in so far as we are Marxists, feel that we
have an excellent protection against these dangers in the materialistic conception of history, so intimately connected with our
proletarian point of view.

The traditional conception of history views political movements
only as the struggle to bring about certain specific political institutions—Monarchy, Aristocracy, Democracy, etc.—which in turn
are represented as the result of specific ethical concepts and
aspirations. But if our conception of history does not advance
beyond this point, if we do not seek the basis of these ideas,
aspirations and institutions, we are soon brought up against the
fact that in the course of the centuries these things suffer only
superficial changes, remaining the same at bottom; that we are
always dealing with the same ideas, aspirations, and institutions,
recurring again and again; that all of history is one long uninterrupted struggle for liberty and equality, which meets again and
again with oppression and inequality, which never is realized, but
is never completely destroyed.

Wherever the champions of liberty and equality have for a
moment been victorious, they have always transformed their vic-

tory into a basis for new oppression and inequality, resulting in the immediate rise of new combatants for liberty and equality. The whole course of history therefore appears as a cycle always returning to its initial point, an eternal repetition of the same drama, with only the costumes changed, and with no real advancement for humanity.

He who holds this view will always be inclined to depict the past in the image of the present, and the more he knows man as he is now, the more he will attempt to depict man in previous ages according to his present model. Opposed to this view of history is another, which does not content itself with a consideration of historical ideas, but seeks to run down their causes, lying at the very basis of society. In applying this method, we again and again encounter the mode of production, which in turn is always dependent on the level of technical progress, although not on that alone.

As soon as we undertake an investigation of the technical resources and the mode of production of antiquity, we at once lose the notion that the same tragicomedy is eternally repeating itself on the world stage. The economic history of man shows a continuous evolution from lower to higher forms, which is, however, by no means uninterrupted or uniform in direction. But once we have investigated the economic conditions of human beings in the various historical periods, we are freed at once from the illusion of an eternal recurrence of the same ideas, aspirations, and political institutions. We now learn that the same words may in the course of centuries alter their meanings, that ideas and institutions resembling each other externally have a different content, having arisen from the needs of different classes and under different circumstances. The freedom which the modern proletarian demands is quite different from that which was the aspiration of the representatives of the Third Estate in 1789, and this freedom in its turn was fundamentally different from that which the Knighthood of the German Empire struggled for at the beginning of the Reformation.

Once we have ceased to regard political struggles as mere conflicts concerning abstract ideas or political institutions, and have revealed their economic basis, we are ready to understand that in this field, as well as in that of technology and the mode of production, a constant evolution toward new forms is going on, that no epoch completely resembles any other epoch, that the same slogans and the same arguments may at various times have very different meanings.

Our proletarian point of view will permit us to grasp more easily than bourgeois investigators those phases of primitive Christianity which it has in common with the modern proletarian movement. But the emphasis placed upon economic conditions, which is a necessary corollary of the materialistic conception of history, preserves us from the danger of forgetting the peculiar character of the ancient proletariat merely because we grasp the common element in both epochs. The characteristics of the ancient proletariat were due to its peculiar economic position, which, in spite of many resemblances, nevertheless made its aspirations entirely different from those of the modern proletariat.

While the Marxist view of history guards us from the danger of measuring the past with the standard of the present and sharpens our appreciation of the peculiarity of each epoch and each nation, it also frees us from the other danger, that of attempting to adapt our presentation of the past to the immediate practical interest we are defending in the present.

Surely no honest man, whatever may be his point of view, will permit himself to be misled into a conscious forgery of the past. But nowhere is the investigator so much in need of an unprejudiced mind as in the social sciences, and in no field is it harder to attain such a standpoint.

For the task of science is not simply a presentation of that which *is*, giving a faithful photograph of reality, so that any normally constituted observer will form the same image. The task of science consists in observing the general, essential element in the mass of impressions and phenomena received, and thus providing a clue by means of which we can find our bearings in the labyrinth of reality.

The task of art, moreover, is quite similar. Art also does not merely give us a photograph of reality; the artist must reproduce that which strikes him as the essential point, the characteristic fact of the reality he sets out to depict. The difference between art and science is in the fact that the artist represents the essential in a physical and tangible form, through which he impresses us, while the thinker represents the essential in the form of a conception, an abstraction.

The more complicated a phenomenon and the smaller the number of phenomena with which it may be compared, the more difficult is it to segregate that which is essential in it from that which is accidental. The more will the subjective characteristic of the investigator and reproducer make itself felt. All the more indispensable is it therefore that his glance be clear and unprejudiced.

There is probably no more complicated phenomenon than human society, the society of humans, each one of whom in himself is more complicated than any other creature that we know. In addition, the number of social organisms that may be compared with each other, on the same level of development, is relatively quite small. It is not a marvel, therefore, that the scientific study of society should have begun later than that of any other sphere of experience; nor is it a marvel that just in this field the views of students should be so widely divergent.

These difficulties are furthermore magnified if the various investigators, as is so frequently the case in the social sciences, have practical interests of very different, often opposed tendencies, in the results of their investigations, which does not mean that these practical interests must be merely personal in their nature; they may be very definitely class interests.

It is manifestly quite impossible to preserve a judicial attitude toward the past while one is interested in any way in the social oppositions and struggles of one's own time, beholding in these present-day phenomena a repetition of the oppositions and struggles of the past. The latter become mere precedents, involving a justification and condemnation of the former, for now the present depends on our judgment of the past. What man who is really interested in his cause could remain fair-minded? The more he is attached to the cause, the more important do those facts of the past become to him—and he will emphasize them as essential —which seem to support his own view, while he relegates to the background those facts that seem to support the opposite view. The student becomes a moralist or an advocate, glorifying or branding specific phenomena of the past because he is an advocate or a foe of similar phenomena of the present, such as the Church, the Monarchy, Democracy, etc.

The case becomes quite different, however, when the student recognizes, as a result of his economic understanding, that there are no mere repetitions in history, that the economic conditions of the past are gone never to return, that the former class oppositions and class struggles are essentially different from those of the present day, and that therefore our modern institutions and ideas, in spite of all their external identity with those of the past, are nevertheless of entirely different content. The student now understands that each epoch must be measured by its own standard, that the aspirations of the present day must be based on present-day conditions, that successes and failures in the past have very little meaning when considered alone, and that a mere invocation of the past in order to justify present-day demands may be downright misleading. The democrats and the proletarians of France found this out time and time again in the last century when they placed their faith more in the "teachings" of the French Revolution than in an understanding of actually existing class relations.

He who accepts the standpoint of the economic conception of history can adopt a completely unprejudiced view of the past, even though he be actively involved in the practical struggles of the present. His work can only sharpen his glance for many phenomena of the past, not render it dim.

Such was the purpose of my presentation of the bases of primitive Christianity. I had no intention of either glorifying or belittling it, merely the desire to understand it. I knew that no matter what results I might arrive at, the cause in which I struggle

could not suffer thereby. In whatever light the proletarians of
the Imperial Era might appear to me, whatever their aspirations,
and the results of those aspirations, there is no doubt they were
completely different from the modern proletariat, struggling and
working in an entirely different situation and with entirely different resources. Whatever the great accomplishments and successes, the petty defects and defeats, of the ancient proletarians,
they could mean nothing in forming an estimate of the nature and
the prospects of the modern proletariat, either from a favorable
or an unfavorable standpoint.

But, this being the case, is there any practical purpose at all
in occupying oneself with history? The common view regards
history as a chart for him who navigates the sea of political
activity; this chart must indicate the cliffs and shallows on which
previous mariners have come to grief, and enable their successors
to sail the seas with impunity. However, if the navigable channels of history are constantly changing, the shallows shifting, and
forming again in other spots, and if every pilot must pick his way
by making new soundings for his own navigation of the channels;
if a mere following of the old chart only too often leads us astray,
wherefore study history at all, except perhaps as a pet hobby?

The reader who makes this assumption is indeed throwing away
the wheat with the chaff.

If we would retain the above figure of speech, we must admit
that history as a permanent chart for the pilot of a ship of state
is indeed of no use; but this does not mean that it has no other
use for him; the utility he will draw from it is of a different
nature. He must use history as a sounding line, as a means of
studying the channels in which he is navigating, of understanding
them and his position in them. The sole way to understand a
phenomenon is to learn how it arose. I cannot understand
present-day society unless I know the manner in which it has
come to be, how its various phenomena: Capitalism, Feudalism,
Christianity, Judaism, etc., have developed.

If I would have a clear idea of the social function, the tasks
and the prospects of the class to which I belong or to which I
have attached myself, I must gain an understanding of the exist-

ing social organism, I must learn to grasp it from every angle, which is an utter impossibility unless I have traced its growth. It is impossible to be a conscious and far-sighted warrior in the class struggle without an understanding of the evolution of society. Without such understanding one remains dependent on the impressions of one's immediate surroundings and of the immediate moment, and one is never certain that these impressions will not tempt one into channels that apparently lead to the goal, but actually bring one among cliffs from which there is no escape.

To be sure many class struggles have succeeded in spite of the fact that the participants have had no clear conception of the essential nature of the society in which they lived. The conditions for such a successful struggle are vanishing in present-day society, just as it is becoming increasingly absurd in this society to permit oneself to be led in one's choice of food and drink by instinct and tradition merely. These guides were perhaps sufficient under simple, natural conditions. The more artificial our conditions of life become, owing to the advance of industry and of the natural sciences, the more they depart from nature, the more necessary for the individual is the scientific knowledge required for choosing, from among the superabundance of artificial products which are available, those that are most suitable for his organism. While men drank water only, it was sufficient to have an instinct leading them to seek good spring water and avoid stagnant swamp water. But this instinct is helpless in the presence of our manufactured beverages; scientific understanding now becomes an absolute necessity.

Very similar is the case in politics and in social activity in general. In the communities of antiquity, often very small, with their simple and transparent conditions, remaining changeless for centuries, tradition and "plain common sense"—in other words, the good judgment which the individual had gained from personal experience—were sufficient to show him his place and his functions in society. But today, in a society whose market embraces the entire world, which is in process of constant transformation, of industrial and social revolution, in which the workers are organizing themselves into an army of millions, and the capitalists are accumulating billions in money, it is impossible for a rising class, a class that cannot content itself with the retention of the *status quo*, which is obliged to aim at a complete reconstruction of society, to conduct its class struggle intelligently and successfully by a mere resort to "plain common sense" and to the detail work of practical men. It becomes a necessity for every combatant to broaden his horizon through scientific understanding, to grasp the operation of great social forces in time and space, not in order to abolish the work in detail, or even relegate it to the background, but in order to align it in a definite relation with the social process as a whole. This becomes all the more necessary since this society, now practically embracing the entire globe, is pushing further and further its division of labor, limiting the individual more and more to a single specialty, to a single operation, and thus tending to progressively lower his mental standard, to make him more dependent and less capable of understanding the process as a whole, which simultaneously is expanded into gigantic proportions.

It then becomes the duty of every man who has made the advancement of the proletariat his life work, to oppose this tendency toward spiritual stagnation and stupidity, and to direct the attention of proletarians to great points of view, to large prospects, to worthy goals.

There is hardly any way of doing this more effectively than by a study of history, by viewing and grasping the evolution of society over great periods of time, particularly when this evolution has embraced immense social movements whose operation continues down to the present day.

To give the proletariat a social understanding, a self-consciousness and a political maturity, to make it capable of forming large mental visions, for this purpose we must study the historical process, with the aid of the materialistic conception of history. Under these circumstances the study of the past, far from being a mere antiquarian hobby, becomes a mighty weapon in the struggle of the present, with the purpose of achieving a better future.

K. KAUTSKY

Berlin, September, 1908.

Part One
THE PERSONALITY OF JESUS

I. THE PAGAN SOURCES

WHATEVER may be our attitude toward Christianity, we must recognize it as one of the most gigantic phenomena in human history as known to us. We cannot regard without intense admiration the Christian Church, which has lasted for nearly twenty centuries, and which we behold still full of strength, in many countries stronger even than the State. Everything, therefore, which can contribute to an understanding of this imposing phenomenon becomes an extremely important present concern of great practical significance; such is our attitude toward the study of the origin of this organization, which will take us back thousands of years in history.

The present strength of Christianity leads us to regard the study of its beginnings with far greater interest than any other historical investigation, even though it take us back only two centuries; [1] but it also makes the investigation of these beginnings more difficult than they would otherwise have been.

The Christian Church has become an organization of domination, either in the interest of its own dignitaries, or the dignitaries of another organization, the State, where the latter has succeeded in getting control of the Church. He who would fight these powers must also fight the Church. The struggle *for* the Church, as well as the struggle *against* the Church, has therefore become a *party cause,* with which the most important economic interests are bound up. Of course, this condition is only too likely to obscure the objective pursuit of an historical study of the Church, and for a long time it has caused the ruling classes to forbid any investigations of the beginnings of Christianity at all, to attribute a divine character to the Church, standing above and beyond all human criticism.

The bourgeois "enlightenment" of the Eighteenth Century

[1] Obviously a reference to the foundation of the Prussian Kingdom in 1701.—TRANSLATOR.

21

finally succeeded in disposing of this divine halo once for all. Not until then was the scientific investigation of the origin of Christianity possible. But strange to say, lay science kept aloof from this field even in the Nineteenth Century, seemed to regard it as still exclusively belonging to the realm of theology, and as no concern of science at all. A great number of historical works, written by the most important bourgeois historians of the Nineteenth Century, and treating of the Roman Imperial Period, timidly steer clear of the most important phenomenon of this epoch, namely, the rise of Christianity. Thus Mommsen, in the fifth volume of his *Roman History,* has a detailed study of the history of the Jews under the Caesars, and is unable to evade some occasional mention of Christianity in this section, but Christianity appears in his work as an accomplished fact, the knowledge of whose existence is presupposed. On the whole, only theologians and their opponents, the freethinking propagandists, have hitherto shown any interest in the beginnings of Christianity.

But it is not necessarily cowardice which has deterred bourgeois historians, in so far as they were producing only history and not also controversial literature, from occupying themselves with the origin of Christianity. Sufficient reason for not going into this question was perhaps the unfortunate meagerness of the sources from which we must draw our knowledge of this subject.

Christianity according to the traditional view is the creation of a single man, Jesus Christ, and this view is by no means entirely superseded. To be sure, at least in "enlightened", "cultured" circles Jesus is no longer considered a God, but he is still regarded as an extraordinary personage, who set out to found a new religion and succeeded in this effort to the remarkable degree that is so generally apparent. This view is held not only by enlightened theologians, but also by radical freethinkers, the latter distinguishing themselves from the theologians only by the criticism which they make of the personality of Jesus, from which they attempt to subtract so far as possible everything that is noble.

However, even before the end of the Eighteenth Century, the English historian Gibbon, in his *History of the Decline and Fall of the Roman Empire* (written from 1774 to 1788), pointed out with delicate irony the striking fact that not one of the contemporaries of Jesus had reported anything about him, in spite of the fact that he was alleged to have performed such marvelous deeds.

"But how shall we excuse the supine inattention of the pagan and philosophic world to those evidences which were presented by the hand of Omnipotence, not to their reason, but to their senses? During the age of Christ, of his apostles, and of their first disciples, the doctrine which they preached was confirmed by innumerable prodigies. The lame walked, the blind saw, the sick were healed, the dead were raised, demons were expelled, and the laws of Nature were frequently suspended for the benefit of the church. But the sages of Greece and Rome turned aside from the awful spectacle, and, pursuing the ordinary occupations of life and study, appeared unconscious of any alteration in the moral or physical government of the world."

According to the Christian tradition, the whole earth, or at least all Palestine, was covered with darkness for three hours after the death of Jesus. This took place within the life of the elder Pliny, who has a special chapter in his *Natural History* on the subject of eclipses; but he says nothing of this eclipse (Gibbon, Chapter xv *Decline and Fall*, London, 1895; vol. ii, pp. 69-70).

But even if we disregard the miracles, it is hard to understand that a character like the Jesus of the Gospels, who, according to report, aroused such commotion in men's minds, could carry on his agitation and finally die as a martyr to his cause without having his pagan and Hebrew contemporaries devote even so much as a word to him.

The first mention of Jesus by a non-Christian is found in the *Jewish Antiquities* of Josephus Flavius. The Third Chapter of the Eighteenth Book, which treats of the Procurator Pontius Pilate, says, among other things:

"About this time there lived Jesus, a wise man, if he may be named a man, for he achieved miracles and was a teacher of men, who gladly accepted his truth, and found many adherents among

Jews and Hellenes. This man was the Christ. Although Pilate
then had him crucified on the accusation of the most excellent
men of our people, those who had first loved him remained faithful to him nevertheless. For on the third day he appeared to
them again, arisen to a new life, as God's prophets had prophesied
this and thousands of other miraculous things of him. From him
the Christians take their name; their sect (φῦλον) has since
then not ceased."

Josephus again speaks of Christ in the Twentieth Book, Ninth
Chapter, 1, saying that the High Priest Ananus, under the rule
of the Governor Albinus (in the time of Nero), had succeeded in
having "James, the brother of Jesus, the so-called Christ (τοῦ
λεγομένου χριστοῦ), haled to court, together with a number of
others, indicted as transgressors of the law, and stoned."

These evidences have always been much esteemed by Christians, for they are the word of a non-Christian, of a Jew and
Pharisee, who was born in the year 37 A.D., and who lived in
Jerusalem, and who therefore might very well have had authentic
information concerning Jesus. Furthermore, his testimony is the
more important, since, being a Jew, he had no cause to color the
facts in favor of the Christians.

But precisely this excessive laudation of Christ by the pious
Jew made this passage in his work seem suspicious even to early
students. Its authenticity was already questioned in the Sixteenth
Century, and it is now certain that it is a forgery and not written
by Josephus at all.[2]

It was added in the course of the Third Century by a Christian
copyist, who evidently was offended at Josephus' failure to give
any information concerning the person of Jesus, while he repeats
the most childish gossip from Palestine. The pious Christian
rightly felt that the absence of any such mention was equivalent
to a denial of the existence, or at least of the importance of his
Savior, and the exposure of his interpolation has practically become an evidence against Jesus.

But the passage concerning James is also of very dubious na-

[2] Compare, among others, Schürer, *Geschichte des jüdischen Volkes im Zeit-
alter Jesu Christi*, vol. i. Third Edition, 1901, p. 544 ff.

ture. It is true that Origen, who lived from 185 to 254 A.D., mentions, in his commentary on Matthew, a passage in Josephus concerning James. He remarks in this connection that it is peculiar that Josephus nevertheless did not believe in Jesus as the Christ. He again quotes this statement of Josephus on James in his polemic against Celsus, and again points out Josephus' skepticism. These words of Origen are one of the evidences showing that Josephus in the original form did not have the passage concerning Jesus in which he recognizes the latter as the Christ, the Messiah. It now appears that the passage concerning James, which Origen found in Josephus, is also a Christian interpolation, for this passage as quoted by Origen is entirely different from that contained in the manuscripts of Josephus that have been handed down. Origen's quotation represents the destruction of Jerusalem as a punishment for the execution of James. This interpolation did not pass into the other manuscripts of Josephus, and has therefore not been preserved. But the passage that has been handed down in our manuscripts of Josephus, on the other hand, is not quoted by Origen, while he thrice mentions the others in various connections. And this in spite of the fact that he had carefully quoted all the evidences in Josephus which were likely to favor the Christian faith. It is therefore reasonable to assume that the passage in Josephus that has been handed down to us is also a forgery, and that it was interpolated by some pious Christian, to the greater glory of God, after the time of Origen, but before that of Eusebius, who quotes it.

Not only the mention of Jesus and James in Josephus, but also that of John the Baptist (*Antiquities,* xviii, Chapter v, 2) is under suspicion as an interpolation.[3]

We therefore find Christian interpolations in Josephus at every step, from the very beginning of the Second Century. His silence concerning the principal personages of the Gospels was simply too striking, and had to be altered.

But even if the statement concerning James were genuine, it would at most show that there was a Jesus who was called the Christ, *i.e.,* the Messiah. It could not possibly prove more than

[3] Schürer, *op. cit.,* pp. 438, 548, 581.

that. "But even if the passage were admitted to be genuine, it would be no stronger than a spider's line, on which critical theology would find it hard to suspend a human form. There were so many pseudo-Christs in the time of Josephus, and far into the Second Century, that we have no more than a summary mention of them. There was a Judas of Galilee, a Theudas, an unnamed Egyptian, a Samaritan, and a Bar Kochba. There may very well have been a Jesus among them. Jesus was a very familiar name among the Jews—Joschua, Josua, the Savior." [4]

The second passage in Josephus informs us at most that among the agitators then operating in Palestine as Messiahs, as the Lord's anointed, there was one called Jesus. The passage tells us absolutely nothing concerning his life and work.

The next mention of Jesus in a non-Christian writer is to be found in the *Annals* of the Roman historian, Tacitus, which were composed about the year 100 A.D. In the Fifteenth Book, the burning of Rome under Nero is described, and we read in Chapter xliv:

"In order to counteract the report (which laid the blame for this conflagration on Nero) he accused persons who were called *Christians* by the people, and who were hated for their misdeeds, of the guilt, and visited the most excruciating penalties upon them. He from whom they had taken their name, Christ, had been executed in the reign of Tiberius by the Procurator Pontius Pilate; but though this superstition was thus for a moment put down, it arose again not only in Judea, the original home of this plague (*mali*), but even in Rome itself, in which city every outrage and every shame (*atrocia aut pudenda*) finds a home and wide dissemination. First a few were seized who confessed, and then on their denunciation a great number of others, who were not, however, accused of the crime of incendiarism, but of that of hating humanity. Their execution was made a public amusement; they were covered with the skins of wild beasts and then torn by dogs or crucified, or prepared for the pyre, and then

---

[4] Albert Kalthoff, *The Rise of Christianity*, translated by Joseph McCabe, London, 1907, pp. 20, 21.

burned as soon as night came, to illuminate the city. For this spectacle Nero lent his gardens, and he even arranged circus games in which he mingled with the people in the costume of a charioteer, or mounted a racing chariot. Although these men were criminals deserving of the severest punishment, there was some public sympathy for them, as it seemed they were being sacrificed not to the general weal, but to the cruelty of a single man."

This testimony surely is not a forgery made by Christians in favor of Christians. To be sure, its truthfulness has been attacked, as Dio Cassius knows nothing of a persecution of the Christians under Nero. However, Dio Cassius lived a century later than Tacitus. Suetonius, who wrote not long after Tacitus, reports in his biography a persecution of Christians, "people who have embraced a new and evil superstition." (Chapter xvi.)

But of Jesus, Suetonius tells us nothing at all, and Tacitus does not even hand down his name. Christ, the Greek word for "the anointed", is nothing more than the Greek translation of the Hebrew word "Messiah". Concerning Christ's activities and the content of his teachings Tacitus has nothing to say.

And that is all that non-Christian sources in the First Century of our era tell us about Jesus.

II. THE CHRISTIAN SOURCES

But do not the Christian sources flow all the more plentifully? Have we not in the Gospels the most minute narrations of the teaching and influence of Jesus?

There is no doubt that they are minute. But their plausibility is quite a different matter. The example of the forgery in Josephus has already made us acquainted with a characteristic trait of the earlier Christian writing of history, namely, its complete indifference to truth. These writers were concerned not with the truth, but with making their point, and they were not at all delicate in the choice of their means.

To be quite just, we must admit that in this respect they were not different from their times. The Jewish religious literature was in no way better, and the "pagan" mystical movements preceding and following the opening of the Christian era were guilty of the same offense. The gullibility of the public, the desire to create an effect, as well as a lack of confidence in their own abilities, the need of clinging to superhuman authorities, the lack of a sense of reality, qualities whose causes we shall examine later, were then vitiating the whole body of literature, especially where it departed from traditional lines. We shall find many proofs of this in Christian and Jewish literature. But the fact is that the mystical philosophers also were inclined in this direction—to be sure, they were closely related with Christianity—as shown, for example, by the Neo-Pythagoreans, a sect which arose in the century preceding the birth of Christ. Their doctrine, a mixture of Platonism and Stoicism, rich in the faith in revelations, hungry for miracles, pretended to be the teaching of the ancient philosopher Pythagoras, who lived in the Sixth Century B.C., and of whom very little was known. It thus became all the easier to attribute everything to him that needed the authority of a great name.

"The Neo-Pythagoreans wished to be considered as true pupils of the ancient Samite philosopher: to make it possible for them to represent their teachings as genuinely Pythagorean, they undertook those countless literary misrepresentations which without hesitation attributed everything, regardless of its newness, or of how well known its Platonic or Aristotelean origin might be, to Pythagoras or to Archytas." [5]

Quite similar is the case with primitive Christian literature, which therefore is in a state of confusion that has required the diligent work of some of the most brilliant minds of the past century for its tidying up, without the achievement of any very remarkable results.

Let us point out in a single case how great is the confusion resulting from the mingling of the most varied conceptions of the origin of primitive Christian writings. The case in point is the Revelation of Saint John, a particularly hard nut to crack. Pfleiderer has the following to say on this subject in his book *Primitive Christianity, Its Writings and Teachings:*

"The Book of Daniel was the earliest of these apocalypses, and set the pattern for the whole series. When a key to the interpretation of the visions of Daniel had been sought in the events of the Jewish war in the time of Antiochus Epiphanes, it was rightly assumed that the Johannine Apocalypse was to be explained from the circumstances of its own time. Accordingly, when the mystical number 666 in Chapter xiii, verse 18, was interpreted almost simultaneously by several scholars (Benary, Hitzig, and Reuss) from the numerical value of the Hebrew letters, as meaning the Emperor Nero, the conclusion was drawn from a comparison of Chapters xiii and xvii that the Apocalypse originated soon after the death of Nero in the year 68. This long remained the prevailing view, especially in the earlier Tübingen School, which, on the presupposition, to which it still held firmly, of the composition of the book by the Apostle John, supposed that the key to the whole book was to be found in the party-conflict between Judaisers and adherents of Paul—an interpretation which could not be carried through in detail without

[5] Zeller, *Philosophie der Griechen,* Part iii, Sec. ii, Leipzig, 1868, p. 96.

great arbitrariness (especially conspicuous in Volkmar). A
new impulse towards the more thorough investigation of the problem was given in 1882 by a pupil of Weizsäcker, Daniel Völter,
who formulated the hypothesis of a repeated revision and extension of a primary document by various authors between 66 and
170 (fixing, later, 140 as the lower limit). The method of documentary criticism here applied underwent in the next fifteen years
the most manifold variations. Vischer assumed a Jewish document as the basis, which had been worked over by a Christian
editor; Sabatier and Schön, on the other hand, assumed an original Christian document into which Jewish materials had been interpolated; Weyland distinguished two Jewish sources, dating
from the times of Nero and Titus, and a Christian editor of the
time of Trajan; Spitta distinguished a Christian primary document of the year 60 A.D., two Jewish sources of 63 B.C. and
40 A.D., and a Christian redactor of the time of Trajan; Schmidt,
three Jewish sources and two Christian redactors; Völter (in a
second work in 1893), an original apocalypse of the year 62, and
four revisions under Titus, Domitian, Trajan, and Hadrian. The
consequence of all these mutually opposed and more or less complicated hypotheses was, finally, that 'the uninitiated received the
impression that nothing is certain and nothing impossible in the
field of New Testament criticism' (Jülicher, *Introd.*, p. 287)." [6]

But Pfleiderer nevertheless believes that the "diligent investigations of the last two centuries" have yielded "a definite result",
yet he hardly dares state this in so many words, but says it
"seems" so to him. Reasonably sure conclusions as to primitive
Christian literature have almost without exception been attained
only in a negative way, in the ascertaining of that which is certainly forged.

It is certain that but a small minority of the primitive Christian writings really were written by the authors to whom they
are attributed, that for the most part they originated much later
than the dates commonly assigned, and that their original text
has in many cases been outrageously distorted by later revisions

---

[6] Pfleiderer, *Primitive Christianity, Its Writings and Teachings in Their
Historical Connections*, London and New York, 1906-1911, vol. iii, pp. 401, 402.

and additions. Finally, it is certain that none of the Gospels or other primitive Christian works was written by a contemporary of Jesus.

The so-called Gospel of Saint Mark is now considered the oldest of the Gospels; it surely was not written before the destruction of Jerusalem, which the author represents as prophesied by Jesus, and which, in other words, must already have been accomplished when the Gospel was written. It, therefore, was probably written not less than half a century after the time assigned as that of Jesus' death. What it has to tell is therefore the product of an evolution of legend during half a century.

After Mark comes Luke, then the so-called Matthew, and finally John, in the middle of the Second Century, and at least a century after the birth of Christ. The further we advance in time, the more miraculous do these Gospels become. To be sure, miracles already occur in Saint Mark, but they are quite innocent as compared with the later ones. Thus, in the case of the awakenings from the dead, Mark has Jesus summoned to the bedside of Jairus' daughter, who is at the point of death. All believe she is already dead, but Jesus says: "The damsel is not dead but sleepeth," and lays his hand upon her, and she arises (Mark, Chapter v).

In Luke, we have in addition the awakening to life of the youth of Nain. He has been dead long enough to be on his way to the cemetery when Jesus meets him; the latter causes him to arise from his bier (Luke, Chapter vii).

For Saint John, these items are not strong enough. In his Eleventh Chapter he records the awakening of Lazarus, who "has been dead four days", and "by this time stinketh". John thus beats the record.

But the Evangelists were extremely ignorant men, their ideas on many subjects concerning which they wrote being quite erroneous. Thus Luke has Joseph travel with Mary from Nazareth to Bethlehem on the occasion of a Roman imperial census, with the result that Jesus is born in Bethlehem. But no such census was taken under Augustus. Furthermore, Judea did not become a Roman Province until after the date assigned to the birth of

Christ. In the year 7 A.D. a census really was taken, but the census gatherers went to the habitations of the population. It was not at all necessary to go to Bethlehem.[7]

We shall have occasion to come back to this point. Furthermore, the court procedure at the trial of Jesus before Pontius Pilate is not in accordance with either Jewish or Roman law. Even in cases therefore, where the Evangelists are not relating miracles, they often present untrue and impossible situations.

And the concoction thus brewed into a "Gospel" suffered many more changes at the hands of later "editors" and copyists for the edification of the faithful.

For example, the best manuscripts of Mark end with Chapter xvi, verse 8, at the point where the women are looking for the dead Jesus in the tomb, but find in his place a youth in a long white garment; whereupon they left the tomb, and "were afraid".

Our traditional versions do not end at this point, but what follows was written much later. Yet, the work could not possibly have ended with verse 8 as above described. Renan already assumed that what had followed had been stricken out in the interest of the good cause, because it contained some material that might have conflicted with a later interpretation.

On the other hand, Pfleiderer and others, after an exhaustive investigation, arrive at the conclusion "that the gospel of Luke originally contained nothing of the supernatural origin of Jesus, but that this story arose later, and was interpolated into the text by the addition of verses 34 ff.[8] in Chapter i, and of the words 'as was supposed' in iii, 23." [9]

In view of the above, it is not a miracle that already in the early part of the Nineteenth Century the Gospels began to be considered by many scholars as completely useless as sources for the biography of Jesus, and Bruno Bauer even went to the point

[7] On this point, see David Strauss, *The Life of Christ, Critically Examined,* London, 1846, vol. i, pp. 200-208.

[8] Then said Mary unto the Angel, How shall this be since I know not a man? And the Angel answered and said unto her, The Holy Ghost shall come upon thee and the power of the Highest shall overshadow thee, etc.

[9] "Being (as was supposed) the son of Joseph." The passage from Pfleiderer is taken from his *Primitive Christianity,* London and New York, 1906-1911, vol. ii, p. 103.

of absolutely denying the historical reality of Jesus. It is natural that the theologians should nevertheless be unable to give up the Gospels, and that even the most liberal of them should make every effort to maintain their authority. What would be left of Christianity if the personality of Christ had to be relinquished? But in order to save the latter, they are obliged to resort to the most ingenious contortions and combinations.

Thus Harnack, in his lectures on the essentials of Christianity (1900), declared that David Friedrich Strauss may have thought that he was knocking the historical reliability of the Gospels into a cocked hat, but the historical and critical work of two generations had nevertheless succeeded in again setting up this reality to a great extent. To be sure, the Gospels are not historical works, not being written in order to present facts as they happened, but being intended as edifying documents. "Yet they are not useless as historical sources, especially since their purpose is not one that was imposed from without, but in many ways coincides with the intention of Jesus." (Page 14.)

But what can we know about the intentions of Jesus, aside from what the Gospels tell us! Harnack's whole reasoning in support of the plausibility of the Gospels as sources for the life of Jesus merely proves how impossible it is to present any sure and decisive evidence in this direction.

Later in his treatise, Harnack himself is forced to admit that everything reported by the Gospels concerning the first thirty years of Jesus' life is unhistorical, as well as all the incidents of later date which can be proved to be impossible or fabricated. But he would nevertheless like to preserve the remainder as a historical fact. He believes that we still retain "a vivid picture of the preaching of Jesus, of the termination of his life, and of the impression he made on his disciples". (Page 20.)

But how does Harnack know that the preaching of Jesus has been so faithfully rendered in the Gospels? Theologians are far more skeptical when they approach the subject of the reproduction of other sermons in those days. Thus we find Harnack's colleague, Pfleiderer, telling us in his book, *Primitive Christianity:*

"To argue about the historicity of this and other speeches in

Acts is really absurd. One need only consider all the conditions which would need to be fulfilled in order to render possible a verbally accurate, or even a generally correct, record of such a speech. It would need to have been immediately written down by someone who was present (indeed, to secure an exact record, it would need to have been taken down in shorthand), and these notes of the various speeches would need to have been preserved by the hearers, who were for the most part Jews or heathen, and were either hostile or indifferent towards what was said, for more than half a century, and finally collected by the historian from the most diverse localities! Anyone who has once made clear to himself all these impossibilities, will realize once for all how he is to look upon all these speeches, that, in fact, in Acts, just as in all secular historians of antiquity, the speeches are free compositions, in which the author makes his heroes speak as he thinks that they might have spoken in the circumstances of the moment." [10]

Quite right! But why should not all this reasoning also apply to the speeches of Jesus, which lay further behind (in time) the authors of the Gospels than the speeches in the Acts of the Apostles? Why should the speeches of Jesus in the Gospels be anything but speeches which the authors of these records wished that Jesus might have delivered? As a matter of fact, the speeches as handed down contain numerous contradictions, expressions that are at times rebellious, and at other times submissive, and which can be explained only by the fact that various tendencies were present among the Christians, each of which adapted the speeches of Christ, in its tradition, to its own needs. I shall give another example of the audacious manner in which the Evangelists proceeded in these matters. Compare the Sermon on the Mount as reported by Luke with the later record in Matthew. In Luke it is still a glorification of the poor, a condemnation of the rich. In the days of Matthew, many Christians no longer liked that kind of thing, and the Gospel of Saint Matthew, therefore, transforms the poor who shall be blessed into

---

[10] *Primitive Christianity*, London and New York, 1906-1911, vol. ii, pp. 234, 235.

those who are poor in spirit, while the condemnation of the rich is entirely omitted. If this was the manner of treating speeches which had already been set down, what reason have we to believe that the speeches Jesus is alleged to have delivered a half century before their recording are faithfully repeated in the Gospels! In the first place, it is absolutely impossible for mere oral tradition faithfully to preserve the wording of a speech that was not set down at once, over a period of fifty years after its delivery. Anyone who, in spite of this obvious fact, sets down speeches transmitted only by hearsay, indicates by this very act his readiness to write down anything that pleases him, or his extreme gullibility in believing at its face value everything he has been told.

On the other hand, it can be proved that many of Jesus' statements do not come from him, but were in circulation before his day.

For instance, the Lord's Prayer is considered as an original contribution by Jesus. But Pfleiderer points out that an Aramaic Kaddish prayer of great antiquity concludes with the words:

"Magnified and sanctified be His great name in the world which He has created after His will. May He erect his Kingdom in your lifetime and within the lifetime of the whole house of Israel." It is apparent that the first part of the Christian Lord's Prayer is an imitation.

But if we can place no faith in the speeches of Jesus, in the early history of his life, and surely not in his miracles, what is there left in the Gospels?

According to Harnack we still have the influence of Jesus upon his disciples, and the story of his Passion. But the Gospels were not composed by the disciples of Christ, they do not reflect the impression made by this *personality,* but rather the impression made by the *narration* of the personality of Christ on the members of the Christian sect. Even the most powerful impression can prove nothing concerning the historical correctness of this narration. Even a tale concerning a fictitious person may make the most profound impression upon a system of society, provided the historical conditions are suitable for the production of such an impression. How great was the impression made by Goethe's novel, *The Sorrows of Werther;* and yet, although everybody knew it was only a novel, Werther had many disciples and successors.

Among the Jews, particularly in the centuries immediately preceding and following the time of Christ, invented personages have often exercised a very great influence, whenever the deeds and teachings attributed to them corresponded to profound needs among the Jewish people. This is shown, for example, by the figure of the Prophet Daniel, of whom the Book of Daniel reports that he lived under Nebuchadnezzar, Darius and Cyrus, in other words, in the Sixth Century B.C., that he produced the greatest miracles, and uttered prophecies that later were fulfilled in an astonishing manner, the last of them being that great misfortunes would befall Judaism, from which it would be redeemed or saved by a redeemer, and again raised to its former prestige. This Daniel never lived; the book treating of him was not written until about the year 165, at the time of the Maccabean insurrection; it is therefore hardly a miracle that all the prophecies alleged to have been uttered by the prophet are correctly applicable to all events preceding the year 165, which convinced the pious reader that the final prophecy of such an infallible prophet must also be fulfilled without fail. The whole business is an audacious invention which nevertheless had the greatest possible effect; the belief in the Messiah, the belief in a redeemer that was to come, found its strongest support in this prophet; he became the model for all later prophecies of the Messiah. But the Book of Daniel also shows how unhesitatingly pious people would resort to humbug in those days whenever they were aiming at producing a strong effect. The effect produced by the figure of Jesus therefore is not a proof of its historical reality.

We therefore have nothing left of what Harnack himself thinks he has rescued as the true historical kernel, except the story of the Passion of Christ. Yet this story, too, is so interwoven with miracles from beginning to end, terminating in the Resurrection and Ascension, that it is almost impossible to discover the historical nucleus in the life of Jesus. We shall have further occasion to become acquainted with the reliability of the story of the Passion.

The case for the rest of primitive Christian literature is no better. Everything apparently written by the contemporaries of Jesus, for instance, by his disciples, has been recognized as a forgery at least in the sense that it is a product of a later age.

The Epistles also that are attributed to Saint Paul do not include a single one whose genuineness has not been disputed; a number have been generally recognized by historical criticism as not genuine. The most brazen of these forgeries is probably that of the Second Epistle to the Thessalonians. In this imitated letter the author who conceals himself under the name of Paul utters the following warning: "That ye be not soon shaken in mind, or be troubled, neither by spirit nor by word, nor by letters as from us" (ii, 2), (*a forged letter is meant*), and finally the forger states: "The salutation of Paul with mine own hand, which is the token in every epistle: so I write." Of course, it is just these words that betrayed the forgery.

A number of other epistles of Paul perhaps constitute the oldest literary products of Christianity, but they mention practically nothing about Jesus aside from the fact that he was crucified and then rose from the dead.

What credence we must give to the Resurrection is hardly a matter that we need discuss with our readers. Therefore, there is practically not a single element in the Christian literature concerning Jesus that will bear the test of examination.

III. THE STRUGGLE FOR THE IMAGE OF JESUS

At best the historical kernel of the primitive Christian reports concerning Jesus does not appear to be more than what Tacitus tells us: namely, that at the time of Tiberius, a prophet had been executed, to whom the sect of the Christians traced their origin. What this prophet taught and what was his influence, this is a subject on which not the slightest positive information has yet been obtained. At any rate, he surely did not attract the attention with which he is credited in primitive Christian records, for otherwise Josephus would surely have reported something about it, for he recounts many things of much less importance. The agitation and execution of Jesus at any rate did not arouse the slightest interest on the part of his contemporaries. But if Jesus really had been an agitator who was worshiped by a sect as its champion and leader, surely the importance of his personality would grow with the growth of this sect. Now a crown of legends began to form about this character, into which pious spirits would weave whatever they wished their model to have spoken and done. But as Jesus thus came to be regarded more and more as a model for the entire sect, the more did each of the numerous contending groups, of which the sect had consisted from the start, attempt to assign to this personality precisely those ideas to which each group was most attached, in order then to be able to invoke this person as an authority. Thus the image of Jesus, as depicted in legends that were at first merely transmitted from mouth to mouth and later set down in writing, became more and more the image of a superhuman personality, the incarnation of all the ideals developed by the new sect, but it also necessarily became more and more full of contradictions, the various traits of the image no longer being compatible with each other.

When the sect had arrived at a fixed organization, had become an all-embracing Church, in which a specific tendency had come to dominate, one of its first tasks was to outline a fixed canon, a catalog of all those primitive Christian writings which it recognized as genuine. Of course only such writings would be so recognized as were written from the point of view of this dominant tendency. All those Gospels and other writings which contained a picture of Jesus that did not agree with this tendency of the Church were rejected as "heretical", as forged, or at least apocryphal, and, being therefore not worthy of confidence, they were not disseminated, but even suppressed as far as possible; the manuscripts were destroyed, with the result that very few remained in existence. The writings admitted to the canon were also "edited" in order to introduce the greatest possible uniformity, but fortunately the editing was so unskillfully done that traces of earlier, contradictory accounts still come to light here and there, and permit us to surmise the course of the book's history.

But the Church did not succeed in its object, which was that of producing in this way a uniformity of views within the Church; this was impossible. The changing social conditions were ever producing new differentiations of views and aspirations within the Church, and thanks to the contradiction which the image of Jesus as recognized by the Church preserved in spite of all the editing and omitting that had been done, these various views always succeeded in finding in the image such points as would serve their purpose. Therefore, the struggle between socially opposed forces within the framework of the Christian Church became ostensibly a mere struggle concerning the interpretation of the words of Jesus, and superficial historians, therefore, are simple-minded enough to believe that all the great and often bloody conflicts within Christendom, which were fought under religious flags, were nothing more than struggles for mere words, and therefore a sad indication of the stupidity of the human race. But whenever a social mass phenomenon is ascribed to a mere stupidity of the men participating, this apparent stupidity in reality is merely the stupidity of the observer and critic, who evidently has not succeeded in finding his bearings among conceptions and opinions foreign to him, or in penetrating to the material conditions and motives underlying these modes of thought. As a rule the war was waged between very realistic interests; when the various Christian sects are disputing over a varying interpretation of the words of Christ it is really such interests that are operative.

The rise of the modern mode of thought and the passing away of the ecclesiastical mode of thought has of course more and more deprived these combats concerning the image of Christ of their practical significance, reducing them to mere quibbles on the part of theologians, who are paid by the state to keep alive the ecclesiastical psychology, and who must make some returns for their salaries.

The modern Bible criticism, applying the historical methods of an investigation of sources to the books of the Bible, gave a new impulse to the effort to create a likeness of the personality of Jesus. This criticism undermined the certainty of the traditional image of Jesus, but, being manipulated chiefly by the hands of theologians, it very rarely advanced so far as the view first proclaimed by Bruno Bauer, and later by others, particularly A. Kalthoff, that it is impossible in view of the present conditions of the sources to set up a new image at all. Criticism has again and again tried to restore this image, with the same result formerly produced by the Christianity of other centuries: each of our theologian friends puts his own ideals, his own spirit, into his image of Jesus. The descriptions of Jesus in the Twentieth Century resemble those written in the Second Century in that they do not depict what Jesus actually taught, but what the producers of these images wish he had taught.

Kalthoff gives us a very neat account of this transformation of the image of Jesus:

"From the social-theological point of view, the image of Jesus is therefore the most highly sublimated religious expression of all the social and ethical forces operative in the era in question; and the transformations which this Christ-image has constantly suffered, its extensions and contractions, the weakening of old traits, and their reappearance in new colors, afford us the most delicate instrument with which to measure the alterations through which contemporary life is passing, from the highest points of its spiritual ideals, to the lower depths of its most material phenomena. This Christ-image will now show the traits of a Greek philosopher, now those of the Roman Caesars, then again those of the feudal lord, of the master of the guild, of the tormented peasant vassal, and of the free burgher, and all these traits are genuine, all are alive until the faculty theologians become possessed with the peculiar notion of proving the individual traits of their particular day as being the original historical features of the Christ of the Gospels. At best, these traits are made to appear historical by the fact that the most varied, even the most opposite, forces were operative in the nascent and constructive periods of Christian society, each one of which forces bears a certain resemblance to the forces that are at work today. But the Christ-image of the present day seems quite full of contradictions at first glance. It still bears to a certain extent the traits of the ancient saint or of the Lord of Heaven, but also the entirely modern features of the friend of the proletarian, even of the labor leader. But this contradiction merely is a reflection of the most fundamental contrasts that animate our modern life." And in an earlier passage:

"Most of the representatives of the so-called Modern Theology use their shears when making excerpts according to the critical method beloved of David Strauss: they amputate the mythical elements in the gospels, and declare the remainder to be the historical nucleus. But even the theologians recognize that this nucleus has waxed too lean under their operations. . . . In the absence of all historical certainty, the name of Jesus has therefore become an empty vessel for Protestant Theology, into which each theologian may pour his own intellectual equipment. One of them will make this Jesus a modern Spinozist; the other, a Socialist; while the official professorial theologians will of course view Jesus in the religious light of the modern state; in fact in recent days they have represented him more and more boldly as the religious advocate of all those aspirations that are now claiming dominance in the greater Prussian, national Theology." [11]

In view of this state of affairs it is no cause for surprise that

---

[11] *Das Christusproblem. Grundlinien zu einer Sozialtheologie,* 1902, pp. 15, 17, 80, 81.

temporal historians have felt but a slight inclination to investigate the sources of Christianity, if these historians begin with the view that Christianity was the work of a single man. If this view were correct, it would of course be reasonable to give up every effort to determine the origin of Christianity, and to leave our theologians in undisputed possession of the field of religious fiction.

But the historian's attitude becomes quite different if he views a world religion not as the product of an individual superman, but as a social product. The social conditions at the time when Christianity originated are well known. And the social character of primitive Christianity can also be determined with some precision from a study of its literature.

The historical value of the Gospels and of the Acts of the Apostles is probably not of higher value than that of the Homeric poems, or of the Nibelungenlied. These may deal with historical personages; but they relate their activities with such poetic license that it is impossible to draw from their accounts even the slightest data for a historical description of these persons, not to mention the fact that they are so interwoven with fabulous elements that we shall never be able on the basis of these poems alone to state which of their characters are historical and which are invented. If we had no information concerning Attila but what is found in the Nibelungenlied, we should have to say of him as we say now of Jesus, that we are not even certain that he ever lived, and that he may have been as mythical a personage as Siegfried.

But such poetic narrations are of incalculable value for the study of the social conditions under which they arose, and which they faithfully reflect, no matter how many liberties their authors may take in their treatment of facts and persons. The extent to which the account of the Trojan War and its heroes is based on historical fact is enveloped in obscurity, and perhaps will always remain so, but we have in the Iliad and the Odyssey two historical sources of the first rank for a study of the social conditions of the Heroic Age.

Poetic works are often far more important for a study of their times than the most faithful historical accounts. For the latter give us only the personal, striking, unusual elements which are least permanent in their historic effect; the former on the other hand afford us a view of the daily life of the masses, which is constant and permanent in its effect, with a lasting influence on society; the historian does not relate these things, because he assumes them to be generally known and self-evident.   It is for this reason that Balzac's novels are one of the most important sources for the social life of France in the first decades of the Nineteenth Century.

Thus, while we may learn from the Gospels, the Acts of the Apostles, and the Epistles, nothing definite about the life and doctrine of Christ, we may obtain very important information concerning the social character, the ideals and aspirations of the primitive Christian congregation.   When Biblical criticism excavates the various deposits that have been gathered in successive layers in these writings, it affords us an opportunity to trace the development of these congregations to a certain extent at least, while the "pagan" and Jewish sources enable us to cast a glance at the social forces that were simultaneously at work on primitive Christianity.   This enables us to recognize and understand the latter as a product of its times; such is the basis of all historical knowledge.   Individual persons may influence society, and the delineation of prominent individuals is indispensable for a complete picture of their times.   But when measured by historical epochs, their influence is temporary at best, furnishes only the surface adornments which, while they may be the first portion of the structure that strikes the eye, reveal nothing to us concerning its foundation walls.   It is the latter that determine the character and permanence of the structure.   If we can reveal *them,* we have accomplished the most important work in an understanding of the edifice.

Part Two
ROMAN SOCIETY IN THE
IMPERIAL PERIOD

I. THE SLAVE-HOLDING SYSTEM

a. Property in Land

THOSE who would understand the opinions which are characteristic of a particular epoch and which distinguish them from the ideas of other epochs, must first of all study the needs and problems peculiar to the period. These are at bottom the outgrowth of the particular mode of production in the period, of the manner in which the society of the time maintained its life.

Let us first attempt to trace from its very beginnings the economic system on which the society of the Roman Empire was based. Only in this way can we understand its peculiar characteristics at the moment of the conclusion of this evolution, namely, under the Imperial Period, and the peculiar tendencies which it showed at that time.

The basis of economic production in the countries of which the Roman Empire was constructed was agriculture, besides which artisan industry and trade in commodities were practiced on a much smaller scale. Production for direct consumption was the general rule. The production of commodities, in other words, production for sale, was still in its infancy. Artisans and merchants in many cases had farms of their own, and these were closely bound up with the domestic life; their chief task was production for the household. Agriculture furnished the foodstuffs for the kitchen and in addition such raw materials as flax, wool, leather, timber, from which the members of the family made their own clothes, utensils and tools. All that could be sold was the surplus—when there was any—over and above the household needs.

This mode of production demands that there be private property in most of the means of production, in all that involves human labor, including therefore the farm land, but not private property in forests and pastures, which may remain a common holding; property in domestic animals, but not in game; finally, it involves private property in tools and raw materials as well as the products resulting from their use.

But with private property we already have the possibility of economic inequality. Fortunate accidents may favor and enrich one establishment while they injure and impoverish another. Establishments of the former variety will grow; their land and cattle will increase; but this condition at once produces a special labor question for the larger establishments, namely, the question of where to get the additional labor that is required for the proper care of the greater herds of cattle and the proper tilling of the more extensive fields.

Class differences and class oppositions make their appearance. The more productive agricultural labor becomes, the greater is the surplus it furnishes over the needs of the farmer himself. This surplus serves on the one hand to feed artisans, who are assigned to the production of certain useful articles, such as smiths and potters; on the other hand the surplus may be used in exchange for useful articles or raw materials that cannot be produced in the region itself, nature not furnishing them, or the necessary skill being absent. Such products are brought by merchants from other regions. The rise of the artisan and of trade tends to increase the inequalities in landed property. In addition to the inequality between large and small holdings we now have also the greater proximity or distance from the points in which workers and merchants congregate in order to exchange their commodities for the surplus produced by the peasants. The poorer the means of traffic, the more difficult does it become to bring products to market, and the greater is the advantage of him who lives close to the market.

We therefore observe the formation of a class of landed proprietors from among all those favored by one or more of these factors, who obtain a greater surplus than the mass of the peasants, and who can in exchange secure more products of trade and industry, and possess more leisure than the average farmer, control more technical resources in labor and in war, receive more mental stimulus by living together with others or by frequent

relations with artists and merchants, and can widen their mental
horizon. This class of fortunate landed proprietors now has the
time, the ability and the means of transacting business exceeding
the narrow limits of the peasant outlook. They have the time
and energy enabling them to weld together a number of peasant
communities into a state, as well as to administer and defend the
state and regulate its relations with neighboring and more distant states.

All these classes, large landed proprietors, merchants, artisans,
live on the surplus from agricultural work, to which is soon added
the surplus from industry. As their functions in society gain in
importance, the merchants and large landowners acquire more
and more of such surplus products. Soon the more powerful
landed proprietors, by virtue of their economic superiority as
well as their powerful position in the state, are able to deprive
the mass of peasants and artisans of the surplus resulting from
their work. They thus obtain wealth far in excess of their peasant or artisan standards and in turn solidify their social power
and their ability to seize further surplus products, and gain
additional wealth.

Thus there grow up, over the heads of the peasants and artisans, a number of strata of great exploiters, landed proprietors,
and merchants, not to mention usurers, of which latter we shall
have occasion to speak in another connection. The increase of
their wealth is accompanied by an increased need of extending
their households, which are still closely bound up with the tilling
of the soil. He who would have a household economy of his
own must at this period still control his own agricultural establishment, which is most secure where it is on his own land. The
general ambition is therefore in the direction of property in
land, even the ambition of artisans, usurers, and merchants. And
the general desire is to increase one's property in land, since production for home use is still predominant; increased prosperity,
a more lavish household, can only be based on an increase in
farm area.

The desire to get and to increase the amount of land which
one owns is the dominant passion of this period, which extends

from the epoch at which society, based on agriculture, ceases to be nomadic, in other words, from the establishment of peasant economy up to the time of the rise of industrial capital. Ancient society even at its culminating point, in the Imperial Period, never passed beyond this stage, which was not superseded until the time of the Reformation.

b. Domestic Slavery

But property in land is useless without workers to till it. We have already pointed out the peculiar labor problem arising from the first formation of large landed estates. Even before the beginning of historic time, we find that the richer individuals are looking for workers who may always be counted upon, in order to add them to the household, in addition to the members of the family, who are bound to the household by ties of blood.

Such workers could not at first be had by offering them wages. To be sure, we find cases of wage labor very early, but it is always an exceptional and temporary phenomenon, for instance, help in gathering the crops. The production tools required by an independent establishment were not so extensive that a competent family could not acquire them as a rule. And family and communal ties were still so strong that any accident befalling a family and depriving it of its property could usually be counteracted by means of assistance from relatives and neighbors.

While there was but a slight supply of wage workers, there was also very little demand for them. For the household and its industry were still closely connected. If additional workers were needed for the establishment, they had to become members of the household, necessarily lacking not only a workshop of their own, but also a family life of their own, being entirely absorbed by the stranger's family. Free workers were not available under these circumstances. Even during the Middle Ages, journeymen consented to accept membership in the family of the master only as a temporary stage, as a transition to mastership and to the establishment of their own families. At this period free men could not be permanently secured by the payment of

wages as additional workers in a stranger's family. Only a compulsory detention could obtain the required additional workers
for the large agricultural establishments. This purpose was
served by *slavery*. Under slavery the stranger had no rights.
And in view of the small size of the community in those days, the
conception of the "stranger" was all-embracing. In war, not
only the captured warriors, but very often the entire population
of the conquered country were enslaved and either divided among
the victors or sold. But there were also means of obtaining
slaves in peace times, particularly through maritime traffic,
which was frequently associated with piracy in its early stages,
one of the most desired booties being capable and handsome
humans, who were captured on coast raids when found defenseless on the shores. In addition, the posterity of male and female
slaves also passed into slavery.

The status of the slaves was at first not very bad, and they
sometimes took their lot lightly. Being members of a wealthy
household, often engaged in tasks contributing to comfort or
luxury, they were not notably overworked. If their work was of
a productive nature, it was often performed—on the big farms—
with the aid of the master, and involved only production for
family consumption, necessarily limited. The lot of the slave
was determined by the character of his master, and by the wealth
of the family to which he belonged. The masters had considerable interest in improving the status of the slaves, because it
involved improvement in their own status. Besides, by constant personal contact with the master, the slave stood in a more
or less human relation with the latter, and might, if he possessed
wit and brightness, even become indispensable to the master, a
friend as it were. Passages can be found in the ancient poets to
show how free the slaves were with their masters and with what
affection both sides often regarded each other. Quite frequently
the slaves would be dismissed with a handsome present for faithful services and others would save enough to buy their freedom.
But not a few preferred slavery to freedom, that is, they preferred life as members of a wealthy family to the lonely, meager,
and uncertain existence away from such a family.

"It must not be supposed," says Jentsch, "that the legal status of the slave, so repulsive to us, was taken seriously in private life and that the slave was neither considered nor treated as a human being; up to the end of the First Punic War the lot of the slave was not a sad one. What has been said of the legal power of the head of the family over his wife and children applies also to his rights over the slaves; although legally unlimited, they were modified by religion, custom, reason, sentiment, and self-interest, and the man who was considered before the law as a commodity, subject without defense to purchase and to his master's caprice, was esteemed as a faithful fellow-worker in the fields and as a companion in the home, with whom one could chat pleasantly by the hearth after working together with him out of doors." [1]

This comradely relation was found not only on the peasant farm; even princes still did more or less work in the Heroic Age. In the Odyssey, the daughter of King Alkinoos does the washing, together with her female slaves; Prince Odysseus does not challenge his rival to a duel, but to a competition in mowing and plowing, and on his return to his homeland he finds his father working in the garden with a shovel. Besides, Odysseus and his son Telemachus are the object of the affectionate regard of their slave, the "divine swineherd" Eumæus, who is firmly convinced that his master would have given him his liberty long ago, and also a farm and a wife, if only his master had returned.

This form of slavery was one of the mildest forms of exploitation known to us. But it changed its character when it became a means of making money, particularly when the large estates, having been separated from the household of the master, began to employ many workers.

c. Slavery in the Production of Commodities

Probably the first such properties were mines. The mining and working of minerals, particularly metallic ores, is ill suited

---

[1] Karl Jentsch, *Drei Spaziergänge eines Laien ins klassische Altertum*, 1900. Third *Spaziergang, Der Römerstaat*, p. 237. Compare also the Second *Spaziergang* in the same book: *Die Sklaverei bei den antiken Dichtern*.

by its very nature for production for household use only. As soon as such industries attain even the smallest degree of development, they yield a great surplus beyond domestic needs; besides, they can attain a certain perfection only by regularly employing the labor of large bodies of workers, because the worker can in no other way acquire the necessary skill and experience, or make the necessary engineering structures profitable. Even in the Stone Age we already find great centers in which the manufacture of stone implements was carried on proficiently and on a large scale, being then distributed by barter from group to group or from clan to clan. These mineral products seem to have been the first commercial commodities. They probably are the very first to have been produced with the intention of serving for barter.

As soon as a mining operation had developed over a deposit of valuable minerals, and had passed beyond the limits of the most primitive surface mining, it required larger and larger bodies of workers. The need for such workers might easily exceed the number of free workers that could be recruited from the ranks of the clan owning the mine. Wage labor could not permanently supply numerous bands of workers; only compulsory labor by slaves or condemned criminals could assure the necessary number of workers.

But these slaves were no longer producing only utensils for the limited personal requirements of their master; they worked so that he might make money. They were not working for his consumption of sulphur, iron or copper, gold or silver, in his own household, but for his sale of the mined products, to put him in possession of money, that commodity that can purchase everything, all enjoyments, all power, and of which one can never have too much. As much labor as possible was ground out of the workers in the mines, for, the more they worked, the more money their owner made. And they were fed and clothed as poorly as possible, for their food and clothing had to be *bought*, had to be paid for in *money;* the slaves in the mine could not produce them. While the owner of a wealthy agricultural establishment could do nothing else with his surplus of articles for consumption than lavish them on his slaves and guest-friends, the case with commodity production was different; the less the slaves consumed, the greater was the gain in money from the industry. Their situation became worse and worse as the industry became larger, thus removing them more and more from the master's household, housing them in special barracks whose dismal bareness contrasted sharply with the luxury of the former household. Furthermore, all personal contact between master and slave ceased, not only because the workshop was now separated from his household, but also because of the great number of workers. Thus it is reported in Athens at the time of the Peloponnesian War that Hipponikos had six hundred slaves working in the Thracian mines and Nikias one thousand. The slave's position now became a terrible scourge for him; while the free wage worker might after all make a certain selection among his masters and might at least under certain favorable circumstances exercise a certain pressure on his master by refusing to work, and thus resist the worst encroachments, the slave who ran away from his master or refused to work for him might be slain on sight.

There was only one reason for sparing the slave, the reason for which one spares cattle: the cost of buying a new one. The wage worker costs nothing, and if the work destroys him another will take his place, but the slave had to be bought; if he died before his time, his master was the loser. But this reason had less and less influence when slaves were cheap, and there were times when the price of a slave was extremely low, when constant foreign and domestic wars threw numerous captives on the market.

Thus in the third war of the Romans against Macedonia, seventy cities were plundered in Epirus, in the year 169 B.C., *on a single day*, 150,000 of their inhabitants being sold as slaves.

According to Böckh, the usual price of a slave in Athens was 100–200 drachmas ($20–$40). Xenophon reports that the price varied between fifty and a thousand drachmas. Appianus says that in the Pontus on one occasion prisoners of war were knocked down at four drachmas (a trifle over 75 cents) each. When

Joseph's brothers sold him to Egypt he brought in only twenty shekels ($4.50).[2]

A good riding horse was much more expensive than a slave, as its price at the time of Aristophanes was about twelve *minae,* or almost $250.

But the very wars which furnished cheap slaves also ruined many peasants, since the peasant militia then constituted the kernel of the armies. While the peasant was waging war his farm would go to pieces for lack of workers. The ruined peasants had no other resource than to take to banditry, unless they had the opportunity to go to a neighboring city and eke out their livelihood as artisans or as part of the *Lumpenproletariat.*[3] Many crimes and criminals were thus produced that had not been known in earlier days, and the pursuit of these criminals furnished new slaves, for jails were as yet unknown, being a product of the capitalist mode of production. Persons not crucified were condemned to compulsory labor.

Over certain periods there were therefore available extremely cheap hosts of slaves whose status was very wretched. The Spanish silver mines, among the most productive of antiquity, are an excellent illustration. "At first," Diodorus says of these mines, "ordinary private individuals undertook the mining and gained great wealth thereby, since the silver ore was not deep in the ground and was present in great abundance. Later, when the Romans had become masters of Iberia (Spain), a large number of Italians were attracted to the mines, gaining great wealth through their avarice, for they bought a number of slaves and handed them over to the mine supervisor. . . . The slaves who have to work in these mines make incredible sums for their masters; but many of them, working far below the ground, exerting their bodies day and night in the shafts, die from overwork. For they have no recreation or recess in their work, but are driven on by the whips of their supervisors, to bear the worst discom-

---

[2] Herzfeld, *Handelsgeschichte der Juden des Altertums,* 1894, p. 193.

[3] This German word, now frequently used in economic works written in English, signifies that portion of the proletariat whose income, though of proletarian dimensions, is not the result of actual labor, but of charity or extortion.—TRANSLATOR.

forts and work themselves to death. A few who possess sufficient physical strength and a patient equanimity, are able to bear this treatment, but this only prolongs their misery, the immensity of which makes death appear more desirable to them than life." [4]

While patriarchal domestic slavery is perhaps the mildest form of exploitation, slavery in the service of greed is surely the most abominable. The technical methods of mining under the given circumstances made it necessary to employ a large-scale production with slaves, in the mines. But in the course of time a demand arose for the production of commodities on a large scale by slaves in other branches of industry. There were communities that were far superior to their neighbors in military power, and these found war so profitable that they never tired of it. Warfare furnished an inexhaustible supply of new slaves which it was sought to put to profitable work. But these communities were always connected with great cities. When such a city, because of its favorable situation, became a great trading place, commerce alone would attract many persons, and if the city was generous in its grants of citizenship to strangers, it soon became richer in population, and also in means, than the other neighboring communities which it subjected. Plundering and exploiting the surrounding country was a further source of increasing wealth for the city and its inhabitants. Such wealth would stimulate the need for great building operations, either of a hygienic nature —sewers, aqueducts; or of æsthetic and religious nature—temples and theaters; or of military nature—encircling walls. Such structures could at that time be best produced by great masses of slaves. Contractors arose, who bought great numbers of slaves and executed various constructions for the state with their labor. The large city also furnished an extensive market for great masses of foodstuffs. With the low price of slaves, the most extensive surplus was produced by agricultural establishments working on a large scale. To be sure, the technical supe-

---

[4] Diodorus Siculus, *Historische Bibliothek*, vol. xxxvi, 38. Compare the quotation from the same work, iii, 38, on the Egyptian gold mines, to which Marx refers in his *Capital*, vol. i, chap. 8, 2, note 43.

riority of large-scale production in agriculture was at that time
by no means an accomplished fact.   In fact, slavery was less
productive than the labor of free peasants, but the slave, since
his labor power did not need to be spared and he could be driven
to death without regret, produced a greater *surplus* over and
above the cost of his maintenance than did the peasant, who had
then not yet learned to appreciate the blessings of overwork and
was accustomed to a life of ease.   In addition, slave labor had
the advantage, precisely in such communities, that the slave was
freed from military service, while the peasant might at any
moment be taken from the plow by the duty of defending his
country.   Thus, in the economic territory of such large and warlike cities, large-scale agricultural production by slaves began.
It was brought to a high level by the Carthaginians; the Romans
became acquainted with it in the wars with Carthage, and when
they annexed large territories from their great rival, they also
annexed the practice of large-scale agricultural production, which
they further developed and expanded.

Finally, in large cities where there were many slaves practicing
the same trade, and also a good market for their products, it was
a simple matter to buy up a large number of such slaves and put
them to work in a common factory, so that they might produce
for the market as wage workers do today.   But such slave manu-
factures attained importance only in the Hellenic world, not in
the Roman.   Everywhere, however, a special kind of slave industry developed together with large-scale agricultural production, regardless of whether such production was a mere plantation
furnishing a certain species such as grain by factory methods for
the market, or whether it chiefly served the home consumption
by the family, by the household, and therefore had to furnish
the very varied products which the latter required.

Agricultural work is peculiar in that it demands a large number of workers only at certain seasons of the year, while at other
seasons—particularly in winter—it requires but a few.   This is
a problem even for modern large-scale agricultural establishments; it was a harder problem under the system of slave labor.

For the wage worker can be dismissed when not needed and re-employed when needed. How he gets along in the interval is his own business. On the other hand, the large-scale farmer could not sell his slaves every autumn and buy new ones in the spring. He would have found such a practice very expensive, for in the fall they would have been worth nothing and in the spring a great deal. He therefore was obliged to try to keep them busy during periods in which there was no farming. The traditions of a combined agriculture and industry were still strong, and the farmer still worked his own flax, wool, leather, timber, and other products of his land into clothes and implements. There-fore the slaves of large-scale agricultural enterprises were em-ployed, during the time when farming was idle, at industrial tasks such as weaving, and the manufacture and working of leather, the making of wagons and plows, the production of pot-tery of all kinds. But, when the production of such commodities had advanced to a high level, they manufactured not only for their own establishment and household, but also for the market.

When slaves were cheap, their industrial products could also be made cheap, as the latter required no outlay in money. The estate, the latifundium, furnished the food and raw materials for the workers, and for the most part even the tools. And as the slaves had to be kept alive in any case during the period in which they were not needed for farming work, all the industrial products which they produced beyond the needs of their own establishment and household constituted a surplus that might allow a profit even at low prices.

It is not to be marveled at that a free and healthy artisan class could not develop in the face of this competition from slave labor. In the ancient world, particularly the Roman world, the artisans remained wretched fellows, working mostly alone with-out apprentices, and usually in the customer's house, with mate-rials furnished by the latter. A healthy artisan class, such as later developed in the Middle Ages, is entirely absent. The guilds remained weak, the artisans constantly at the mercy of their customers, most of whom were large landed proprietors, as whose clients they often led a very parasitic existence on the threshold of the *Lumpenproletariat.*

But large-scale production with slave labor was only powerful enough to prevent a healthy growth of free industry and a development of its technique, which always remained at a low level in ancient times, as was natural in view of the artisan's poverty; but the artisan's skill might on occasion become highly developed, his tools remaining wretched and primitive. But the case in the large-scale enterprises was no different; here also slavery had the same inhibitive effect on all technical development.

d. The Technical Inferiority of the Slave-Holding System

Large-scale production in agriculture did not yet involve the same condition for higher efficiency as in mining. To be sure, the increasing production of commodities did bring about a division of labor even in agriculture; many farms turned to grain-raising, while others took up cattle-breeding, etc. As the large-scale establishment developed, it became possible to have it managed by scientifically trained men with more ability than the routine peasant; we therefore actually find in those countries that introduced this large-scale agricultural economy, in other words among the Carthaginians and later the Romans, a fully developed science of agriculture at about the same level as that of European agriculture in the Eighteenth Century. But the workers were lacking whom this science might have used to lift the large-scale establishment beyond the practices of the peasant establishment. Even the wage laborer is not as much interested or solicitous in his work as the free landed proprietor; employing a wage laborer is profitable only in places where the large-scale establishment is technically far superior to the smaller establishment. But the slave employed in a large-scale establishment, no longer living in patriarchal family conditions, is a far more unwilling worker, in fact, his efforts are directed chiefly to the detriment of his employer. Even in domestic slavery, the work of the slave was not considered as productive as that of the free proprietor. Already Odysseus says:

"Servants, no longer spurred on by the imperious master,
Negligent at once they become, to do the work that he gives them.
Fully one half of his virtue the divine providence of Zeus
Takes from a man as soon as the day of serfdom overtakes him!"

How much worse was the case with slaves who were daily tortured to the quick, and whose attitude towards their master was one of desperation and hatred! It would have required an immense superiority on the part of large-scale production over small production, for the former to achieve the same results as the latter with the same number of workers. But large-scale production not only was not superior; it was in many ways inferior. The slaves, who were themselves maltreated, gave vent to all their rage in their treatment of the cattle, which needless to say did not thrive. Similarly, it was impossible to allow them to handle delicate tools. Marx has already pointed this out. He says of "production based on slavery":

"This is one of the circumstances that makes production by slave labor such a costly process. The laborer here is, to use a striking expression of the ancients, distinguishable only as *instrumentum vocale*, from an animal as *instrumentum semivocale*, and from an implement as *instrumentum mutum*. But he himself takes care to let both beast and implement feel that he is none of them, but is a man. He convinces himself with immense satisfaction, that he is a different being, by treating the one unmercifully and damaging the other *con amore*. Hence the principle, universally applied in this method of production, only to employ the rudest and heaviest implements and such as are difficult to damage owing to their sheer clumsiness. In the slave-states bordering on the Gulf of Mexico, down to the date of the civil war, plows constructed on old Chinese models, which turned up the soil like a hog or a mole, instead of making furrows, were alone to be found. . . . In his *Sea Board Slave States*, Olmsted tells us: 'I am here shown tools that no man in his senses, with us, would allow a laborer, for whom he was paying wages, to be encumbered with; and the excessive weight and clumsiness of which, I would judge, would make work at least ten per cent greater than with those ordinarily used with us. And I am assured that, in the careless and clumsy way they must be used by the slaves, anything lighter or less rude could not be furnished them with good economy, and that such tools as we constantly give our laborers and find our profit in giving them, would not last out a day in a Virginia cornfield—much lighter and more free from stones though it be than ours. So, too, when I ask why mules are so universally substituted for horses on the farm, the first reason given, and confessedly the most conclusive one, is that horses cannot bear the treatment that they always must get from negroes; horses are always soon foundered or crippled by them, while mules will bear cudgeling, or lose a meal or two now and then, and not be materially injured, and they do not take cold or get sick, if neglected or overworked. But I do not need to go further than to the window of the room in which I am writing, to see at almost any time, treatment of cattle that would ensure the immediate discharge of the driver by almost any farmer owning them in the North.' " [5]

Unintelligent, sulky, malicious, eager for an occasion to injure the hated tormentor, whenever the opportunity served, the slave labor of the latifundium produced far less than the peasant farm. Pliny, in the First Century of our era, already pointed out how fruitful the fields of Italy had been when the farmer had not yet scorned to till them himself, and how intractable Mother Earth had become when fettered and branded slaves were permitted to maltreat her. This kind of farming might under certain circumstances provide a greater surplus than the peasant farm, but it could by no means maintain as many people in prosperity. However, so long as the condition of war continued, with which Rome was constantly disturbing the entire world that surrounded the Mediterranean Sea, the expansion of peasant operation also continued, but side by side with it there proceeded the decline of the peasant economy oppressed by it, since the wars furnished rich booty to the great landed proprietors that were waging them, besides new lands and endless numbers of cheap slaves. We thus find in the Roman Empire an economic process that bears

[5] *Capital,* London edition, 1887, vol. i, p. 178, footnote.

a striking similarity to that of modern times: decline of petty industry, progress of large-scale production, and a still greater increase of the great landed estates, the latifundia, which expropriate the peasant and, whenever they cannot replace him by means of plantation methods or other large-scale production, at least reduce him from a free proprietor to a dependent tenant.

Pöhlmann, in his *History of Ancient Communism and Socialism,* quotes among other things "The Lament of the Poor Man against the Rich Man" from the pseudo-Quintillian Collection of Declamations, in which the growth of the latifundia is excellently narrated. It is the lament of an impoverished peasant, who wails:

"I have not always been the neighbor of a rich man. All around me there once were on many farms independent farmers, equally rich, who tilled their humble lands in neighborly peace. How different is it now! The land that once fed all these citizens is now a single great plantation, belonging to one rich man. His estate has expanded in all directions; the peasant homes which it has devoured have been razed to the ground and the figures of the ancestral gods destroyed. The former proprietors have had to take leave of the patron gods of their ancestral house and proceed to foreign parts with their wives and children. A great uniformity of work prevails over the wide expanse. Everywhere wealth incloses me as with a wall. Here is the rich man's garden, there are his fields; here his vineyards, there his forests and pastures. I, too, would gladly have departed but I could not find a single spot of ground where I should not have had rich men as neighbors. For where do we not find the private estates of the wealthy? They are no longer satisfied with extending their estates until they meet with a natural boundary, as the nations do, in the form of a river or a mountain, but they take possession of the most remote mountain wastes and forests. And nowhere does this expanse encounter any limit, any barrier, except when the rich man's land meets the land of another rich man. And another element of the contempt which these rich men have for us poor is that they do not even consider it worth while to deny their actions if they have been guilty of any violation of our rights." (*Geschichte des antiken Kommunismus und Sozialismus*, vol. ii, pages 582, 583.)

Pöhlmann considers the above to be a characterization of the tendencies "of extreme capitalism in general". But the similarity of this evolution with that of modern capitalism and its concentration of funded wealth is merely superficial and it is absolutely misleading to compare the two. He who studies the subject more deeply will rather find a sharp opposition between the two developments. First of all, in the fact that the tendency to concentration, the effort on the part of larger enterprises to displace smaller ones, as well as the drift to increasing dependence of the smaller enterprises on the possessors of great wealth is at the present day chiefly proceeding in industry, and much less so in agriculture, while in ancient times just the opposite was the case. Furthermore, the subjection of the smaller enterprises by the greater ones proceeds today in the form of competition, which enables the greater productivity of the establishment working with immense machines and plants to have its full effect. In antiquity, this subjection took the form of a weakening of the free peasants, oppressed by military service, and of a greater cheapness of labor power at the disposal of the possessors of great resources of money in the shape of an immense slave supply, and finally owing to usury, of which we shall speak later. All of which are factors which decreased the productivity of labor instead of raising it. The necessary conditions were lacking in antiquity for a development and utilization of machinery. As yet the free artisan class had not developed to such a high level as to be able to furnish immense quantities of free skilled labor, ready to hire themselves out permanently for pay, in great numbers, laborers who would have been required for the production of machines and their manipulation. Therefore the necessary incentive to thinkers and investigators to invent machines was also lacking, since such machines would have remained without practical use. Once machines have been invented, however, that are capable of successful utilization in production, and as soon as numerous free laborers appear, eager for employment in the production and manipulation of these machines, the machine becomes one of the most important weapons in the competition of the entrepreneurs among themselves. A constant perfection and an increased size of the machine are the result, increasing the productivity of labor, increasing the surplus over the wage paid to the laborer, increasing also the necessity of hoarding or accumulating a portion of this surplus with the object of providing new and better machines; and also increasing finally the necessity of constantly widening the market, since the improved machinery continues to deliver more and more products which must be gotten rid of. This leads to an uninterrupted increase of capital so that the production of means of production assumes an increasingly important rôle in the capitalist system of production, with the result that the latter, in order to dispose profitably of the increased articles of consumption created simultaneously with the increased means of production, must seek more and more new markets, so that it may be said that in the course of a single century, namely the Nineteenth, it conquered the entire world.

Quite different was the course of events in antiquity. We have seen that the slaves employed in large establishments could be given only the coarsest tools, that only the crudest and most unintelligent workers could be put to work, and that therefore it was only the extreme cheapness of the slave material that made the large-scale establishment reasonably profitable. This stimulated among the entrepeneurs of the large-scale establishments a constant tendency toward war, this being the most effective means of obtaining cheap slaves, and towards a continual expansion of the national boundaries. Beginning with the wars against Carthage, this tendency became one of the mightiest moving forces of the Roman policy of conquest, which in the course of two centuries subjected all the countries surrounding the Mediterranean Sea, and in the time of Christ, after having put Gaul—which is now France—under the yoke, was preparing to subjugate Germany, whose robust population furnished such excellent slaves.

This insatiable and constant tendency to increase the area exploited made the ancient large-scale enterprise somewhat similar

to that of modern days; but there was nevertheless a great difference in the manner in which the surplus products yielded by
the increasing hosts of slaves were applied.   The modern capitalist, as we have seen, must save up his profits to a great extent,
in order to improve and expand his enterprise, unless he wishes
to be overtaken and defeated by his competitors.   The ancient
slave-holder felt no such need.   The technical basis on which his
production rested, was not higher, it was rather lower than that
of the small peasants whom he was forcing out.   This technical
basis was not being constantly revolutionized and broadened, but
remained always the same.   All the surplus products beyond the
costs once incurred, and the replacement or deterioration of
tools, cattle and slaves, were at the disposal of the slave-holder
for his enjoyment, even if he was not a wastrel.   To be sure,
money might be invested in trade and usury or new tracts of
land, and might thus become a source of increased profit, but
even this new profit could be put to no other use than that of
enjoyment.   The accumulation of capital for purposes of producing new means of production beyond the given quantity would
have been ridiculous, for these new means of production could
not have been put to new application.

The more the peasants were displaced by the latifundia, the
greater were the quantities of lands and of slaves that were
brought together under a single ownership, and the greater became
the surplus, the treasures which were at the disposal of individual
persons, and which the latter could put to no other use than
consume them for their own gratification.   While the modern
capitalist is characterized by his tendency to *accumulate capital,*
the aristocratic Roman of the Imperial Period is marked by his
pursuit of enjoyment: it was in this period that Christianity arose.
The modern capitalists have accumulated funds that make the
wealth of the richest citizen of ancient Rome ridiculous in comparison.   The Crœsus of the ancient Romans was Narcissus,
Nero's freed slave, who had a fortune of over $20,000,000.   But
what are $20,000,000, as compared with the $1,000,000,000 that
Mr. Rockefeller is said to own?   But the extravagance prac-

ticed by the American multi-millionaires cannot be compared, in spite of all its madness, with the extravagance of their Roman predecessors, who served nightingales' tongues at their banquets and dissolved precious pearls in vinegar.

With the growth of luxury the number of domestic slaves used for personal service also increased, all the more when the slave material became cheaper. Horace in one of his Satires says that the smallest number of slaves a man can hold in order to be tolerably comfortable is ten. In an aristocratic establishment their number might run into thousands. While the barbarians were put into the mines and on large farms, the more finely trained, particularly the Greek slaves, were with the "city families", in other words, lived in the town house. Not only cooks, scribes, musicians, pedagogues, actors, but even physicians and philosophers were held as slaves. In contrast with the slaves who served to increase the owner's wealth, these educated slaves for the most part had very little labor to perform. The greater number were now as great idlers as their masters themselves. But the two conditions which had formerly served to contribute to decent treatment for the family slave now disappeared: his high price, which had made it necessary to spare him, and the relation of comradeship with his master, who had worked together with the slave. Now, in view of the great wealth of the master and the cheapness of the slaves, no one felt the slightest obligation to spare the latter. Furthermore, all personal relation with the master ceased for the great mass of the domestic slaves; the master hardly knew them. And if master and slave came into personal contact, it was not over their work, which was a source of mutual respect, but in revels and vices such as are produced by idleness and arrogance, and which inspired masters and servants with mutual contempt. Idle, often pampered, the slaves of the house were nevertheless exposed without defense to every illhumor, every angry outburst, which often assumed dangerous proportions for them. The cruel act of Vedius Pollio is well known: the slave had broken a crystal vessel, for which offense Pollio ordered him to be thrown as food to the muræne, which he kept in a pond, as these eels were much esteemed as a delicacy.

The increase in the number of these domestic slaves meant an increase in the number of unproductive elements in society, whose hosts were simultaneously being swelled by the growth of the *Lumpenproletariat,* recruited partly from the main body of the freed peasants. And this process was going on while at the same time the driving out of free labor by slave labor was considerably decreasing the productivity of labor in many productive occupations.

But the greater the number of members in a household, the easier it became for the products to be prepared for the household by its own workers, products which the smaller household had been obliged to purchase, such as certain garments and utensils. This led to a renewed development of production for home consumption within the family. But this latter form of the family economy of the rich should not be confused with the primitive simple family economy, which was based on the almost complete absence of community production, and which itself produced precisely the most important and indispensable articles among its needs, purchasing only tools and articles of luxury. This second form of production for household consumption within the family, as we encounter it at the end of the Roman Republic and in the Imperial Period, in the households of the wealthy, was based precisely on community production, on the production of the mines and latifundia for the market; this home production was first and foremost a production of luxuries.

This new development of production for home consumption was a danger to the free artisan, to whom the industrial enterprises of the cities and latifundia, manned by slaves, were already doing harm enough. The free artisan class was bound to decrease *relatively,* in other words, the number of free workers could but go down as compared with that of the slaves, even in artisan work. But in a number of trades the free workers might still be increasing in number *absolutely,* thanks to the increase of extravagance, which created an increased demand for objects of art and of art industries, but also for mere articles of vanity, such as cosmetics and pomades.

He who would judge the prosperity of society by such extravagances, who would take the same narrow-minded standpoint as that assumed by the Roman Caesars and the great landed proprietors and their retinue of courtiers, artists, and literati, may very well estimate the social conditions of the period of the Emperor Augustus as excellent. Boundless wealth was being accumulated in Rome for the sole purpose of serving personal gratification; pleasure-seeking wealthy wastrels staggered from banquet to banquet, scattering with lavish hands the abundance which it was impossible for them to consume all for themselves. Many artists and scholars received very generous grants of money from the *mœcenates*, great structures were put up, the immense size and artistic proportions of which are the object of our admiration to this day; the whole world seemed to be perspiring wealth from all its pores—and yet this society was already doomed to destruction.

e. The Economic Decline

A foreboding of the fact that things were on the downward path arose rather early among the ruling classes, shut out as they were from all activities, all their work, even that of scholarship and of politics, being done by slaves. In Greece, slave labor had at first served the purpose of granting great leisure to the masters, for the administration of the state, and for meditation concerning most of the important problems of life. But the more the surplus products increased, which were being united in the hands of single individuals by the concentration of landed property, the expansion of the latifundia, and the increase in the masses of slaves, the greater became the tendency to regard the practice of enjoying, of wasting these surpluses, as the most aristocratic social functions of the ruling classes, the more they burned with the zeal of competition in extravagance, the emulation to outdo each other in splendor, luxury, and idleness. In Rome this process was accomplished more easily than in Greece, since the latter country was somewhat backward in its cultural level when it reached this mode of production. The Greek military power had expanded chiefly at the expense of barbarian tribes, while in Asia Minor and Egypt it had encountered really powerful opposition.

Their slaves were barbarians from whom the Greeks could learn nothing, to whom they could not intrust the administration of the state. And the wealth which it was possible to extract from the barbarians was comparatively insignificant. The Roman rule on the other hand, rapidly spread over the ancient sites of civilization in the East, going as far as Babylonia (or Seleucia): from these newly conquered provinces the Romans not only drew immense wealth, but many slaves who were superior to their masters in knowledge, and from whom the latter had much to learn, and to whom they could afford to intrust the administration of the state. The administrators of the state, who formerly had been great land-holding aristocrats, were more and more succeeded in the Imperial Period by slaves of the imperial house and by former slaves of the emperor, freedmen who remained faithful to their former masters.

The only functions in society remaining to the owners of the latifundia and to their numerous retinue of parasites was that of enjoyment. But man becomes unresponsive to a stimulus that continues to operate on him for a long period, to pleasure as well as to pain, to voluptuous impulses as well as to the fear of death. Mere uninterrupted pleasure, unrelieved by labor, resulted at first in a constant pursuit of new enjoyments, in which it was sought to outdo former experiences, to goad the jaded nerves anew, which led to the most unnatural vices, to the most exquisite cruelties, and which also raised extravagance to the highest and most senseless heights. But there is a limit to everything, and once the individual had gotten to the point where he was no longer able to increase his pleasures, either through a lack of resources, or of strength, or as a consequence of financial or physical bankruptcy, he was visited with the most extreme nausea, with an aversion to the mere idea of pleasure, even with complete disgust with life; all earthly thoughts and images now seemed vain—*vanitas, vanitatum vanitas*. Despair, the desire for death, was the result, but also the desire for a new and higher life. So deep-rooted in many minds, however, was the aversion to work, that even this new ideal life was not conceived as a life of joyous labor, but as an absolutely inactive state of bliss, which drew all its pleasure from its complete detachment from all the pains and disillusionments of physical needs and physical enjoyments.

But among the best individuals in the exploiting class there arose also a feeling of shame at the fact that their pleasure was based on the destruction of numerous free peasants, on the maltreatment of thousands of slaves in the mines and the latifundia. Their qualms of conscience also awakened a sense of sympathy with the slaves—in peculiar contradiction with the ruthless cruelty with which the lives of the slaves were then regarded—we need only to refer in passing to the gladiatorial combats. Finally the sick conscience also aroused an aversion toward the lust for gold, for money, which at that time was already ruling the world.

"We know," cries Pliny in the Thirty-third Book of his *Natural History*, "that Spartacus (the leader of a slave uprising) forbade anyone in his camp to have gold or silver in his possession. How far our runaway slaves outshine us in greatness of mind! The orator Messala writes that the Triumvir Antonius had made use of golden vessels for his lowest bodily needs. . . . Antonius, who so degraded gold, making it the lowest thing in nature, would have deserved to be declared an outlaw. But only a Spartacus could have outlawed him."

Down below, under this ruling class, of which a part was wrecking itself in a mad pursuit of enjoyment, lust for money and cruelty, while another part was filled with sympathy for the poor, with an aversion for gold and pleasures, even with the desire for death, there extended an immense host of toiling slaves, who were more wretchedly treated than beasts of burden, recruited from the most varied tribes, debased and vulgarized by constant abuse, by working in chain gangs under the cracks of the whip, full of sullen rage, desire for revenge, and hopelessness, ever ready for violent insurrection, but incapable—owing to the backwardness of the barbarous elements which constituted the majority of them—to overthrow the establishment of the mighty state system and set up a new system, although single outstanding spirits among them may have pursued such ambitions. The only kind of liberation that they might succeed in attaining was not by means of overthrowing the existing society, but by escaping from that society, by flight either into the criminal classes, into banditry, whose numbers they were continually swelling, or by escaping over the imperial boundary and joining the enemies of the empire.

Somewhat above these millions of the most wretched of all humans was a class of slaves consisting of many hundreds of thousands, who often lived in luxury and plenty, and who always witnessed and suffered from the most exaggerated and outrageous passions, who served as accessories in every conceivable form of corruption, becoming either subject to such corruption themselves and therefore just as depraved as their masters, or—again resembling some of their masters, and often earlier in the game than the latter, since they had to suffer the evils of the life of pleasure far sooner—profoundly disgusted with depravity and mere pleasure seeking, and full of a longing for a new, purer, higher life.

And side by side with all these there were also swarms of hundreds of thousands of freed citizens and freed slaves, also numerous impoverished remnants of the peasantry, down-and-out tenants, wretched urban artisans and burden-carriers, as well as, finally, the *Lumpenproletariat* of the large cities, having the energy and self-reliance of the free citizen and yet having become economically superfluous in society, homeless, without any sense of security, depending absolutely on the crumbs which the great lords would throw to them of their own superfluity, moved either by generosity, or fear, or by the desire for peace.

When the Gospel of Saint Matthew represents Jesus as saying of himself: "The foxes have holes, and the birds of the air have nests; but the Son of Man hath not where to lay his head" (viii, 20), this is merely expressing in the case of Jesus a thought which Tiberius Gracchus had expressed 130 years before the birth of Christ for the whole proletariat of Rome: "The wild animals of Italy have their caves and their lairs in which they may rest, but the men who struggle and die for Italy's greatness possess nothing but light and air because they cannot be robbed of these. Homeless and shelterless they wander about with their wives and children." Their misery and the constant insecurity of their existence must have enraged them the more with the increasing shameless-ness and luxury which the wealth of the great was constantly placing before their eyes. There ensued a violent class hatred on the part of the poor for the rich, but this class hatred was of an entirely different kind from that of the modern proletariat.

All of present-day society is based on the labor of the proletarian. He has only to stop working and society quakes in its foundations. The ancient proletarian outcast performed no labor and even the labor done by the remnants of the free peasants and the artisans was not indispensable. Society did not live on the proletariat at that time; the proletariat lived on society. The proletariat was completely superfluous and might have disappeared entirely without injuring society. On the contrary, the disappearance of the proletariat could only have rendered the social system more secure. The work of the slaves was the basis on which society was built up.

The oppositions between the capitalist and the proletarian are today fought out in the factory, in the workshop. The question is: who shall control the products, the owner of the means of production, or the owner of the labor power? The struggle involves the entire system of production; it is a struggle to put a higher mode of production in place of that now in force.

The ancient impoverished proletarian was not concerned with this struggle. As a matter of fact, he did not work and did not want to work. All he wanted was a share in the enjoyments of the rich, a different distribution of pleasures, not of means of production, a plundering of the rich, not an alteration of the mode of production. The sufferings of the slaves in the mines and plantations left him as unmoved as did those of common animals.

Still less could the peasants and artisans think of attempting to install a higher mode of production. These classes do not aspire to any such thing even now. Their dream was at best to restore the past, but they were so closely related to the *Lumpenproletariat,* and the aspirations of the latter were so enticing even to them, that they also had no other wish or ambition than did these impoverished proletarians: a life without labor, led at the expense of the rich; communism by plundering the rich.

Roman society at the end of the Republic and during the Imperial Period, therefore, may present immense social oppositions, much class hatred and many class struggles, insurrections, and civil wars, a boundless longing for a different, better life, and the abolition of the existing order of society, but it does not show that any effort is being made in the direction of introducing a new and higher mode of production.[6]

The moral and intellectual prerequisites for such a movement were not present; no class possessed the knowledge, the energy, the joy in labor and the unselfishness required for the exerting of effective pressure in the direction of a new mode of production; and also, the material prerequisites were lacking, without which even the idea of such a thing could not arise.

We have seen above that the slave-holding economy technically involved not an advance but a retrogression, that it not only effeminized the masters and made them unfit for labor, that it not only increased the number of unproductive workers in society, but in addition lowered the productivity of the productive workers and retarded the advances in practical technique—with the possible exception of certain luxury trades. Anyone who compared the new mode of production under the slave-holding economy with that of the free peasantry which it displaced and oppressed, could not but behold in it a decline, certainly not an advance. People began to feel that the old times had been the better times, the Golden Age, and that each succeeding epoch was relatively a degeneration. The capitalistic era is characterized by the notion of an unlimited progress of mankind, owing to capitalism's constant effort to improve its means of production, resulting in a tendency to view the past in gloomy colors and to see only a roseate future; but in the Roman Imperial Period we

[6] Pöhlmann, in his already quoted *Geschichte des antiken Kommunismus und Sozialismus,* very stupidly places the class struggles of the ancient proletarians, even those of the debt-ridden agrarians, the renunciation of debts to the land-owning class, the plunderings and distributions of land by the disinherited, on the same level with Socialism in modern times, in order to prove that the Dictatorship of the Proletariat cannot under any circumstances have any other result than murder, violence, incendiarism, dividing up and revelry. The wisdom of this Erlangen professor is that of the late Eugen Richter, adorned with great numbers of Greek quotations.

find the opposite view, namely, that of a ceaseless progressive deterioration of humanity, and of a conṣtant longing to restore the good old days. Whenever social reforms and social ideals in the imperial days were at all concerned with an improvement of production conditions, they aimed only at a restoration of the ancient mode of production, namely, that of a free peasantry, and rightly so, for this mode of production was relatively higher. Slave labor led into a blind alley. Society would have to be placed once more on the basis of peasant operation before it could begin a fresh ascent. But Roman civilization was incapable of taking even this step, for it had lost the necessary peasants. It was necessary for the migration of nations to throw great masses of free peasants into the Roman Empire before the remnants of the civilization which that empire had created could again be used as the basis for a new social evolution.

Like every mode of production based on mutual hostility, the ancient slave-holding economy was digging its own grave. In the form which it finally attained in the Roman Empire, this economy was based on war. Only ceaseless victorious wars, a continued subjection of new nations, and uninterrupted expansion of the imperial territory could furnish the immense quantities of cheap slave material which it needed.

But war cannot be waged without soldiers and the best material for soldiers was the peasant. Accustomed to uninterrupted hard work in the open air, in heat and cold, in the blazing sun and in the driving rain, he could best bear the hardships which war lays upon the soldier. The impoverished city proletarian, no longer accustomed to work, as well as the dexterous artisan, weaver or goldsmith or sculptor, were far less suited for such use. The disappearance of the free peasants meant the disappearance of soldiers for the Roman armies. It became necessary more and more to replace the number of soldiers liable to militia service by mercenary volunteers, professional soldiers, who were willing to serve beyond their military period. Soon these also no longer sufficed, unless other than Roman citizens were also accepted. Already in the days of Tiberius, the emperor declared in the Senate that there was a lack of good soldiers, all sorts of rabble and vagabonds had to be accepted. More and more numerous became the barbarian mercenaries in the Roman armies, recruited from the subjected provinces; finally the breaches in the army had to be filled up by recruited foreigners, enemies of the empire. Under Caesar we already find Teutons in the Roman armies.

With the decreasing opportunity to recruit soldiers for the army from among the dominant race, and with the increasing rarity and cost of the soldiers, the Roman love of peace necessarily increased, not because of any change in ethical conceptions, but for very material reasons. Rome had to be sparing with its soldiers, but also it could no longer afford to extend the imperial boundaries; it was glad enough to be able to get a sufficient number of soldiers to hold the existing boundaries. It is just at the time in which Jesus lived, namely, under Tiberius, that the Roman offensive, viewed in the large, comes to a standstill. There now begins an effort in the Roman Empire to hold it together against the enemies threatening from without. And the difficulties of this situation were at this moment beginning to become more serious, for the more foreigners, particularly Teutons, were serving in the armies of Rome, the more did Rome's barbarian neighbors become acquainted with her wealth and her mode of warfare, not to mention her weaknesses, and the more did they become inspired with the ambition to penetrate into the empire, not as mercenaries and servants, but as conquerors and masters. Instead of undertaking more hunts for barbarians, the Roman masters soon found themselves obliged to retire before the barbarians or to purchase peace from them. Thus, in the First Century of our era, the influx of cheap slaves came to an abrupt stop. More and more it became necessary to *breed* slaves.

But this was a very expensive process. The training of slaves was profitable only in the case of domestic slaves of the higher types, capable of performing skilled labor. It was impossible to continue administering the latifundia by the use of trained slaves. The use of slaves in farming was becoming less and less frequent and even mining was on the decline, numerous shafts becoming unprofitable with the cessation of the supply of slaves captured in war, who did not need to be spared.

But the downfall of the slave-holding economy did not provide a new renascence of the peasantry. The necessary stock of numerous peasants, economically solvent, was lacking, and in addition, private property in land was an obstruction. The owners of the latifundia were not willing to give up their ownership, but merely lowered the scale of their larger operations. They placed a portion of their lands at the disposal of small tenants, renting them out to tenants or to *coloni*, under the condition that the latter should devote a portion of their labor power to the master's farm. Thus there arose a system of farming which even later, in the Feudal Period, remained the ambition of the great landed proprietors, until capitalism supplanted it with the capitalist lease-hold system.

The laboring classes from which the *coloni* [7] were recruited were partly rural slaves and poverty-stricken peasants, partly proletarians, free artisans and slaves from the great cities, no longer able to make a living in the latter, since the yields of the slave-holding establishments in agriculture and mining were going down, with the result that the magnanimity and luxuriousness of the rich were suffering a setback. In addition, these laboring forces were also swelled by inhabitants of the border provinces who were being driven out of their holdings by the advancing barbarians and fleeing toward the central provinces of the empire, where they found homes as *coloni*.

But this new mode of production could not hold back the process of economic decay resulting from the lack of a slave supply. This new method also was technically backward as compared with the free peasantry, and was a hindrance to technical development. The work which the *colonus* was obliged to perform on the farm remained a compulsory task, approached with the same sullenness and negligence, with the same contempt for cattle and tools, as was the case in slave labor. To be sure, the *colonus* did work on a farm of his own, but he was given such a small one that he was in no danger of waxing insolent, or getting more than a mere livelihood out of it, and besides, the rent, which was paid in kind, was made so excessive that the *colonus* had to

[7] See *colonus,* in the *Standard Dictionary.*—TRANSLATOR.

deliver to his master all that he produced beyond the bare needs of life. The wretchedness of the *coloni* was perhaps comparable with that of the petty tenants in Ireland, or perhaps of the peasants of present-day Italy, where a similar mode of production is still in force.

But the present-day agricultural regions at least have the safety-valve of emigration to regions which are industrially prosperous. There was no such thing for the *coloni* in the Roman Empire. Industry then served only in a small measure for the production of means of production, but was principally devoted to articles of consumption and luxury. As the surplus earnings of the possessors of the latifundia and mines went down, industry in the towns went backward and their population rapidly decreased.

But the population of the provincial regions was also decreasing. The petty tenants could not support large families, for the yield of their farms in normal times was barely enough to keep them alive. Crop failures found them without supplies and without money to purchase that which was lacking. Starvation and misery necessarily had a rich harvest; the ranks of the *coloni* were decimated, particularly those of their children. The decreasing population of Ireland within the past century is a parallel to the decrease in population of the Roman Empire.

"It is easy to understand that the economic causes which were bringing about a decrease in the population of the entire Roman Empire necessarily operated most perceptibly in Italy, and more at Rome than anywhere else. If the reader asks for figures, let him assume that the city of Rome in the time of Augustus had attained about 1,000,000 inhabitants, that it remained at about the same level during the first century of the Imperial Period, and then in the age of the Severi went down about 600,000; after this the number continued to decrease rapidly." [8]

Eduard Meyer, in his excellent work, *The Economic Evolution in Ancient Times* (1895), prints in a supplement the description given by Dio Chrysostom (born about 50 A.D.), in his Seventh Oration, on the conditions in a small town in Euboea, the name

[8] Ludo M. Hartmann, *Geschichte Italiens im Mittelalter*, 1897, vol. i, p. 7.

of which he does not give. It is a drastic presentation of the decrease in the population of the Empire.

"The entire surrounding district belongs to the town and pays tribute to the town. Almost all the land, if not all of it, is owned by rich people, who are the proprietors of extensive parcels, which are used both for pasture and for tilling. But the land is entirely desolate. 'Almost two-thirds of our land,' a citizen declared in the Popular Assembly, 'lies fallow because we cannot work it, and because our population is too small. I myself have as many acres as anybody else, not only in the mountains, but down in the plains. If I could find anyone who was willing to till them, I should not only let him have them without payment, but should gladly pay him money into the bargain. . . .' The speaker went on to say that desolation was now at the very gates, 'the land is absolutely idle and presents a sad spectacle, almost as though it were in the midst of the desert and not right outside the gates of the city. But within the walls of the city, most of it is used as pasture. . . . The gymnasium has been transformed into a plowed field, so that Hercules and the other statues of gods and heroes are hidden by the grain in summer, and the speaker who preceded me drives out his cattle every morning to graze in front of the town hall and the town offices, with the result that strangers who visit us laugh at us or mourn for us.'

"Accordingly, we find that many houses in the town itself are empty; the population is evidently decreasing. A few purple-fishers live down by the Capharic Rocks; otherwise there is not a soul to be found far and wide in the whole region. Formerly all this territory belonged to a rich citizen 'who had great herds of horses and cattle, many pastures, many fine plowed fields and much other property.'" Because of his wealth, the emperor ordered him killed, his herds were driven away, including the cattle which belonged to his herdsman, and since then all his land has been lying idle. Only two herdsmen, freemen and citizens of the city, have remained here and are now supporting themselves on the chase and on a little farming and cattle-holding. . . .

"The conditions here depicted by Dio—and throughout Greece

things were about the same even in the earliest days of the Imperial Period—are the same conditions that developed in the course of the centuries immediately following in Rome and in its surroundings, and which have placed their mark on the Campagna to this very day. In this district also we find that the country towns have disappeared, the land lies barren in every direction, and is used only for cattle-raising (also for grape-raising along the sides of the hills), and finally Rome itself becomes empty of its inhabitants, its houses unoccupied and collapsing, and its great public structures in the Forum and on the Capitol giving pasture to cattle. The same conditions have begun to appear in our century (the Nineteenth) in Ireland, and cannot fail to strike any visitor who comes to Dublin or travels through the country." (*Op. cit.*, pp. 67-69.)

The fertility of the soil was also going down. Stall-feeding was as yet little used, and necessarily was little resorted to under the slave-holding system, as here it meant bad treatment of the cattle. But no stall-feeding meant no manure, and the failure to fertilize the soil, or to farm it intensively, meant that it was being deprived of the ability to provide further yields. Profitable crops could be obtained only from the best soils by this mode of farming. But the number of such good lands was constantly decreasing, with the ever recurring crops, the soil becoming more and more exhausted.

A similar phenomenon was witnessed in America in the course of the Nineteenth Century, where in the Southern States, where slave-holding was also practiced, the soil was not fertilized and therefore rapidly deteriorated, and the use of slaves was profitable only on the most favorable soils. In that country the slave-holding system could only maintain itself by a constant expansion westward, absorbing more and more new land, and leaving behind the barren soil that had been already used up. The case is the same in the Roman Empire, and this constituted one of the reasons for the constant land-hunger of that empire's masters, and for their effort to conquer new land by war. Southern Italy, Sicily, Greece, were already agriculturally exhausted at the beginning of the Imperial Period.

An exhausting of the soil, coupled with an increasing lack of workers, as well as an irrational use of the latter, could have no other result than a constant decrease in the crops.

But simultaneously the nation's ability to purchase foodstuffs abroad was also decreasing. Gold and silver were less and less in evidence, for the mines were yielding little, as we have seen, laborers being few. And such gold and silver as was available was flowing more and more into foreign channels, some of it to India and Arabia, to purchase articles of luxury for those wealthy persons who still remained, but chiefly as tribute to the barbarous tribes of the border. We have seen that soldiers were being drawn in increasing measure from these tribes; and the number of soldiers was increasing who would take back their pay with them, or at least what remained of it, when their period of service was over. As the military power of the Empire declined, it was more and more necessary to appease dangerous neighbors, and keep them in good humor, which was most easily attained by the payment of heavy tribute. Failing in this, the territory of the Empire was often invaded by hostile tribes, who came for plunder. This also served to decrease the wealth of the Empire, and the last remnant of this wealth was dissipated in an effort aiming at its protection. As the military strength of the Empire went down, as domestic recruits became less and less frequent, as the necessity for importing recruits from abroad became more urgent, and the influx of hostile barbarians therefore more extensive, all these causes producing an increased demand for mercenaries, while the supply was decreasing; the wage that had to be paid them went higher and higher. Beginning with Caesar, this wage was 225 *denarii* ($50), in addition to which the soldier received 4 *modii* of grain per month (or 2/3 *medimnus* or 36 liters), and later the monthly allowance even rose to 5 *modii*. A slave who lived on grain only, received the same monthly allowance. In view of the moderation in food that is observed among southerners, most of their needs could be filled with grain. Domitian raised the wage to 300 *denarii* ($65), and under the later emperors even arms were furnished free. Septimius Severus and after him Caracalla made additional increases in the soldiers' pay.

But the purchasing power of money was then much higher than it is today. Seneca, a contemporary of Nero, tells us that a philosopher could live on half a *sestertius* (less than 3 cents) per day. The cost of 40 liters of wine was 6 cents; a lamb cost 10 cents; a sheep about 40 cents.

"It is apparent that the wage of the Roman legionary was very high in view of the prevailing prices. And in addition to his pay he received presents in money at the accession of new emperors; in the days when a new emperor was set up by the soldiers every few months, this made quite a difference. Upon the expiration of his service the soldier obtained a bonus at discharge, which in the days of Augustus was 3,000 *denarii* ($650); Caligula reduced this amount by one-half, while Caracalla again raised it, this time to 5,000 *denarii* (over $1,000)." [9]

And besides, the size of the standing army had to be increased in proportion as the attacks on the imperial boundaries became more numerous from every quarter. At the time of Augustus its strength was 300,000 men, later more than twice as much.

These are immense figures when we recall that the population of the Empire was very thin, owing to the low level of agriculture, and the surplus of their labor was very meager. Beloch estimates the population of the entire Roman Empire, the size of which was about four times that of the present German Empire, as being about 55,000,000 in the days of Augustus. Italy, which alone now contains 33,000,000, then counted only 6,000,000. These 55,000,000, with their primitive technical methods, were obliged to support an army as large as that which is a heavy burden even for the present German Empire, in spite of the enormous technical progress that has since taken place; and this army of recruited mercenaries was far better paid than the German warrior of today. [10]

And while the population was decreasing and growing poorer, the burdens of militarism were increasing.

[9] Paul Ernst, *Die sozialen Zustände im römischen Reich vor dem Einfall der Barbaren. Die Neue Zeit*, vol. xi, No. 2, pp. 253 ff.
[10] In 1908.

There were two causes for this; together they completed the economic collapse.

The two chief functions of the state in those days were warfare and the construction of edifices. If it would increase the outlay for the former, without increasing taxes, it must necessarily neglect the latter, and this it did. In the period of its wealth, and when there was a great surplus produced by the labor of great numbers of slaves, the state had been rich enough to execute great building operations, which served not only for luxury, for religion, for hygienic purposes, but also for economic needs. With the aid of the enormous masses of peasants that were at its disposal, the state constructed those colossal works which we have not ceased to admire to this day, those temples and palaces, aqueducts and cloacas, and also the system of excellent roads connecting Rome with the most remote possessions of the Empire, a mighty medium of economic and political unification and international traffic, not to mention great irrigation and drainage operations. Thus, by draining the Pontine swamps south of Rome, an immense region of fruitful soil, amounting to 100,000 hectares, was opened to agriculture, and at one time included not less than thirty-three towns. The construction and maintenance of the drainage plant for the Pontine swamps constituted a constant source of worry for those in power at Rome. This plant fell into such decay that to this day this entire swamp region and the land around it are a barren waste.

When the financial power of the Empire weakened, its rulers preferred to neglect the maintenance of all these constructions rather than place a curb on militarism. The impressive edifices became impressive ruins, and their disappearance was hastened by the increasing lack of labor power, which made it easier to take building materials for such new structures as had to be raised, from the ruins of the old structures, than obtain it from the remote quarries. This method of building did more harm to the works of ancient art than did the devastations of the invading Vandals and other barbarous tribes.

"The spectator, who casts a mournful view over the ruins of ancient Rome, is tempted to accuse the memory of the Goths and

Vandals for the mischief which they had neither leisure, nor power, nor perhaps inclination, to perpetrate. The tempest of war might strike some lofty turrets to the ground; but the destruction which undermined the foundations of those massy fabrics was prosecuted, slowly and silently, during a period of ten centuries. . . . The monuments of consular, or Imperial, greatness were no longer revered as the immortal glory of the capital; they were only esteemed as an inexhaustible mine of materials, cheaper and more convenient than the distant quarry." [11]

Not only works of art were wasted by this decay, but also public structures serving economic or hygienic uses, roads and water supply systems. This general ruin, a consequence of the universal economic débâcle, in its turn aided in accelerating that débâcle.

But the military burdens were increasing in spite of everything, finally becoming unbearable and accomplishing the ultimate destruction. The total sum of public burdens—payment in kind, payment in labor, money taxes—remained as large, or increased, while the population and its wealth were decreasing.

More and more irksome became the burdens imposed upon the individual by the state. Each man sought to shift this burden to weaker shoulders; most of this shifting was in the direction of the wretched *coloni,* and their already disconsolate situation became a desperate one, as is shown by numerous uprisings, such as those of the Bagaudi, Gallic *coloni,* who first insurrected under Diocletian, 285 A.b., were put down after some successes at the start, but again and again expressed the immensity of their misery by engaging in renewed attempts at insurrection and rebellion.

Meanwhile other classes of the population were also being oppressed more severely, though not as badly as were the *coloni.* The *fiscus* took everything it could lay its hands on; the barbarians were not worse plunderers than the state. A constant process of social disintegration set in, an increasing disinclination and incapacity of the various members of society to perform even

[11] Gibbon, *History of the Decline and Fall of the Roman Empire,* chap. 36, London, 1898, vol. iv, p. 19.

the most necessary functions for the commonwealth and for each other.

What had once been regulated by custom and by economic need, now required the forceful intervention of the state for its realization. Compulsory measures became more numerous after Diocletian. Some of these laws bound the *colonus* to the soil, thus transforming him into a serf; others obliged the landed proprietors to share in the administration of the city, the function of which was chiefly to collect taxes for the state. Other such laws organized the artisans in compulsory unions and forced them to furnish their services and commodities at fixed prices; and the state bureaucracy needed for carrying out these compulsory measures became larger.

Bureaucracy and army—in other words, the state power—thus were placed in an increasing condition of opposition, not only to the exploited classes but also to the exploiters. For the latter the state was ceasing to be a protecting and encouraging institution and becoming a plundering and devastating power. The hostility to the state increased; even the rule of the barbarians was considered a relief. The population of the border would escape to the free barbarian peasants, and finally the latter were invited by the border population as saviors and redeemers from the prevailing order of government and society, and welcomed with open arms.

A Christian writer of the later Roman Empire, Salvianus, writes the following on this subject in his book, *De gubernatione dei*:

"A great portion of Gaul and Spain is already Gothic, and all the Romans living there are animated only by the desire not to become Romans again. I should only be surprised if all the poor and needy should not desert to them, if it were not for the fact that they feel that they cannot leave their property and families behind. And we Romans consider it a wonder that we cannot overcome the Goths, while we Romans prefer to live among them rather than among our own people." The migration of nations, the inundation of the Roman Empire by hosts of rude Germans did not mean the untimely destruction of a flourishing, advanced civilization, but merely the termination of a process of dissolution of a dying civilization and the laying of the basis for a new cultural growth, which, to be sure, proceeded for centuries in a very slow and uncertain manner.

In the four centuries that lie between the foundation of the imperial authority by Augustus and the migration of nations, Christianity took shape: in the period which begins with the highest culmination attained by the ancient world, with the most colossal and most intoxicating accumulation of wealth and power in a few hands; with an immense heaping of the greatest misery on slaves, declining peasants, artisans and the lowest proletarians; with the most violent class oppositions and the most cruel class hatred—and which ends with the complete impoverishment and desperation of the whole system of society.

All these conditions have put their marks on Christianity and left their traces in its form.

But Christianity also bears the marks of other influences arising from the national and social life of the times, which was built upon the basis of the mode of production above described, and which in many ways even magnified the effects of this mode of production.

II. THE LIFE OF THE STATE

a. *The State and Trade*

In addition to slavery there were two other modes of exploitation in ancient society which also reached their culmination about the time of the origin of Christianity, sharpened class antagonisms to the utmost, and then progressively accelerated the destruction of society and of the state: *usury,* and the *plundering* of the subjected *provinces* by the all-conquering central power. Both of these institutions are closely bound up with the character of the state as then constituted, which in general is so closely interwoven with the economic situation of the times that we have had to mention the state repeatedly in our discussion of the basis of state and society, namely, the mode of production. Our first duty is therefore to present a short outline of the ancient state.

The democracy of antiquity never reached out beyond the limits of the town community or the clan. The clan was formed by one or more villages who owned and administered a certain territory in common. This was done by direct levies on the part of the people itself, in its assembly of all the adult members of the clan. This condition necessarily required that the commune or clan be not too extensive; its territory might be just large enough to enable each member to travel from his farm to the popular assembly without undue exertion and loss. It was impossible in ancient times to develop any democratic organization beyond these proportions, the necessary technical and economic conditions for such expansion being absent. Only modern capitalism with its printed books and its post-offices, with newspapers, railroads, and telegraphs has been able to weld the modern nations into units not only as to language, as were the ancient nations, but also into solid political and economic organisms. This process remained essentially incomplete until the Nineteenth Century. Only England and France were enabled by special circumstances to become nations in the modern sense at an earlier date, and to establish a national parliamentarism, the basis of democracy on any larger scale than that of the commune. But even in these countries this condition was made possible only by the leadership of two great centers, London and Paris, and as late as 1848 the national democratic movement was dominated by the movement of certain outstanding communities—Paris, Vienna, Berlin.

In antiquity, with its far less advanced transportation facilities, democracy remained limited to the extent of the commune. Transportation between the countries on the Mediterranean was, it is true, of rather respectable proportions in the First Century of our era, even going so far as to place two languages in a position of international importance, namely, Greek and Latin. But unfortunately this was accomplished precisely at the time when democratic and political life as a whole were on the downward path—unfortunately, we say, but not as the consequence of an unfortunate accident. The evolution of traffic between the communities was at that time necessarily connected with conditions that were bringing about the death of democracy.

It is not our task to prove this in the case of the countries of the Orient, in which democracy, limited to the commune, became the basis for a special kind of despotism. We shall here only consider the specific course of events in the Hellenic and Roman worlds, and shall examine only one example, that of the Roman community. Here the tendencies of the ancient evolution are emphatically evident, because here that evolution proceeded more rapidly and on a more gigantic scale than in the case of any other of the city communities of the ancient world. But in all these communities the same tendencies were at work, though perhaps on a more modest and petty scale.

The extent of each clan and commune had very narrow boundaries, beyond which it could not push out, and which caused the various clans and communes to remain fairly equal so long as a purely peasant economy prevailed. Nor were there at this stage many causes for jealousies or conflicts between them, as each clan and commune produced in general all that it needed.

At the worst an increase in population might cause a lack of land. But the increase in population could not lead to an extension of the clan boundaries, for the latter could not become so broad as to prevent each member from being able to travel to the legislative popular assembly without excessive effort and loss. Once all the arable land of the clan was actually under cultivation, the excess number of young men capable of bearing arms would set out to emigrate and establish a clan of their own, either by driving out other weaker elements, or by settling in regions where there was still a lower mode of production, with a consequently thinner population and more available space.

Therefore the individual communes and clans remained of fairly equal strength. But this condition changed as soon as trade began to operate side by side with the peasant economy.

We have already seen that the trade in commodities begins very early, going back into the Stone Age. In regions where a number of much desired raw materials were easily attainable, while elsewhere they occurred infrequently or not at all, it was natural that the inhabitants of such regions should acquire more of such raw materials than they consumed, and that they should develop greater skill in the winning and manipulation of such articles. They would then give their surplus in exchange for other products to their neighbors, who in turn would transmit it further. In this process of exchange from tribe to tribe many products were able to cover incredibly great distances. The presupposition for this trade was a nomadic mode of life on the part of individual hordes who frequently came in contact with each other in their roamings and on such occasions exchanged their surpluses.

Such opportunities ceased when man took to settling down, but the need for an exchange of commodities did not cease; particularly, the need for tools or at least the material of which to make them, which was easily accessible in a few deposits only, and therefore hardly obtainable except through the trade in commodities, necessarily grew. To satisfy this need, a peculiar class of nomads had to be formed, the *merchants*. These were either nomadic tribes of *cattle-breeders*, who now devoted themselves to supplying goods from districts in which they were abundant, and therefore cheap, to other districts where they were rare and therefore expensive, with the aid of their beasts of burden, or they were *fishermen,* who sailed in their boats along the coast or even from island to island. But as trade thrived more and more, even peasants were induced to take it up. As a rule, the landed proprietor class had an arrogant contempt for trade; the Roman aristocracy considered usury to be a decent occupation, but not trade; all of which does not prevent the landed proprietor from occasionally drawing great advantages from trade operations. Trade follows certain routes which therefore are more frequently traveled. Towns lying on such roads receive their commodities with greater ease than do others, and in the merchants they find purchasers for their wares. At many points, where it happens to be impossible to turn aside from the road, and which cannot be circumvented, and which in addition are in a position fortified by nature, the inhabitants and masters of such places are enabled to stop the merchants and mulct them, by imposing taxes upon them. On the other hand, other points become storing places where commodities must be transshipped, for instance, seaports or crossroads, where merchants arrive in large numbers from the most varied quarters and commodities often lie stored for some time.

All the communes thus favored by nature in the matter of trade necessarily develop beyond the proportions of peasant communes, and while the population of a peasant commune soon reaches a limit in the extent and fertility of its territory, the population of a trading town is independent of the fertility of the soil it owns and may reach out far beyond it. For in the commodities which it controls it possesses the means of purchasing everything it needs, in other words, of also obtaining foodstuffs from beyond the clan boundaries. With the trade in agricultural tools, in raw materials and tools for industry, and in industrial luxury products, there also develops the trade in the foodstuffs required by city dwellers.

But the expansion of trade itself does not encounter any fixed limits, and by its nature it continues reaching out beyond the boundaries already obtained, ever seeking new customers, new producers, new deposits of raw materials, new industrial regions, new purchasers for its products. Thus the Phœnicians very early in history passed out of the Mediterranean and reached North as far as England, while in the South they rounded the Cape of Good Hope.

"At an incredibly early period we find them in Cyprus and Egypt, in Greece and Sicily, in Africa and even on the Atlantic Ocean and the North Sea. The field of their commerce reached from Sierra Leone and Cornwall in the west, eastward to the coast of Malabar. Through their hands passed the gold and pearls of the East, the purple of Tyre, slaves, ivory, lions' and panthers' skins from the interior of Africa, frankincense from Arabia, the linen of Egypt, the pottery and fine wines of Greece, the silver of Spain, tin from England, and iron from Elba." [12]

The artisans naturally prefer to settle in the trading towns, in fact the latter furnish the only market for many classes of artisans, thus encouraging the formation of such classes: on the one hand there are the merchants who are seeking goods, and on the other hand there are the peasants from the surrounding villages who travel to town on market days in order to sell their foodstuffs and purchase tools, weapons, and adornments with the proceeds. The trading town also assures the artisans of the necessary supply of raw materials, without which they cannot practice their trade.

In addition to the merchants and artisans a class of wealthy landed proprietors also arises in the city community. The members of the original commune of this city, who hold ownership in the city lands, now become rich, as real-estate is in demand among the new arrivals, becoming valuable and constantly rising in price. They further profit by the fact that among the commodities brought by the merchant there are also slaves, as we have already seen. Certain families of landed proprietors who, for one reason or another, pass beyond the stratum of common peasants by their greater property in land or their wealth, are now enabled to extend their agricultural plant by the accession of

[12] Theodor Mommsen, *History of Rome*, New York, 1895, vol. ii, p. 132.

slaves, in fact they may even have this land operated by slaves only, themselves retiring to the city and devoting themselves to urban business, city administration, or warfare. A landed proprietor of this type, who formerly had only a farm in the surrounding territory, may now also build a town house and live in it. Such landed proprietors continue to base their economic strength and their social position on their property in land and agriculture, but in addition they become city-dwellers and increase the city population by their numerous households, which in time, with the addition of slaves for purposes of luxury, may become very extensive, as we have seen.

Thus the trading town constantly increases in wealth and population, but as its strength grows, its warlike spirit and the desire for exploitation also grow. For trade is not the peaceful thing that bourgeois economics would teach us, and this was least of all true in the days of its beginnings. Trade and transportation were then not yet divorced. The merchant could not sit in his office, as he does today, receive the orders of his customers in writing, and fill them with the aid of the railroad, the steamship, and the mails. He had to carry his wares to market himself, and this required strength and courage. Through pathless fields, on foot or on horseback, or over stormy seas on small open boats, he was obliged to be on the road for months, often for years, far from home. This involved burdens not inferior to those of a campaign, to which only strong men were equal.

Nor were the dangers of the trip less serious than those of warfare. The merchant was threatened at every moment not only by nature, with her billows and cliffs, her sandstorms, her lack of water or nutrition, icy cold or pestilential heat. The valuable treasures which the merchant carried with him constituted a booty which invited the stronger to take them from him. While trade at first had passed only between tribe and tribe, it was later practiced only by extensive bodies of men, by caravans on land, by commercial fleets on sea. And every member of such an expedition had to be armed and capable of defending his possessions, sword in hand. Thus trade became a school for the warlike spirit.

But while the great value of the commodities which he carried with him obliged the merchant to develop the strength of a warrior in order to defend them, this warlike strength in turn became a temptation to apply it for purposes of attack. The profit of trade resulted from obtaining cheap and selling dear. But the cheapest way of obtaining anything was unquestionably that of taking what one wanted without giving compensation. Robbery and trade are therefore at first closely connected. Wherever he felt himself the stronger, the merchant easily became a bandit, when valuable booty was in sight—and not the smallest of such booty was man himself.

But the merchant needed his warlike strength not only in order to enable him to make his purchases and acquisitions as cheaply as possible, but also in order to keep competitors away from the markets that he was frequenting; for the greater the number of buyers, the higher the price of the commodities which he wanted to buy; and the greater the number of sellers, the lower the prices of commodities which he was carrying to market; in other words, the greater the resulting difference between the price of purchase and that of sale, which means the profit. Wherever a number of large commercial cities arise in close proximity, wars soon develop among them, the victor having the prospect not only of driving his competitors off the field, but also of transforming the competitor from a profit-robbing factor into a profit-bringing factor; either in the most radical manner, not capable of frequent repetition, of absolutely plundering the opponent's city and selling its inhabitants into slavery, or by the less radical method, involving fresh gain each year, of incorporating the vanquished city into the state as an "ally" who is under the obligation to furnish taxes and troops and to refrain from injuring the victorious competitor in any way.

Certain trading towns, particularly favored by their situation or by other circumstances, may in this way combine many other cities, with their territories, into a state organization, without necessarily preventing the continued existence of a democratic constitution in each such town. But the totality of these cities, the state as a whole, is nevertheless not governed democratically, for the single victorious city is alone in control while the others must obey without having the slightest control in matters of legislation and administration of the state as a whole.

In Greece we find a great number of such city states, the most powerful of them being Athens, but none of the victorious cities was strong enough to subject all the others permanently, to gain final control of all its rivals. Therefore the history of Greece is nothing but an eternal war between the various cities and city states among themselves, very rarely interrupted by a common defense against a common enemy. These wars immensely accelerated the downfall of Greece, as soon as the consequences of the slave-holding economy, already described, made themselves felt. But it is ridiculous to become morally indignant at this situation as do some of our professors. The struggle against the competitor is a necessary corollary of trade. The forms of this struggle change, but the struggle necessarily enters the war phase when sovereign commercial cities stand face to face. The spectacle of Greece rending her own flesh was therefore unavoidable as soon as trade began to make its cities great and powerful. But the final goal of every competitive struggle is the driving out or suppression of the competitor, monopoly. No city in Greece became strong enough to attain this goal, not even powerful Athens. That was reserved for an Italian city, Rome, which became the ruler of the entire system of civilization about the Mediterranean Sea.

b. Patricians and Plebeians

Competition with rivals is not the only cause for which a great commercial city may wage war. Where its territory is contiguous with that of robust peasants, particularly cattle-raising peasants in the mountains, who are usually poorer than farming peasants in fruitful plains, but less definitely fixed to the soil, men accustomed to bloodshed and hunting, an excellent school for war—the wealth of the city may easily arouse the desire for booty on the part of the peasants. The latter may pass carelessly by the smaller country towns, serving only the local trade of a limited area and sheltering a few petty artisans besides, but the treasures of a great trading center must necessarily attract and tempt them to band together in masses for a predatory attack on the wealthy community. On the other hand, the latter is constantly at an effort to extend its possessions in land and the multitude of its subjects. We have seen that the growth of the city is accompanied by the development of an extensive market within it for the products of agriculture, and that the soil which is producing commodities for the city becomes valuable, stimulating the desire for more land and for laborers who may till this newly acquired land for its conquerors. A constant struggle between the city and the surrounding peasant tribes is the result. If the latter are victorious the city is sacked and must start all over again. But if the city is victorious, it takes away a portion of the land of the defeated peasants, turning it over to its own landowners, who sometimes settle their landless sons on it, but for the most part have the conquered land tilled for them by compulsory labor, which is also furnished by the defeated community, in the form either of tenants or serfs or slaves. Sometimes, however, a gentler procedure is taken; the subjected population is not only not enslaved, but even admitted to citizenship, in the victorious city; not to full citizenship, to be sure, for the full citizens rule the city and the state in their assembly, but to citizenship of the second class, enjoying full freedom and all the legal protection of the state, but without any share in its government. Such new citizens were much needed by the city as its wealth and consequently its burden of war increased, since the families of the old-time citizens were no longer capable of furnishing the required number of citizen soldiers. Military duty and the rights of citizenship are at first very closely connected. There was no way of rapidly increasing the number of warriors except by having the state receive new citizens. Not the least of the reasons for Rome's rise to greatness was in the fact that it was very generous in the bestowal of citizenship on immigrants as well as on the neighboring communities which it had defeated.

The number of such new citizens could be extended at will. The limits imposed upon the number of old-time citizens did not apply to the new citizens. These limits were in part of a physical nature. Since the city administration was the function of the Assembly of the old citizens, this Assembly might not be made so large as to make it impossible to transact business, nor could the citizens live so far from the place of assembly as to render it impossible for them to travel to that place without difficulty and without neglecting their farms at certain periods. But such objections did not apply in the case of the new citizens. In cases where certain political rights were given them, even the right of voting in the Assembly of citizens (which rarely was the case at their first admission to citizenship), it was not at all necessary —from the point of view of the old citizens—that the new citizens should be able to take part in these Assemblies. The more the old citizens had things their own way, the more they liked it.

The limits imposed upon the numbers of the latter therefore had no application to the numbers of the new citizens.

The number of new citizens could be increased as much as desired; it was limited only by the size of the state and by the state's need of reliable soldiers. For even when the duty of supplying troops was imposed upon the subjected provinces, the army still needed a nucleus that assured its trustworthiness, and such a nucleus could only be supplied by a strong contingent of citizen soldiers. Thus there arises in the growing city a second form of undemocratic organization for the state. While on the one hand the great city community becomes the absolute mistress of numerous communes and provinces, there arises within the citizenship of the commune, now extending far beyond the limits of the former city territory and the city lands, an antagonism between the old-style citizens or full citizens (*patricians*) and the new citizens (*plebeians*). Both of these processes transform the democracy into an aristocracy, not by limiting the circle of citizens with full privileges, or by elevating a few privileged persons above them, but by the growth of the state itself, in which this circle remains the same while all new elements joining the ancient community or clan have fewer rights or no rights at all. But these two modes of evolving aristocracy out of democracy do not pursue exactly the same course. One of these types of exploitation and control of the state by a privileged minority, the rule of one community over an entire empire, may be constantly increasing in extent, as is shown by the example of Rome; and it must increase, so long as the state still has vital energy and is not overthrown by a superior power. But the case with the new citizens without political rights is quite different. As long as these citizens are peasants only, they accept their restricted rights more or less calmly. Owing to the great distance between their farms and the city, they are for the most part not able to leave home early in the morning, attend the Assembly of citizens on the city market place at noon, and return home again by evening. And with the growth of the state, its internal and external conditions become more and more complicated, politics and even warfare becomes a business requiring a previous training not accessible to the peasant. He therefore has no understanding whatever of all the personal and technical questions that are discussed in the political assemblies of the city, and consequently feels very little need of demanding the right to have a part in them.

But the body of new citizens does not remain limited to peasants. Foreigners who take residence in the city and are considered useful to the city are made citizens. Nor do the conquered districts upon which citizenship is conferred include only mere villages; they even embrace cities with artisans and merchants as well as great landed proprietors who own a town house in addition to their country house. As soon as the latter acquire the rights of Roman citizenship, they begin to feel the need of moving from the smaller town to the large city, in which they are now more than tolerated and to which they are attracted by the easier opportunities for employment and the more interesting amusements. Meanwhile, in the manner already indicated, more and more peasants are being expropriated by war and the requirements of slavery. The best asylum for such disinherited elements is again the large city, of which they are citizens, and in which they attempt to make their way as artisans or burden-carriers, as peddlers, or as mere parasites of some rich master whose *clients* they become for every possible sort of service, and whose courtiers they are—the *Lumpenproletariat*.

Such elements have far more time and opportunity than the peasants to concern themselves with city politics, the effects of which upon them are far more perceptible and direct. They have an active interest in obtaining an influence in politics, in substituting an Assembly of the entire citizenry for an Assembly of old citizens only, and in achieving for all the citizens the right of electing state officers and passing laws.

As the city grew, the number of all these elements continued growing, while the circle of old citizens did not increase. Therefore this circle became relatively weaker and weaker, the more since it did not possess any military power separate from that of the entire citizenry, and since the new citizens as well as the old citizens were soldiers, bearing arms, and trained in their use. Thus we have in all the cities of this kind a bitter class struggle between old citizens and new citizens, invariably terminating sooner or later with the victory of the latter, therefore of democracy, which amounts to nothing more nor less, however, than an expansion of the aristocracy, as the disfranchisement and exploitation of the provinces possessing no citizen rights continues. Indeed, very often, increases of territory take place, sometimes even accompanied by a severer exploitation of the provinces, at the same time that democracy is making progress within the ruling city.

c. The Roman State

All these struggles, which are characteristic of every flourishing commercial city of antiquity, are found fully developed in Rome when that city first appears in history.

Rome was much favored by its situation in becoming a staple center for commodities. The city lies on the Tiber, at some distance from the seacoast, which in those days was no obstacle to maritime trade, because ships were very small; in fact, it was an advantage, for, being further from the coast, the city was better protected against pirates and floods than cities on the coast. It is no accident that so many of the older great commercial cities did not arise on the seacoast itself, but on navigable rivers at some distance from their mouth—Babylon and Bagdad, London and Paris, Antwerp and Hamburg.

The city of Rome arose at a point where the Tiber was still navigable and where two hills, easily fortified, came down to meet the river, thus assuring protection and security for the storehouses used by ships discharging or loading. The district in which Rome was situated was still rude, inhabited only by peasants, but to the North and South of it there were lands in an advanced stage of economic development, Etruria and Campania, with an active industry, extensive trade, and already having an agricultural economy based on compulsory labor. And from Africa the Carthaginians, who were at about the same stage of civilization as the Etruscans and the Greek colonies of Southern Italy, came with their wares.

This geographic position was very favorable to Rome. The commercial city seemed to the peoples of its immediate environment, the Latins and Volscians, to represent a higher culture; but to those of the more remote surroundings, the Etruscans and Italic Greeks, the Romans remained a mere rude peasant folk. As a matter of fact, agriculture remained the chief source of livelihood for the Romans, in spite of all the increase in trade. Not being near the sea, they knew nothing of navigation and shipbuilding, but left to foreign merchants and skippers the task of sailing to Rome and carrying on its trade. This condition remained unchanged and partly explains the fact that the Jews constituted such an important colony in Rome at the time of Caesar and his immediate successors, in other words, about the time of the origin of Christianity. They had succeeded at that time in getting control of a portion of the Roman trade. A similar condition may still be noted today in Constantinople, where trade is chiefly in the hands of non-Turks.

The more prosperous Rome became by reason of its trade, the more it came into conflict with its neighbors. The market for foodstuffs, which was opened by trade, stimulated the Roman landed proprietors to extend their possessions at the expense of their neighbors, while the latter were inspired with greed for the wealth of the city. On the other hand, competitive struggles

arose with the Etruscan cities. A series of long and severe wars
was fought by the young community, but it came out of them
victorious, thanks to its peculiar double position, which we have
already mentioned. The higher technical resources and the firm
organization of the large city triumphed over the peasants; but
the Etruscans, who had already lost some of their military power
as a consequence of the displacement of a free peasantry by compulsory labor, were defeated by the toughness and endurance of
the Roman peasant.

As soon as Rome had become strong enough to dispose of the
Etruscans, it learned in this procedure what an excellent business
war might be. Far more wealth was to be gained by warfare
than by trade, since the latter was mostly in the hands of foreigners, or by agriculture, which, owing to peasant operation,
yielded very slight profits each year. If the wars were successful, and were waged against wealthy cities and nations, much
plunder and tribute resulted. Trade and banditry are closely
associated from the very start, but probably not another commercial city has so much emphasized the banditry phase, or made
it even a national institution, if not a basis of the greatness of
the city, establishing all the national institutions on this basis,
as did Rome.

As soon as it had conquered and plundered the Etruscan cities
and made them its tributaries, Rome turned toward those rich
neighbors in the South whose growing wealth had also involved
a loss of their military power, for reasons that have often been
stated in these pages, with the result that the booty was at the
same time more desirable and more easy to take. But this wealth
was simultaneously attracting the glances of another peasant
people, the Samnites, who had to be defeated before the Greek
cities in Southern Italy could be taken by Rome. It was a case
of peasant tribe fighting peasant tribe, but the Samnites had no
large city, like Rome, at their center, which might have given a
centralized organization to the peasant fighting forces. Therefore they succumbed, and thus the path was cleared for Rome to
plunder and subject the wealthy cities of Southern Italy.

It was but a single step from Southern Italy to Sicily, which, no less wealthy than the Greek portion of Italy, also strongly attracted the predatory Roman hosts. But in this field the Romans encountered a serious enemy, the Carthaginians. Carthage, a powerful commercial city not far from present-day Tunis, had, under the influence of the same predatory instinct as Rome, subjected the western half of the North African coast, as well as Spain, and was now trying to do the same with Sicily. Carthage was a colony of the Phœnicians, who had been forced at an early period by the nature of their country to take up navigation, and had attained their great supremacy in this field. Carthage also attained its greatness and its wealth by means of navigation; Carthage produced sailors, not peasants. In the place of a *peasant* economy it developed the *latifundia* system with cheap captured slaves, and also some mining. It therefore lacked a popular peasant army. As soon as Carthage was forced to penetrate from the coast-line into the interior, in order to consolidate its conquests and develop military power on land, it had to resort to the hiring of mercenaries.

The struggle between Rome and Carthage, the three so-called Punic Wars, began in 264 B.C., and was not definitely ended until Carthage was destroyed in 146 B.C. Of course this struggle had already been decided by the defeat of Hannibal, which brought about the end of the Second Punic War in 201 B.C. These struggles became wars between mercenary armies and peasant armies, between professional and militia forces. Often the former were successful; under Hannibal, Rome came close to defeat, but the militia army, defending its own homes, finally turned out to be more enduring, and forced Rome's opponent to its knees at the end of the mighty conflict. Carthage was razed to the ground, its population destroyed; its immense resources in latifundia, mines, conquered cities, were the victor's booty.

Thus fell Rome's most serious opponent; Rome now ruled without interference in the western half of the Mediterranean; it was soon to rule also the eastern half, whose nations had already advanced far on the ancient road to destruction, which means the displacement of free peasants by the compulsory labor of slaves or serfs, and the impoverishment of the peasant by un-

ending wars, and the replacement of the militia forces by mercenaries. The nations of the Eastern Mediterranean were now
so weak from a military point of view as to be unable to offer
any serious resistance to Rome's armies. The latter subjugated
one city after the other, without difficulty, one country after the
other, in order to plunder them and condemn them to pay eternal
tribute. From this time on, Rome was to be the mistress of the
ancient world until the Teutonic barbarians succeeded in preparing the same fate for Rome that Rome had already prepared for
the Greeks, although the latter were far superior to Rome as far
as art and learning were concerned. Not only in economics and
politics, but also in philosophy and art, the Romans never were
more than the plunderers of the Greeks. Rome's greatest thinkers and poets were almost all of them plagiarists.

The richest lands of the then known world, which had accumulated the countless treasures of a civilization lasting for centuries,
or as in the case of Egypt, for thousands of years, were now
exposed to be plundered and robbed by Rome.

The enormous exertion of military force which brought about
this imposing result, was at Rome's disposal only when Rome was
a democracy, a city in whose existence all classes of the population
—although not all in equal degree—had a serious interest. In a
long and dangerous struggle, lasting from the Sixth to the Fourth
Century B.C., the new citizens, or plebeians, had succeeded in
wresting from the old citizens, the patricians, privilege after privilege, until finally all legal differences between the two estates had
disappeared and the popular assembly of all the citizens had the
privilege of adopting the laws and electing the highest officials,
the consuls, prætors, ædiles, who subsequently entered the Senate
after the expiration of their term of office; and the Senate was
the actual government of the whole state.

But the Roman people did not thus acquire control of the
state, but only the right of electing the rulers. And the more
the *Lumpenproletariat* predominated in the population of the city
of Rome, the more did this democracy really become an instrument of gain, a means of extorting largess and amusements from

the candidates. We have already become acquainted with the *clientes,* who hired themselves out to rich masters for services of every kind. In the case of those *clientes* who had the right to vote, one of the most important of their services was that of voting according to the desires of their patrons. Every wealthy Roman, every wealthy family, thus controlled numerous votes in the popular assembly, which they manipulated in the interests of the clique to which they belonged. A few cliques of rich families in this manner kept the government of the state in their hands and again and again would succeed in securing the election of the members of their families to the higher state offices, and therefore ultimately to the Senate. Democracy did not change anything in this system except in that it also permitted wealthy barbarian families to penetrate into the favored circle, which was limited to patricians while the aristocratic régime endured.

After their election, the consuls and prætors were obliged to spend the first year of their official activity in Rome. In the second year each of them assumed the administration of a province and tried in this new field to recover the expenses that had been incurred by candidacy for the office, and also to realize some profit on the investment; for these officials received no salaries; the offices were "offices of honor". On the other hand, the prospect of the profit which could be realized in the provinces by extortion and bribery, often also by outright robbery, was a cause for pressing one's candidacy for office most emphatically, with the result that the various candidates outvied each other in their gifts and amusements for the people.

But the more the various modes of purchasing votes increased the prospects of gain from the sale of the privileges of citizenship by the *Lumpenproletariat,* the greater was the temptation for those peasants who held the rights of Roman citizens to give up their wretched, laborious and oppressed condition in the country and travel to Rome. This tendency in turn increased the numbers of the rabble holding the franchise, and also the demands made on the candidates. In the time of Caesar there were not less than 320,000 Roman citizens in Rome who were receiving grain gratis from the state; the number of votes that could be purchased was therefore probably about 320,000. It may be imagined what enormous sums were used up in an election.

In the year 53 B.C., the purchase of votes created such a demand for cash, that interest on capital rose considerably and a crisis ensued.[13]

"The nobility (the office-seeking nobility) had to pay through the nose," observes Mommsen. "A gladiatorial combat cost 720,-000 sesterces (about $40,000). But they were glad to pay, as they were thus keeping out of office all persons who had not much money."[14]

Indeed, they paid frequently, for there were new elections each year. They did not pay, however, from any idealistic motive, but because they knew they were thus purchasing permission to engage in a far more profitable plundering of the provinces and therefore making a very good trade.

"Democracy", or the rule over the population of the entire Roman Empire, consisting of fifty or sixty million inhabitants, by a few hundreds of thousands of Roman citizens, thus became one of the most effective means of exaggerating in the highest degree the plundering and draining of the provinces, by immensely increasing the number of persons participating in this operation. Not only did the governors do all they could in the way of extortion, but each of them would take over a host of "friends" with him, who had helped him in the election, and who now set forth, as a reward, to rob and plunder under his protecting wing.

But this was not all; the usurious money capital of Rome also was unleashed against the provinces, in which it had every opportunity to develop its destructive power to the full, and to attain a position of importance which it did not enjoy in any other portion of the ancient world.

d. Usury

Usury itself is extremely ancient, being almost as old as trade. While it cannot be traced back to the Stone Age, it is nevertheless probably older than the use of money. As soon as a number

[13] Salvioli, *Le capitalisme dans le monde antique*, 1906, p. 243.
[14] *History of Rome*, New York, 1895, vol. iii, p. 42.

of households were formed, with definite possessions for every family, it was possible for one family to become wealthier than others in cattle, in land, in slaves, while other families might become poor. It was therefore natural for peasants in embarrassed situations to borrow of the superfluity of a wealthier neighbor, either grain or cattle, which the borrower had to promise to replace after an interval, together with an additional quantity, or to perform a certain task in exchange—this is the beginning of debtors' slavery. Such transactions in usury are possible, and actually occur, in an economy based on natural products alone, even without the use of money. The ownership of large estates, and usury, are closely associated from the very start; and usurious capital—today termed "high finance"—and large landed property have in many cases been on the best of terms. In Rome also the great proprietors were usurers as far back as we can go in history, and the struggle between patricians and plebeians was not only a struggle between the landed proprietors and the peasants for the use of the state commons, but also a struggle between usurers and debtors.

But the productivity of peasant labor, and therefore the surplus produced by it, were so slight that the exploitation of great masses of men was necessary in order to provide the exploiters with any considerable wealth. While the Roman aristocrats were exploiting by their usury only the peasants in the immediate surroundings of Rome, they might oppress these peasants considerably without gaining very much for themselves. But the affairs of the Roman usurers necessarily flourished more satisfactorily and yielded more considerable wealth, as they gradually obtained access to the entire world of their day.

But this involved also a division of labor. The taking of usurious interest from neighbors was not a business requiring much attention, and the aristocrats were able to take care of it without neglecting the management of their estates or the administration of the state. On the other hand, it was difficult to exploit Spain and Syria, Gaul and Northern Africa, while at the same time conducting the destinies of the enormous Roman state. The business of usury now begins to be differentiated more and more from that of government. By the side of the official nobility, which was robbing the provinces in its capacity as generals and governors, not disdaining at the same time to make a little money on the side, there now developed a special class of usurious capitalists who also formed a special social organization, the class of "knights." But the more numerous the class of money capitalists became, who were exclusively engaged in financial transactions, the more varied were the types of these transactions.

One of the chief means of plundering the provinces was that of *farming out their taxes*. As yet there existed no bureaucracy that might have taken charge of the collection of taxes, and the most convenient way of collecting them was to assign this duty for a particular province to a Roman financier, who would deliver to the state the total amount of the tax and was left to indemnify himself as well as he could. This was a system of taxation similar to that still practised in many parts of the Orient with such disastrous results. The tax farmer, of course, will not content himself with the amount that is rightfully his; the inhabitants of the provinces are at his mercy and are bled white.

It very often comes to pass that certain cities or tributary kings are unable to pay the sums that have been imposed upon them. In this case Roman financiers are ready to make advances to them, for interest of course. Thus, for example, the great republican, Junius Brutus, made "excellent speculations by lending money to the King of Cappadocia and to the city of Salamis. He made a loan to the latter at 48 per cent interest." (Salvioli, *op. cit.*, page 42.) This was not an unusually high rate of interest; Salvioli in his book reports loans made to cities at rates as high as 75 per cent. In cases of unusual risk, the rate of interest would be even higher. Thus, the great banking house of Rabirius in the time of Caesar lent the exiled King Ptolemy of Egypt all its own resources and those of its friends, at the interest rate of one hundred per cent. It is true that Rabirius made a bad investment, for when Ptolemy regained his throne, he failed to pay and had his importunate creditor, who claimed the entire Egyptian state as his domain, thrown into prison. The financier escaped to

Rome, however, and Caesar gave him a chance to make a new fortune in contracts for the African Wars.

These contracts were another form of money-making. The tributes that were gathered in the Roman coffers from the subjected provinces were enormous. But the ceaseless wars also cost a lot of money, they became means by which the financiers succeeded in pouring into their bottomless purses much of the booty taken in the provinces that had not gone to the financiers directly but been delivered to the state. They made deliveries of war supplies to the state—a frequent source of money-making, even in our day. But they would also undertake to apply usury to their own state, when the latter happened to be financially embarrassed, which was not unusual, for the more booty the state succeeded in dragging from the provinces, the higher rose the claims on the state by all the various kinds of parasites. Great sums had sometimes to be advanced to the state, greater sums than any individual possessed. For this purpose, the formation of joint-stock companies was very useful. Usury is not only the earliest form of capitalistic exploitation, it is also the first function of the joint-stock companies.

Rome's financiers "founded companies, corresponding to our joint-stock banks, having directors, cashiers, agents, etc. Under Sulla the Asiani Company was formed with a capital that was so enormous that the company was able to lend the state twenty thousand talents, or twenty-five million dollars. Twelve years later it increased this loan to one hundred and twenty thousand talents. . . . Smaller resources were invested in shares of the great companies with the result, as Polybius tells us (vi, 17), that the entire city (Rome) was a participant in the various financial undertakings headed by a few prominent firms. The smallest savings had their share in the enterprises of the publicans, which farmed out taxes and leased state lands, and yielded enormous profits." (Salvioli, *op. cit.*, pages 40, 41.)

All this sounds very modern to us, and it is an indication at least of the fact that Roman society at the time when Christianity was being born had advanced to the threshold of modern capitalism, and yet, the effects of this ancient capitalism were entirely different in kind from those of modern capitalism.

The methods we have described here are about the same as those which resulted in the formation of modern capitalism, the methods characterized by Marx as those of "primitive accumulation": expropriation of the peasant population, plundering of the colonies, slave trade, commercial wars, and national debts. In modern times we find these methods producing the same destructive and devastating effects as they did in antiquity. But the difference between modern and ancient times lies in the fact that antiquity was able to develop only the destructive influences of capitalism, while the capitalism of the modern epoch begins with destruction in order to develop the conditions for the erection of new and higher modes of production. The method by which modern capitalism developed is surely not less barbarous and cruel than that pursued by ancient capitalism; but at least modern capitalism creates a basis for an advance beyond this cruel, destructive activity, while ancient capitalism never could transcend that limitation.

We have already seen the reasons for this in the preceding chapter. The accumulations made by modern capitalism, by plunder and extortion and other acts of violence, are used only in small part for purposes of consumption, are devoted chiefly to the production of new and higher means of production, thus increasing the productivity of human labor. The capitalism of the ancient world did not find the necessary preliminary conditions for this task. Its influence on the mode of production was limited to a substitution of the labor of slaves for that of the free peasants, which was equivalent to a backward step economically in the most important fields of production, a decrease in the productivity of social labor, an impoverishment of society.

Those gains of the Roman financiers, as well as the booty of Roman generals and officials, that were not put to new employment in usury, in other words in the service of new plunder, either had to be lavished, on the one hand, in enjoyments, as well as in the production of means of enjoyment—and we must reckon not only palaces, but also temples among these means of enjoyment—or

these gains, if we ignore those drawn from the few mining operations, might be devoted to the acquisition of property, in other
words to the expropriation of free peasants and their substitution
by slaves.

The plundering and devastation of the provinces therefore only
served to give the financiers of Rome a means for permitting the
decrease in the productivity of social labor, owing to the spread
of slavery, to proceed more swiftly than might otherwise have
been the case. Destruction in one field was not counteracted by
economic prosperity in another field, as is at least sometimes the
case with modern capitalism, but destruction in the provinces also
accelerated the decline of Rome. Therefore, as a result of Rome's
world dominion, the general impoverishment of the ancient world
begins to move faster after the beginning of the Christian era,
than it could otherwise have done.

But for a long time the symptoms of economic bankruptcy
were thrown in the shade by the dazzling splendor of Rome's
situation. In a few decades, Rome had gathered together almost
all the objects that centuries, even thousands of years, of diligent
artistic work had created, in all the centers of civilization around
the Mediterranean Sea. The political bankruptcy of the system
became evident far sooner than its economic bankruptcy.

e. Absolutism

Rome destroyed political life in all the regions conquered by it,
by breaking their capacity for resistance and depriving them of
all independence. The entire policy of this tremendous empire
was concentrated in the city of Rome alone. But who were the
persons who had become the bearers of political life in that city?
They were financiers who thought only of accumulating interest
upon interest; aristocrats who staggered from one enjoyment to
another enjoyment, who scorned all regular labor, all exertion,
even the exertion of governing and waging war; and finally, the
Lumpenproletariat, who lived by selling their political power to
the highest bidder.

Thus, Suetonius reports in his biography of Caesar, concerning
the latter's gifts after the civil wars:

"He gave to each man of the population, in addition to ten *modii* of grain and ten pounds of oil, the three hundred sesterces which he had previously promised, together with one hundred sesterces as interest on the arrears. (In other words, $20 at a time when one could live on three cents a day. *K.*) He also undertook to pay (for those living as tenants in premises, *K.*) their annual rent, in Rome up to two thousand sesterces per family ($100), and in Italy up to five hundred sesterces ($25). In addition he gave a banquet (for two hundred thousand persons, *K.*) and distributed meat gratis; after the victory over Spain he also gave two public breakfasts, for the former seemed to him to be too scant and therefore not worthy of his generosity; he accordingly arranged for a second breakfast, five days later, which was a gorgeous feast." (Chapter xxviii.)

He also arranged games of unheard of splendor. One actor, Decimus Labirius, received five hundred thousand sesterces, or $25,000, for a single performance!

Suetonius says concerning Augustus:

"Often he distributed gifts to the people, not always of the same amount, sometimes four hundred sesterces ($20), sometimes three hundred sesterces ($15), sometimes only two hundred and fifty sesterces ($12) per man. And he did not even overlook the younger boys, although in other distributions they had received nothing unless they were over eleven years of age. Likewise, in famine years he often had grain distributed to the entire population at a very low price, and doubled his instructions for the distribution of money." (*Octavius,* Chapter xiv.)

Of course a proletariat that permitted itself to be purchased in this way, that had organized its venality into a system and paraded it openly, lost its political independence entirely. It was now only a tool in the hands of the highest bidder. The struggle for authority in the state became a competition between a few bandits who had been able to accumulate the greatest booty and who enjoyed the most extensive credit with the financiers.

This factor was also considerably emphasized by the rise of the mercenary system, which was making the army more and more the mistress of the Republic. After the mercenary system was extended, the warlike prowess of the Roman citizen declined—or rather, the decline in this prowess caused the increase in the application of the mercenary system. All the elements of the population capable of military service were to be found in the army; the population outside of the army lost more and more of its fighting ability and fighting spirit.

Two factors particularly were working in the direction of lowering the army more and more to be a willing tool of any general that would offer or promise it sufficient pay and booty, and to its being dominated less and less by political considerations. The first factor was the increasing number of non-Romans, of provincials, even of foreigners, in the army, elements that had no rights as citizens, elements that were therefore entirely excluded from any participation in political life; the second factor was the increasing disinclination of the pleasure-loving, effeminate aristocrats to take part in military service. This class had hitherto supplied the military officers, who were now yielding ground more and more to the professional officers; the latter were not economically independent, as were the aristocrats, and had no interest whatever in the conflicts of the Roman parties, which were in reality struggles between the various cliques of the aristocracy.

As the non-Romans in the army increased more and more, while the aristocratic officers continued to be replaced by professional officers, the greater became the army's readiness to sell itself to the highest bidder and make him the ruler of Rome.

Thus the foundation was laid for Caesarism, the condition that enabled Rome's richest man to buy out the Republic, purchasing the political authority for himself, and this in turn was a motive that would stimulate a successful general, having control of the army, to seek to become the wealthiest man of Rome, which he could best achieve by expropriating his opponents, confiscating their possessions.

The political life of the last century of the Republic in the last analysis consists of nothing but civil wars—a very erroneous term, as the citizens have nothing at all to do with these wars. They were not wars of citizens, but wars of individual politicians among themselves, most of whom were simultaneously both greedy financiers and prominent generals, and who mutually slew and robbed each other until Augustus finally succeeded, after overcoming all competition, in establishing his permanent autocracy.

To a certain extent Caesar had already succeeded in this before the days of Augustus; Caesar, an aristocratic adventurer who was deeply in debt, had conspired with two of the wealthiest Roman financiers, Pompey and Crassus, for the purpose of seizing the state power. Mommsen characterizes Crassus as follows: "His fortune was based on land purchases during the revolution; but he scorned no means of making money: he conducted building operations in the capital that were as magnificent as they were wise; he was associated with his freedmen in the most varied enterprises; both in and out of Rome he would act as banker, directly or through his friends; he advanced money to his colleagues in the Senate and would undertake, for their account, to carry out public works or bribe judicial bodies, whatever might be required. He was not delicate in his choice of money-making. . . . He would not hesitate to accept an inheritance because the testament in which his name was written was a notorious forgery." [15]

But Caesar was no better; no means of making money seemed too low for him. Suetonius, whom we have already quoted a number of times, has the following to tell us in his biography of the Caesar whom Mommsen later glorified:

"He showed no unselfishness either as a general or as a ruler of the state. For as we know from several sources, he received money from our allies when he was Proconsul in Spain; begged from them in order to pay his debts, and sacked several cities in Lusitania, pretending they were hostile, although they had complied with his orders and opened their gates on his arrival. In Gaul he robbed the temples and sanctuaries, richly stored with gifts; he destroyed cities more frequently for their booty than for their transgressions. He therefore had so much gold that he had it offered and sold at three thousand sesterces ($150) a pound

[15] *History of Rome*, New York, 1895, vol. iv, pp. 275, 276.

in Italy and in the provinces.[16]   In the period of his First Con-
sulate he stole three thousand pounds of gold from the Capitol,
replacing it with an equal weight of gilded copper.   He sold
alliances and kingdoms for money; thus he took from Ptolemy
(King of Egypt) alone for himself and Pompey nearly six thousand talents ($7,500,000).   Later he defrayed the most oppressive
disbursements of the civil wars, triumphs and festivities, by the
most outrageous extortions and temple robbings." (*Julius Caesar*,
Chapter liv.)

The war against Gaul, which had until then been free from
Roman oppression and therefore not subject to plunder, was
chiefly undertaken by Caesar for the sake of gain.   The rich
booty obtained in that country enabled him to get on his feet
and to break with his associate Pompey, with whom he had until
then shared the business of government.   The third partner,
Crassus, had fallen in Asia in a predatory campaign against the
Parthians, in which he had, as Appian tells us, "hoped to obtain
not only much fame but much money" [17]—in the same manner
that had been so successfully applied by Caesar in Gaul.

After the death of Crassus only Pompey still stood in Caesar's
way; Pompey was surrounded by the remnants of the aristocracy
that were still politically active.   The great Julius disposed of
them in a series of campaigns, which also were not unprofitable
in booty.

"It is reported that in his triumphal procession (at the end of
the civil war) he exhibited sixty thousand talents of silver as
well as 2,822 golden crowns weighing 2,414 pounds.   Immediately after his triumph he applied these treasures to satisfying
the claims of his army, giving each soldier five thousand Attic
drachmas (more than $1,000), twice as much to each non-com-
missioned officer, and to the higher officers twice as much as to
the non-commissioned officers, thus far exceeding his original

[16] The value of a pound of gold was ordinarily four thousand sesterces.
Caesar's plundering in Gaul forced it down a full quarter of its value in Italy.

[17] *History of the Civil Wars*, Book ii, chap. iii.   Appian informs us that the
Parthians had not been guilty of the slightest hostility.   The war with them was
therefore in reality a mere predatory campaign.

promises." [18] We have already reported, from Suetonius, the gifts Caesar then made to the proletarians of Rome.

From that time on Caesar's sole authority was not publicly disputed, and the Republicans were unable to voice their protests except by assassination. Caesar's heirs, Antony and Augustus, then gave them their quietus.

Thus the Roman Empire became the possession of a single individual, the Caesar or Emperor. All political life ceased. The management of this dominion was the private affair of its owner. Like all other possessions, it of course was frequently disputed; bandits, in other words successful generals, with a strong army behind them, quite frequently attacked the actual possessor, who was in many cases slain by his own bodyguard, in order that the vacant throne might be sold to the highest bidder. But this was a financial transaction, not worse than some other such transactions of the same period, and not a political act. Political life completely ceased; soon we find, at first among the lower classes, later also in the upper classes, not only indifference to the state, but even hatred for the state and its dignitaries, for its judges, its tax officials, its soldiers, for the emperors themselves, who were really no longer able to protect anyone, who became a scourge even for the possessing classes, to escape from which the latter sought refuge among the barbarians.

There were very few places left in the Roman Empire that retained any remnants of political life after Caesar's victories, and these remnants also were soon wiped out by Caesar's successors. A vigorous political life was kept alive longest of all in Jerusalem, the largest city of Palestine. The most serious exertions were required to overthrow this last stronghold of political freedom in the Roman Empire. After a long and stubborn siege the city of Jerusalem was razed to the ground in the year 70 A.D., and the Jewish people made homeless.

[18] Appian, *History of the Civil Wars,* Book ii, chap. xv.

III. CURRENTS OF THOUGHT IN THE ROMAN
IMPERIAL PERIOD

a. *Weakening of Social Ties*

WE have seen that the age in which Christianity originated was
one of complete disintegration of the traditional forms of production and of the state. The traditional forms of thought accordingly were also more or less moribund. There was a general
seeking and groping for new modes of thought. The individual
felt that he was a unit in himself, for the entire social background
which the individual had formerly possessed in his community
or in his clan, and the moral views handed down by them, were
now being dissolved. Therefore one of the most prominent
features of the new mode of thought was *individualism*. Of course
individualism may never involve a complete isolation of the individual from his social connections; that would be entirely impossible. The human individual can exist only in society and
through society. But individualism at least may go so far as to
cause the social bond in which the individual has grown up, and
which therefore seems natural and self-evident to him, to lose its
power, thus facing the individual with the task of now making
his way outside of this *former* social relation. The individual
can only achieve this by uniting with other individuals with
similar interests and requirements, forming new social organizations. The nature of these organizations will of course be determined by the existing circumstances and not by the caprice of
the individuals concerned. But these institutions do not approach
the individual in the form of ready-made traditional organizations,
but must be created by him in association with others of like
aspirations, which may be accompanied by numerous mistakes
and the greatest possible differences of opinion, until finally new
organizations arise out of the conflict of opinions and experiments

which new organizations, corresponding to the new conditions, will last and offer as firm a security for later generations as did the former organizations to which they succeeded. In such transitional periods it may appear that society does not condition the individual, but that the individual conditions society, that the social forms, their problems and aspirations, are entirely dependent on his volition.

Such an individualism, an individual seeking and groping for new modes of thought and new social organizations, is characteristic, for example, of the period of liberalism which followed upon the dissolution of the feudal organizations, without immediately replacing them with other new social organizations, until finally the new organizations of the workers and employers developed more and more into the dominant factors of capitalist society.

The first centuries of the Roman Imperial Era are very similar to the Nineteenth Century in this dissolution of whole social organizations and the creation of new ones. But these periods also resemble each other in the fact that in both periods the disintegration of the old social relations proceeded most rapidly and most perceptibly in the large cities, the entire social life being gradually determined more and more by these cities.

The peasant in the period of his strength and self-sufficiency was offered little opportunity for thought by the social life of the times, as life was definitely fixed for him by custom and habit. But he was obliged to devote considerable attention to nature, with whom he was constantly at war, who daily provided new surprises for him, on whom he was completely dependent, and whom he had to overcome in order to live. The question as to the *wherefore* of the various natural phenomena was therefore one that forced itself upon him. He first sought to answer it very naïvely by personifying various natural forces, by assuming the existence of numerous gods operative in nature, but in this way of putting the question we already have the beginnings of the *natural sciences*, which are based on the same question, the question of the *wherefore*, of the *causes* of all things. As soon as man began to understand that the relation between cause and effect in natural phenomena is a regular and necessary relation, that it is not dependent on the caprice of individual divinities, the path was cleared for a real knowledge of the natural sciences. Of course this recognition could not be achieved by peasants, who were absolutely dependent on nature. The peasant yielded without resistance to the natural forces, being unable to control them through *knowledge,* but inclined to *propitiate* them by *prayers* and *sacrifices.* A scientific study of nature is possible only in the cities, where man is not made to feel so directly and emphatically his dependence on nature, with the result that he may begin to work as a detached observer of nature. Only in the cities did a class arise with sufficient leisure for observation, and not subject to the impulse to utilize its leisure only in bodily enjoyments, like the great landed proprietors in the country, where bodily strength and endurance are such an important element in production, with the result that leisure and abundance create amusements only of the most coarsely physical kind, such as the chase and the banquet.

Natural philosophy begins in the cities, but gradually many cities grew so large that their populations began to be cut off from any relation with nature, thus losing all interest in the subject. The course of events was gradually assigning to these cities more and more of the leadership in the mental and economic life of large regions. Simultaneously this same course of development was weakening all the social bonds that had hitherto bound the individual to the traditional organizations and modes of thought. But the same process was sharpening class antagonisms, unleashing an ever more savage class struggle, which sometimes even assumed the form of an overthrow of existing relations. It was not *nature,* it was now *society* that was daily providing man with new surprises in the large cities, daily facing him with new, unheard-of problems, daily obliging him to answer the question: "What shall we do next?"

It was not the question as to the *wherefore, in nature,* but that of the *should, in society,* not the knowledge of necessary natural *relations,* but the apparently free choice of new social *goals;* this it was that now took up man's thoughts chiefly. In the place of *natural philosophy* we now have *ethics;* the latter assumed the form of a search for the *happiness of the individual.* This was already the case in the Hellenic world after the Persian wars. We have already seen that the Roman world was only the plagiarist of Greece in art and science, not having attained the possession of its mental (nor of its material) treasures by labor, but by plunder. The Romans became acquainted with Greek philosophy when the latter was already more concerned with ethical interests than with an interest in the study of nature. Roman thought therefore never devoted much attention to natural philosophy; Roman philosophy from the very outset busied itself with ethics.

Two philosophical tendencies were particularly prevalent in the earliest centuries of the Imperial Era, that of *Epicurus,* and that of *Stoicism.*

Epicurus called philosophy an activity which brings about a happy life by means of conceptions and proofs. He thought he could attain happiness through the pursuit of pleasure, but only through the pursuit of rational, permanent pleasures, not through the desire for temporary and exaggerated sensual joys, which lead to the loss of health and fortune, and therefore to unhappiness.

This was a philosophy that was quite well suited to the uses of an exploiting class, which had no other use to which to put their wealth than to consume it; what they needed was a rational regulation of the life of pleasure. But this doctrine gave little satisfaction to that constantly increasing number of persons who already had suffered a physical, mental or financial breakdown, to the poor and wretched, nor did it afford consolation to the over-sated, to those already nauseated by enjoyment. Nor could it give pleasure to those who still had some interest in the traditional forms of the communal life, and were still pursuing purposes that transcended their own personal needs, to those patriots who were witnessing the decay of state and society, full of impotent grief, but unable to retard the process. To all these groups the pleasures of this world seemed vain and shallow. They turned to the Stoic doctrine, which exalts *virtue,* not *pleasure,* as the highest good, as the only bliss. Mere external goods, health, riches, etc., the Stoics declared to be matters of as great indifference as were the external evils.

This finally led many persons to turn away completely from the world, to scorn life, even to desire death. Suicide became a habit in Imperial Rome, it was for a time quite the fashion.

But it was remarkable that simultaneously with a desire for death there also developed in Roman society a veritable terror of death. A citizen of any of the communities of classic antiquity felt himself to be a portion of a great whole which would survive after his death, and which was immortal by comparison with himself. He would continue to live in his community; it would bear the traces of his life; he needed no other immortality. As a matter of fact we either do not find among the ancient nations, who had but a short period of cultural development behind them, any ideas at all of a life after death, or their idea is that of a life of shades, an idea produced by the need of explaining the appearance of deceased persons in dreams: this life of shades was a lamentable existence for which no person had any desire at all. We know the lament of the shade of Achilles:

> "Rather I should till my field as a day laborer,
> For a needy man, having no land or possessions,
> Than rule the entire host of the vanished dead!"
>
> (*Odyssey*, xi, 489-491)

The assumption of a shadowy existence after death was, we repeat, a naïve hypothesis required for the explanation of certain dream phenomena, and not the result of a real need of the spirit.

But things changed when the community was on the downward path and the individual was breaking away from it. The individual was no longer possessed by the feeling that his activity would endure in the state; for his attitude toward the state was that of indifference or even hostility; and yet the thought was intolerable to him that he would be completely annihilated. There arose a fear of death such as had hitherto been unknown in antiquity. Cowardice flourished, Death became an image of terror, whereas he had formerly been considered as the brother of Sleep.

More and more the need began to be felt for a doctrine which would maintain the immortality of the individual, not as a disembodied shade, but as a joyous spirit. Soon blessedness was no longer sought in earthly joy, nor even in earthly virtue, but in the achievement of a better hereafter, for which this life was merely a preparation. This conception found a powerful support in Plato's doctrine, and such was the direction also taken by the Stoic school.

Plato already assumed a life in the future, in which the souls, liberated from their bodies, would continue to live and would be rewarded and punished for their activities on earth. In Chapter xiii of Book x of his *Republic*, Plato tells us of a Pamphylian who had fallen in war, and who, when he was about to be incinerated on the twelfth day after his death, suddenly came to life again and reported that his soul, after leaving his body, had been in wondrous places, with great clefts extending into the sky above and downward into the bowels of the earth. Judges sat in that place, to judge the souls on their arrival and to conduct to the right those found to be righteous, to Heaven, where boundless beauty reigned; while the unrighteous were directed to the left, down into the bowels of the earth, into a subterranean chasm, where they had to atone tenfold for their sins. Those who were incorrigibly wicked were there seized by savage men who looked like images of fire, and who chained and tortured them. But the rest of those who were assigned to the subterranean chasm, as well as those who were living in Heaven, were to begin a new life after the lapse of a thousand years. The Pamphylian who had seen all this maintained he was instructed to report it, whereupon he had been returned to life by a miracle.

Who is there that is not reminded at once of Heaven and Hell in the Christian sense, of the sheep on the right and the goats on the left, of the eternal fire that is prepared in Hell (Matthew xxv, 33, 41) and of the dead who shall live again "until the thousand years are finished" (Revelation of Saint John, xx, 5), etc.? And yet Plato lived in the Fourth Century before Christ. Not less Christian is the impression produced by the words:

"The body is the burden and punishment of the spirit; it oppresses the spirit and holds it captive."

It was not a Christian who wrote these words, but the teacher and master of Nero, the persecutor of the Christians, the Stoic philosopher Seneca.

Very similar is another passage:

"By this fleshly envelope is the soul concealed, disguised, separated from that which is its own and the truth, and cast into deception; the soul's entire struggle is with the flesh that oppresses it. The soul strives thitherward whence it was sent forth; there it is attended by eternal peace, where it preserves that which is pure and clear after the confused and intricate appearances of this world."

In other passages of Seneca we also find a striking number of turns of phrase that also occur in the New Testament. Thus Seneca says on one occasion: "Put ye on the spirit of a great man." Bruno Bauer rightly compares this expression with that contained in the Epistle of Paul to the Romans: "But put ye on the Lord Jesus Christ" (xiii, 14), and in that to the Galatians: "For as many of you as have been baptized into the Christ have put on Christ" (iii, 27). These coincidences have led some persons to conclude that Seneca was using Christian sources, even that Seneca was a Christian; the latter is the product of the Christian imagination. As a matter of fact, Seneca wrote before the various parts of the New Testament were composed; if there was any borrowing at all, therefore, we may rather assume that the Christians were drawing upon the widely disseminated writings of the fashionable philosopher of that day. But it is just as reasonable to assume that both were using, independently of each other, turns of phrase that were in vogue at the time.

Particularly with regard to the expression "putting on Christ", Pfleiderer points out that it is borrowed from the Persian cult of Mithra, which was much in favor in Imperial Rome. He tells us concerning the influence of this cult on Christian conceptions, among other things:

"The Mithra sacraments also included a sacred meal, at which the sanctified bread and a cup of water or even wine served as mystic symbols of the distribution of the divine life to the Mithra-believers. At such celebrations, the latter appeared in animal masks indicating by these representations attributes of their god

Mithra; the celebrants had 'put on' their god, which meant that they had entered into a community of life with him. This, too, is paralleled closely by Paul's teaching of the Lord's Supper as a 'communion' of the blood and of the body of Christ (I Cor. x, 16), which he who had been baptized, has 'put on' (Gal. iii, 27)." [1]

Seneca is not the only philosopher of his time who devised or used turns of phrase that appear to us as Christian.

Particularly the notions with which we are dealing at this moment, those of the immortality of the soul and the life hereafter, were finding more and more adherents at the time in which Christianity originated. Thus the Alexandrian Jew Philo, who lived early in the Christian era, ends his First Book on the Allegories of the Law with the sentence: "Heraclitus also has said, 'We live the deaths of them (the gods) and have died their lives'; for, as we live, the soul has died and is encased in the body as in a mound, whereas the soul lives its own life after we have died, and is liberated from the evil and the corpse of the life to which it had been chained."

The preparation for the life hereafter began more and more to be regarded as more worthy than the struggle for the goods of this world. The Kingdom of God took the place of the wealthy of this world: but how find this kingdom? Formerly the citizen had possessed three distinct and reliable guides in conduct, in the form of tradition, the popular will, the needs of the community. These were now absent. Tradition had resolved itself into an empty shadow; the people no longer had any united will; the citizen was now indifferent to the needs of the community. Concerned only with himself, the individual was helpless in the torrent of new ideas and relations that was inundating society, and cast about for a firm anchor, for doctrines and teachers that would teach him the truth and a correct philosophy of life, pointing out to him the right path to the Kingdom of God.

As in every case when a new need arises, there were numerous persons who sought to satisfy this demand. The preaching of individual morality began, the morality by means of which the individual could, without altering society, elevate himself out of

[1] Pfleiderer, *Christian Origins,* New York, B. W. Huebsch, 1906, p. 158.

and above society and become a worthy citizen of a better world.

In what other activity could oratorical and philosophical talents engage? All political activity had ceased; the interest in the study of the causes of things, in scientific work therefore, had lessened. What was left for the ambition of orators and philosophers, besides conducting litigations for the acquisition of property, or preaching the doctrine of contempt for property, becoming therefore either jurists or preachers? Both these fields, as a result, were very extensively cultivated in the Imperial Era, and the Romans were exceedingly productive at that time both in declamations concerning the emptiness of the goods of this world, as well as in legal paragraphs devised for the protection of these goods. It became the fashion to deliver edifying speeches and to fabricate edifying maxims and anecdotes. The Gospels also are nothing more or less than a compilation of such collections of maxims and anecdotes.

Of course this era may not be judged merely by its moralizing rhetoric. There is no doubt that the new morality with its contempt for this world answered certain strong mental needs, which in turn were produced by very real social conditions. But in fact it was impossible to escape from the world; the world always turned out the stronger. There resulted that contradiction between moral theory and moral practice which is inevitable in any moral doctrine of this stamp.

A classic example of this is Seneca, whom we have already mentioned several times. This excellent Stoic delivered himself of moral sentiments against taking part in politics, and censured Brutus who had violated, he said, the fundamental principles of Stoicism by taking part in such activity. But the same Seneca who rebukes the Republican Brutus for participating in political conflicts was an accessory to all the bloody deeds of Agrippina and Nero and played pander to the latter, for the sole purpose of retaining his position as minister. This same Seneca thundered in his writings against wealth, avarice and the love of pleasure, but in the year 58 A.D. he was obliged to hear Suilius accuse him in the Senate of having accumulated his millions by forging testaments and engaging in usury. According to Dio Cassius, the insurrection of the Britons under Nero was partly caused by the fact that Seneca had made them a loan of ten million *denarii* ($2,200,000) at a high rate of interest, and later had suddenly tried to collect the entire sum in the most brutal manner. This eulogist of poverty left behind him a fortune of three hundred million sesterces ($15,000,000), one of the greatest fortunes of those times.

In the face of this magnificent example of true hypocrisy, it is almost an understatement of the case when the satirist Lucian, a century later, ridicules, in his *Hermotimus,* a Stoic philosopher invented by him, who preaches contempt for money and enjoyments, and gives assurance that his teaching results in a noble equanimity in all the vicissitudes of life, and who nevertheless sues his scholars in the courts if they are unable to pay him the tuition agreed upon, who gets drunk at banquets and becomes so heated in disputes that he casts a silver beaker at the head of his opponent.

Moral preaching had become the fashion in the Imperial Era. But people sought not only for *moral teachings* that could be a support to weak spirits who were not independent, who had lost all their background together with their common public activities and traditions; the need was also felt for a *personal* support. We already read in Epicurus: "We must seek for ourselves a noble man to have him constantly before our eyes, that we may live as if he watched and act as if he beheld it." Seneca quotes this passage and then continues: "We need a guardian and teacher. A great number of sins will disappear if the stumbling man has a witness by his side. The spirit must have someone whom it venerates with a respect that sanctifies also its innermost kernel. The mere thought of such a helper has a guiding and corrective power. He is the guardian, model, and rule, without which one cannot rectify that which is wrong."

Thus people became accustomed to choosing a deceased great man as their patron saint. But some persons even went so far as to subject their conduct to the control of persons still living, moral preachers who pretended that they were superior, owing to their magnificent morality, to the rest of humanity. Stoicism had already declared the philosopher to be free from error and defects. By the side of sanctimoniousness and hypocrisy, a pharisaical arrogance of the moral teacher now began to develop —qualities which were unknown in classic antiquity, which were the outgrowth of a period of social decay, and which necessarily became more and more prominent, as science was being replaced in philosophy by ethics, in other words, as the *investigation of the world* was being displaced by the drawing up of *demands upon the individual*.

Moral preachers now arose for each social class, preachers who claimed to be able to elevate man to a greater moral perfection through the example of their own sublime personalities. The chief teachers of this kind for the proletarians were philosophers of the School of the Cynics, successors to the famous Diogenes, who preached in the streets, lived by begging, and found happiness in filth and frugality, which made it unnecessary for them to engage in any work, which they hated and despised as a terrible sin. Christ and his apostles are sometimes represented as mendicant street preachers. The Gospels have no place for work; in this they all agree, in spite of all their contradictions.

But the aristocrats had their own personal moralists, most of whom belonged to the Stoic School.

"After the manner of the great since the time of the Scipios, Augustus kept his own philosopher about him in the person of Areus, a Stoic from Alexandria, and Livia also became his disciple in order to obtain consolation from him after the death of her son Drusus. Augustus had Areus with him in his retinue when he entered into Alexandria after the battle of Actium, and introduced him to his fellow citizens in a speech (in which Augustus promised the Alexandrians to pardon them for having supported Antony) as being one of the motives for his clemency. Similar spiritual guides served the spiritual needs of the great in other palaces and houses. Having formerly been the teachers of some new theory, they had become for the Romans, after the civil wars, practical spiritual guides, mental directors, consolers in misfortune, confessors. They would accompany the victims of the imperial caprice to their death and give them their last ministrations. Canus Julius, who received his death sentence from the Emperor Caligula with an expression of thanks, and who died with calm and composure, was accompanied on his last journey by 'his philosopher'. Thrasea admitted his son-in-law Helvidius and the Cynic Demetrius, the latter practically his domestic clergyman, to the chamber where he caused his own veins to be opened, and in the torment of his slow death he kept his eyes fixed upon him." (Bruno Bauer, *Christus und die Cäsaren*, pages 22, 23.)

Thus, even before the rise of Christianity, we find the *father confessor* entering upon the scene, and, owing to the force of the new circumstances, not to the teachings of any individual person, a new historic power arises in the countries of Europe, *priestly rule*. To be sure, there had for a long time been priests among the Greeks and Romans, but they had been of very slight importance in the state. Not until the Imperial Era do we begin to find the conditions in the countries of Europe ripe for priestly rule, which had already existed in early antiquity in many countries of the Orient. We now find even in the Occident the necessary preliminary conditions for a clergy, for the *priestly caste* as rulers of men, which by the sanctimoniousness and arrogance of many of its members is already beginning to develop the traits that are characteristic of a priesthood, and which, in all ages down to the present day, have caused it to be hated by all the vigorous elements of society which have no need of any guardianship.

Plato had already declared that the state would not be properly governed until the philosophers controlled it and the remaining citizens no longer had anything to say. Now his dream was being fulfilled in a manner that would, of course, not have been much to his taste. But these moral preachers and father confessors were by no means sufficient for the weakened generation then living. The state was moving irresistibly toward destruction. Louder and louder was the knocking of the barbarians at the gates of the Empire, whose flesh was often rent by the bloody disputes of its own generals. The poverty of the masses increased; depopulation was progressive. Roman society was brought face to face with its end; but this generation was too corrupt, too weak in body and spirit, too cowardly, too spineless, too completely at variance with itself and with its surroundings to be able to make an energetic attempt to free itself from these intolerable conditions. It had lost faith in itself, and the only support that preserved it from complete despair was the hope for assistance from some higher power, some *redeemer*.

They first considered the Caesars to be this redeemer. In the days of Augustus a prophecy from the Sybilline books was in circulation, promising a redeemer in the near future.[2] Augustus was regarded as a prince of peace leading the disorganized Empire, after the civil wars, toward a new epoch of splendor and prosperity, with "peace on earth for men of good-will".

But the Caesars brought neither permanent peace nor economic or moral advancement, in spite of all the confidence that was placed in their divine powers, great though this confidence actually was.

They were actually classed with the gods; before the doctrine of the god turned man had originated, the notion of the man turned god was accepted, in spite of the obviously greater difficulty of this latter procedure. Where all political life has been extinguished, the lord of the state rises so majestically above the mass of the population that he really must impress them as supreme, since he alone appears to unite within himself the entire force and power of society and to direct it according to his will. On the other hand, the gods were conceived in a very human manner in antiquity. The transition from superman to god was therefore not a very difficult one.

The degenerate Greeks of Asia and Egypt had begun several centuries before our era to consider their despots as gods or the offspring of gods; they even venerated their philosophers as such. Within the lifetime of Plato there had already arisen the legend mentioned in the funeral discourse delivered by his nephew Speusippus, that his mother Periktione had conceived him not from her husband, but from Apollo. When the Hellenic realms

[2] Merivale, *The Romans Under the Empire,* 1862, vol. vii, 349.

became provinces of Rome, they transferred their divine worship of their kings and philosophers to the Roman governors.

But Julius Caesar was the first man who dared demand of the Romans what the cowardly Greeks offered him: to be worshiped as a god. He boasted of his divine origin; his ancestress was no less a person than the goddess Venus, as Virgil, the court poet of Caesar's nephew Augustus, later explained in detail in his long epic, the *Æneid*.

When Caesar returned to Rome from the Civil War, as a victorious triumphator, it was resolved in Rome "to erect a number of temples to him as to a god, including one to be sacred to him and to the goddess of clemency, in which he was represented as clasping the hand of this goddess." [3]   By this cunning device it was attempted to appeal to the clemency of the victor. After his death the "divine Julius" was formally admitted by decision of the people and the Senate of Rome to the galaxy of the Roman gods. And this was done, says Suetonius, "not superficially only, by a mere resolution, but because of the inner conviction of the people. For did not a comet appear during the games that his successor Augustus provided for the people, the first after Julius had become a god, for seven days in succession, rising about the eleventh hour (between five and six o'clock in the afternoon)? It was believed that this was the soul of Cæsar, who had risen heavenward. Therefore he is still depicted with a star over his head." (Chapter lxxxix.)   Does this not recall the star which indicated the divinity of the Christ child to the wise men of the East?   From the time of Augustus it was considered as self-evident that each emperor should be admitted to divinity after his death. In the eastern portion of the Empire he therefore was given the Greek name *Soter*, meaning *redeemer*.

But these canonizations (apotheoses) were not limited to deceased emperors, but were also bestowed on their relations and favorites. Hadrian had fallen in love with a handsome Greek youth, Antinoos, who "became in *every manner* the favorite of the Emperor," as Hertzberg delicately expresses it in his *Geschichte*

[3] Appian, *Civil Wars of Rome*, ii, 16.

des römischen Kaiserreichs (page 369).[4]   After his lover had
drowned in the Nile, Hadrian at once had him placed among the
gods, as a reward for his versatile services, had a splendid city
built not far from the scene of the accident, which he named
Antinoopolis, and in this city a magnificent temple for his singular
saint.   The worship of this youth rapidly spread throughout the
Empire; in Athens festive games and sacrifices were arranged
in his honor.   But Suetonius reports concerning Augustus:
"Although he knew that temples were dedicated even to Pro-
consuls (governors) he nevertheless did not accept this honor in
any province unless the temple was dedicated to both him and
Roma together.   Within Rome he always emphatically rejected
this honor."   (Chapter lii.)

But Augustus was comparatively modest.   The third emperor
of the Julian dynasty, Gaius, nicknamed Caligula (*little boot*),
caused himself to be worshiped in Rome while still alive, not only
as a demigod, but as a full god, and felt himself to be such.

"Even as those," he once said, "who must guard sheep and
oxen, are neither sheep nor oxen but have a higher nature, so
also are those that have been placed as rulers over men not men
as others, but gods."   It is in truth the sheepish nature of men
which produces the divinity of their rulers.   This sheep-like quality was very strongly developed in the Imperial Era.   And therefore the divine worship of the emperors and their favorites was
taken as seriously as some persons today take the gift of a bit
of ribbon for their buttonholes, ascribing miraculous effects to
such a bestowal.   Of course this divine worship involved a good
deal of servility; in this respect the Imperial Era has not been
excelled even to this day, and that means a good deal.   But in
addition to servility, *credulity* also played a great part.

b.   Credulity

This credulity was also an outgrowth of the new conditions.
From his earliest beginnings, man is forcibly made to observe

---

[4] The English translation of this book (*Imperial Rome*, Philadelphia, 1905)
tactfully omits both the delicacy and indelicacy of this reference (p. 149, footnote).—TRANSLATOR.

nature closely, to avoid being deceived by any of her phenomena and to grasp clearly a number of relations of cause and effect. His whole existence depends on this ability; where he does not succeed, his destruction only too often results.

Man's whole conduct is based on the experience that certain definite causes are followed by certain definite results, that the stone thrown by man will kill the bird on striking it, that the meat of this bird will appease his hunger, that two bits of wood rubbed against each other will produce fire, that fire gives warmth, while it also consumes wood, etc.

Man will then judge other natural events on the basis of his own conduct as determined by such experiences, where these events are more or less impersonal. He beholds in them the effects of the actions of individual personalities, endowed with superhuman powers, the gods. The latter are not at first workers of miracles, but producers of the regular natural course of events, of the blowing of the wind, the surging of the sea, the destructive power of lightning, but also of men's ideas, wise as well as stupid. It is well known that the gods make blind them whom they would destroy. The production of such results continues to remain the principal function of the gods in primitive natural religion.

The charm of this religion is in its naturalness, in its acute observation of persons and things, which to this day makes the Homeric poems, for example, unexcelled as works of art.

This acute observation and constant investigation for the where-fore, for the causes of things in the external world, became more delicate with the development of the cities and that of natural philosophy in the cities, as we have seen. The urban observers now became able to discover impersonal phenomena in nature, very simple indeed, but of such rigid regularity that they were easy to recognize as necessary relations, altogether transcending the realm of the caprice that is associated with the conception of personal divinities. It was particularly the motion of the *stars* that gave rise to the conception of law and necessity in nature. Natural science begins with *astronomy*. These ideas are then applied also to the rest of nature; everywhere a search begins for necessary relations of law. The regular recurrence of a certain experience is the basis for this mental activity.

But this condition changes, when, in response to the causes already indicated, the interest in the scientific investigation of nature recedes and is replaced by the *ethical* interest. The human spirit is no longer preoccupied with such simple motions as the paths of the stars, for example, which furnish an easy point of departure; it is concerned exclusively with itself, with the most complicated, most variable, most intangible phenomenon, one that resists scientific study longest of all. Furthermore, ethics no longer involves a knowledge of that which is and was, of what is present in *experience,* and usually in a regularly recurring experience; ethics concerns itself with plans and obligations in the *future,* as yet entirely beyond experience, constituting therefore a field of absolute free-will that lies before us. In this field the wish and the dream have the freest play, the imagination may disport itself unbridled and rise above all the barriers of experience and criticism. Lecky correctly observes in his *History of the Spirit of Rationalism*: "The philosophy of Plato, by greatly aggrandizing the sphere of the spiritual, did much to foster the belief; and we find that whenever, either before or after the Christian era, that philosophy has been in the ascendant, it has been accompanied by a tendency to magic." [5]

Simultaneously, life in the large cities deprives their population, now the dominant mental element in the entire population, of a direct contact with nature, frees them both from the necessity and the possibility of observing and understanding nature. The conception of that which is natural and that which is possible begins to waver; the population loses its standard for the absurdity of the impossible, the unnatural, the supernatural.

The more impotent the individual feels himself to be, the more timidly he seeks for a firm support in some personality that stands out from the ordinary average; and the more desperate the situation becomes, the more a miracle is needed to save him—the more

[5] Lecky, *History of the Rise and Influence of the Spirit of Rationalism in Europe,* New York and London, 1910, vol. i, p. 43 (vol. i, p. 7 of the *Truth Seeker* edition, New York, 1910).

likely will he be to credit the person to whom he attaches himself as a rescuer, as a savior, with the performance of miracles. In fact, he will demand these miracles as a test to prove that his savior really possesses the power to rescue him. Reminiscences of divine legends of an earlier period may also play a part; motives borrowed from such legends are frequently embodied in the new myths. But the latter are quite different from the former. Superhuman powers were assigned to the old gods in order to afford an explanation of actual events that had been very precisely and correctly observed. Now superhuman powers were assigned to men, in order to enable them to produce effects that no one had yet observed, that were entirely impossible. Such wondrous phenomena might have been developed by an over-active imagination even in the most ancient times from the old legends of the gods; but the old legends *are not based* on such miraculous events. The miracle constitutes the point of departure for the new forms of myths.

One of the points in which the older and later legends most coincided was the begetting of the hero by a god. In early times men loved to exalt the splendor of their ancestors, to represent the man from whom their race took its origin (to make him appear very splendid) as a superman, a demigod. According to the mode of thought then in vogue, which sought a god behind all things, he could of course obtain the necessary power only from a god. And since these gods, in spite of all their superhuman qualities, were conceived in a very human manner, with very human emotions, it was natural to assume that the mother of the ancestral hero had inspired a tender passion in a god, the fruit of which was this brave hero.

Similarly, the later legends also had the redeemers of the world produced by mortal mothers, but with divine fathers. Thus, Suetonius tells us:

"In the book of Asklepiades of Mendes concerning the gods, I read that Atia, the mother of Augustus, had once gone at midnight to a solemn service in honor of Apollo, and had fallen asleep in her litter while waiting for the arrival of the other women. Suddenly a serpent joined her on the couch, leaving her soon after; on awaking she had the same feeling as if her husband had been with her and therefore cleansed herself. Immediately a spot appeared on her body, of the form of a serpent, which was ineradicable, causing her thenceforth to absent herself from the public baths. In the tenth month later Augustus was born, wherefore he was considered as a *son of Apollo*." (*Octavius*, Chapter xciv.)

An intrigue with a god seems at that time to have been considered by the Roman ladies as not only possible, but also as quite distinguished. Josephus tells a pretty story in this connection. At the time of Tiberius there lived in Rome a lady by the name of Paulina, whose beauty was as great as her chastity. A wealthy knight, Decius Mundus, fell mortally in love with her and offered her two hundred thousand drachmas for a single night, but was rejected. But a liberated female slave was able to help him; she had learned that the beautiful Paulina was a zealous worshiper of the goddess Isis, and accordingly laid her plans. She bribed the priests of this goddess by paying them forty thousand drachmas, to cause Paulina to be informed that the god Anubis desired her. "This lady was delighted and boasted to her friends of the honor Anubis was thus bestowing on her. She also told her husband that Anubis had invited her to dine and cohabit with him. The husband gladly consented, knowing his wife's virtue. Thereupon she went to the temple, and after having supped, bedtime having come, the priest extinguished all the lights and locked the door. Mundus, who had already been concealed in the temple, now joined her and waited for no invitation. He had his will with her all night, because she thought he was the god. Having sated his lust, he departed in the morning, before the priests entered the temple, and Paulina returned to her husband, informing him that the god Anubis had been with her, and also boasting of it to her friends."

But the noble knight Decius Mundus carried his impudence to the point of upbraiding his lady some days later, on meeting her in the street, for having given herself up to him for nothing. The pious lady, now disillusioned, was of course terribly indignant, made straightway for Tiberius and succeeded in having the priests of Isis crucified, their temple destroyed, and Mundus banished.[6]

This little story is rendered the more amusing by reason of the fact that it follows immediately upon the passage we mentioned at the beginning, in which the praises of the miraculous Christ are enthusiastically sung. The juxtaposition of these two passages did not fail to attract pious commentators at a very early day; they saw a connection between Christ and Madame Paulina's adventure, beholding in it a disguised slander by the wicked Jew Josephus on the virginity of Mary and the simplicity of her betrothed Joseph, a slander which of course would be hardly compatible with the recognition of the miracles of Christ that is contained in the passage immediately preceding. But as Josephus actually knows nothing of these miracles, and as the passage concerning them is a later Christian interpolation, as the reader now knows, this insinuation against the holy Virgin and her submissively acquiescent betrothed is entirely unintentional. It proves only the stupidity of the Christian forger, who chooses precisely this passage as the most suitable companion-piece for his testimony concerning the son of God.

To be a son of God was a portion of the business of a redeemer, whether he was a Caesar or a street preacher. But it was also no less necessary to perform miracles, which in both cases were invented along the same lines.

Even Tacitus, who was not at all inclined to exaggeration, reports (*Histories*, iv, Chapter lxxxi) concerning Vespasian, that the latter had worked many miracles in Alexandria, proving Heaven's good will to the Emperor. Thus he had moistened the eyes of a blind man with saliva and thereby made him to see. Likewise, he had stepped upon the lamed hand of another and thus cured it.

The power of performing such miracles was later transferred from the pagan emperors to the Christian monarchs. The kings of France possessed the remarkable gift of being able to cure scrofula and goiter at their coronation by a mere touch. As late as 1825, at the coronation of Charles X, the last Bourbon to occupy the French throne, this miracle was duly performed.

[6] *Antiquities of the Jews,* xviii, 3.

Similar healings by Jesus are of course reported more than once. The pious Merivale [7] assumes that Vespasian's miracle had been performed according to the Christian model—a view that does not seem plausible when we consider how insignificant and unknown Christianity was at the time of Vespasian. Bruno Bauer, on the other hand, declares in his book, *Christus und die Cäsaren*: "I shall delight the learned theologians of the present day with my assertion that the later author of the Fourth Gospel, and later still, the editor of the primitive Gospel contained in the St. Mark version, borrowed the application of saliva in the miraculous healings of Christ from this work of Tacitus." (John ix, 6; Mark vii, 33; viii, 33.)

But in our opinion it is not necessary to assume even this case of borrowing. Every epoch that believes in miracles also has its peculiar notions of how they are produced. In the later Middle Ages it was generally assumed that a compact with the devil had to be signed with warm blood; two writers might both make use of this treatment in the same way in their stories, without one necessarily having borrowed from the other; similarly, in Vespasian's day, and later, saliva may have been considered a proper material for use in miraculous healings, with the result that it was natural not only for the sober reporter of the temporal redeemer on the throne of the Caesars to ascribe healing by this method to the person to be glorified, but also for the more ecstatic reporter of the redeemer on the throne of the millennial kingdom; neither author needs to have borrowed from the other. Surely Tacitus did not invent this treatment, but found the legend in general circulation.

Not only the Caesars were operating miracles then, but also a great many of their contemporaries. Tales of miracles were then so common that they ceased to receive any particular attention. Even the narrators of the Gospels do not represent the miracles and tokens of Jesus as producing the profound impression which we, with our modern attitude, should expect them to produce. Even after the miraculous feeding of the five thousand, Christ's disciples remain incredulous. Furthermore, not only Jesus but

[7] *The Romans Under the Empire.*

also the apostles and disciples performed many miracles. In fact, people were so credulous that it never occurred to Christians to have doubts as to miracles emanating from persons whom they considered impostors. They escaped from the difficulty by the simple device of ascribing such miracles to the power of the devil and evil spirits.

Miracles grew like mushrooms, every founder of a religious sect or a philosophical school brought them forth as his letter of recommendation. For instance, we have the example of the Neo-Pythagorean, Apollonius of Tyana, a contemporary of Nero.

Of course, even his birth is miraculous. When his mother was pregnant the god Proteus, the wise god understood by none, appeared to her; but she asked him without fear what child she should bear. Whereupon he answered: "Me." [8] The young Apollonius grows up, a prodigy of wisdom, preaching a pure moral life, distributes his fortune among his friends and poor relatives, and travels about in the world as a mendicant philosopher, but he is even more impressive by his miracles than by his frugality and morality. The miracles have a striking resemblance to those of Christ; thus we are given an example from the time of his sojourn in Rome:

"A virgin had died on the day of her wedding, at least she was considered dead. The bridegroom followed her bier, lamenting, and Rome lamented with him, for the maiden was of a very aristocratic family. Now when Apollonius encountered the procession, he said: 'Set down the bier, I shall stop your tears over this maiden.' When he asked her name, the multitude thought he intended to deliver one of the customary funeral orations, but he touched the dead girl, speaking a few words that were not understood, and awakened her from her trance. But she lifted up her voice and returned to her father's house." [9]

According to the legend Apollonius boldly opposes the tyrants Nero and Domitian, is made a prisoner by them, succeeds in freeing himself without difficulty from his fetters, but does not flee,

[8] *Apollonius of Tyana,* translated from the Greek of Philostratus, with notes by Ed. Baltzer, 1883, i, 4.
[9] *Op. cit.,* iv, 45.

awaiting his trial in prison; he delivers in court a long speech in his own defense, and then, before judgment is spoken, disappears mysteriously from the court chamber in Rome, suddenly putting in his appearance a few hours later at Dikæarchia, near Naples, whither the gods had forwarded him with the speed of an express train.

Apollonius possesses in a high degree the gift of prophecy which was indispensable to the business of a redeemer, as well as the ability to see things going on in other parts of the world. When Domitian was murdered in his palace at Rome, Apollonius at Ephesus beheld the act as clearly as if he had been on the spot, immediately informing the Ephesians of it. This is a feat of wireless telegraphy compared with which Marconi is a cheap amateur.

He ended by disappearing into a temple whose doors had opened to receive him, and closed behind him. "From within they heard songs of maidens which sounded as if they were inviting him to rise heavenward, with the words: 'Come out of the dark of earth, enter into the light of Heaven, come.' " [10]

Apollonius' body was never found. It was therefore manifest that this redeemer also had ascended heavenward.

A sharp competition soon set in between the miracles believed by the adherents of Christianity and those performed by Apollonius. Under Diocletian, one of the later governors, Hieroclis by name, wrote a book against the Christians, in which he pointed out that the miracles of Christ were as nothing when compared with those of Apollonius and furthermore, not equally well attested. Eusebius of Cæsarea wrote a reply to this book, in which he expressed not the slightest doubt of the reality of the miracles of Apollonius, but merely attempted to belittle them by designating them not as divine acts, but as acts of magic, the work of the spirits of darkness.

In other words, even where it became necessary to oppose miracles, no one thought of doubting them.

And this credulity rose with the increasing disintegration of society, with the decline in the spirit of scientific investigation,

[10] *Op. cit.,* p. 378.

and the luxuriant spread of moral preaching. The increase in credulity was accompanied by an increased love of miracles. All sensations cease to produce an effect when too often repeated. Stronger and stronger stimuli must be applied in order to make an impression. In our first chapter we saw how this rule is applied in the Gospels, where it can be definitely traced in the example of the awakenings from the dead, which are simpler in the older Gospels than in the later ones.

The youngest Gospel, that of Saint John, adds to the older miracles, which were reported by the earlier Gospels, the miraculous production of wine at the wedding at Cana; John goes so far as to say that a sick man healed by Jesus had been sick for thirty-eight years, while a blind man whom he causes to see was born blind; in other words, the miracles are made more outrageous at every point.

In the Second Book of Moses, xvii, 1-6, we read the story that Moses struck water from a rock in the desert in order to give drink to the thirsty Israelites. This was not enough of a miracle for the Christian period. We learn from the First Epistle of the Apostle Paul to the Corinthians (x, 4), that the rock from which the Jews received water had traveled through the desert with them in order that they might never lack water—a nomadic gushing rock.

Particularly crude are the miracles appearing in the so-called "Acts of the Apostle Paul". In a competition of miracles with the magician Simon, the apostle restores life to a salted herring.

On the other hand, perfectly natural events were miracles in the eyes of men in those days, evidences of the arbitrary intervention of God in the course of nature, not only convalescences and deaths, victories and defeats, but every-day amusements such as wagers. "When in a horse-race at Gaza, in which the horses of a pious Christian and a pious pagan were competing, 'Christ defeated Marnas', many pagans caused themselves to be baptized." [11]

[11] Friedländer, *Roman Life and Manners Under the Early Empire*, London (Routledge), vol. iii, p. 197.

But the natural event that was interpreted as a miracle was not always susceptible to one interpretation only.

"During the war against the Quadi (173-4) in the reign of Marcus Aurelius, the Roman army, overcome by the heat of the blazing sun, found itself surrounded by a superior force, and threatened with annihilation. Then suddenly thick clouds gathered together, rain fell in torrents, and a fearful storm wrought havoc and confusion in the ranks of the enemy; the Romans were saved and gained the victory. The effect of this event was overwhelming: according to the custom of the time it was immortalized by pictorial representation, was generally regarded as a miracle, the memory of which lasted till the last days of antiquity, and for centuries afterwards was appealed to by both Christians and pagans as a proof of the truth of their respective faiths. . . . The marvelous deliverance of the army appears to have been generally attributed to the emperor's prayer to Jupiter; others, however, asserted that it was really due to the art of an Egyptian magician Arnuphis, a member of his suite, who had drawn down rain from heaven by calling upon the gods, especially Hermes.[12] But according to the account of a Christian contemporary, the miracle had been wrought by the prayers of the Christian soldiers of the twelfth (Melitenian) legion. Tertullian also (197) refers to the Christian version as well known, and appeals to a letter of Marcus Aurelius in support of it."

The eagerness for miracles, and the popular credulity, assumed larger and larger proportions, until finally in the period of the greatest degradation, in the Fourth and Fifth Centuries, the monks practiced miracles compared with which those of Jesus, as reported in the Gospels, are very unimpressive.

"A believing age was easily persuaded that the slightest caprice of an Egyptian or a Syrian monk had been sufficient to interrupt the eternal laws of the universe. The favorites of Heaven were accustomed to cure inveterate diseases with a touch, a word, or a distant message; and to expel the most obstinate dæmons from the souls, or bodies, which they possessed. They familiarly accosted, or imperiously commanded, the lions and serpents of the

12 Friedländer, op. cit., vol. iii, p. 123.

desert; infused vegetation into a sapless trunk; suspended iron on the surface of water; passed the Nile on the back of a crocodile, and refreshed themselves in a fiery furnace." [13]

An excellent characterization of the mental attitude of the time in which Christianity arose is that drawn by Schlosser, in his *Weltgeschichte*, of Plotinus, the most famous Neo-Platonic philosopher of the Third Century of our era.

"Plotinus, who was born in 205 at Lycopolis in Egypt, and who died in 270 in Campania, was for eleven years a diligent pupil of Ammonius, but buried himself so deeply in thought on the subject of divine and human nature that, not contented with the Egyptian-Greek mystic teachings of his predecessor and teacher, he reached out also for Persian and Indian wisdom, and attached himself to the army of the younger Gordianus and went to Persia with him. . . . Plotinus later went to Rome, where he found the prevalent inclination for Oriental mysticism very much to his purpose, and played the prophet for twenty-five years, until shortly before his death. The Emperor Gallienus and his wife regarded him with such superstitious veneration that it is said that they even had the intention of establishing a philosophical state in one of the cities of Italy, to be governed according to the principles of Plotinus. Equally great was the approval Plotinus received from the most respected families of the Roman citizenry; some of the most prominent men of the city became his most zealous champions and received his teaching as a message from Heaven.

"The spiritual and moral weakening of the Roman world and the generally prevalent inclination toward hysterical rapture, toward monkish morality and toward supernatural and prophetic qualities, are nowhere expressed so clearly as in the impression produced by Plotinus and in the respect which his doctrine received, for the very reason that it was incomprehensible.

"The means used by Plotinus and his pupils to disseminate the new philosophy were the same as those used at the end of the Eighteenth Century by Mesmer and Cagliostro in France to mys-

[13] Gibbon, *History of the Decline and Fall of the Roman Empire,* chap. xxxvii, London and New York, 1898, vol. iv, p. 75.

tify the decayed nobility, and by Rosicrucians, spirit charmers, and the like in Germany to mystify a pious Prussian king. Plotinus practiced magic, summoned spirits to appear before him, and even stooped to the activity practiced in this country only by a despised class of persons, that of revealing those guilty of petty thefts, when asked by his acquaintances.

"Plotinus' writings were also conceived in the prophetic manner; for according to the testimony of his most famous pupil he set down his alleged inspirations without ever deigning to glance at them again, or even to correct the language. The masterpieces of the ancient Greeks had not been written thus! Even the most rudimentary rules of thought, what we are accustomed to call 'method', is lacking both in the writings and in the oral discourses of this man, who demanded of everyone who would attain philosophical knowledge a sloughing off of his own nature or an emergence from the natural state of thought and feeling, as his first condition.

"In order to convey an idea of the nature of his teaching and of the effect it produced, we need only give a few data concerning the contents of his writings. Living with men and among men is always represented as sinful and unnatural, while true wisdom and bliss consists, according to him, in a complete separation from the world of the senses, in meditation and in a brooding and dismal isolation of one's own spirit, and a concentration on higher things. . . . This theory of life, which undermines all activity, and flies in the face of all experience and of all human relations, and which furthermore is expounded with the strongest contempt for all those having different views, is accompanied by a purely theoretical conception of nature and its laws, based only on overheated mental vagaries. Aristotle had based his ideas of nature on experience, observation and mathematics; there is not a trace of these in Plotinus. Plotinus considered himself to be a philosopher illuminated by God; he therefore believed that all his knowledge was derived from an internal source of inspiration, and that he needed to mount no ladder in order to attain knowledge, for his pinions bore him over the earth and through all the realms of space. . . .

"Plotinus had three pupils who put in tolerable shape the words he had delivered in the form of oracles, and who disseminated his teachings as his apostles: Herennius, Amelius, and Porphyrius. All three were quite talented, and Longinus mentions the latter two as the only philosophers of his time whose writings are readable, although Longinus was in most matters very hostile to any philosophy that turned its back on life and sound reason.

"But we may best judge how low was their *love of truth* by the biography of Plotinus written by Porphyrius. Porphyrius relates the silliest stories of his lord and master, and as Porphyrius had too much sense to believe them himself, he must have *fabricated them intentionally and knowingly* in order to raise the credit of Plotinus' oracular dicta".[14]

c. The Resort to Lying

Duplicity is a necessary complement to credulity and the love of miracles. Thus far we have given only examples in which the reporters relate miracles concerning the deceased, but there was no lack of persons who also reported the greatest marvels concerning themselves, such as Apion of Alexandria, the Jew-baiter, "the 'world's clapper' (*cymbalum mundi*), as the Emperor Tiberius called him, full of big words and still bigger lies, of the most assured omniscience and unlimited faith in himself, conversant, if not with men, at any rate with their worthlessness, a celebrated master of discourse as of the art of misleading, ready for action, witty, unabashed, and unconditionally loyal".[15]

Men of this stamp were usually loyal—meaning servile. This loyal scamp had the impudence to conjure up Homer from the underworld in order to question him concerning his place of birth. And he even maintained that the spirit of the poet had appeared to him and answered his question, but bound him to secrecy!

A more outrageous swindler was Alexander of Abonuteichos (born about 105 A.D., died about 175 A.D.), who practiced magic with the crudest means, for instance, slaughtered animals and

14 *Weltgeschichte*, 1846, vol. iv, 452 *ff*.
15 Mommsen, *The Provinces of the Roman Empire from Caesar to Diocletian*, London, 1886, vol. ii, pp. 193, 194.

hollow images of the gods, in which humans were concealed. This man established an oracle which would give information for a fee, and Lucian estimates the income from this business at about $15,000 a year. He even succeeded in obtaining an influence through the Consular Rutilianus over the "philosophical" Emperor Marcus Aurelius. The swindler died rich and full of honors, and a statue erected in his memory is said to have given forth prophecies even after his death. Another well managed deception seems to have been the following.

"Dio Cassius relates that in the year 220 a *spirit,* which called itself that of Alexander the Great, exactly resembled him in form and features and wore a similar dress, marched with a retinue of 400 persons clothed as Bacchants, from the Danube to the Bosporus, where it disappeared: no official ventured to stop it, but *on the contrary lodging and food were everywhere provided at the public expense.*" [16]

Our heroes of the fourth dimension and even the more material Captain of Köpenick must hide their faces in shame when they think of these achievements.[17]

But not only swindlers and mountebanks engaged in the practice of conscious lying and deception; even serious thinkers, and other persons who meant well, made frequent use of it.

The historical literature of antiquity was never characterized by an excess of severely critical method; it was not yet a science in the narrower sense of the word, it was not yet used for the investigation of the laws of the evolution of society, but for *pedagogical* and *political* purposes. Its object was to edify the reader, or to prove to him the correctness of the political tendencies favored by the historian. The great deeds of their ancestors must be made to elevate the minds of the coming generations and inspire them to similar actions—this made a work of history merely an echo in prose of the heroic epic.

But the later generations had also to be taught from the experiences of their ancestors what they themselves were to do and

[16] Friedländer, *op. cit.,* vol. iii, p. 306.
[17] In 1906, a poor laborer named Voigt, in the town of Köpenick, near Berlin, disguised himself as a military officer and secured the aid of several soldiers in robbing the town treasury at the City Hall.—TRANSLATOR.

not do. It is easy to understand that many a historian, particularly when the purpose of edification and inspiration was the
chief one, was not over-delicate in the selection and criticism of
his sources; he may even have permitted himself, in the interest
of his artistic effect, to fill out gaps in his tale with the aid of the
imagination. Each historian considered it to be particularly his
privilege to improvise freely the speeches which he had his characters deliver. But the classical historians took pains not to be
consciously and intentionally misleading in their depiction of the
activity of the persons they treated. They had to be all the more
careful in avoiding this fault since they were treating a public
political activity, which made their records subject to a close
checking up.

But with the decline of ancient society, the task of the writer
of history changed. The people ceased to demand political instruction, for politics was becoming more and more indifferent,
more and more repulsive to them. Nor did they continue to require examples of manly courage and devotion to country; what
they wanted was amusement, a new stimulus for their jaded
nerves, gossip and sensations, miracles. One slight inaccuracy
more or less did not matter to the reader. Furthermore the
checking up of recorded facts became more difficult, for *private*
destinies were now in the foreground of the reader's interest,
events which had not taken place in the full light of publicity.
Literary history resolved itself more and more, on the one hand
into narrations of scandals, and on the other hand into outrageous
exaggerations of the Munchausen type.

This new tendency became manifest in Greek literature about
the time of Alexander the Great, concerning whose deeds Alexander's courtier Onesikritos wrote a book that simply swarms
with lies and exaggerations. But there is only a single step between lying and forgery. This step was accomplished by
Euemeros, who in the Third Century brought home inscriptions
from India, which he alleged were of great age, but which the
good man had fabricated himself.

But this excellent method was not limited to literary history
alone. We have seen how the interest in the things of this world

was gradually dying down among students of philosophy, while that in the next world was becoming stronger. But how should a philosopher convince his pupils that his views of the hereafter were more than mere imaginings? The simplest means of producing such conviction was of course to invent a witness who was represented as having come back from the country "from whose bourne no traveler returns", and reporting on its general conditions. Even Plato did not scorn to use this device, as we have seen in the case of the excellent Pamphylian whom we have already mentioned.

Furthermore, the decreasing interest in the natural sciences, and their displacement by a meditation on ethics, involved also an abandonment of the critical spirit which aims to test the correctness of each proposition by *actual experience,* and a further weakening of the intellectual stamina of the various individuals, thus producing an increased desire to find a support in the person of some great man. Men were moved now not by *actual proofs* but by *authorities,* and anyone desiring to produce an impression upon them had to see to it that he was supported by the necessary authorities. If these authorities did not provide the required passages, it became necessary to doctor them a little, or to create one's authorities out of whole cloth. We have already had occasion to note authorities of this kind in the cases of Daniel and Pythagoras. Jesus was such an authority, also his apostles, Moses, the Sibyls, etc.

The writer did not always take the pains to write a whole book under the false name; often it was sufficient to interpolate a single sentence in a genuine work by a recognized authority, making this sentence express the writer's own beliefs, and thus conquering this authority for his argument. This was rendered easier by the fact that printing had not yet been invented. Books circulated only in written copies, made either by their owner or for him, by a slave, if the owner was wealthy enough to support a slave for this purpose. Besides, there were publishers who made their slaves copy books, which were then sold with great profit. It was very easy in such a copy to omit a sentence that seemed inconvenient, or to insert another that was needed, particularly if the author had already died, which, in those careless and credulous days, made the likelihood of a protest very remote. Later copyists would then see to it that this forgery was preserved to posterity.

The Christians found this method of procedure easier than did the other historians. Whoever the first teachers and organizers of the Christian congregations may have been, it is certain that they rose from the lowest strata of the population, that they could not write and left no written records. Their doctrines were at first disseminated only by word of mouth. If any of their adherents would invoke the authority of the earliest teachers of the congregation, in any discussion that might arise, it was difficult to contradict him, unless he outraged tradition too crudely. Soon the most varied versions of the words of "the master" and his apostles were necessarily in circulation. And in view of the heated state of conflict which prevailed in the Christian congregations at the outset, these various versions were first advanced not for the purpose of an objective historical record, but for utilization in controversy, being later recorded and collected in the Gospels. The later copyists and rewriters were also animated chiefly by controversial aims, which caused them to strike out an inconvenient sentence here and insert another in its place in order to be able to use the entire record as a proof of the fact that Christ or his apostles had advocated one view or another. This polemical tendency is encountered at every step in an examination of the Gospels.

But soon the Christians no longer contented themselves with adapting and forging their own sacred writings in this manner, as their needs demanded. This method was too convenient not to be applied also to other, to "pagan" authors, as soon as there was a sufficient number of educated persons among the Christians to cause some weight to be given to prominent writers outside the Christian world; when there was a sufficient number of such persons, it became worth while to have special fabricated copies prepared for them, which were greeted with satisfaction by them and circulated further. Many of these forgeries have been preserved to the present day.

One such forgery has already been mentioned, namely, Josephus' testimony on Jesus. The next writer, with Tacitus, to speak of the Christians as their contemporary, is the Younger Pliny, who wrote a letter concerning them to Trajan, at the time when Pliny was Proprætor of Bithynia (probably 111-113 A.D.), which has been preserved in the collection of his letters.[18] In this letter, Pliny asks for instructions as to what he shall do with the Christians in his province, concerning whom he knows no evil report, but who cause all the temples to be empty. This view of the innocence of the Christians does not harmonize well with the opinion of Pliny's friend Tacitus, who emphasizes their "hatred for the entire human race". It is equally striking for us to learn that Christianity was already so widespread in Bithynia under Trajan, that it was capable of emptying the temples, "which had already long been desolate, whose solemnities had long been in disuse, whose sacrificial beasts rarely found a purchaser". We should have been inclined to suppose that such conditions would have aroused as much attention as would be given now to the fact, if it should so happen, that only Socialist votes were being cast in Berlin. There would surely have been a general commotion. But Pliny does not hear of the existence of the Christians until someone denounces them. This and other reasons make us assume that this letter is a *Christian forgery*. Semler, as early as 1788, already assumed that this entire letter of Pliny was invented by a Christian at a later date, for the magnification of Christianity. But Bruno Bauer is of the opinion that the letter was really written by Pliny, was not originally at all flattering to the Christians, and therefore had been "fixed up" by a later Christian copyist.

These forgeries became more impudent when the Teutonic barbarians inundated the Roman Empire in the period of the great migrations. These new masters of the world were simple peasants, full of peasant cunning to be sure, and sober and sophisticated enough in things that were not too deep for them. With all their simplicity they were less thirsty for miracles and less credulous than the heirs of the ancient civilization, but of reading

[18] *C. Plinii Cæcilii Epistolarum libri decem,* Book x, Letter 97.

and writing they knew nothing. These arts became the privilege of the Christian clergy, which was now the only cultured class. The clergy had no need to fear that its forgeries in the interest of the Church would encounter criticism, and so these forgeries multiplied more luxuriantly than ever before, and they were no longer limited, as before, to matters of doctrine, no longer served only in the discussion of theoretical, technical or organizational disputes, but now became a means of *acquiring property*, or legally justifying an accomplished seizure of property. The most outrageous of these forgeries surely were the *Constantine Donation* and Isidor's *Decretals*, both of which were manufactured in the Eighth Century. In the former document, Constantine (306-337 A.D.) hands over to the Popes the unlimited and eternal dominion of Rome, Italy and all the provinces to the West. Isidor's *Decretals* are a collection of ecclesiastical laws ostensibly gathered by the Spanish Bishop Isidorus in the beginning of the Seventh Century, which proclaim the sole authority of the Pope in the Church.

This great mass of forgeries is not the least important of the causes that make the history of the origin of Christianity so obscure to this day. Many of these forgeries are not hard to detect; many were exposed centuries ago; for instance, Laurentius Valla revealed in 1440 that the *Constantine Donation* was a forgery. But it is not equally easy to detect the existence of a grain of truth in one of these forgeries, and to fix the outline of this truth.

The picture that we are recording is not a pleasant one: general decay in every quarter, economic, political, and also scientific and moral. The ancient Romans and Greeks had considered the full and harmonious development of manhood in the best sense of the word as a virtue. *Virtus* and *Arete* had signified bravery and endurance, but also manly pride, sacrifice and unselfish devotion to the common weal. But as society sank deeper into bondage, submission became the supreme virtue, and from it were derived all the noble qualities to which we have devoted our attention: aversion to the common weal and concentration on individual interests, cowardice and lack of self-confidence, longing for redemption by an emperor or a God, not by one's own strength or the strength of one's class; self-debasement before the powerful, priestly impudence toward inferiors; *blasé* indifference and disgust with life, yielding to a yearning for sensations, for marvels; hysteria and ecstasy, together with hypocrisy, lying and forgery. Such is the picture afforded us by the Imperial Era, and its traits are reflected in the product of the era, which is Christianity.

d. Humanitarianism

But the champions of Christianity will say that this picture is one-sided and therefore untrue. We must admit that the Christians were only human beings, and could not entirely protect themselves against the degrading influences of their surroundings, but this is only one side of Christianity. On the other hand, we must also observe that it expounds a morality which is far superior to that of antiquity, a sublime humanity, an infinite mercy, toward everything bearing the human form, the lowly and the exalted, strangers and comrades in the clan, enemy as well as friend; that it preaches a fraternization of all classes and races. This teaching is not to be explained on the basis of the times in which Christianity arose; it is all the more remarkable for being taught in a period of the most profound moral corruption; the materialistic interpretation of history here fails us; we are here dealing with a phenomenon that can only be explained by the sublimity of an individuality that is completely independent of the conditions of time and space, a God-Man, or to use the modern cant term, a Superman.

That is the way our "idealists" put it.

But what are the facts? Let us first consider the charity toward the poor and the humanity toward slaves; are these two phenomena really to be found only in Christianity? It is true that we do not find much charity in classic antiquity, and the reason is not far to seek: charity implies the existence of poverty on a vast scale. The intellectual life of antiquity was deeply rooted in communistic conditions, and in a common ownership of the clan lands, of the community, of the household, which gave their members a *right* to their common products and their common means of production. The giving of *alms* was rarely necessary.

The reader should not confuse hospitality with charity. Hospitality was a very general trait in ancient times; but it is a relation between *equals*, while charity implies a social *inequality*. Hospitality rejoices both guest and host; but charity exalts him who gives and debases and humiliates him who receives.

In the course of events various large cities began to have a mass proletariat, as we have seen. But this proletariat either possessed or achieved *political power*, and made use of the latter in order to conquer for itself a share in the foodstuffs which were flowing into the storehouses of the wealthy and of the state as a product of slave labor and the exploitation of the provinces. Thanks to democracy and its political power, even these proletarians did not need charity. Charity implies not only a great wretchedness of the masses, but also a proletariat without political rights and powers, conditions that did not obtain on a large scale before the Imperial Era. It is not surprising that the notion of charity should only then have begun to dominate Roman society. But it was not a result of the superhuman morality of Christianity.

In the early days of their rule, the Caesars considered it to be still advisable to buy up by means of bread and games not only the army, but also the proletariat of the capital. Nero particularly was very successful in this practice. In many of the large provincial cities this method was also used to pacify the lower strata of the population.

But this procedure did not last long. The increasing impoverishment of society forced a retrenchment in the national expenditures, which the Caesars naturally applied first to the proletariat, no longer feared by them. Probably the desire to remedy the increasing lack of labor power also decreased their generosity toward the proletariat. If there were no gifts of grain, the proletarians capable of physical labor had to look for work, and perhaps bound themselves over to the great landed proprietors as *coloni* or tenants.   But precisely this lack of sufficient labor caused the rise of new forms of public gifts.

In the Imperial Era, all the ancient social organizations are disintegrating, not only the clans, but also the households of the larger families.   Each man thinks only of himself, family ties are dissolved as well as political ties, the readiness to sacrifice oneself for one's relatives becomes extinct, as does also the devotion to community and to state.   Orphaned children suffered particularly from this condition.   To be without parents now made them defenseless; there was no one who would look after them. The number of children having no relatives ready to support them was further increased by the fact that the general indigence and the lowering of the spirit of sacrifice was causing an increasing number of persons to evade family burdens.   Some achieved this by not marrying, by resorting to prostitutes only; male prostitution, by the way, was in a flourishing condition; others, although married, sought to avoid the begetting of children.   Both these practices naturally aided in the depopulation of the country, in producing a lack of laborers, and therefore increasing the general poverty.   And many persons having children found it most convenient to dispose of them by abandoning them.   This excellent practice assumed enormous proportions; no prohibitions were of any avail; two burning questions became ever more urgent: the care of children not supported by relatives, and the care of the children of the poor, still living with their parents; these questions necessarily received much attention from the early Christians. The latter were constantly concerned over the question of the support of orphans.   Not only compassion, but also the need for labor power and soldiers, led to an effort to assure the bringing up of orphans, foundlings, and proletarian children.

Under Augustus we already find efforts being made in this direction; in the Second Century of our era they begin to assume practical form.   The Emperors Nerva and Trajan were the first to establish such institutions in the Italian provinces, by having the state either purchase a number of estates and sublease them, or transfer them on mortgages.   The yield in the rent or interest on mortgages was to be used for the training of poor children, particularly orphans.[19]

Hadrian, immediately after his accession, extended this institution, which had been planned under Trajan for about 5,000 children; later emperors developed it further, but this national charity was also accompanied by communal charity, as it had been preceded by private charity. The oldest private boarding institution of which we have any information dates from the time of Augustus. Helvius Basila, who had held the prætorship, bequeathed $22,000 to the citizens of Atina in Latium for supplying grain to a number of children, the number being unfortunately not stated.[20]

Later, under Trajan, numerous such institutions are mentioned. A rich lady, Cælia Macrina, of Tarracina, on the death of her son, donated a million sesterces (more than $50,000), from the interest of which 100 boys and girls were to be supported; the Younger Pliny founded a boarding establishment in the year 97 in his native city of Comum (now Como), which was to receive the annual income of an estate valued at 500,000 sesterces, and devote it to the nourishing of poor children. He also established schools, libraries, etc.

Of course all these foundations did not succeed in counteracting the depopulation of the empire; for this depopulation was due to causes that lay too deep in the economic conditions; and therefore it increased as the economic decay progressed. The general impoverishment advanced to the point of consuming the resources necessary for continuing this child welfare work; poverty bankrupted not only the feeding institutions, but the state itself. Concerning the development of the feeding institutions we learn from Müller:

"Their life may be traced for almost 180 years. Hadrian improved the allotments to the children. Antonius Pius appropriated new sums for this purpose. In 145 A.D. the boys and girls of Cupramontano, a city in Picenum, who were his beneficiaries,

[19] Cf. B. Matthias, *Römische Alimentarinstitutionen und Agrarwirtschaft.* *Jahrbuch für Nationalökonomie und Statistik,* 1885, vol. i, pp. 503 ff.
[20] A. Müller, *Jugendfürsorge in der römischen Kaiserzeit,* 1903, p. 21.

erected a grateful epitaph to him, as did those of Sestinum in Umbria in 161. A similar dedication at Ficulea in Latium testifies to the similar activity of Marcus Aurelius. The latter establishment seems to have reached its culmination early in the reign of this emperor; from then on the general disintegration of the Empire was paralleled in the history of the institution. Marcus Aurelius, owing to the embarrassments which war was constantly putting upon him, and which even forced him to auction off the crown jewels, insignia, and other valuables of the Imperial Dynasty, seems to have gone so far as to confiscate the endowment funds of this institution and guarantee the payment of interest from the State Treasury. Under Commodus, the Treasury was unable for nine years to fulfill this obligation, and Pertinax, unable to pay the arrears, repudiated them. But it seems that the fortunes of the institution later improved. An official in charge of it is still mentioned in the Third Century; but its existence terminated about that time. We no longer hear of it under Constantine." [21]

Increasing poverty might wipe out the charitable institutions, but it could not destroy the concept of charity, which necessarily became stronger and stronger in view of the increasing wretchedness. But this notion is by no means a characteristic of Christianity alone; Christianity shares it with its epoch, which resorted to it not because of the moral sublimity of the times, but because of their economic decay.

The appreciation and admiration for charity also resulted in the rise of another less amiable quality: that of *boasting* of the alms one had given. Pliny, already mentioned above, is a good example. All our information concerning his charitable institutions is derived from him alone: he described them in great detail in books that were intended for publication. When we behold Pliny nursing his sublime emotions and evincing immense admiration for his own nobility of character, it seems to us that this is less an indication of the moral greatness of the "Golden Age" of the Roman Empire, of its most happy period, as Gregorovius and most of his colleagues term it,[22] than of the silly

[21] *Op. cit.*, pp. 7, 8.   [22] *Der Kaiser Hadrian*, 1884.

vanity of that era, an edifying counterpart of its priestly arrogance and its pious hypocrisy.

The severest censure that has been spoken of Pliny, as far as we know, is Niebuhr's, which accuses him of "childish vanity" and "dishonest humility".[23]

As in the case of charity, we have been told that the humane treatment of slaves is peculiar to Christianity.

We must first of all point out that Christianity, at least in the form under which it became the state religion, never in any way undertook to combat slavery as a principle. It never exerted any influence toward the abolition of slavery. If the exploitation of slaves for purposes of profit ceased in the time of Christianity, the reasons for this had nothing whatever to do with religious conceptions. We have already had occasion to observe these reasons: Rome's military decline was cutting off the cheap supplies of slaves and thus making the exploitation of slaves unprofitable. But the keeping of *luxury* slaves on the other hand continued to be practiced until long after the Roman Empire; in fact, simultaneously with Christianity, there arose in the Roman world a new variety of slaves, the Eunuchs, who played an important part particularly under the *Christian* emperors, beginning with Constantine. They are already found, however, at the court of Claudius, Nero's father.[24]

But the free proletarians themselves never thought of doing away with slavery. They sought to improve their condition by increasing their bleedings of the rich and of the state without doing any work themselves, which was impossible except on the basis of the exploitation of slaves.

It is an interesting fact that in the communistic state of the future which Aristophanes derides in his *Ekklesiazusæ*, slavery continues to exist. The difference ceases between those who have possessions and those who have none, but only in the case of freemen; everything becomes common property for them, including the slaves, who continue the business of production. Of

23 *Römische Geschichte*, 1845, vol. v, p. 312.
24 Suetonius, *Tiberius, Claudius, Drusus*, chap. xxviii, 44.

course Aristophanes intends this as a joke, but it is fully in accord with ancient thought.

We find a similar attitude expressed in a pamphlet concerning the sources of the general Attic prosperity, written in the Fourth Century B.C., to which Pöhlmann calls attention in his history, already quoted in this work.

This polemic demands, as Pöhlmann puts it, "an immense extension of the general economy of the state for purposes of traffic and production," and particularly, that the state purchase slaves for working the silver mines. The number of these state slaves is to be increased to such an extent that each citizen will ultimately have three slaves. The state will then be in a position to grant each of its citizens at least the minimum comforts of life.[25]

Professor Pöhlmann declares that this fine proposal is characteristic of "collectivistic radicalism" and "democratic socialism", which aims at nationalizing all the means of production in the interest of the proletariat. In truth it is characteristic of the peculiar attitude of the ancient proletariat, and its interest in the preservation of slavery; but Pöhlmann's understanding of this demand is characteristic of the narrowness of bourgeois learning, which considers every nationalization of property, even property in men, as an example of "collectivism", every measure adopted in the interest of the proletariat as an example of "democratic socialism", regardless of whether this proletariat is to be counted as an exploiter or as the exploited.

An indication of the fact that the proletarians were interested in preserving slavery is to be found in the fact that even the revolutionary practice of the Roman proletarians never presented an opposition in principle to the ownership of human beings. The slaves, in turn, are occasionally ready to be used in putting down a proletarian insurrection. Slaves led by aristocrats dealt the death blow to the proletarian movement under Caius Gracchus. Fifty years later, Roman proletarians led by Marcus Crassus struck down the rebellious slaves under Spartacus.

Quite independent of the idea of a general abolition of slavery,

[25] Pöhlmann, *Geschichte des antiken Kommunismus,* vol. ii, p. 252 *ff.*

which no one took seriously, is the manner in which slaves were treated. And here we must admit that a great improvement in the views concerning slavery, a recognition of the human rights of the slaves, is indeed evinced in Christianity, which is in sharp contrast with the wretched situation of the slaves at the beginning of the Imperial Period, when life and limb of the slave, as we have seen, were subject to every caprice of his master, who often made the most cruel use of this privilege.

Christianity, indeed, sharply opposed this way of regarding slaves. But this would not be equivalent to saying that Christianity thus was in opposition to the spirit of its times, that it stood alone in this attitude on slaves.

What was the class that claimed the right of a limitless maltreatment and execution of slaves? Of course it was the class of the rich landed proprietors, particularly the aristocracy.

But the democracy, the lower classes having no slaves themselves, were not as much interested in the privilege of maltreating slaves as were the great slave owners. To be sure, as long as the class of petty peasants, themselves owning slaves, or at least the traditions of this class, prevailed among the Roman people, the latter did not feel impelled to defend the slaves.

But a change in sentiment was slowly being prepared, not as the consequence of an improved moral teaching, but as the consequence of the altered composition of the Roman proletariat. Fewer and fewer freeborn Romans, particularly petty peasants, were found among the people, while the number of freed slaves, also participating in the rights of Roman citizens, was increasing enormously; under the Imperial Period the majority of the population of Rome were of the latter class. Slaves were freed for many reasons. Many a man who had no children, which was frequently the case, owing to the desire to escape the burdens of marriage and offspring, was induced, by caprice or good-nature, to provide in his will for the liberation of his slaves after his death. Others sometimes would liberate a slave during their own lives, as a reward for special services or through vanity, for anyone who could afford to liberate many slaves came to be regarded as a rich man. Others were liberated by political calculation, for the freedman usually remained dependent on his master, as his client, in spite of his political rights. The slave, therefore, increased the political influence of his master. Also, slaves were permitted to save money and buy their freedom with their savings, and many a master was driving a very good bargain when a slave, after having been worked to a skeleton, would buy his freedom at a price permitting the master to purchase a new one, whose strength was as yet intact.

With the increase of the number of slaves in the population, the number of freedmen also increased. The free proletariat, however, was being recruited more and more from the *slave* class, and not from the *peasants*. But this proletariat was also politically opposed to the slave-holding aristocracy and attempted to wrest political rights and powers from it, which meant the prospect of an attractive economic gain. It is therefore no cause for surprise to find a sympathy with the slaves beginning to make itself felt among the Roman democracy just at the time when the excesses of the slave-holders toward their human work-horses had reached their culmination.

But another factor must also be taken into account.

When the Caesars attained power, their households, like that of any distinguished Roman, were administered by slaves and freedmen. Degraded as the Romans had become, a freeborn citizen would nevertheless have considered it beneath his dignity to consent to perform personal services even for the most powerful of his fellow-citizens. The household of the Caesars now became the *Imperial Court,* their domestic servants became imperial courtiers. A new mechanism for administering the state was developed from among them, in addition to the staff inherited from the Republic. And the former mechanism was more and more entrusted with the actual business of state, and ruled the state, while the offices handed down from the Republican period became more and more empty titles, perhaps satisfactory to personal vanity, but not involving real power.

The slaves and freedmen in the Imperial Court became the rulers of the world, and through their embezzlements, extortions and bribes, its most successful exploiters. Friedländer describes this condition excellently in his splendid book, *Roman Life and Manners under the Early Empire,* which we have cited more than once: "The wealth which came to them by reason of their privileged position was a chief source of their strength. At a time when the riches of the freedmen had become proverbial, there surely were not many persons who could compare with these imperial servants. Narcissus had 400,000,000 sesterces ($21,000,-000), the greatest fortune known to the ancient world; Pallas, 300,000,000 ($16,000,000). Callistus, Epaphroditus, Doryphorus and others had treasures of hardly smaller size. When the Emperor Claudius once complained of the low state of the imperial finances, Roman gossip had it that he would have a superfluity if his two freedmen (Narcissus and Pallas) would take him as a third partner."

In fact, many an emperor found an excellent source of income in the practice of obliging rich slaves and freedmen to share with him the proceeds of their embezzlements and extortions.

"Owing to their possession of such enormous wealth, the imperial freedmen exceeded the Roman aristocrats in luxury and splendor. Their palaces were the most magnificent in Rome. That of Claudius' eunuch Posides was more brilliant than the Capitol, according to Juvenal, and the rarest and costliest things the earth could show adorned it in lavish profusion. . . . But the imperial freedmen also adorned Rome and the other cities in the monarchy with splendid and useful structures. Cleander, the powerful freedman of Commodus, utilized a proportion of his immense wealth in the construction of houses, baths, and other establishments useful to individuals as well as to entire cities."

This sudden prosperity of the many slaves and former slaves was the more striking when compared with the simultaneous financial decay of the land-owning aristocracy. It has a parallel today in the rise of the Jewish financial aristocracy. And just as the bankrupt aristocrats by birth at the present day at the bottom of their hearts hate and despise the rich Jews, but flatter them when they need them, so also was the treatment of the imperial slaves and freedmen.

"The highest aristocracy of Rome would outvie each other in

their efforts to do honor to the powerful servants of the emperor, no matter how sincerely these offspring of ancient and famous families despised and abhorred these persons of hated origin who were indelibly stamped with the mark of slavery and who in more than one respect were legally of lower station than the free-born beggar."

Socially, the position of the imperial servants was a very modest one, quite subordinate to that of the highborn dignitaries.

"But in reality the relation was quite a different one, in fact was often exactly the opposite, and the infinitely despised 'slaves' had the satisfaction that 'free men and nobles admired and envied them,' that Rome's most distinguished families humiliated themselves profoundly before them; few dared treat them as servants. . . . Crude flattery devises a family tree for Pallas which traces his origin from the King of Arcadia of the same name, and a descendant of the Scipios proposed a vote of thanks in the Senate because this scion of a royal house had subordinated his ancient nobility to the weal of the state and condescended to become a prince's servant. On the proposal of one of the consuls (in the year 52 A.D.) he was offered the prætorian insignia and a sizable purse of money (15,000,000 sesterces)." Pallas accepted only the former.

The Senate hereupon adopted a resolution of thanks to Pallas. "This decree was publicly exhibited on a bronze tablet by the side of a statue of Julius Caesar in full armor, and the possessor of 300,000,000 sesterces was lauded as a pattern of austere unselfishness. L. Vitellius, father of the emperor of the same name, a man in very high position, although his virtuosity in rascality aroused comment even in those days, worshiped among his domestic gods golden images of Pallas and Narcissus. . . .

"But nothing can so definitely indicate the position of these former slaves than the fact that they were permitted to marry the daughters of aristocratic families, even those related to the imperial house, at a time when the pride of the nobility in its ancient lineage and in a long series of illustrious forebears was very great." [26]

[26] Friedländer, *op. cit.,* vol. i, pp. 43-48. Routledge edition, London.

The Roman citizens, masters of the world, had therefore descended to being governed by those who were or had been slaves, and to bow their heads before them.

It is manifest how great must have been the reaction of this condition on the current views of the times. The aristocrats might hate the slaves the more, as they were obliged to yield the more to them; the popular masses were induced to respect the slaves, and the slaves themselves began to feel their oats.

On the other hand, Caesarism had risen in the struggle which democracy, itself consisting in great part of former slaves, was waging against the aristocracy of great slave-owners. The latter, not so easily to be purchased as the penniless masses of the people, were the only serious competition which the rising Caesars had to meet in fighting for the state power; the great slave-owners were the Republican opposition in the imperial realm, if we may speak of any such opposition at all. But the slaves and freedmen were the emperor's most faithful supporters.

All these influences necessarily produced an attitude more or less friendly to the slaves, not only in the proletariat, but in the imperial court, and in the circles which followed the court; this attitude was very emphatically expressed both by the court philosophers as well as by the proletarian street preachers.

We shall not take up any lengthy quotations expressing such opinions, but shall simply report one very characteristic incident: the clemency of the tyrant Nero toward slaves and freedmen. Nero was constantly at odds with the aristocratic Senate, which, while it was very subservient toward individual powerful freedmen, nevertheless always demanded the severest measures with regard to slaves and freedmen in general. Thus the Senate in the year 56 A.D. demanded that the "arrogance" of the freedmen be broken by granting the former owners of slaves the right to deprive of their freedom such freedmen as had acted "impudently," i.e., not abjectly enough, toward these former owners. Nero emphatically opposed this motion. He pointed out how high was the status now attained by the freedmen, many knights and even senators having come from their ranks, and recalled

the ancient Roman principle that whatever might be the differences between the various classes of the people, liberty must remain the common possession of all. Nero proposed a substitute
motion that the rights of the freedmen be not curtailed, and
forced the cowardly Senate to pass his motion.

In the year 61 the situation became more hazardous. Pedanius
Secundus, Prefect of the City, had been murdered by one of his
slaves. According to the ancient aristocratic law, this deed required retribution in the form of the execution of all the slaves
present in the house at the time of the murder, in this case not
less than 400 persons, including women and children. But public
opinion was in favor of a more lenient procedure. The masses
of the people were decidedly in favor of the slaves; it seemed as
if the Senate itself would be carried away by the general frame
of mind. Then Caius Cassius, Republican opposition leader in
the Senate, a descendant of one of Caesar's murderers, took the
floor, and admonished the Senate in a fiery speech not to be in-
timidated, and to yield no ground to mercy. The scum of humanity could be kept in check only by fear. This firebrand's
speech was very effective; no one in the Senate contradicted him;
even Nero was forced to yield, considering it wisest to keep his
peace. The slaves were all executed. But when the Republican
aristocrats, emboldened by this victory, introduced an additional
motion in the Senate to deport from Italy all the freedmen
who had ever lived under the same roof with the condemned
slaves, Nero rose from his seat and declared that though mercy
and compassion might not be permitted to soften the ancient law,
the latter should not, however, be aggravated; this caused the
defeat of the motion.

Nero went so far as to appoint a special judge, according to
Seneca, to "investigate maltreatments of slaves by their masters
and to impose limits upon the cruelty and caprice of the masters
as well as upon their niggardliness in supplying things to eat."
The same emperor decreased the number of gladiatorial combats, and sometimes insisted, according to Suetonius, that none
of those participating, not even condemned criminals, be slain.

We have a similar report concerning Tiberius. The facts cited above clearly show how unfruitful is a moralizing or political record of history, which considers it to be its task to measure the men of the past by the moral and political standards of our day. Nero, murderer of his mother and wife, indulgently grants their lives to slaves and criminals. The tyrant takes liberty under his protection when it is threatened by the Republicans; the insane voluptuary practices the virtues of humanity and charity toward the saints and martyrs of Christianity, feeds the hungry, gives drink to the thirsty, clothes the naked—let the reader recall his princely generosity to the Roman proletariat—and espouses the cause of the poor and miserable: this historical figure mocks any attempt at evaluating it by ethical standards. But difficult and foolish though it may be to attempt to ascertain whether Nero was at bottom a good man or a rascal, or both, as is commonly assumed today, it is nevertheless easy to *understand* Nero and his actions, those that are sympathetic to us as well as those that are repellent to us, if we proceed from the standpoint of his epoch and his social position.

The clemency shown by the imperial court, as well as by the proletariat, toward the slaves, must have been emphatically strengthened by the fact that the slave had ceased to be a *cheap commodity*. On the one hand, the phase of slave labor that had always been productive of the most terrible brutalities, namely, its exploitation for profit, had come to an end. There remained only the luxury slaves who by the very nature of their employment usually received better treatment. These slaves became a relatively more important element as slaves became rarer and dearer, as the loss caused by the untimely death of a slave became greater, as the slave became more difficult to replace.

Finally, other influences were working in the same direction: the increasing disinclination to military service, which was causing an increasing number of city dwellers to recoil from bloodshed; also the theory of internationalism, which taught that each man must be esteemed without regard to descent, thus obliterating the national differences and oppositions.

e. Internationalism

We have already pointed out how great was the development of world traffic under the Imperial Era. A system of excellent roads united Rome with the provinces and the latter among themselves. Commercial traffic between them was particularly stimulated by the peace within the Empire which followed upon the eternal wars between the various cities and states, and the later civil wars which had filled the last few centuries of the history of the Republic. Thanks to this condition, the national naval power in the Imperial Era was entirely available for combating piracy; the latter, never entirely absent from the Mediterranean before this, now ceased. Measures, weights and moneys were now made uniform over the entire Empire; all these factors greatly aided intercourse between its various portions.

And this intercourse was preëminently personal in character. Postal communications, at least as far as private letters are concerned, were then but slightly developed; anyone having business to do abroad found himself obliged, more often than now, to conduct such business personally by traveling to the spot.

Thus the peoples dwelling around the Mediterranean were brought more closely together and their local peculiarities were ironed out more and more. To be sure, the entire Empire never progressed to the point where it consisted of an altogether uniform mass. It was possible always to distinguish two halves, the *Western,* which spoke Latin, and had a Romanizing influence, and the *Eastern,* which spoke Greek, and had a Hellenizing influence, and when the power and the world rule of Rome and its traditions were extinguished, when Rome was no longer the capital of the Empire, these two sections were separated both in a political as well as in a religious sense.

But in the early days of the Imperial Era there was as yet no possibility of a serious attack on the unity of the Empire. This was the moment at which the distinction between the subjugated nations and the dominant city was disappearing. As the population of Rome lost its virility, the Caesars began no longer to consider themselves as the rulers of the entire Empire, as the masters of *Rome and the provinces*, as the lords of the provinces in the name of Rome. Rome—both aristocracy and people—fed by the provinces, but unable to produce from its own resources enough soldiers and officials to control the provinces, Rome now was not an element of power in the Empire of the Caesars, but an element of weakness. What Rome took from the provinces did not go to the Caesars, and there was no compensating gain to the latter. The emperors were therefore impelled by their own interest to oppose and finally to abolish Rome's privileged position in the Empire.

The right of Roman citizenship was now generously bestowed on the inhabitants of the provinces. We find the latter entering the Senate and occupying high office. The Caesars were the first to put to a practical application the principle of the equality of all men without regard to their descent: all men were equally subject to them and were valued by them only in accordance with their usefulness, without respect of person, whether they were senators or slaves, Romans, Syrians, or Gauls. By the beginning of the Third Century, the welding and leveling down of the races had progressed so far that Caracalla could afford to bestow rights of Roman citizenship on all the inhabitants of the provinces, thus simultaneously abolishing all the former differences between the former rulers and ruled, all of these differences having as a matter of fact long ceased to exist. It was one of the most wretched emperors who thus openly expressed one of the most elevated thoughts of the epoch, a thought that Christianity claims as its own; and the cause which moved the despot to make this decision was a wretched one—*financial distress.*

Under the Republic, Roman citizens had been free of taxes from the time when booty had begun to pour in plentifully from the conquered provinces. "Æmilius Paullus brought back, after defeating Perseus, 300,000,000 sesterces of the Macedonian booty, for the Treasury, and from this time on the Roman people paid no taxes." [27] But beginning with the time of Augustus, the increasing financial distress had made it necessary gradually to restore taxation in the form of new burdens even on Roman citi-

[27] Pliny, *Natural History*, xxxiii, 17.

zens. Caracalla's "Reform" now made Roman citizens of the provincials, in order to oblige them to pay taxes as Roman citizens in addition to their regular taxes, the former being simultaneously doubled by this imperial financial genius. The other side of the story is that he increased the army budget by $15,000,000. We are not surprised that his "Financial Reform" was of little use, and that he had to resort to other means, of which the most important and most audacious was an inflation and forging of money.

The general disintegration was favorable in another respect to the dissemination of ideas of internationalism and the disappearance of national prejudices.

The depopulation and corruption in Rome, proceeding so rapidly with the Romans, having ceased to provide *soldiers* soon also ceased to produce suitable *officials*. We can trace this defect even in the emperors. The first emperors were still the descendants of ancient Rome's aristocratic families, of the Julian and the Claudian gens. But the third emperor of the Julian dynasty, Caligula, was insane, and Nero is an indication of the complete bankruptcy of the Roman artistocracy's power to govern. Nero's successor, Galba, was also of a Roman patrician family, but he was followed by *Otho*, of a distinguished *Etruscan* family, and Vitellius, a plebeian from Apulia. Vespasian, finally, who founded the Flavic dynasty, was a plebeian of Sabine origin. But the Italic plebeians soon showed themselves to be just as corrupt and incapable of government as were the Roman aristocrats, and the wretched Domitian, Vespasian's son, was followed after the short reign of Nerva by the Spaniard Trajan. With the latter begins the rule of the Spanish emperors, which lasted almost a century, until they also gave evidence of political bankruptcy, in the person of Commodus.

Septimius Severus, after the termination of the Spanish line, founded an Afro-Syrian dynasty. Already after the murder of the last emperor of this line, Alexander Severus, the crown passed to a Thracian, of Gothic descent, Maximin, being offered to him by the legions, a harbinger of the time when the Goths would rule at Rome. The provinces were more and more attacked by the general process of decay, and it became more and more necessary to reinvigorate them with barbarian, non-Roman blood, in order to infuse new life into the dying Empire, and soldiers now had to be sought farther and farther from the main centers of civilization, and not only soldiers, but even emperors.

We have already seen slaves ruling as courtiers over free men; now we behold provincials, even barbarians, who have been placed on the throne as emperors, as creatures entitled to divine worship. All the race and class prejudice of pagan antiquity necessarily disappeared, and a feeling of equality was bound to assert itself more and more.

Many minds evinced this attitude at an early stage, before the conditions above described made it a frequent phenomenon. Thus Cicero already writes (*De officiis*, iii, 6): "He who maintains that we must have consideration for our fellow-citizens, but not for strangers, is making a breach in the universal ties of the human race, and thus fundamentally abolishing charity, generosity, kindliness and justice." Our ideological historians here again confuse cause and effect and attempt to use such sentences (which the "pious" find in the Gospels, and the "enlightened" in the pagan philosophies) as causes to explain the softening of customs and the extension of the concept of the nation to include all humanity. The only difficulty is that they are faced with the fact that the noble and sublime spirits who are alleged to have brought about this revolution in men's minds are headed by bloodthirsty criminals and voluptuaries like Tiberius, Nero, Caracalla, as well as a galaxy of foppish fashionable philosophers and swindlers, like Seneca, the Younger Pliny, Apollonius of Tyana, and Plotinus.

The aristocratic Christians, we must remark in passing, did not find it very difficult to adapt themselves to the society of this noble band; let us give one example only. Among the many female and male concubines kept by the Emperor Commodus (180-192 A.D.)—a harem of 300 girls and 300 boys is mentioned —the honor of occupying the first place fell to Marcia, a pious Christian, the goddaughter of Hyacinthus, Presbyter of the Christian congregation at Rome. Her influence was so great that she secured the liberation of a number of deported Christians. But finally she found her imperial lover somewhat of a nuisance; perhaps she feared his bloodthirstiness would cost her her life. In short, she took part in a conspiracy against the emperor's life and undertook to carry out the assassination. In the night of December 31, 192, this pious Christian lady handed her unsuspecting lover a cup of poison, and as the latter did not take effect quickly enough, the emperor, already unconscious, was strangled.

Equally characteristic is the story of Callistus, who enjoyed Marcia's protection.

"Callistus had had special gifts for financial work in his earlier years, and had kept a bank. He was at first the slave of a prominent Christian, who handed over to him a considerable sum which he was to put out at interest. On the strength of his master's solidity he secured the moneys of widows and others, came at last to the verge of bankruptcy, and was then asked for an account by the master. He fled, but was captured, and sent by the master to the treadmill. Obtaining his liberty through the entreaties of his Christian brethren, then sent by the prefect to the Sardinian mines, he won the favor of Marcia, the most powerful mistress of the Emperor Commodus. At her request he was restored to liberty, and was shortly afterwards appointed Bishop of Rome." [28]

Perhaps Kalthoff considers it possible that the two tales in the Gospels concerning the faithless steward who "makes to himself friends of the Mammon of unrighteousness" (Luke xvi, 1-9) and the sinful woman, who is forgiven her sins, "which are many; for she loved much" (Luke, vii, 36-48), were included in the Gospels in order "to provide an ecclesiastical interpretation and sanction" for the dubious characters of Marcia and Callistus, who were so prominent in the Christian congregation at Rome. This may also serve as a contribution to the history of the origin of the Gospels.

Callistus was not the last Bishop and Pope to owe his office to a paramour, and the murder of Commodus was not the last

[28] Kalthoff, *The Rise of Christianity,* translated by Joseph McCabe, London, 1907, p. 171-172.

act of Christian violence. The bloodthirstiness and cruelty of many popes and emperors, beginning with the times of Constantine the Holy, are too well known to require mention.

The "softening and ennobling of manners" which accompanied the introduction of Christianity were therefore of somewhat peculiar nature. To understand their limitations and contradictions, it is necessary to study their economic roots; the fine moral doctrines of the times will not explain them.

And the same statement holds good of the internationalism of that day.

f. The Tendency to Religion

World-wide traffic and a political leveling process were two powerful causes of the increase in internationalism; yet this increase could hardly have reached the proportions it did, were it not for the dissolving of all those bonds which had cemented the old communities, simultaneously isolating them from each other. The organizations which had determined the entire life of the individual in antiquity, and had afforded him a support and guide, lost most of their significance and force in the Imperial Period. This applies not only to such organizations as were based on ties of blood, as the brotherhood of the gens, including even the family, but also to those based on a territorial unity, on a dwelling together on the same soil, as in the case of the clan and the community. This, as we have seen, resulted in a general seeking, on the part of persons who had thus lost their moral support, for models and leaders, even for redeemers. But it also stimulated men to seek to establish new social organizations, that might better answer the new needs than did the traditional forms, which were becoming more and more a mere burden.

Already toward the end of the Republic we find a general tendency toward the formation of clubs and associations, particularly for political purposes, but also for the purpose of giving beneficiary aid. These were dissolved by the Caesars, for despotism fears nothing so much as social organizations. The power of despotism is greatest when the state power represents the only social organization, while the citizens of the state face that power as scattered individuals only.

Caesar already "dissolved all societies, with the exception of those that were of hoary antiquity," reports Suetonius (*Caesar*, Chapter xlii), while he says of Augustus:

"Many parties (*plurimæ factiones*) organized under the name of a new collegium for carrying out all possible atrocities. . . . These collegiums he dissolved, with the exception of those that were very old and legally recognized." [29]

Mommsen finds these provisions to be quite laudable. No doubt, for the accomplished and unconscionable swindler Caesar appears to him as a genuine statesman who "served the people not for reward, not even for the reward of their love," but "for the blessing of posterity, and above all for the permission to save and renew his nation". [30] To understand this estimate of Caesar, the reader must recall that Mommsen's work appeared in the years immediately following the June Battle (the first edition came out in 1854), when Napoleon the Third was exalted by many liberals, particularly Germans, as the savior of society, and Napoleon made a certain cult of Caesar fashionable.

After the cessation of political activity and of the political associations, those desiring social intercourse turned to more innocent societies, particularly professional societies and beneficiary associations for sick and death benefits, aids in poverty, volunteer fire associations; but merely sociable bodies, dining clubs, literary societies, and the like, also grew up like mushrooms. But the Caesars were so suspicious that they could not tolerate even such organizations, for the latter might serve as a cloak for more dangerous associations.

In the correspondence between Pliny and Trajan we may still read letters in which Pliny speaks of a conflagration which had devastated Nicomedia, and recommends that the establishment of a volunteer fire association (*collegium fabrorum*) of not more than 150 men be permitted; such a number could easily be kept

[29] *Octavianus Augustus,* chap. xxxii.
[30] *History of Rome,* vol. v, p. 324.

under surveillance. But Trajan found even this much to be dangerous and refused the permission that had been asked.[81]

Later letters (No. 117 and No. 118) show us that even gatherings of persons on the occasions of marriages or other festivities of rich people, at which money was distributed, seemed to Pliny and Trajan as involving danger to the state.

But our historians exalt Trajan as one of the best emperors.

The instinct for organization found itself compelled under these circumstances to engage in underground activities. The discovery of such, however, meant the death penalty for those participating. It is evident that mere amusements or even advantages accruing only to the individual, though they involved an improvement in his personal situation, could not be strong enough to impel any man to risk his neck. Only such organizations could maintain themselves as had for their goal something that transcended mere personal advantage, that would endure even if the individual perished; but such organizations could only gain in power if this goal corresponded to a strong and universally appreciated *social interest* and *need*, a class interest or a general interest, an interest most profoundly felt by great masses, and therefore capable of moving its most energetic and unselfish members to risk their lives in order to satisfy its demands. In other words, only such organizations could maintain themselves in the Imperial Period as pursued a far-reaching social object, a high ideal. No mere striving for practical advantages, for the safeguarding of momentary interests, but only the most revolutionary or idealistic enthusiasm could then give life and vigor to any organization.

This idealism had nothing in common with philosophical idealism. The pursuit of great social goals may be the result of a materialistic philosophy also, in fact only the materialistic method, basing itself on experience, on the study of the necessary relations of cause and effect in our experiences, may lead to the proposal of great social goals that are free from illusions. But all the necessary prerequisites for the existence of such a method were lacking in the Imperial Period. The individual could rise

[81] Pliny, *Letters*, x, 42 and 43.

beyond himself only by means of a moralizing mysticism, and thus attain the vision of goals transcending personal and temporary well-being, in other words, only by means of that mode of thought which is known as *religious*. Only religious associations maintained themselves in the Imperial Period. But we should have an erroneous understanding of them if their religious form, their moralizing mysticism, should make us overlook the social *content* inherent in all these organizations, which gave them their strength: the longing for a cessation of the existing sad conditions, for higher social forms, for a close coöperation and a mutual support for these many individuals now mentally homeless, who drew new courage and joy from having banded together for high achievement.

But these religious organizations involved a new line of cleavage in society, at the very moment when the concept of *nationality* was expanded, at least as far as the Mediterranean countries were concerned, to that of *humanity*. The purely economic organizations which aimed to help the individual only in one particular respect or other, did not weaken the individual's attachment to existing society and gave him no new interest in life. But it was different with the religious societies, which pursued a great social ideal under a religious garb. This ideal was diametrically opposed to the existing system of society, not in one point only, but in every possible respect. The advocates of this ideal spoke the same language as their surroundings, and yet were not understood by them, and at every step the two worlds, the old and the new, encountered each other in a hostile manner, although both lived in the same land. Thus a new opposition arose between men. At the very moment when the Gaul and the Syrian, the Roman and the Egyptian, the Spaniard and the Greek, were beginning to lose their national identity, there arose the great difference between believers and unbelievers, saints and sinners, Christians and pagans, which was soon to divide the world as with a gulf.

As this contrast became sharper, as the struggle became more emphatic, intolerance and fanaticism also increased, a necessary accompaniment of any struggle, constituting, like the struggle itself, a necessary element of progress and evolution, if they give animus and energy to the forces of progress. But let the reader note that we use the word "intolerance" not as meaning a forcible suppression of propaganda for all inconvenient opinions, but an energetic rejection and criticism of all different views, accompanied by an energetic defense of one's own views. Only cowardice and indolence could be "tolerant" in this sense, where great and universal life questions are at stake.

To be sure, these interests are subject to constant change. A question of life and death yesterday, may today be a matter of indifference, hardly worth fighting for. Therefore a fanatical advocacy of such a point, yesterday still a necessity, may today become an occasion for wasted energy, and thus have very unfortunate effects.

Thus the religious intolerance and religious fanaticism of many of the Christian sects that were gaining strength at this time constituted one of the forces which accelerated the social evolution, as long as social goals were accessible to the masses only when clothed in religious garb; in other words, from the Imperial Era to the Era of the Reformation. But these qualities became reactionary and constituted only a means of retarding progress, when the religious mode of thought was superseded by the methods of modern science, with the result that it is cherished only by backward classes and strata of the population, or backward regions, and may not in any manner continue to serve as an envelope for new social goals.

Religious intolerance was an entirely new trait in the mode of thought of ancient society. Intolerant though the latter may have been from a nationalistic standpoint, slight as was its respect for strangers, not to mention foreigners, whom it enslaved or slew, even though they may not have fought as soldiers, ancient society nevertheless did not dream of despising anyone for his religious convictions. Those cases that may perhaps be regarded as religious persecutions, as, for example, the trial of Socrates, may be explained as the results of *political* accusations that were not religious in character.

The new mode of thought arising in the Imperial Era was the

first to bring religious intolerance with it, and it did this on both sides, Christian as well as pagan, on the pagan side, of course, not involving intolerance to all foreign religions, but only toward that which was preaching a new social ideal under a religious cloak, an ideal absolutely opposed to the existing order of society.

In all other cases, the pagans retained the religious tolerance they had formerly practiced; in fact, it was precisely in these imperial days of international intercourse that a certain internationalism of religious cults became established. Foreign merchants and other travelers always took their gods with them wherever they went, and strange gods were then more highly regarded than the native gods; for the latter had not been of much use; they had shown their impotence. The same feeling of desperation which resulted from the general disintegration also led to a loss of faith in the old gods, impelling many of the bolder and more independent spirits to turn to atheism and skepticism, to doubts of all divinity, and even of all philosophy. The more timid, the weaker elements, however, were moved to seek a new redeemer, as we have seen, in whom they might find a support and a hope. Many thought they had found this quality in the Caesars, who were made gods. Others thought it wiser to turn to gods that had long been venerated as such, but had not yet been given a trial in their adopted country. The result was that foreign religions became popular.

In this international competition of divinities, however, the Orient defeated the Occident, partly because the oriental religions were less naïve, more imbued with the rich philosophy of the large cities, for reasons that we shall learn later, but partly also because the East was defeating the West in the industrial field.

The ancient civilization of the Orient was far superior to that of the Occident when it was plundered first by the Macedonians and later by the Romans. Perhaps the reader may think that the international leveling down which had then begun would also have involved an industrial equalization, necessarily raising the West to the level of the East, but the opposite was what actually resulted. We have seen that beginning with a certain point there is a general process of disintegration in the ancient world, a consequence in part of the predominance of compulsory labor over free labor, in part of the plundering of the provinces by Rome and by usurious capital. But this decay proceeds more rapidly in the West than in the East, with the result that the cultural superiority of the latter for many centuries, beginning with the Second Century of our era, and extending to about 1000 A.D., does not decrease but increase. Poverty, barbarism, depopulation, make more rapid strides in the West than in the East.

The cause of this phenomenon is to be found above all in the industrial superiority of the East and the constant increase in the exploitation of the working classes throughout the Empire. The surplus profits yielded by the latter flowed for the most part to Rome, the seat of all the great exploiters, from all the provinces. But of all of the surplus accumulated in Rome, which took the form of money, the lion's share flowed to the East. For it was the East alone that produced all the articles of luxury desired by the great exploiters. It was the East that furnished the luxury, slaves, and also industrial products, such as glass and purple in Phœnicia; linen and embroidered cloths in Egypt; fine woolens and leathers in Asia Minor; rugs in Babylonia. And the decreasing fertility of Italy was making Egypt a granary of Rome, for, thanks to the overflowings of the river, covering the soil of Egypt with a new fruitful mud each year, the agriculture of the Nile Valley was inexhaustible.

To be sure, much of what the Orient furnished was being taken by force in the form of taxes and usurious interest, but there still remained a considerable quantity which had to be paid for with the yield of the exploitation of the West, whose poverty was increasing.

The traffic with the East was beginning to extend beyond the boundaries of the Empire. Alexandria became wealthy, not only through the sale of Egyptian industrial products, but also by serving as an intermediary in the trade with Arabia and India, while a commercial route to China started from Sinope on the Black Sea. Pliny estimated in his *Natural History* that about 100,000,000 sesterces (more than $5,000,000) was taken out of the Empire annually to pay for Chinese silks, Indian jewels and Arabian spices, without any noteworthy compensation in the form of commodities, and also without in any way obligating foreign lands to pay tribute or interest. The whole amount had to be paid in precious metal.

But with the oriental merchandise, the oriental merchants also came to the West, bringing their forms of worship with them. These were quite acceptable to the needs of the West, by reason of the fact that similar social conditions had already existed in the Orient, though perhaps not developed to such disastrous proportions as had now been reached throughout the Roman Empire. The idea of redemption by a divinity whose good graces were acquired by a renunciation of earthly pleasures was peculiar to most of these cults which now rapidly spread throughout the Empire, particularly to the Egyptian cult of Isis, and the Persian cult of Mithra.

"Isis particularly, whose worship had begun in Rome at the time of Sulla, and had gained imperial favor under Vespasian, was now spreading to the furthest point West, and had gradually attained an enormous, all-embracing significance, first as a goddess of healing, particularly in the narrow physical sense. . . . Her worship was rich in magnificent processions, and also in chastisements, atonements, and strict observations, particularly in mysteries. It was precisely the religious longing, the hope for forgiveness of sins, the desire for severe penances and the hope to gain a blessed immortality by complete surrender to a divinity, that encouraged the spread of such exotic cults in the Greek or Roman Olympus, which formerly had been rather indifferent to such mysterious ceremonies, enraptured ecstasies, magic practices, self-denials, boundless surrender to divinity, renunciation and penance as a condition for purification and holiness. Still more powerful was the secret worship of Mithra, which was particularly disseminated by the armies, and which also laid claim to redemption and immortality; this cult first became known under Tiberius." [32]

[32] Hertzberg, *Geschichte des römischen Kaisereichs*, p. 451. The English translation of this book, *Imperial Rome* (Philadelphia, 1905), omits this passage. —TRANSLATOR.

East Indian views also became current in the Roman Empire; for example, Apollonius of Tyana, whom we have already had occasion to mention, took a special trip to India to study the philosophical and religious doctrines current in that country. We have also heard concerning Plotinus that he traveled to Persia in order to become better acquainted with Persian and Indian lore.

All these views and cults did not fail to leave a trace among the Christians who were striving for redemption and exaltation; they were one of the most powerful influences on the early stages of the cult and the legends of Christianity.

"Eusebius, a Father of the Church, treated this Egyptian cult contemptuously as a 'wisdom of beetles', and yet the myth of the Virgin Mary is only an echo of the myths originating on the banks of the Nile.

"Osiris was represented on earth by the steer Apis. Just as Osiris himself had been conceived by his mother without the intervention of a god, so was it also necessary for his representative on earth to be conceived by a virgin cow without the assistance of a bull. Herodotus informs us that the mother of Apis was fructified by a sunbeam, while according to Plutarch she conceived from a moonbeam.

"Like Apis, Jesus had no father, having been begotten by a beam of light from Heaven. Apis was a steer, but he represented a god; Jesus was a god represented by a lamb. But Osiris himself was also represented as having the head of a ram." [33]

As a matter of fact, a scoffer remarked, perhaps in the Third Century, when Christianity was already quite strong, that there was no very great difference in Egypt between Christians and pagans: "Those who worshiped Sarapis in Egypt are also Christians, and those who call themselves Christian Bishops are also worshipers of Sarapis; every grand rabbi of the Jews, every Samaritan, every Christian priest in Egypt, was at the same time a sorcerer, a prophet, a mountebank (*aliptes*). Even when the

[33] Lafargue, *Der Mythus von der unbefleckten Empfängnis, Die Neue Zeit,* vol. xl, No. 1, p. 49.

Patriarch comes to Egypt, some want him to pray to Sarapis, while others want him to pray to Christ." [34]

Furthermore, the story of the birth of Christ, as found in Luke, has certain Buddhist traits.

Pfleiderer points out that the author of the Gospel could not have invented this tale out of whole cloth, unhistorical though it may be, but must have taken it from legends "which had come to his knowledge in some way", possibly ancient legends which were common to all the Western Asiatic peoples. "For we find the same legends with at times strikingly similar earmarks, in the story of the childhood of the East Indian Savior Buddha (who lived in the Fifth Century B.C., K.). He also is born miraculously by the Virgin Queen Maya, whose immaculate body had been entered by Buddha in his character as a light of Heaven. At his birth also, celestial spirits appear and intone the following song of praise: 'A wondrous hero, an incomparable hero has been born. Hail to the world, full of mercy, today thou spreadest out thy benevolence over all the things of universal space! Let joy and satisfaction come to all creatures, that they may be calm, masters of themselves and happy.' Buddha also is then brought by his mother to the temple so that the legal customs may be complied with; there he is found by the old hermit Asita, who has been induced by a premonition to descend from Himalaya; Asita prophesies that this child will be the Buddha, the redeemer from all evils, a guide to freedom and light and immortality. . . . And finally we have a summary account of how the royal child gains daily in mental perfection and bodily strength and beauty—which is precisely what is said of the child Jesus in Luke ii, 40 and 52." [35]

"Examples of early wisdom are also told of the growing Gautama; among other stories, it is told that, during a festival of his people, the boy was lost and, after an eager search, he was found by his father in a circle of holy men lost in pious reflection,

[34] Cited by Mommsen, *The Provinces of the Roman Empire,* London, 1886, vol. ii, p. 266.
[35] *Primitive Christianity,* London, 1906-1911, vol. ii, pp. 108-110.

whereupon he admonished the marveling father to seek after higher things." [36]

In the book mentioned above, Pfleiderer points out additional elements that were taken by Christianity from other forms of worship; for example, from the worship of Mithra. We have already cited Pfleiderer's reference to the precedent for the Lord's Supper, which was "one of the Mithra sacraments" (page 158). There are probably pagan elements also in the doctrine of the Resurrection.

"Perhaps Paul was influenced by the popular idea of the god who dies and returns to life, dominant at that time in the Adonis, Attis and Osiris cults of Hither Asia (with various names and customs, everywhere much alike). At Antioch, the Syrian capital, in which Paul had been active for a considerable period, the main celebration of the Adonis-feast took place in the springtime; on the first day (in the Osiris celebration it was the third day after the death, while in the Attis celebration it was the fourth day), the death of Adonis, 'the Lord', was celebrated, while on the following day, amid the wild songs of lamentations sung by the women, the burial of his corpse (represented by an image) was enacted; on the next day, proclamation was made that the god lives and he (his image) was made to rise in air," etc.[37]

But Pfleiderer rightly points out that Christianity did not merely take over these pagan elements, but adapted them to suit its unified system of belief. For Christianity could not grant asylum to the strange gods without transforming them; its monotheism alone would have been sufficient to prevent such a procedure.

g. Monotheism

But even monotheism, the faith in a single god, was not characteristic of Christianity alone. In this case also we have an opportunity to reveal the economic roots on which the idea is based. We have already seen how the inhabitants of large cities became estranged from nature, how all the traditional organiza-

[36] Pfleiderer, *Christian Origins*, New York, 1906, p. 229.
[37] *Op. cit.*, p. 175.

tions, which had formerly afforded a firm moral support to the individual, were dissolved; and, finally, how a preoccupation with the *ego* became the principal task of philosophy, which gradually shifted its ground from the investigation of the external world into a brooding on the individual's own feelings and needs.

The gods had at first served as explanations for the processes of nature whose causal connections were not yet understood. These processes were very numerous and of the most varied kinds; they therefore required for their explanation the creation of the most manifold and various gods, gruesome and cheerful, brutal and tender, male and female. Then, with the advance in the knowledge of the causal relations in nature, the individual gods became more and more superfluous. But in the course of thousands of years they had taken too firm a root in man's thought, and become too closely associated with his daily occupations, while the knowledge of nature was still by no means so complete as to wipe out the faith in the gods entirely. The gods now found themselves driven out of one field of activity after the other; from having been constant companions of men, they now became extraordinary miraculous phenomena; having once been inhabitants of the earth, they were now assigned to regions above the earth, in the sky; having been vigorous, energetic workers and fighters, who tirelessly kept the world in commotion, they now became meditative observers of the universal scene.

Probably the advance in natural science would finally have abolished them altogether, if the rise of the large city and the economic decline that we have already described had not brought about an estrangement from nature and caused the foreground of thought to be occupied chiefly by the study of the spirit by the spirit; in other words, not by a scientific study of the sum of all the mental phenomena that had been experienced, but by a study in which the spirit of the individual became the source of all wisdom concerning itself, and this wisdom in turn was made the key to all the wisdom of the world. But manifold and changeable though the feelings and needs of the soul might be, the soul itself was assumed to be an indivisible unit. And the souls of others were conceived to be of exactly the same texture as the soul of the perceiving individual. A scientific attitude would have drawn the inference of the necessary subjection of all mental operations to uniform laws. But just at that time the ancient moral props were beginning to dissolve, with the result that man lost his former background and seemed now to be free; the individual seemed to possess freedom of the will. The uniform nature of the spirit in all men seemed then susceptible only of the explanation that this spirit was everywhere a portion of the same spirit, of a single spirit whose emanation and counterfeit constitutes the inscrutable and uniform spirit in all individuals. Spaceless, as the individual soul, was also this universal soul. But this soul was conceived as being present and active in all persons, in other words, as omnipresent and omniscient; the most secret thoughts could not be concealed from it. The greater attention that was being given to the moral interest, as opposed to the interest in nature, which gave rise to the assumption of this universal soul, also imparted a moral character to the universal soul. The latter came to embody all the moral ideas then occupying the minds of men. But in order to attain this state, the soul had to be divorced from the bodily nature inherent in the soul of man and obscuring its morality. We thus have the development of a new divinity. This divinity was necessarily a single unit, corresponding to the unity of the soul of the individual, as opposed to the manifold nature of the gods of antiquity, which corresponded to the complexity of the natural processes going on around us. And this new single divinity stood beyond nature and above nature; it existed before nature, which is one of its creations, as opposed to the ancient gods, who had been a portion of nature and possessed no seniority over nature.

But while the new spiritual interests of men were purely psychic and moral in character, they could not entirely neglect nature. And as the natural sciences were falling into disuse, it again became more customary to assume the intervention of super-human personal elements in order to explain natural events. The superior beings who now were represented as intervening in the universal process were no longer sovereign gods, as they once had been, but were subordinated to the universal spirit as nature was subordinated to God, and the body to the spirit, according to the conception of those days. They were creatures that stood somewhere between God and men.

This view of things was further supported by the course of events in the political field. The destruction of the Republic of the gods in Heaven went hand in hand with the downfall of the Republic in Rome; God became the almighty Caesar of the hereafter; like Caesar he had his court, the saints and the angels, and his Republican opposition were the devil and his hosts.

Finally the Christians went so far as to divide God's celestial bureaucracy, the angels, according to rank, into classes corresponding to the divisions made by the Caesars among their earthly bureaucracy, and the angels seem to have been subject to the same pride of place as the officials of the emperor.

Beginning with Constantine, the courtiers and state officials were divided into a number of ranks, each of which had the right to use a certain title. We find the following titles: 1. the *gloriosi*, namely, the highly celebrated, who were the Consuls; 2. the *nobilissimi*, or most noble; these were the princes of the blood; 3. the *patricii*, the barons. In addition to these ranks of nobility there were also ranks among the upper bureaucracy; 4. the *illustres*, or the illustrious ones; 5. the *spectabiles*, or respectable ones; 6. the *clarissimi*, or famous ones; and below these we have: 7. the *perfectissimi*, or most perfect ones; 8. the *egregii*, or distinguished ones; 9. the *comites*, or "privy councilors".

Our theologians will bear me out when I say that the celestial court is organized in exactly the same manner.

Thus, for example, the *Church Lexicon of Catholic Theology* [38] (issued by Wetzer and Welte, Freiburg in Breisgau, 1849) mentions in its article "Angel" the enormous number of angels and goes on to say:

"Following the precedent of Saint Ambrosius, many teachers believed that the ratio between the number of angels and the number of men is as 99 to 1; for instance, the lost sheep in the Parable of the Good Shepherd (Luke xii, 32) stands for the

[38] In German.—TRANSLATOR.

human race, while the 99 sheep that are not lost represent the angels. The angels of this countless host are grouped in a number of classes, and the Church—opposing even the opinion of Origen, who held that all spirits are like unto each other as to substance, strength, etc.—came out frankly in favor of distinctions between the angels, at the Second Council at Constantinople in 553 A.D. The Church recognizes nine choirs of angels, which are grouped in choruses of three choirs each. These nine orders are: 1. the Seraphim, 2. the Cherubim, 3. the Throni (*thrones*), 4. the Dominationes (*rulers*), 5. the Virtutes (*virtues*), 6. the Potestates (*mighty ones*), 7. the Principatus (*principalities*), 8. the Archangeli (*archangels*), 9. the Angeli (*common angels*).[39]

"It seems beyond all doubt that the angels constitute in the narrow sense of the word the lowest and most numerous class, while the Seraphim are the uppermost and least numerous class." Things on earth are not much different: there are not many officials with high titles, but we have a large number of common letter carriers.

The above article also contains the following information: "The angels live in intimate and personal communion with God and their relation with God is therefore one of infinite worship, of humble submission, of untiring affection that renounces all love aside from the love of God, of a complete and joyous surrender of their entire being, of steadfast fidelity, unfaltering obedience, profound respect, gratitude without end, ardent prayer, as well as ceaseless laudation, of constant magnification, of awesome praise, of holy jubilation, and rapturous rejoicing."

Similar joyous submission was required by the emperors on the part of their courtiers and officials. Such was the ideal of Byzantinism.

It is apparent that the image of the sole God as it grew up in Christianity was not less a product of imperial despotism than of philosophy, which since the days of Plato had turned more and more toward monotheism.

This philosophy was so much in accord with the general feeling and the general needs that it soon became a part of the popular

[39] The word *angelus* at first signifies simply *a messenger*.

consciousness. Thus, for example, we already find in Plautus, a writer of comedies, who lived in the Third Century, B.C., and whose ideas were those of a cheap popular philosophy, such passages as the following statement of a slave, who is asking for a favor:

> "Yet there is a God, hearing and seeing all that is done by us men,
> He will do by your son as you here have done by me.
> He will reward good deeds and also requite deeds of evil."
>
> (*The Prisoners of War*, Act II, Scene 2.)

We are already face to face with a conception of God that is quite Christian. But this monotheism was extremely naïve, thoughtlessly permitting the old gods to continue existing by its side. Nor did it occur to the Christians themselves to question the existence of the ancient gods, since they accepted so many pagan miracles without question. But the Christian God tolerated no other gods but him; he would be sole ruler. If the pagan gods would not submit to him and consent to be enrolled among his court, there was no other rôle left them but that played by the Republican opposition under the earlier emperors, which for the most part was a very sorry rôle. It consisted merely in occasional efforts to play some trick on the Almighty Lord, to incite his virtuous subjects against him, without any hope of ever overthrowing the master, but with the sole prospect of occasionally irritating him.

But even this intolerant monotheism, sure of its victory, which doubted not for a moment the superiority and omnipotence of its God, was already in existence when Christianity came upon the scene. To be sure, not among the pagans, but among a small nation of peculiar character, the Jews, who developed *the belief in a redeemer*, and the obligation of *mutual aid*, and of a firm solidarity, to a far greater extent, and who satisfied much better the strong need felt at that time for such doctrines, than did any other nation or class of society in that era. The Jews, therefore, imparted a mighty impetus to the new doctrine arising from these needs, and contributed to it some of its most important elements. In order to reveal completely all the roots from which Christianity grew, we must add to our general study of the Roman-Hellenic world, under the Imperial Era, a specific study of the Jewish people.

Part Three
THE JEWS

I. THE PEOPLE OF ISRAEL

a. *Semitic Tribal Migrations*

THE beginnings of the history of Israel are involved in profound obscurity, perhaps even more than is the case with Greek and Roman history. For not only were these early stages transmitted through many centuries by word of mouth alone, but even when the old legends began to be collected and recorded, they were distorted in the worst propaganda manner. Nothing would be more erroneous than the assumption that biblical history is a record of actual happenings; the Bible stories may contain a historical nucleus, but this nucleus is extremely difficult to determine.

It was only after the return from the Babylonian Exile, in the Fifth Century, B.C., that the "sacred" scriptures of the Jews were given the form in which we have them today. All the ancient traditions were at that time manipulated and supplemented by fabrications, with the greatest audacity, in order to answer the requirements of the rising priestly caste. All of the ancient history of the Jews was thus turned topsy-turvy; this is particularly true of what we are told concerning the religion of Israel before the Exile.

When the Jews founded a community of their own, after the Exile, in Jerusalem and in the surrounding country, this community soon impressed other tribes by its peculiarities, as a number of records show. But with regard to the period before the Exile no such records have been preserved. Before the destruction of Jerusalem by the Babylonians, the Israelites were considered by other peoples as a nation not unlike other nations; no particular traits seemed to distinguish them from others; and there is every reason to assume that the Jews until then actually presented no exceptional qualities.

It is impossible, in view of the scantiness and unreliability of the available sources, to draw an accurate picture of ancient Israel. Protestant Bible criticism, as practiced by the theologians, has already proved that much has been forged and invented, but far too much is still accepted at its face value, merely because it has not yet been revealed as a manifest forgery.

We have practically nothing but hypotheses to go by in our attempt to outline the development of Israelitic society. The reports of the Old Testament will give us valuable service wherever we are able to compare them with descriptions of peoples in similar situations.

The historical existence of the Jews does not begin until they penetrate into the country of the Canaanites. All the tales of their nomadic period are either ancient tribal legends, with propaganda adornments, or fairy tales, or later inventions. They first appear in history as participants in a great Semitic migration of nations.

Migrations of nations play the same part in the ancient world that revolutions do today. In the preceding section we considered the downfall of the Roman Empire and traced the stages preliminary to its inundation by the Teutonic barbarians, which event is called the "migration of nations". This is not an unparalleled phenomenon. The ancient Orient had already known it on repeated occasions, on a smaller scale, but as a result of similar causes.

In many of the fruitful basins of the great oriental rivers, agriculture developed at an early time, providing a considerable surplus of foodstuffs, and permitting the existence and activities of a numerous population devoted to other occupations besides that of agriculture. The arts, crafts, and sciences flourished, and an aristocracy developed, with the opportunity to devote its time exclusively to the arts of war, and this aristocracy became all the more necessary as the wealth of the river region began to entice warlike nomadic neighbors to engage in predatory incursions. The peasant who wished to till his fields in peace needed the protection of such an aristocracy, for which he had to pay. But as the aristocracy grew stronger, it easily succumbed to the temptation to employ its warlike strength for the purpose of increasing its income, particularly as the progress of the arts and crafts gave rise to all sorts of luxuries which could only be obtained by the possessors of wealth. The peasants begin to be oppressed, and campaigns begin to be made by the aristocrats, more skilled in arms, and their vassals, against neighboring peoples for the purpose of capturing them as slaves. Compulsory labor begins, and gradually pushes society into the same blind alley which was later to be the final stage of society in the Roman Imperial Era also. The free peasant is ruined, he is replaced by forced labor; simultaneously the basis of the Empire's warlike strength is destroyed. Likewise, in spite of their superiority in arms, the aristocracy lose their warlike prowess, being undermined by the increase in luxury.

They lose the ability needed for the discharge of the functions demanded by their social position: that of defending the commonwealth against the invasions of predatory neighbors. These neighbors gradually become thoroughly aware of the rich and enticing booty so near at hand, they gradually press closer and closer upon the boundaries, finally overflowing them and thus inaugurating a tendency which embraces more and more tribes pushing behind them, with the result that the movement does not terminate for some time. Some of the invaders take possession of land and thus create a new free peasantry. Others, the more powerful ones, establish a new warlike aristocracy, while the older aristocracy, the guardian of the arts and sciences of the ancient civilization, may continue to maintain a superior status to that of the barbarian conquerors, but it is no longer a caste of warriors but rather a caste of priests.

When this migratory movement has ceased, the course of evolution again passes through the same cycle, which may perhaps be compared with the cycle of prosperity and crisis in capitalist society; but the older cycle was not merely a cycle recurring each decade, but one covering many centuries, a cycle which was not superseded until the capitalistic mode of production intervened, just as the cycle of crises of today will not be overcome until socialistic production is installed.

In the various regions of Asia and Northern Africa this course of evolution continued for thousands of years; it was most perceptible in spots where broad, fruitful river valleys produced immense wealth, but this wealth resulted in a profound corruption and enervation. The less favored regions produced poor but warlike nomadic tribes, ever ready to change their domicile when booty called, and who at a favorable opportunity could gather swiftly in countless numbers at any single point in order to penetrate violently and destructively into the region. The valleys of the Hoang-Ho and Yangtse-Kiang, in which the Chinese nation developed, are examples of this condition; also the valley of the Ganges, where enticing wealth was concentrated; those of the Euphrates and Tigris, where the mighty empires of Babylonia and Assyria arose; and finally the valley of the Nile, which is Egypt.

But in one case we have Central Asia, and in the other Arabia, which were inexhaustible reservoirs of warlike nomads who were a constant menace to their neighbors and sometimes made use of their weakness as an opportunity to begin immense immigrations.

From Central Asia, at such periods of weakness, streams of Mongols, and on certain occasions also of so-called Indo-Germans, would break through the barriers of civilization. From Arabia came those tribes which are included under the general name of Semites. The goals of the Semitic invaders were Babylonia, Assyria, Egypt, and the intermediate region of the Mediterranean.

Somewhat more than a thousand years before Christ, one of these great Semitic migrations begins; it advances toward Mesopotamia, Syria, Egypt, and perhaps closes some time in the Eleventh Century B.C. Among the Semitic tribes who conquered neighboring cultural territory at that time were the Hebrews. In view of their Bedouin-like wanderings they may perhaps have encountered the Egyptian boundaries and Mt. Sinai before this, but it is only after they settled down in Palestine that the Hebrew community took definite form, leaving behind the stage of nomadic instability, under which there was no possibility for the formation of a large nation.

b. Palestine

From this time on, the history and the characteristics of the Israelites are no longer determined only by the qualities acquired in the Bedouin stage, and perhaps retained for some time after, but also by the character and the situation of Palestine.

We must be on our guard against overestimating the influence of the geographic factor in history. In historic times the geographic factor—situation, contour of the soil, climate—does, to be sure, continue on the whole the same in most countries; this factor is present before history begins and surely has a powerful influence on the latter. But the manner in which the geographic factor will influence the history of a country frequently depends on the level attained by technical skill and social conditions in that country.

Thus, for example, the English would surely not have reached their dominant position in the world in the Eighteenth and Nineteenth Centuries, if it had not been for the peculiar character of their country, with its wealth in coal and iron and its insular position. But so long as coal and iron did not play the important part in industry which they played in the age of steam, these natural treasures of the soil were of slight importance. And before America and the sea-route to India were discovered, before Spain, France, Germany became highly civilized; while these countries were still inhabited by mere barbarians, and European trade was concentrated around the Mediterranean and carried on chiefly by ships propelled by oars, England's insular position was still a factor which cut it off from European civilization and maintained it in a condition of weakness and barbarism.

The same peculiarities of a country may therefore have very different results under different social conditions; even where the nature of the country has not been transformed by a change in the mode of production, its influence will not necessarily be the same. We again and again encounter as the deciding factor the sum total of all the economic conditions.

The history of Israel was therefore determined not by the

nature and situation of Palestine, considered absolutely, but by the latter under certain definite conditions of society.

The peculiar situation of Palestine was that it constituted a border region in which hostile elements were brought together and fought each other. It lay at a point where, on the one hand, the Arabian desert ended and the land of Syrian cultivation began, and where, on the other hand, the spheres of influence of those two great empires collided, which stand at the beginning of our civilization and dominate that beginning, namely, the Egyptian, originating in the Nile valley, and the Mesopotamian, originating on the Euphrates and the Tigris, with its center now at Babylon, now at Nineveh.

As a final element, Palestine was traversed by extremely important commercial roads. It dominated the traffic between Egypt on one side and Syria and Mesopotamia on the other, as well as the Phœnician trade with Arabia.

Let us first consider the effect of the former factor. Palestine was a fruitful country; its fruitfulness was by no means exceptional, but necessarily seemed unusually luxuriant when compared with the neighboring desolate, stony and sandy regions. Its inhabitants considered it as a land overflowing with milk and honey.

The Hebrew tribes came as nomadic cattle-breeders, in constant conflict with the inhabitants of Palestine, the Canaanites, from whom they conquered one city after another, subjecting them more and more to their rule. These Hebrew tribes gradually settled down. But what they had conquered in constant warfare had to be held by constant warfare, for other nomads were pushing behind them, equally eager for this fruitful land, the Edomites, Moabites, Ammonites, and others.

In the conquered country the Hebrews remained shepherds for a long time, although they now had definite homes. But they gradually acquired the agriculture that had been practiced by the original inhabitants, the raising of grain, grapes, the cultivation of olive and fig trees, and intermarried with the earlier inhabitants. But they long retained the characteristics of the nomadic Bedouin life that had been theirs.

The nomadic cattle-breeding of the desert seems to be particularly unfavorable to technical progress and social development. The present-day mode of life of the Bedouins of Arabia still vividly recalls that found in the ancient Israelitic legends of Abraham, Isaac and Jacob. The eternal recurrence of the same activities and tribulations, the same needs and ideas, over thousands of years, from generation to generation, finally produces a tenacious conservatism, which is more deeply rooted in the nomadic shepherd than even in the farmer, and is very favorable to the preservation of ancient customs and institutions, even after great alterations have intervened. We may probably consider the fact that the hearth had no definite place in the house of the Israelitic peasant, and no religious significance, as an expression of this nomadic tradition. "In this point the Israelites resemble the Arabs and are distinguished from the Greeks, to whom they stand much nearer in other matters of daily life," says Wellhausen, adding: "Hebrew may hardly be said to have a word for 'hearth,' the word *ashphot*, characteristically enough, acquired the significance of 'garbage-heap.' This is quite different from the Indo-European hearth, the domestic altar; the Hebrews have the eternal lamp instead of a never-extinguished hearth fire." [1]

Among the customs retained by the Israelites from their Bedouin period, the inclination and predilection for trade in commodities is perhaps the most important.

We have already indicated above, in our study of Roman society, how early is the development of trade between peoples, as compared with that between individuals. The first to practice trade probably were nomadic shepherds living in the wilderness. Their manner of gaining a livelihood forced them to wander about without fixed domicile from one pasture to another. The scant resources of their country must have stimulated earliest among them the need for the products of other more favorably situated countries whose boundaries they encountered. Probably they exchanged grain, oil, dates, or tools of wood, stone, bronze, and iron, for cattle, which they produced in abundance. But their mobility also permitted them not only to acquire products for themselves from afar, but also to exchange products that were

[1] Wellhausen, *Israelitische und jüdische Geschichte*, pp. 87, 88.

much in demand, and easily transported, for the account of others; in other words, not for the purpose of retaining such products for their own use or consumption, but for passing them on in further transactions. They thus became the first merchants. As long as there were no roads and navigation was poorly developed, this form of trading was necessarily predominant and might lead to the acquisition of great wealth by those who practiced it. Later, as maritime commerce increased, and as permanent and practicable roads were built, the commerce formerly conducted by the nomads necessarily decreased, and the latter were again limited to the products of their wilderness and became poorer. It is to this condition that we must attribute at least in part the great decline of the ancient civilization of Asia after the discovery of the sea-route to India. Arabia had already become impoverished for the same reason; its nomads had carried on a very profitable trade with the Phœnician cities when the latter were most flourishing. They furnished to the Phœnician looms, which produced for export to the West, the highly prized wool of their sheep; but they also brought to them the products of the southern, rich and fruitful "Happy" Arabia, frankincense, spices, gold, and precious stones, and in addition they brought from Ethiopia, separated from Happy Arabia only by a narrow strait, such valuable goods as ivory and ebony. The trade with India also passed for the most part through Arabia, along whose coasts, facing the Persian Gulf and Indian Ocean, the merchandise was brought on ships from Malabar and Ceylon, thereupon to be transported through the desert to Palestine and Phœnicia.

All the tribes through whose territory this trade passed were much enriched by it, partly through their profit as merchants, partly through the taxes which were imposed upon goods in transit.

"It is a common phenomenon to find very wealthy tribes among these races," says Heeren. "None of the tribes among the Arabian nomads seem to have made enormous profits earlier by means of the caravan trade than the Midianites, who were accustomed to travel along the northern boundary of this country, near Phœnicia therefore. It was a caravan of Midianite merchants, laden with spices, balsam, and myrrh, on its way from Arabia to Egypt, to which Joseph was sold. (*Genesis* xxxvii, 28.) The booty (captured by Gideon when he repelled an invasion of the Midianites into Canaan) which the Israelites took from this people in the form of gold was so great as to cause astonishment, and this metal was so common among them that they made of it not only adornments for themselves, but even the neck-pieces for their animals were of gold." Thus, we read in the Book of Judges, viii: "And Gideon arose and slew Zebah and Zalmunna, and took away the ornaments that were on their animals' necks. . . . And Gideon said unto them, I would desire a request of you, that you would give me every man the earrings of his prey. (For they had golden earrings, because they were Ishmaelites.). . . . And the weight of the golden earrings which he requested was one thousand and seven hundred shekels [2] of gold; besides ornaments, and collars, and purple raiment that was on the kings of Midian, and besides the chains that were on their animals' necks."

Heeren now discusses the Edomites and continues: "The Greeks classed all the nomadic tribes that wandered about Northern Arabia under the name of the Nabatæan Arabs. Diodorus, who excellently describes their mode of life, also does not fail to mention their caravan trade with Yemen. 'A not inconsiderable number of them,' he says, 'make it their business to bring to the Mediterranean Sea the incense, the myrrh, and other precious spices which they receive from them that come from Happy Arabia.'" (Diodorus, ii, page 390.)

"The wealth thus acquired by the various desert tribes was great enough to arouse the greed of Greek warriors. One of the staple centers for the merchandise passing through the territory of the Edomites was the fortified town of Petra, after which Northwestern Arabia is named Arabia Petra. Demetrius Poliorketes attempted to assault and plunder this town." [3]

We must consider the Israelites in their nomadic period as resembling their neighbors the Midianites. Even Abraham is

[2] One shekel of gold equals 16.8 grammes or about $11.
[3] Heeren, *Ideen über die Politik, den Verkehr, und den Handel der vornehmsten Völker der alten Welt*, 1817, vol. i, II, pp. 84-86.

reported to have been very rich, not only in cattle, but also in silver and gold. (*Genesis* xiii, 2.) Nomadic shepherds could have obtained wealth only by trade. But their later condition in Canaan was by no means calculated to restrict or weaken the commercial spirit acquired by them from their nomad condition. For the situation of this country permitted them to continue their part in the trade between Egypt and Babylonia, and to profit by this trade, partly by conducting and advancing it, partly by disturbing it, by falling upon trading caravans from their mountain fortifications, and plundering or imposing toll upon them. It must not be forgotten that trade and banditry were then two closely related professions.

"Even before the Israelites came to Canaan, trade was highly developed in this country. In the Tell-el-Amarna Letters (of the Fifteenth Century before Christ) caravans are mentioned that traveled through the country under armed protection." [4]

But we have a record as early as the year 2000 B.C. concerning the intimate commercial relations between Palestine and Egypt as well as the countries on the Euphrates.

Jeremias (a Privatdozent at the University of Leipzig, not the Hebrew prophet) cites the contents of a papyrus of that period in his own words as follows:

"The Bedouin tribes of Palestine are therefore in intimate contact with the cultural land of Egypt. Their sheiks, as we learn from the papyrus, occasionally frequent the court of Pharaoh and are informed as to conditions in Egypt. Envoys travel to and fro with written messages between the Euphrates territory and Egypt. These Asiatic Bedouins are by no means barbarians. The barbarous tribes combated by the Egyptian King are expressly mentioned as in contrast to them. The Bedouin sheiks also joined together for the purpose of making military campaigns against 'the princes of peoples'." [5]

In his *Commercial History of the Jews in Antiquity*, Herzfeld treats in detail the caravan routes passing through or in the vicinity of Palestine. He surmises that these communications "were

[4] Franz Buhl, *Die sozialen Verhältnisse der Israeliten*, 1899, p. 76.
[5] Jeremias, *Das alte Testament im Lichte des alten Orients*, 1906, p. 300.

perhaps of even greater commercial importance in antiquity than our railroads are to us".

"Such a route led from Southwestern Arabia, parallel to the coast of the Red Sea and its Ælanitic Gulf, carrying the products of Happy Arabia as well as of Ethiopia and a number of the latter's *hinterlands*, as far as Sela, later called Petra, about seventy kilometers to the South of the Dead Sea. Another caravan route brought Babylonian and Indian products from Gerrha, on the Persian Gulf, straight across Arabia, likewise to Petra. From Petra three routes branch out: one to Egypt with branches on the left to the Arabian ports on the Mediterranean, a second to Gaza, with an important continuation to the North; a third along the eastern shores of the Dead Sea and the Jordan, to Damascus. Ailat, at the very head of the Ælanitic Gulf, to which it gave its name, had already become a staple center for the merchandise of the countries further to the South, and also was connected by a short route with Petra. The route going from Gaza to the North, already mentioned, passed through the lowlands of Judea and Samaria, terminating in the plains of Jisreel, where it met another route from the East and proceeding to Acco. Of the merchandise flowing in by these manifold routes, that intended for Phœnicia was partly transshipped in the Arabian seaports above mentioned, or at Gaza and Acco, for the road from the latter town to Tyre and Sidon was a very rocky one and not rendered practicable for land transportation until much later. The much-frequented caravan route from the East, already mentioned, went from Babylon to the middle course of the Euphrates, then through the Arabian-Syrian desert, in which Palmyra later flourished, and after proceeding for a short distance along the eastern bank of the Upper Jordan, it crossed this river and ran through the plains of Jisreel until it reached the sea. Shortly before touching the Jordan, it entered the route already mentioned, leading from Gilead, which we have seen was already used in the time of Joseph; and we have already learned that this route was met in the plains of Jisreel by the route from Gaza; but presumably the road which passed from Palestine to Egypt according to Genesis xxxvii, 25; xli, 57, also started from Gaza. . . . We cannot prove that these (these commercial routes and the fairs held at their intersections) for a long time had any influence on the Israelites, from any facts recorded in history, nor can we estimate such an influence, but there is no doubt that it necessarily was present, and this assumption will shed light on many a modest old passage reflecting such influence." [6]

Luxury and export industries, and also art, flourished much less among the Israelites than did trade, possibly because the Israelites had ceased to be nomads at a time when handicraft had already been developed to a high level among their neighbors. Articles of luxury obtained by trade were better and cheaper than those manufactured by domestic artisans. The result was that such work was limited to the simplest articles. Even among the Phœnicians, who became a cultural nation at a much earlier date, the progress of industry was retarded by the competition of the Egyptian and Babylonian goods in which the Phœnicians traded. "It is hardly likely that the Phœnicians were superior in the field of industry to the inhabitants of the rest of Syria. Herodotus is probably right when he says that the first Phœnicians who landed on the coast of Greece offered their wares, which were not products of their home, but of Egypt and Assyria, in other words of the *hinterland* of Syria. The large cities of Phœnicia did not become predominating industrial cities until they had lost their political independence and a considerable portion of their commercial relations." [7]

Perhaps the development of handicraft was really hindered also by the eternal condition of war. At any rate it is certain that handicraft did not develop far. The prophet Ezekiel, in his lament over Tyre, very fully describes the latter's trade, including that with Israel. The exports of the Israelites were exclusively agricultural in nature: "Judah, and the land of Israel, they were thy merchants: they traded in thy market wheat of Minith, and Pannag, and honey, and oil, and balm" (xxvii, 17).

When David made Jerusalem his capital, King Hiram of Tyre sent him "cedar trees, and carpenters, and masons: and they

[6] *Handelsgeschichte der Juden*, pp. 22-25.
[7] R. Pietschmann, *Geschichte der Phönizier*, 1889, p. 238.

built David an house" (II Samuel v, 11). The same thing took place in the time of Solomon at the building of the Temple. Solomon in exchange paid Hiram annually 20,000 measures of wheat and twenty measures of pure oil (I Kings, v, 11).

Without highly developed luxury crafts, in other words without art crafts, no plastic or graphic arts can flourish and attain even the presentation of the human form, transcend the mere indication of the human type, individualize and idealize its subjects.

Such an art can be based only on a high level of trade, providing the artist with the most varied materials in many qualities, and thus enabling him to choose those most suitable for his purposes. Furthermore, a far-reaching specialization, and a host of experiences accumulated by generations in the treatment of these various materials, coupled finally with a high regard for the artist, elevating him above the level of being obliged to labor, and granting him leisure, joy and energy, are also necessary.

We find all these elements united only in great commercial cities with a vigorous and ancient handicraft. In Thebes and Memphis, in Athens, and later, beginning with the Middle Ages, in Florence, Antwerp and Amsterdam, the graphic arts attained their highest development on the basis of an energetic handicraft system. This the Israelites lacked, and this lack had an effect also on their religion.

c. The Conception of God in Ancient Israel

Conceptions of divinity among the natural primitive peoples are extremely vague and confused, by no means so sharply defined as we later find them in the mythologies turned out by the scholars. The various divinities are neither conceived in clear outlines, nor even sharply distinguished one from another; they are unknown, mysterious personages, having an influence on nature and man, bestowing happiness or unhappiness upon the latter, but actually more hazy and more indefinite in outline, at first, than the visions of dreams.

The only definite distinctions between the various divinities consist in their localizations. Every locality that especially stimulates the imagination of primitive man seems to him to be the seat of a specific divinity. High mountains or single cliffs, groves in peculiar positions and sometimes even a single ancient tree, springs, and caves, thus acquire a sort of sanctity as the homes of gods. But even a peculiarly shaped stone or bit of wood may be considered the domicile of a divinity, a sacred object, the possession of which assures to them that own it the aid of the god it shelters. Each tribe, each race tried to acquire such a sacred object, such a fetish. This is true also of the Hebrews, whose conception of God was at first on the level we have just described, and far removed from monotheism. The sacred relics of the Israelites seem at first to have been nothing more or less than fetishes, beginning with the "idol" (*teraphim*), which Jacob steals from his father-in-law Laban, up to the Ark of the Covenant, in which Yahveh dwells, and which bestows victory and rain and wealth upon him who rightly holds it. The sacred stones worshiped by the Phœnicians and Israelites were named "Bethel" or *House of God*.

The divinities of the various localities and fetishes are not yet definitely individualized at this stage; often their names are not different; for instance, among the Israelites and Phœnicians many gods were called *El* (plural *Elohim*), while others were named *Baal* ("the master") by the Phœnicians. "In spite of their identical names all these Baals were originally considered to be absolutely distinct creatures. We frequently find there is no other way of distinguishing them than by adding to their names the name of the place in which the god in question was worshiped." [8]

A more distinct differentiation between the various divinities in the popular consciousness did not become possible until after the graphic and plastic arts were developed far enough to undertake to individualize and idealize human forms, to create definite figures with personal characteristics, but also involving a charm, a majesty, a greatness, or an awfulness, that made them superior to the forms of common men. Thus polytheism was given a material foundation; the invisible ones now became visible, and therefore capable of being present in the same manner in the minds

[8] R. Pietschmann, *Geschichte der Phönizier*, pp. 183, 184.

of all; now the various gods were permanently differentiated from each other, all confusion between them having disappeared. From now on it became possible to distinguish and individualize from the mass of innumerable spiritual beings dwelling in wild confusion in the imaginations of primitive man, certain specific characters.

In Egypt we can distinctly trace the increase in the number of specific gods as the graphic and plastic arts proceed in their development. Nor is it an accident that we find that Greece not only attains the highest development of the art industries and of the depiction of human beings in plastic art, but also the most manifold and distinct individualization of its divinities, both of these attainments being achieved simultaneously.

The advance made by industrially and artistically developed nations, in displacing the fetish, the habitation of the spirit or god, by the *image* of the god, was not accomplished by the Israelites owing to the backwardness of their industry and art. In this respect also their evolution came to a stop on the level of the Bedouin mode of thought. It never occurred to them to represent their own gods in images. Such divine images as they became acquainted with were only the images of gods of foreign tribes, of enemies, gods imported from abroad or imitated from foreign models. Hence the hatred shown by patriots for these images.

This was due to a retarded development, which simultaneously, however, made it easier for the Israelites to accomplish the step that freed them from polytheism when they became acquainted with the philosophical and ethical monotheism that arose in various large cities, at the culmination of ancient civilization, for reasons which we have already pointed out. Where the image of the god had taken firm root in the imagination of the people, a firm foothold had thus been gained by polytheism, which was not easily weakened. On the other hand the vagueness of the divine image, as well as the identity of names of divinities in the most varied localities, paved the way for a popularization of the idea of a single god, as opposed to whom all other invisible spirits are only subordinate creatures. It is at any rate not an accident that all the monotheistic national religions are derived from nations who were still at the nomadic stage of thought and had developed no important industry or art: besides the *Jews*, it was the *Persians* and later the Islamic *Arabs* who accepted monotheism as soon as they came in contact with a higher urban culture. Not only Islam but also the Zend religion must be reckoned with the monotheistic religions. The latter also knows only a single Master and Creator of the world, Auramazda. Angromainju (Ahriman) is a lesser spirit somewhat like Satan.

The fact that backward stages more easily accept and develop progress, than do those stages that are further advanced, may seem paradoxical, but it is a fact of which we have evidence even in the evolution of physical organisms. Highly evolved forms are frequently less adaptable and perish more easily, while lower forms, whose organs are less specialized, may be able to adapt themselves more readily to changed conditions, and are therefore in a better place to further the course of evolution.

But the development of man's organs is not only an unconscious one; in addition to his bodily organs, man consciously develops other artificial ones, whose construction he may *learn* from others. So far as these artificial forms are concerned, individual persons or groups may therefore skip entire stages in evolution, but of course only after the higher stage has already been reached before them by others from whom they acquire it. It is a matter of common knowledge, for instance, that electric illumination was more quickly introduced in many peasant villages than in the large cities, which had already invested large quantities of capital in gas illumination. The peasant village could make the leap from the oil lamp to the electric light by skipping the stage of illuminating gas; but this was rendered possible only by the fact that technological progress in the large cities had already acquired the ability to produce electric light. The peasant village would not have developed this knowledge of its own account. Thus monotheism was more readily accepted by the masses of the Jews and Persians than by the masses of the Egyptians, Babylonians and Hellenes, but the notion of monotheism had first to be constructed by the philosophers of these highly advanced cultural nations.

But the period we are treating now, namely, the period before the Exile, had not yet reached the monotheistic stage. A primitive world of the gods still prevailed.

d. Trade and Philosophy

Trade develops different mental faculties than handicraft and art.

In his *Critique of Political Economy* and later in his *Capital*, Karl Marx points out the twofold character of labor as represented in commodities. Each commodity is both an article of consumption and an article of exchange, and therefore the labor involved in it may be simultaneously considered both as a special, specific kind of labor—such as the labor of weaving, or pottery, or forging—and as abstract human labor in general.

The specific productive activity which produces specific articles of consumption is particularly interesting to the consumer, who requires such specific consumption values. If he needs cloth, he is interested in the labor applied in the production of this cloth for the simple reason that it *is* this specific cloth-producing labor. But to the producer of the goods also—meaning as a rule, in the stage of evolution which we are now treating, not yet wage laborers, but independent peasants, artisans, artists, or their slaves —labor is important only as the *specific activity*, enabling the producer to produce *specific* products.

But the attitude of the merchant is different. His activity consists in purchasing cheap to sell dear. What specific variety of commodities he buys or sells is indifferent to him in the last analysis, provided only he finds a purchaser. To be sure, he is interested in the quantity of labor which is socially necessary, both at the point of purchase and the point of sale, as well as at the time of purchase and at the time of sale, for the production of the commodities in which he deals, for this element has an effect in determining their price, but he is interested in this labor only as general human labor imparting value to commodities, abstractly, not concrete labor, producing specific consumption values. Of course the merchant does not think of the matter in so many words, for it has taken man a long time to reveal the determination of value by universal human labor. As a matter of fact, it required the genius of a Karl Marx, at a highly advanced stage in the production of commodities, to analyze this condition completely. But even thousands of years before him, abstract general human labor acquires a tangible expression as contrasted with the concrete forms of labor, to grasp which not the slightest power of abstraction is necessary, namely, in money.[9] Money is the representative of the general human labor involved in every commodity; it represents not a specific kind of labor, not the labor of the weaver or potter or smith, but any labor, all labor, today one kind, tomorrow another. But the merchant is interested in the commodity only as representing *money,* not in its specific *usefulness,* but in its specific *price.*

The producer—peasant, artisan, artist—is interested in the peculiar nature of his work, the peculiarity of the material which he is to manipulate; and he will increase the productivity of his labor the more, as he becomes more specialized in it. His specific work chains him, however, to a specific place, to his land or his workshop. Therefore the special limitation of the work on which he is engaged will produce a certain mental limitation in him to which the Greeks gave the name *banausia* (derived from *banausos,* the *artisan*). "Though the smiths, carpenters, and shoemakers may be skilled in their specialties," says Socrates in the Fifth Century before our era, "most of them are slavish souls; they know not what is beautiful, good and righteous." The Jew Jesus Sirach about the year 200 B.C. expressed the same thought. Useful though handicraft may be, he says, the artisan is nevertheless useless in politics, in jurisprudence, in the dissemination of moral culture.

[9] Money appears as a measure of value earlier than as an instrument of circulation. It is used as such even in the days of barter: thus we read of Egypt that men were accustomed "to make use of bars of copper (*utes*) weighing 91 grams, not yet in the form of actual money, for which all other commodities could be exchanged, but already as a measure of value in the exchange of commodities, by means of which the commodities being exchanged could be estimated. Thus, once in the New Empire an ox, valued at 119 *utes* is paid for by means of a cane with inlaid work valued at 25 *utes,* another at 12 *utes,* eleven jugs of honey at 11 *utes,* etc. Later the Ptolemaic copper currency was established on this basis." (Eduard Meyer, *Die wirtschaftliche Entwicklung des Altertums,* 1895, p. 11.)

Only the machine will make it possible to abolish this mental limitation for the masses of the workers; but only the abolition of the capitalistic mode of production will create the conditions under which the machine may fulfill in the most complete manner its magnificent task of liberating the working masses.

The merchant's activities have an entirely different effect on him than have those of the artisan. He cannot afford to content himself with the knowledge of a special branch of production in a special region; the farther his interest extends, the more branches of production it embraces, the more regions, with their specific conditions of production and their specific requirements, the better will he be able to choose those commodities whose sale at the moment is most profitable; those markets, in which he can buy most profitably as well as those where he can make the most profitable sales. But in spite of the great value of the products and markets with which he is concerned, he is interested in the last analysis only in price conditions, in other words, in the conditions of various quantities of abstract human labor, in other words, in abstract numerical relations. As trade develops more and more, as purchase and sale are further removed from each other in space and in time, the more varied the money conditions with which the merchant must deal, the greater the divergence between the purchase and payment times, and the more advanced the stage of development of the credit system and interest payment, the more complicated and varied do these numerical relations become. Therefore trade must stimulate *mathematical* thought, and simultaneously *abstract* thought. But while trade at the same time extends the horizon beyond local and occupational limitations, imparting to the merchant a knowledge of the most varied climates and soils, the most varied stages of civilization, and modes of production, it stimulates him to institute comparisons, enables him to discover the general element in the mass of particular details, the necessary element in the mass of accidentals, the recurring element which will result again and again from certain conditions. The power of abstraction is thereby immensely developed, as well as by mathematical thought, while handicraft rather develops the sense for the concrete, but also for the surface rather than for the essence of things. It is not the "productive" activities, agriculture and handicraft, but "unproductive" trade, which develops those mental faculties that lie at the basis of scientific study.

But this does not mean that trade of itself creates such scientific investigation. Disinterested thought, the search for truth, not for personal advantage—these are precisely most lacking in the merchant. The peasant as well as the artisan live by the labor of their hands only. The wealth accessible to them has very definite limits; but within these limits it is certain to be obtained by any healthy average individual, unless war or overpowerful natural forces undermine and impoverish the entire community. To have aspirations that look higher than the average is under such conditions neither necessary nor promising. These callings are therefore characterized by a cheerful acceptance of their inherited status, so long as capital, usually in the form of usurious capital, does not conquer and oppress them or their rulers.

But trade, with its manipulation of general human labor, proceeds quite differently than does handicraft, with its concrete, useful labor. The success of the latter is strictly limited by the capacity of the individual; the success of trade knows no bounds. The profit in trade finds its limits only in the quantity of money, of capital, which the trader possesses, and this quantity may be extended indefinitely. On the other hand, this trade is exposed to far greater vicissitudes and dangers than is the constant monotony of peasant artisan labor in simple commodities production. The merchant is constantly hovering between the extremes of the most luxurious wealth and absolute ruin. The passion for gain is in such cases stimulated far more effectively than among the producing classes. The merchant is characterized by insatiable avarice, but also by the most brutal cruelty both toward his competitors and toward the objects of his exploitation. To this day, this condition is most repulsively apparent to those who live by their own labor, in all places where the exploiting tendency of capital does not encounter vigorous resistance; for instance, in the colonies.

This is not a mode of thought that encourages a personal disinterested, scientific study. Trade develops the necessary *ability* for this purpose, but not its *application* for scientific purposes. On the contrary, where trade secures an influence over learning, its effect is only in the direction of doctoring the results of learning for its own purposes, of which our present-day bourgeois learning presents numerous examples.

Scientific thought could only be developed in a class that was endowed with all the gifts, experiences and knowledge involved in trade, but also liberated from the necessity of earning a living, and therefore possessing the necessary leisure, opportunity, and pleasure in disinterested investigation, in the solution of problems without regard to their immediate, practical, and personal outcome. Philosophy was developed only in great commercial centers, and only in those centers in which other elements besides trade were present, whose wealth or whose social position gave them leisure and freedom. In a number of Greek commercial cities these were the great landed proprietors, whose slaves freed them from the need to work, and who lived not in the country, but in the city, who were not limited to the rude physical prowess of the country squire, but also were subject to the influences of the town and its large-scale trade.

Such a class of large landed proprietors, living and philosophizing in the cities, seems to have appeared only in maritime towns whose *hinterland* was just large enough to produce such a country nobility, but not large enough to keep the latter away from the town and to turn their attention to extending their possessions in land. These conditions are found particularly in the Greek seaport towns. But the *hinterland* of the Phœnician seaport towns was too insignificant to produce such great estates. In these communities, everyone lived by trade.

In those cities, on the other hand, that were surrounded by large land territory, the great landed proprietors seem to have remained more under the influence of country life, to have developed rather the mode of thought of the country squire. In the great commercial centers of Central Asia, the greatest degree of liberation from labor, and the smallest exposure to the claims of practical business, were enjoyed by the priests of various places of worship. Not a few among these places became important and wealthy enough to be able to support permanently a number of priests of whom little work was demanded. The same social task that fell to the aristocracy in the Greek seaport towns was the lot of the priests at the places of worship in the great commercial centers of the oriental continent, particularly Egypt and Babylonia; namely, the development of scientific thought, of philosophy. But this condition imposed a limitation on oriental thought from which Greek thought remained free: connection and reference to religious worship. Philosophy's loss was religion's gain, and the gain of the priests. While the priests in Greece were simple attendants at worship, guardians of the places of worship and performers of religious rites in them, they became in the great commercial centers of the Orient the preservers and administrators of all knowledge, scientific as well as social: mathematics, astronomy, medicine, history, and law. Their influence on state and society was thereby enormously increased. But religion itself was enabled in these regions to achieve a spiritual intensification such as Greek mythology was not capable of, as Hellenic philosophy soon rejected the mythology, making no attempt to imbue its naïve conceptions with more profound knowledge, or to reconcile the two.

The religion of ancient Greece probably received its sensual, vigorous, and joyous artistic character by reason of the elevation that had been reached by the reproductive arts, as well as by reason of the fact that its philosophy steered clear of the priests. On the other hand, in a region with a vigorous international trade, but not possessing the reproductive arts, without a secular aristocracy having intellectual inclinations and needs, but with a fully developed priesthood, a religion that had not brought forth an early development of polytheism, with sharply defined divine personalities, would more easily assume an abstract and spiritual character, while the divinity might more easily change from a personality into an idea or conception.

e. Trade and Nationality

Trade has another influence upon human thought in addition
to the one just analyzed. It is an immense stimulus to national
feeling. We have already mentioned the limitations of the peasant and bourgeois horizon as opposed to the wide horizon of the
merchant. The latter acquires this wide horizon by reason of
the fact that his ambitions are constantly increasing, taking him
away from the place in which the accident of birth has placed
him. This is made most clear in the case of the maritime nations, in ancient times the Phœnicians and Greeks, the former
venturing far beyond the Mediterranean into the Atlantic Ocean,
the latter opening up the Black Sea. Trade by land did not permit
such extensive expeditions. And maritime trade presupposed a
high degree of skill, particularly in ship-building; it was a trade
between superior and inferior nations, the latter easily subdued,
leading to the foundation of colonies by the commercial people.
Trade by land was earliest and most easily conducted by nomads
who visited more highly developed tribes, among whom they
already found a surplus of products of agriculture and industry.
There was no possibility in such cases of founding colonies by
means of isolated expeditions. Occasionally a number of nomadic tribes might unite in order to plunder or conquer the more
wealthy and advanced country, but even then they did not come
as colonists, as the bearers of a higher culture. But such unions
of nomadic tribes were very rarely realized, and then only under
extraordinary circumstances, since the very nature of nomadic
cattle-breeding isolates the various tribes and gentes, even families,
from each other, scattering them over great distances. The traders belonging to these tribes could as a rule penetrate into the
rich and powerful community with which they were trading, only
as *tolerated supplicants*.

This is true also of the traders belonging to the small tribes who
had settled down on the thoroughfare of nations between Egypt
and Syria. Like the Phœnicians and Greeks, these tribes also
established settlements in the countries with which they were trading, from Babylonia to Egypt, but they are not colonists in the

strict sense of the word, not powerful cities, not instruments for the control and exploitation of barbarians by a civilized nation, but weak communities of supplicants, surrounded by powerful and highly civilized cities. It was all the more necessary for the members of these communities to remain closely associated together as opposed to the strangers among whom they lived, and all the stronger became their desire to secure power and prestige for their own nation, as their own safety and prestige among strangers and therefore also the conditions of their commercial activity, depended on such recognition.

Everywhere, even in the Nineteenth Century, as I have already pointed out in my book on Thomas More,[10] the merchant class is simultaneously the most international and most national section of society. But in the case of merchants belonging to small races, who were exposed without defense to much ill-usage abroad, this national feeling, this longing for a national cohesion and a national prestige, as well as their hatred for strangers, necessarily increase more strongly.

Such was the situation of the Israelitic traders. The Israelites probably went to Egypt rather early in their history, perhaps when they were merely wandering cattle-breeders, long before they became permanent inhabitants of Canaan. We have evidences concerning Canaanitic immigrants into Egypt that are of very early date, perhaps extending back into the third millennium before Christ. Eduard Meyer says, on this subject:

"A famous painting in the grave of Khnemhotep, in Benihassan, shows us a Bedouin family consisting of thirty-seven persons, led by their chieftain Basha, traveling toward Egypt in the sixth year of the reign of Usertesen III.[11] They are called *Amu*, which means Canaanites, and their facial outlines clearly designate them as Semites. They wear the many-colored garments which had been popular in Asia from the most ancient times, are armed with bows and lances, and lead asses and goats with them; one of them also is able to play the lyre. They bring with them the

[10] *Thomas More und seine Utopie*, by Karl Kautsky. Stuttgart: J. H. W. Dietz, Nachf., 1888.—TRANSLATOR.

[11] A monarch of the twelfth dynasty, which extended approximately from 2100 to 1900 B.C., possibly beginning a few centuries earlier.

precious possession of *meszemut* to dye the eyebrows. They now demand admission, in which connection they apply to the Count of Menatchufu, Khnemhotep, to whom the mountain lands are subject. A royal scribe Neferhotep introduces them to the latter for further dispatch and to report to the king. Other scenes like those depicted here might often have taken place, and doubtless Canaanitic traders and artisans settled down in the Eastern cities of the Delta in great numbers, where we shall have occasion to find them again. *Vice versa,* Egyptian traders surely came quite often to Syrian cities. Even though it had to pass through the hands of many intermediaries, Egyptian trade very probably extended as far as Babylonia even at this early period."

A few centuries after this time, about the year 1800 b.c., at a time when Egyptian society was disintegrating, Northern Egypt was conquered by the Hyksos, doubtless Canaanitic wandering tribes, who were enticed and enabled by the weakness of the Egyptian Government to invade the rich land of the Nile, where they maintained themselves for more than two centuries. "The importance of the rule of the Hyksos for world history consists in the fact that it was they that established the active connection between Egypt and the Syrian provinces that has never since been broken. Canaanitic merchants and artisans came to Egypt in great numbers, Canaanitic proper names and forms of worship are therefore encountered in the New Empire, Canaanitic words began to penetrate into the Egyptian language. How active this intercourse was is shown by the circumstance that a medical work written about the year 1550 b.c. contains a prescription for the eyes written by an Amu from Kepni, most probably the Phœnician city of Byblos." [12]

We have no reason to assume that the Amu, the Semitic Bedouins and city-dwellers to the East and Northeast of Egypt, who went to Egypt, did not also include Hebrews, even though the latter are not specifically named. On the other hand, it is difficult to determine today what would be regarded as the historical nucleus of the legends of Joseph, the sojourn of the Hebrews in Egypt, and their departure under Moses. To assume

[12] Eduard Meyer, *Geschichte des alten Aegyptens,* 1887, pp. 182, 210.

that they are identical with the Hyksos, as Josephus does, is not feasible.   But so much seems to be certain, that not all of Israel, but certain families and caravans of Hebrews came to Egypt at an early date, where, depending on the varying conditions of affairs in the country, they were treated more or less favorably, now being received with open arms, and then tormented and driven out as "undesirable" foreigners.

This is the typical lot of such setttlements of foreign traders, coming from weak tribes, after settling in powerful empires.

The "Diaspora," the dispersal of the Jews throughout the world, certainly does not begin as late as the destruction of Jerusalem by the Romans, nor with the Babylonian Exile, but much earlier; it is a natural consequence of trade, a phenomenon shared by the Jews with most commercial peoples.   But it should not be forgotten that agriculture, as in the case of most of these tribes, remained the principal source of livelihood for the Israelites also, up to the time of their Exile.   Formerly trade had constituted only an avocation for the nomadic cattle-breeders.   After they had settled down and a division of labor had been introduced, and the traveling merchant became differentiated from the peasant, who lived on the soil, the number of merchants remained relatively small, the peasant determining the character of the people.   And the number of Israelites who lived abroad was small in any case as compared with those who remained at home.   The Hebrews were not different from the other peoples in this respect.

But they were living under conditions which caused the hatred for strangers and the strong national feeling, even national sensitiveness, which had been stimulated in the merchant, to be transmitted to the body of the population more than is usually the case among peasant peoples.

f. Canaan, a Thoroughfare of Nations

We have seen how great was the importance of Palestine for the trade between Egypt, Babylonia and Syria.   From time immemorial these states had therefore been at an effort to secure possession of this country.

In their struggle against the Hyksos, who have been already

mentioned (about 1800 B.C. to 1530 B.C.) a warlike spirit had been developed in Egypt, but the Hyksos had simultaneously much advanced the trade between Egypt and Syria. Therefore, after the driving out of the Hyksos, the desire for warlike expansion arose among the Egyptians, particularly with the purpose of controlling the commercial route to Babylonia. They advanced up to the Euphrates and occupied Palestine and Syria. From the latter country they were soon driven back by the Cheta, but in Palestine they maintained themselves longer, from the Fifteenth to the Twelfth Centuries B.C. There they also held a number of strongholds, among which was Jerusalem. But finally the warlike power of Egypt declined, and beginning with the Twelfth Century, Egypt was no longer able to hold Palestine, while simultaneously the Syrian Chetites were weakened by the incipient spread of the Assyrians, and prevented from penetrating further to the south.

Foreign rule in Palestine was thus abandoned for a time. This was the opportunity for a group of Bedouin tribes, under the general name of Israelites, to enter the country as conquerors and gradually to occupy it. As yet they had not fully completed this process, and were still engaged in active conflict with the former inhabitants of the country, when new enemies arose to face them in the form of other Bedouin tribes, who were pressing behind them toward the "promised land." Simultaneously, however, they encountered on their front line an enemy in the form of the inhabitants of the plains separating the mountain country under Israelitic control from the sea. These were the Philistines. The latter must have felt themselves seriously threatened by the advance of so aggressive a people as the Israelites. On the other hand the coast plain must have been particularly inviting in the eyes of the Israelites, for through this plain there passed the main road connecting Egypt with the North. Whoever controlled this road therefore simultaneously controlled the entire foreign trade of Egypt with the North and East. The maritime commerce of Egypt on the Mediterranean Sea was at that time very unimportant. But if these dwellers on the hills that skirted along the plain should turn out to be a combative and predatory people, they must necessarily remain a constant menace to trade to and from Egypt, and to the riches yielded by that trade. And they were combative and predatory. We are often told of the formation of bands of robbers in Israel, for instance, Jephtha, to whom "vain men were gathered, and went out with him." (Judges iii, 3.)   We often hear also of bandit invasions into the country of the Philistines. Thus, we read concerning Samson, that "the Spirit of the Lord came upon him and he went down to Ashkelon, and slew thirty men of them, and took their spoil and gave change of garments unto them which expounded the riddle" (Judges xiv, 19), which means that he was robbing them in order to pay a debt. David is also represented in his beginnings as the leader of a band of robbers. "And everyone that was in distress, and everyone that was in debt, and everyone that was discontented, gathered themselves unto him; and he became a captain of them: and there were with him about four hundred men." (I Samuel, xxii, 2.)

It is not to be wondered at that a condition of almost con-stant feud prevailed between the Philistines and the Israelites, with the result that the former exerted every effort to put down their troublesome neighbors. Pressed on the one side by the Bedouins, and on the other by the Philistines, Israel was forced into a condition of dependence and distress. It succumbed to the Philistines the more readily since the mountain territory in-habited by them encouraged the formation of a local particularis-tic spirit, a splitting up of clans, while the plains were more likely to favor a unification of the various tribes and communities of the Philistines for a single great operation. Only when the powerful military kingdom of David succeeded in welding the various tribes of Israel into a firm unit, did Israel cease to be oppressed.

Now the Philistines were overthrown, and the last fortified cities in the table-land of Canaan, which had still resisted the Israelites, were conquered, including Jerusalem, an unusually well-situated, almost impregnable spot, which had offered the longest resistance to the Israelites, and which controlled all the roads entering Palestine from the South. It became the capital of the kingdom and the seat of the Federal fetish, the Ark of the Covenant, in which the war-God Yahveh dwelt.

David now gained control of the entire trade passing between Egypt and the North, and this trade yielded him rich booty, enabling him to increase his warlike resources and expand the boundary of his state northward and southward. He subjected the predatory Bedouin tribes as far as to the Red Sea, rendered secure the commercial routes to that sea, and with the aid of the Phœnicians, for the Israelites had no knowledge of navigation, he began to carry on trade on the Red Sea, which had formerly passed by the land route from Southern Arabia (Saba) northward. It was the golden age of Israel, which, owing to its dominating position over one of the most important commercial routes of that era, was enabled to achieve an intoxicating degree of power and wealth.

And yet precisely this favorable position was destined to effect its ruin. For the economic importance of this situation was not a secret to the great neighboring states. The more the country flourished under David and Solomon, the more it necessarily aroused the greed of its powerful neighbors, whose warlike strength was again undergoing an improvement just at that time; in Egypt particularly, by reason of the fact that the peasant militia was being replaced by mercenaries who could more easily be used in wars of aggression. To be sure, Egypt did not have sufficient strength to conquer Palestine permanently. But so much the worse for Israel. Instead of being placed in a state of permanent dependence on a great nation, whose power would at least have afforded it peace and protection against external enemies, it became the play-ball of competing Egyptians and Syrians, later of Assyrians also, and Palestine constituted the theater of war on which the battles of these hostile powers were fought. In addition to the devastation of the wars which it had now to fight in the defense of its own interests, there now were also the devastations of the great armies that were combating there for interests that were absolutely foreign to the inhabitants of the country. And the burdens of obligatory tribute and dependence, which were now imposed upon the Israelites from time to time, were not softened by the fact that these burdens were not always imposed by the same masters, that the masters were changing constantly with the varying fortunes of war, and that each master considered his possession to be a short-lived one, that must be exploited to the full at once.

Palestine was at that time in a position somewhat similar to the position of Poland in the Eighteenth Century, or Italy, particularly Northern Italy, from the Middle Ages down into the Nineteenth Century. Italy and Poland, in these later situations, like Palestine at an earlier day, found themselves incapable of enforcing a policy of their own, and therefore offered a theater of war and an object of exploitation to foreign powers; Poland had this relation toward Russia, Prussia, and Austria; Italy towards Spain and France, as well as toward the masters of the German Empire, later of Austria. And as in the case of Italy and Poland, in Palestine also a national schism was taking place, probably due to the same reason: in Palestine, as in Italy, the various portions of the country were variously influenced by neighboring races. The northern portion of the territory, occupied by the Israelites, was most menaced, also most ruled, by the Syrians, and later by the Assyrians. The southern portion, including Palestine and the surrounding country, in other words, approximately the territory of the tribe of Judah, was rather subject to being menaced by or dependent on Egypt, as the case might be. Israel proper therefore seemed sometimes to require a different external policy than did Judea. This difference in foreign policy probably became the chief cause of the splitting of Israel into two empires, as opposed to the former condition, in which the foreign policy had been the cause for the uniting of the twelve tribes against the single common enemy threatening all in equal manner, namely, the Philistines.

But the similar situations of Palestine, Italy and Poland necessarily produced similar effects in another field also: in all these countries we find the same nationalistic chauvinism, the same national sensitiveness, the same hatred for foreigners, which are somewhat more intense than the corresponding feelings produced by national oppositions in other races of that day. And this chauvinism must increase, as the unbearable situation of the country continues, subjected ceaselessly to the caprices of its great neighbors, making it the theater of war for their bandit invasions.

In view of the importance attained in the Orient by religion, for reasons that have been already assigned, chauvinism necessarily expressed itself even in religion. The active trade relations with its neighbors also brought their religious views, forms of worship, and divine images into Israel, but the hatred for foreigners, on the other hand, also took the form of a hatred for their gods, not because their existence was doubted, but because they were considered to be effective aids to the enemy.

This point does not distinguish the Hebrews from other oriental peoples. The ancestral god of the Hyksos in Egypt was Sutech. When the Hyksos were finally driven out, the ancestral god also was deposed. He was identified with the God of Darkness, Seth or Sutech, whom the Egyptians regarded with abhorrence.

The patriots of Israel and their leaders, the prophets, probably were just as much enraged against the foreign gods as German patriots in the days of Napoleon were enraged against French fashions and French words in the German language.

g. Class Struggles in Israel

But the patriots were not contented with merely hating strangers. They also felt obliged to rejuvenate the state, to infuse it with greater strength. As oppression became more severe from without, social disintegration within the Israelitic community increased. The growth of trade since the time of David brought great wealth into the country. But, as everywhere else in antiquity, in Palestine also agriculture remained the basis of society, and property in land was the most secure and honorable form of possession. As in other places, those elements in Palestine that had become rich sought to acquire property in land, or, already possessing it, to increase it. Here also we note the beginnings of a tendency toward forming latifundia. This tendency was encouraged by the fact that, as in other countries, the peasant was "going to the dogs" under the new conditions. While the struggles of the Israelites had formerly been mere petty local feuds, not requiring the absence of the peasant militia soldier for a long time, nor at long distances from his home, this condition was altered as soon as Israel became a great state, and involved in the conflicts of great states. Military service was now ruining the peasant and making him dependent on powerful neighbors who owned money and who now faced him as usurers, with the power of driving him out of his land or permitting him to remain on it as an indebted slave, working off his debt. Probably the latter means was often preferred, for we read little in Palestine of slaves belonging to other races. If purchased slaves are to be more than an expensive luxury for the private household, if they are to become a profitable means of investment in production, they necessarily presuppose constant successful wars, allowing plentiful cheap material in slaves. There was no possibility of this process among the Israelites. They belonged for the most part to those unhappy tribes who furnished slaves, not made them. The owners of latifundia, who needed cheap and dependent labor hands, would necessarily much prefer the debtor's slavery of their own fellow countrymen, a system which in other countries also— for instance, in Russia at the present time,[13] since the abolition of serfdom—meets with favor among the great landed proprietors who are in need of slaves or serfs.

As this evolution progressed, the military strength of Israel necessarily decreased simultaneously with the decrease in free peasants, with a resulting weakening of its power of resistance to external enemies. Therefore the patriots united with the social reformers and populists, in order to check this disastrous tendency. They summoned the people and the kingdom to combat both the foreign gods as well as the enemies of the peasants in their own country, and prophesied the destruction of the state if it should not be possible to put an end to the oppression and the impoverishment of the peasantry.

"Woe unto them!" cried Isaiah, "that join house to house, that lay field to field, till there be no place, that they may be placed alone in the midst of the earth! In mine ears said the Lord of

[13] The reader will recall that Kautsky wrote these words in 1908, when Russia was still ruled by a Tsar.—TRANSLATOR.

Hosts: Of a truth many houses shall be desolate, even great and fair, without inhabitant." (v, 8 and 9.)

And the Prophet Amos proclaimed:

"Hear this word, ye kine of Bashan, that are in the mountains of Samaria, which oppress the poor, which crush the needy, which say unto their masters: 'Bring and let us drink.' The Lord God hath sworn by his Holiness, that, lo, the days shall come upon you that he will take you away with hooks, and your posterity with fish hooks." (iv, 1 and 2.)

"Hear this, Oh ye that swallow up the needy, even to make the poor of the land to fail, saying: When will the new moon be gone, that we may sell corn? and the Sabbath that we may set forth wheat, making the ephah small, and the shekel great, and falsifying the balances by deceit? That we may buy the poor for silver, and the needy for a pair of shoes; yea, and sell the refuse of the wheat? The Lord hath sworn by the excellency of Jacob: Surely I will never forget any of their works. Shall not the land tremble for this, and everyone mourn that dwelleth therein?" (Amos viii, 4-8.)

"The fact that the possessors and rulers were utilizing the government apparatus for giving sanction to the new order of things in the form of levies, is clear from the ceaseless laments of the prophets as to the existing laws: 'Woe unto them,' cries the eloquent Isaiah, 'that decree unrighteous decrees, and that write grievousness which they have prescribed; to turn aside the needy from judgment, and to take away the right from the poor of my people' (x, 1). 'Zion shall be redeemed with judgment' (Isaiah i, 27). 'The pen of the scribes is in vain' (Jeremiah viii, 8). 'For ye have turned judgment into gall and the fruit of righteousness into hemlock.' (Amos vi, 12.)" [14]

Luckily for the prophets, they did not live in Prussia or Saxony! They would never have seen an end of their court trials for inciting to violence, *lèse-majesté,* and high treason.

But energetic though their agitation was, and pressing as were the needs from which it sprang, it was impossible for the

---

[14] M. Beer, *Ein Beitrag zur Geschichte des Klassenkampfes im hebräischen Altertum. Die Neue Zeit,* vol. xi, 1, p. 447.

prophets to meet with any success in society, at least of a permanent kind, though they might occasionally succeed in forcing legislation for the alleviation of distress or for the ironing out of social contrasts. They could aim only at restoring the peace, at holding back the tide of economic evolution. It was impossible to do this; the similar efforts of the Gracchi in Rome were doomed in advance to failure.

The destruction of the peasantry, and of the state together with the peasantry, was proceeding as irresistibly in Israel as was later the case in Rome. But the destruction of the state did not proceed by the same slow process of dissolution as in the Roman world-empire. Mighty opponents, superior in strength, suddenly wiped it out, long before it had reached the end of its native vigor. These opponents were the Assyrians and Babylonians.

h.   The Downfall of Israel

The imperialistic policy of the Assyrians begins to operate in the grand manner about the time of Tiglath-Pileser I (about 1115-1050 B.C.), and in spite of temporary interruptions, it brings the Assyrian armies closer and closer to Canaan. But these powerful conquerors brought with them a new method of treating the vanquished, which was to have a very disastrous effect on the Israelites. During their nomad stage, the entire people were naturally interested in any military campaign that resulted in an advantage to each man among them. Such a campaign was intended either for mere plunder, or for the conquest of a fruitful country, in which the victors would settle down as the aristocratic exploiters of the native population. But in the stage of fixed agriculture, the masses of the population, the peasants and artisans, no longer had any interest in a war of conquest; but their interest in any successful war of defense naturally became larger, for in such a war they were menaced with a loss of their liberties and their lands in case of defeat. The great merchants, however, were in favor of outward expansion by force, for they needed security for their commercial routes and markets abroad, which could be attained in most cases only by a military occupation of at least a few foreign places. The landed nobility also was eager for warlike expansion, for it wished more land and new slaves; equally warlike were the kings, eager for an increase in the tax receipts.

But so long as there was no standing army and no bureaucracy which could be cut off from home and transferred to any point, a permanent occupation and administration of conquered territory by the victor was attended with great difficulties at this economic stage. The victor therefore contented himself as a rule with a thorough plundering and weakening of the defeated people, and with the promise of the latter to support him and pay certain definite tribute to him, but left the ruling classes of the captured country in their social position, making no alterations in the country's political institutions.

The disadvantage of this situation was in the fact that the vanquished would seize the first opportunity that offered to shake off the hated yoke, so that a new military campaign would be required to subject him anew, and such a campaign naturally did not end without the infliction of the most extravagant punishments upon the "rebels."

The Assyrians devised a method that promised to give greater permanence to their conquests: wherever they encountered stubborn resistance, or were met with repeated insurrections, they would weaken the people by cutting off its head; in other words, by depriving it of its ruling classes, banishing the most distinguished, most wealthy, intelligent and warlike inhabitants, particularly of the capital, to some remote region, where the deported persons, possessing no subordinate stratum which they could rule, were absolutely powerless. The remaining peasants and petty artisans, however, now constituted an incoherent mass, incapable of offering any strong resistance to the conquerors.

Salmanassar II (859-825 B.C.) was the first Assyrian king who penetrated into Syria proper (Aleppo, Hamath, Damascus), and also the first to give us any news of Israel. In a cuneiform report of 842 B.C. he mentions, among other things, a tribute paid by the Israelitic king, Jehu. And he has a picture representing the consignment of this tribute, which is the oldest pictorial representation of Israelitic individuals that we now possess. From that time on Israel came into ever closer contact with

Assyria, either in its payments of tributes, or in its insurrections, while at the same time the above-described practice of banishing the upper classes of defeated, particularly of rebellious peoples, was developing more and more among the Assyrians. It was only a question of time when Israel's destruction also would come at the hands of the unconquered and apparently unconquerable Assyrians. No particularly unusual gift of prophecy was needed to be able to predict this consummation which the Jewish prophets saw so vividly in advance.

The northern portion of their realm met with its fate under King Hosea, who refused tribute to Assyria in 724 B.C., relying upon aid from Egypt, which did not come. Salmanassar IV proceeded to Israel, defeated Hosea, made him a prisoner, and besieged his capital Samaria, which could not be taken, however, until after a three years' siege by Sennacherib's successor Sargon (722 B.C.). The "flower of the population" (according to Wellhausen), 27,290 persons, according to the Assyrian reports, were now carried away to Assyrian and Median cities. The King of Assyria put in their place persons brought from rebellious Babylonian cities, "and placed them in the cities of Samaria instead of the children of Israel: and he possessed Samaria and dwelt in the cities thereof" (II Kings xvii, 24). Not the entire population of the ten northern tribes of Israel were therefore carried off, but only the most distinguished inhabitants of the cities, which were then populated with strangers, but this was quite sufficient to destroy the nationality of these ten tribes; for the peasant alone is incapable of constructing a specific communal life. The Israelitic city dwellers and aristocrats who were transplanted to Assyria and Media, on the other hand, disappeared in their new environment in the course of generations, becoming fused with it.

i. The First Destruction of Jerusalem

There remained of the people of Israel only the city of Jerusalem with its province of Judea. It appeared as if this small remnant would soon share the fate of the greater mass, and that the name of Israel would thus disappear from the face of the earth. But the Assyrians were not destined to take Jerusalem and destroy it. To be sure, the fact that the army of the Assyrian Sennacherib, who set out against Jerusalem in 701 B.C., was forced to return home because of disturbances in Babylon, thus sparing Jerusalem, was merely a postponement. Judea remained an Assyrian vassal state that might be swallowed up at any moment.

But beginning with the time of Sennacherib the attention of the Assyrians was being gradually diverted northward, for there warlike nomads were advancing more and more menacingly, requiring more and more military strength in order to repel them: the Cimmerians, Medes, and Scythians. The latter entered Western Asia about 625 B.C., advancing in their course of plunder and devastation up to the boundary of Egypt, but scattered, some twenty-eight years later, without having founded an empire of their own. But they did not disappear without leaving considerable traces behind them; their invasion shook the Assyrian monarchy to its foundations. The latter was therefore exposed to a more successful attack by the Medes; Babylon seceded and became free, while the Egyptians made use of the situation to gain control of Palestine. The Judean King Josiah was defeated and killed by the Egyptians at Megiddo (609 B.C.), whereupon Necho, King of Egypt, appointed Jehoiachin as his vassal in Jerusalem. Finally, in 606 B.C., Nineveh was destroyed by a coalition of Babylonians and Medes, and the Assyrian Empire had come to an end.

But this did not save Judea. Babylonia now followed in the footsteps of Assur and immediately attempted to gain control of the route to Egypt. In this effort the Babylonians under Nebuchadnezzar were opposed by Necho, who had advanced as far as Northern Syria. The Egyptians were defeated in the battle of Karkemish (605 B.C.), and Judea was made a vassal state of Babylonia soon thereafter. Judea was apparently passing from hand to hand, having lost all independence. Incited by Egypt, Judea in 597 B.C. refused to pay tribute to the Babylonians, but this rebellion collapsed almost without a struggle; Jerusalem was besieged by Nebuchadnezzar and surrendered unconditionally.

"And Nebuchadnezzar king of Babylon came against the city,

and his servants did besiege it.   And Jehoiachin the king of Judah
went out to the king of Babylon, he, and his mother, and his
servants, and his princes, and his officers: and the king of Babylon
took him in the eighth year of his reign, and he carried out thence
all the treasures of the house of the Lord, and the treasures of the
king's house, and cut in pieces all the vessels of gold which Solomon, king of Israel, had made in the temple of the Lord, as the
Lord had said, and he carried away all Jerusalem, and all the
princes, and all the mighty men of valor, even ten thousand captives, and all the craftsmen and smiths: none remained save the
poorest sort of the people of the land.   And he carried away
Jehoiachin to Babylon, and the king's mother, and the king's
wives, and his officers, and the mighty of the land.   Those carried
he into captivity from Jerusalem to Babylon.   And all the men of
might, even seven thousand, and craftsmen and smiths a thousand, all that were strong and apt for war, even them the king
of Babylon brought captive to Babylon."   (II Kings xxiv, 12-16).

Babylon was continuing to practice the old Assyrian method,
again not making off with the entire population, but only with the
royal court, the aristocrats, the men capable of bearing arms and
the wealthy urban citizens, 10,000 persons in all.   The "poorest
sort of the people of the land," probably also of the city, were
left behind, surely including also a portion of the ruling classes.
Yet Judea was not destroyed.   It was given a new king by the
master of Babylon.   And again, for the last time, the old cycle
was repeated.   The Egyptians incited the new king, Zedekiah,
to secede from Babylon.

Thereupon Nebuchadnezzar appeared outside of Jerusalem,
conquered it and completely wiped out this city, which was so
intractable and disturbing an element by reason of its dominant
position along the thoroughfare of nations from Babylon to Egypt
(586 B.C.).

"And in the fifth month came Nebuzar-adan, captain of the
guard, a servant of the king of Babylon, unto Jerusalem, and he
burned the house of the Lord, and the king's house, and all the
houses of Jerusalem, and every great man's house burned he with
fire.   And all the army of the Chaldees that were with the captain

of the guard brake down the walls of Jerusalem round about. Now *the rest of the people that were left in the city,* and the fugitives that fell away to the king of Babylon, with the remnant of the multitude, did Nebuzar-adan the captain of the guard carry away. But the captain of the guard left of the poor of the land to be *vinedressers* and *husbandmen.*" (II Kings xxv, 8-12.)

Likewise, we read in Jeremiah xxxix, 9, 10: "Then Nebuzaradan the captain of the guard carried away captive into Babylon the remnant of the people that remained in the city, and those that fell away, that fell to him, with the rest of the people that remained. But Nebuzar-adan the captain of the guard left of the poor of the people, which had nothing, in the land of Judah, and gave them vineyards and fields at the same time."

A number of peasant elements therefore remained. For it would have been senseless to depopulate the country entirely, to leave it without farmers, for then it could not have paid any taxes. The Babylonians evidently wished to take away particularly that part of the population, as was their practice, which was capable of uniting and leading the nation and might thereby become dangerous to Babylonian supremacy. The peasant alone has rarely been able to liberate himself from foreign rule.

The information given in Jeremiah xxxix becomes easy to understand if we recall the formation of latifundia which had been taking place in Judea also. It was natural that the latifundia should now be broken up and parceled out to the expropriated peasants, or that the debtor slaves and tenants should become free owners of the soil they cultivated. For their tyrants had been the leaders of Judea in its struggle against Babylon.

According to the Assyrian report, the population of Judea under Sennacherib was 200,000, not counting that of Jerusalem, which may be estimated at 25,000. The number of the large landed proprietors is put at 15,000; 7,000 of these were taken away by Nebuchadnezzar after the first conquest of Jerusalem.[15] He therefore left 8,000 behind. Yet the Book of II Kings, xxiv, 14, reports that already then only "the poorer sort of the people of the land" remained. These 8,000 were subsequently taken

[15] Compare F. Buhl, *Die sozialen Verhältnisse der Israeliten,* pp. 52, 53.

away at the second destruction. Probably it was their vineyards and fields that were given to the "poor of the people, which had nothing."

Very probably the entire population was not taken away this time either; but all of the population of *Jerusalem* was taken away. At any rate, most of the country population was left. But what was left ceased to constitute a specific Jewish community. The entire national life of the Jews was now concentrated in the city-dwellers now living in exile.

This national life now obtained a peculiar tinge, owing to the peculiar situation of the urban Jews. While the Israelites had hitherto been a race that did not differ strongly from the other races surrounding it, and therefore had not aroused any particular attention among these races, its remnants, which now continued to lead a separate national life, developed into a race unlike any other in existence. It was not as late as the destruction of Jerusalem by the Romans, but as early as the destruction of Jerusalem by Nebuchadnezzar, that we have the beginnings of the abnormal situation of the Jews which makes them a unique phenomenon in history.

II. THE JEWS AFTER THE EXILE

a. *Banishment*

APPARENTLY Judea had met with the same fate after the destruction of Jerusalem as had the tribes of Israel after the destruction of Samaria, but the same fate that eliminated Israel from history raised Judea from insignificant oblivion to be one of the most powerful factors in the history of the world, owing to the circumstance that by reason of the greater distance from Assyria, of the natural fortifications of Jerusalem, as well as of the invasion by northern nomads, the destruction of Jerusalem took place one hundred and thirty-five years later than that of Samaria.

The Jews were exposed for four generations longer than the ten tribes to all those influences mentioned by us as stimulating national fanaticism to the highest degree. For this reason, if for no other, the Jews went into exile with far more developed national feelings than did their northern brothers. But another factor working in the same direction was the fact that the Jewish community consisted at bottom of a single large city only, together with the surrounding territory, while the northern empire had been an aggregation of ten tribes, by no means closely connected with each other. Judea therefore constituted a far more unified and compact mass than Israel.

Nevertheless, the Judeans would also have lost their nationality in exile if they had remained under foreign rule as long as the ten tribes. He who is exiled among strangers may long for his old home and be unable to strike roots in his new surroundings. His exile may even strengthen his national feelings. But it is very unusual to find such strong national feelings among the children born in exile, who grow up in the new surroundings and know the old conditions only through the tales of their fathers, unless the prospect of an early return to their former home is kept alive by deprivation of rights, or by unfavorable treatment in the foreign country. The third generation, in turn, will hardly remember its nationality, unless, as we have already stated, it is constantly maintained in subordination to its surroundings, cut off by force from the rest of the population as a separate and inferior race, and thus exposed to oppression and maltreatment by the dominant race. This seems not to have been the case with the Jews transplanted to Assyria and Babylonia, and they would therefore have probably lost their nationality and disappeared among the Babylonians, if they had remained among them for more than three generations. But very soon after the destruction of Jerusalem the victorious empire began to totter, and the banished groups were permitted to hope for an early return to the land of their fathers, and already in the course of the second generation this hope was fulfilled, the Jews being enabled to return to Jerusalem from Babylon. For the tribes which had pressed upon Mesopotamia from the North and destroyed Assyria were not very quickly pacified. The most powerful among them was the nomadic tribe of the Persians, which destroyed the two heirs of Assyrian rule, the kingdoms of the Medes and Babylonians, and not only reëstablished the Assyrian-Babylonian Empire in a new shape, but even enormously extended it, conquering Egypt and Asia Minor into the bargain, and creating for the first time a military system and a national administration capable of assuring a firm basis of world empire, cementing it firmly together and maintaining permanent domestic peace within.

The conquerors of Babylon had no reason to continue to keep away from their homes those who had been conquered and exiled abroad by this state. In 538 B.C. Babylon was conquered by the Persians without a sword-stroke, which shows how weak the city must have been; and in the next year Cyrus, the Persian king, already permits the Jews to return home. Their exile had not lasted half a century, and yet, so many of them had already adapted themselves to the new conditions that only a portion took advantage of the permission, not a few remaining in Babylon, where they felt more at home. There is very little doubt that the Jews would have completely disappeared if Jerusalem had shared the fate of Samaria, if the period between its destruction and the conquest of Babylonia by the Persians had been a period of one hundred and eighty years instead of fifty years only.

But short as was the period of Jewish exile, it nevertheless produced the most far-reaching changes in Judaism, causing a number of tendencies and small beginnings that had been previously produced by conditions in Judea to develop and strengthen to the full, and imparting extremely characteristic forms to these traits, owing to the peculiar situation in which the Jews were placed from this time on.

In exile they continued to exist as a nation, a nation without peasants, a nation consisting exclusively of urban dwellers. To this day this is one of the most important characteristics of the Jews, on which their most essential "race traits" are based, which actually represent nothing more than the ordinary customs of city dwellers accentuated by a long period of urban life, and by the absence of new elements supplied by a peasantry, as I pointed out as early as 1890.[16]

This condition changed but slightly and only temporarily after their return to Palestine from their banishment, as we shall learn in the sequel.

But the Jews now became not only a nation of *city dwellers,* but also of *traders.* Industry was not highly developed in Judea, as we have seen; it was barely sufficient for simple household needs. Among the industrially advanced Babylonians, the Jews were therefore at a disadvantage. Military service and government administration were also closed to the Jews owing to the loss of their independence: what other livelihood remained to city dwellers but trade?

While trade had been very important in Palestine from the earliest days, it necessarily became the chief occupation of the Jews in their banishment.

But with the increase in their trade there necessarily was involved an increase in the intelligence of the Jews, their mathematical sense, their power of mental combination and abstraction. But their national misfortune simultaneously provided their in-

[16] *Das Judentum, Die Neue Zeit,* vol. viii, p. 23 *ff.*

creased acumen with nobler objects than mere personal gain. In their foreign surroundings the members of the tribe become even more closely united than at home. Their feeling of coherence as opposed to strangers becomes stronger, as the individual feels himself weaker and more menaced when standing alone. The social feelings, the ethical compassion, become more powerful, impregnating Jewish ingenuity with the most profound thoughts as to the causes of the national misfortune and the means of rehabilitating the nation.

Simultaneously, however, Jewish thought was necessarily much stimulated by the splendor of the metropolitan city of Babylon, its world traffic, its ancient civilization, its science and philosophy. As in the first half of the Nineteenth Century, German thinkers were elevated and inspired to their highest and best achievements by a sojourn in the Babylon on the Seine, so a sojourn in the Babylon on the Euphrates in the Sixth Century B.C. must necessarily have similarly influenced the Jews and suddenly widened their horizon immensely.

But of course, as in all the oriental commercial centers not lying on the shores of the Mediterranean but in the interior of the continent, science remained affiliated with religion—fettered to religion—in Babylon also, for reasons we have already indicated. Therefore all the powerful new impressions expressed themselves in a religious form among the Jews; in fact, religion now necessarily became the more prominent among the Jews by reason of the fact that the destruction of their national independence left only their common national worship as the sole bond still uniting the nation. The priesthood of this worship now constituted the only central organization retaining any authority in the eyes of the entire people. The tribal organization appears to have attained new energy in banishment, the state constitution having disappeared.[17] But tribal particularism was not a factor cementing the nation. Judea now sought to maintain and rescue its nation in religion, and the priesthood obtained leadership among them as a result.

[17] Compare Frank Buhl, *Die sozialen Verhältnisse der Israeliten*, p. 43.

The Judean priesthood borrowed from the Babylonian priesthood their arrogant claims, but also many of their notions of worship. Quite a number of the Biblical legends are of Babylonian origin; for instance, those of the creation of the world, Paradise, the fall from grace, the construction of the Tower of Babel, the Deluge. Nor is the strict observance of the Sabbath less Babylonian in its origin. The Sabbath was not so strongly emphasized by the Jews before the period of banishment.

"The emphasis thus placed by Ezekiel on keeping the Sabbath holy is something *entirely new*. None of the earlier prophets lays such stress on the celebration of the Sabbath. For Jeremiah xvii, 19 *ff.* is not a genuine passage." [18]

Even after the return from banishment in the Fifth Century B.C., it was very difficult to enforce Sabbath observance, "as it was too strongly opposed to the old habits".[19]

But we may assume that the Jewish priesthood probably acquired from the highly developed Babylonian priesthood, not only popular legends and customs, but also a higher and more spiritual conception of divinity, even though we have no direct evidence to this effect.

The conception of divinity among the Israelites had for a long time been quite crude. Great as was the care shown by later collators and editors of the old stories, to eliminate all traces of paganism from them, we still have a number of such traces in the versions of these stories that have come down to us.

Let us recall, for example, the stories connected with Jacob. His god not only gives him assistance in questionable transactions of every kind, but even lowers himself to the point of wrestling with Jacob, in which combat the god is defeated by the human: "And Jacob was left alone; and there wrestled a man with him until the breaking of the day. And when he saw that he prevailed not against him, he touched the hollow of his thigh; and the hollow of Jacob's thigh was out of joint as he wrestled with him. And he said: Let me go, for the day breaketh. And he said: I will not let thee go except thou bless me. And he said unto him:

[18] B. Stade, *Geschichte des Volkes Israel,* vol. ii, p. 17.
[19] *Op. cit.,* p. 187.

What is thy name? And he said, Jacob. And he said: Thy name shall be called no more Jacob, but Israel: for as a prince hast thou power with God and with man, and *hast prevailed*. And Jacob asked him and said: Tell me, I pray thee, thy name. And he said: Wherefore is it that thou dost ask after my name? And he blessed him there. And Jacob called the name of the place Peniel: for I have seen God face to face and my life is preserved." (Genesis xxxii, 24-30.)

The Great Unknown with whom Jacob wrestled victoriously and whose blessing he obtained by force, was therefore a god subdued by a man, very much as in the combats of gods and men in the Iliad. But when Diomedes succeeds in wounding Ares, it is with the aid of Pallas Athenæ, while Jacob disposes of his god without the assistance of any other god.

While the conceptions of God among the Israelites were very naïve, the civilized nations surrounding them in many cases had priestly classes that had advanced as far as monotheism, at least in their occult teachings. This condition was at one time emphatically evident among the Egyptians.

"We are not yet able to present in detail or enumerate chronologically all the manifold vagaries of speculation, all the phases which the history of thought (among the Egyptians) passed through. But we are finally brought to the point of recognizing that in the occult teaching even Horus and Re, the son and the father, are absolutely identical, and that the god begets himself by his own mother, the goddess of Heaven, and that she herself remains merely a product, a creation, of the single eternal god. This doctrine is not expressed clearly and unambiguously, with all its consequences, before the beginning of the New Empire (after the driving out of the Hyksos, in the Fifteenth Century B.C.); but it already begins to take form in the period beginning with the end of the sixth dynasty (about the year 2500 B.C.), and the ideas lying at the base of it have already been definitely fixed in the Middle Empire (about 2000 B.C.).

"The new doctrine originated in Anu, the City of the Sun (Heliopolis)." [20]

[20] Eduard Meyer, *Geschichte des alten Aegypten,* pp. 192, 193.

To be sure, this doctrine remained a secret doctrine, but it had at least one practical application. This occurred before the Hebrews had entered Canaan, under Amenhotep IV, in the Fourteenth Century B.C. It appears that this prince was in conflict with the priesthood, whose wealth and power threatened to overshadow him. He knew of no other way of combating them than by taking their secret doctrine seriously, ordering that only one god be worshiped, and relentlessly persecuting all other gods, which amounted in fact to his confiscating the immense wealth of the priesthood assigned to the other gods.

We have no information concerning the details of the struggle between priesthood and monarchy. It lasted over a long period, but one hundred years after Amenhotep IV, the priesthood was completely victorious and had completely reëstablished the worship of the old gods.

This whole story shows to what a point monotheistic views had already advanced in the secret priestly doctrines of the civilized centers of the ancient Orient. We have no reason to assume that the Babylonian priests were more backward than those of Egypt, for they seem to be equals in all the arts and sciences. Even Jeremias speaks of a "latent monotheism" in Babylon. Marduk, creator of Heaven and earth, was also the lord of the gods, whom he "pastures as sheep," all the various gods were only special appearances of the one and only god. Thus we read in a Babylonian text concerning the various gods: "Ninib: Marduk of Strength. Nergal: Marduk of Battle. Bel: Marduk of Government. Nabu: Marduk of Business. Sin: Marduk illuminating the Night. Samas: Marduk of Law. Addu: Marduk of Rain."

Precisely at the time of the Exile of the Jews, when a sort of monotheism was also arising among the Persians who had come into contact with Babylon, we have indications that "in Babylon also a beginning was made toward monotheism, which probably showed very strong similarities with the Pharaonic sun worship, of Amenophis IV (Amenhotep). At least an inscription belonging to the period shortly before the fall of Babylon represents the moon-god as having a rôle similar to that of the sun-god

Amenophis IV, which would be fully in accord with the importance of moon-worship in Babylonia." [21]

But while the priestly collegia in Babylonia as well as in Egypt had a real interest in withholding their possibly monotheistic views from the people, since their entire power and wealth depended upon the traditional polytheistic worship, the case was quite different with the priesthood of the Federal fetish at Jerusalem.

Even before the destruction of Jerusalem this fetish had increased in importance, for Samaria had been destroyed and the Northern Empire of Israel had gone down with it. Jerusalem was now the only large city of Israelitic nationality; the country territory dependent upon it remained relatively unimportant. The prestige of the Federal fetish which had been great in Israel, particularly in the tribe of Judea, and perhaps since as long ago as the time before David, now began to overshadow and outshine all the other sacred possessions of the people, as Jerusalem outshone all the other towns in Judea. Likewise the priesthood serving this fetish necessarily attained a dominant position over the other priests in the country. There arose a struggle between the country priests and the priesthood of the capital, which ended in the assignment to the fetish at Jerusalem of a monopoly position, perhaps even before the Exile. At least that is what is indicated in the tale of Deuteronomy, the "Book of Doctrine", which a priest maintained he had "found" in the Temple in the year 621 B.C. It contained the divine command to destroy all places of worship outside of Jerusalem, and King Josiah faithfully carried out this command: "And he put down the idolatrous priests whom the kings of Judah had ordained to burn incense in the high places in the cities of Judah, and in the places round about Jerusalem; them also that burned incense unto Baal, to the sun, and to the moon, and to the planets, and to all the host of Heaven. . . . And he brought all the priests out of the cities of Judah, and defiled the high places where the priests had burned incense, from Geba to Beer-sheba. . . . Moreover, the altar that was at Beth-el, and the high place which Jeroboam the son of Nebat, who made

[21] H. Winckler, *Die babylonische Geisteskultur.* 1907, p. 144.

Israel to sin, had made, both that altar and the high place he brake down, and burned the high place, and stamped it small to powder, and burned the grove." [22]

Not only the places in which foreign gods were worshiped, but those places sacred to Jehovah himself, including the oldest of his altars, were thus desecrated and destroyed.

But possibly this entire story, like so many others of those in the Bible, is only an invention of the post-Exile period, an attempt to justify events that took place after the Exile, by representing them as repetitions of earlier events, inventing precedents for them, or at least inflating and exaggerating such precedents. At any rate, we may assume that even before the Exile jealousies between the priests of the capital and those of the provinces existed which temporarily may have led to a shutting down of holy places that constituted an inconvenient competition. In the case of the exiled Jews, the majority of whom came from Jerusalem, it was not difficult to secure the recognition of the monopoly rights of the Temple at Jerusalem. Under the influence, on the one hand, of Babylonian philosophy, and on the other hand, of the national misfortune—and possibly also of the Persian religion which was developing in about the same direction as the Jewish religion, and, furthermore, coming into contact with it at about this time, imparting stimulus to the Jewish religion and possibly also receiving such stimulus—the priesthood were encouraged in the taking of a new step. The ambition which they had brought with them from Jerusalem to place their fetish in a monopoly position, began, under the influence of all these conditions, to develop a tendency toward an ethical monotheism, in which Jehovah would no longer appear merely as the specific ancestral god of Israel, but as the sole God of the world, the personification of the Good, the incarnation of all morality.

Later, when the Jews returned to Jerusalem from their Exile, their religion had developed and become spiritualized to the extent that the crude conceptions and forms of worship of the Jewish peasants who had remained behind necessarily appeared as a repulsive pagan abomination. Unless this step had been taken

[22] II Kings xxiii, 5, 8, 15.

at an earlier date, it would now have been easy for the priests and masters of Jerusalem to secure the final elimination of these competitive provincial forms of worship, and to establish the monopoly of the priesthood of Jerusalem on a permanent basis.

Such was the beginning of Jewish monotheism. It was ethical in its character, as was also the monotheism of Plato's philosophy. But in the case of the Jews the new conception of God did not arise as with the Greeks outside of religion, it was not supported by a class standing outside of the priesthood. Thus the single God did not appear as a new god, standing above and beyond the old world of gods, but as a concentration of the ancient group of gods into a single most powerful God, who furthermore was nearest to the thoughts of the inhabitants of Jerusalem, the old warlike ancestral and local God Jehovah, who was anything rather than ethical.

This process introduced a number of serious contradictions into the Jewish religion. As an ethical God, Jehovah is a God of all humanity, for good and evil are conceptions that are understood in an absolute manner, valid for all persons equally. And being an ethical God, a personification of the moral idea, this single God is omnipresent, as morality is considered as equally valid everywhere. But religion, in other words, the worship of Jehovah, was also the strongest national bond among the Jews of Babylonia; and the entire possibility of a restoration of the national independence was indissolubly connected with the restoration of Jerusalem. The erection of the Temple at Jerusalem, and its subsequent maintenance, now became the slogan to which the Jewish nation would rally. The priesthood of this Temple had simultaneously become the highest national authority of the Jews, a class having every interest in maintaining the monopoly of worship for this Temple. Thus the lofty philosophical abstraction of a single omnipresent God, who asks only for a pure heart and a sinless mode of life, not for sacrifices, remained peculiarly associated with the ancient primitive fetishism, which domiciled God in a specific place, the only place where offerings of all sorts could be effectively presented for consideration. The Temple at Jerusalem remained the exclusive home of Jehovah, to which every Jew had to turn his thoughts, the goal of his longings.

Not less peculiar was another contradiction: God had become the incarnation of the moral demands that had equal validity for all men, and yet he remained the ancestral God of the Jews. It was attempted to reconcile this contradiction by declaring God to be indeed the God of all men, by making it the duty of all men to love and honor him, but also making the Jews the only people he had chosen as a manifestation of this love and honor, the only people to whom he had revealed his splendor, leaving the pagans to remain in blindness. It is precisely during the time of Exile, at the lowest point in their humiliation and despair, that this peculiar feeling of superiority over the rest of humanity first appears among the Jews. Formerly, Israel had been a people not unlike other peoples, and Jehovah a god resembling other gods; perhaps stronger than the other gods, just as it was natural to believe that one's own nation was stronger than other nations, but surely not the only true God, and Israel surely not the sole possessor of the truth.

"The God of Israel was not the All-Powerful, but only the most powerful among the gods. He was on the same level with them and had to struggle against them; Kamos and Dagon and Hadad were fully on a par with him, less powerful but not less genuine than he. 'What your God Kamos has given unto you to conquer,' Jephthah sends this message to the neighboring peoples who are violating the boundaries, 'that belongs unto you, and what our God Jehovah has conquered for us, that is ours.' The dominions of the gods are therefore as clearly distinguished as those of the peoples, and no god has any rights in lands worshiping another god." [23]

But now this condition changed. The author of Isaiah, beginning with chapter xl, who wrote at the end of the period of Exile or shortly thereafter, has Jehovah proclaim:

"I am the Lord; that is my name; and my glory will I not give to another, neither my praise to graven images. . . . Sing unto the Lord a new song, and his praise from the end of the earth,

[23] Wellhausen, *op. cit.*, p. 32.

Ye that go down to the sea, and all that is therein; the isles, and the inhabitants thereof. Let the wilderness and the cities thereof lift up their voice, the villages that Kedar doth inhabit: let the inhabitants of the rock sing, let them shout from the top of the mountains. Let them give glory unto the Lord, and declare his praise in the islands." [24]

There is no longer any mention of limiting God's authority to Palestine, or even to the single city of Jerusalem. But the same author has Jehovah say:

"But thou, Israel, art my servant, Jacob whom I have chosen, the seed of Abraham my friend. Thou whom I have taken from the ends of the earth, and called thee from the chief men thereof, and said unto thee, Thou art my servant; I have chosen thee and not cast thee away. Fear thou not; for I am with thee; be not dismayed, for I am thy God. . . . They that war against thee shall be as nothing, and as a thing of nought. . . . The first shall say to Zion, Behold, behold them: and I will give to Jerusalem one that bringeth good tidings." [25]

These are peculiar contradictions, but they are contradictions due to the actual life of the times, due to the anomalous position of the Jews in Babylon, who had been transplanted into a new civilization, the immense impressions of which were revolutionizing their entire mode of thought, while all the conditions of their lives still forced them to maintain their old traditions, since this was the only means of retaining their national existence, more important to them than to other tribes; for a painful situation that had lasted for centuries had developed their national sensitiveness in a particularly keen and emphatic manner.

It now became the task of Jewish thinkers to unite the new ethics with the ancient fetishism, to reconcile the philosophy and wisdom of the immense civilization which centered at Babylon and embraced many races, with the narrowness of a little tribe of mountaineers that regarded foreigners with disfavor. And it was necessary to achieve this reconciliation on the basis of religion; in other words, the traditional faith. It was their duty

[24] Isaiah xlii, 8, 10-12.
[25] Isaiah xli, 8-25.

therefore to prove that the new was not new, but extremely ancient, that the truth of these strangers, which seemed irresistible, was neither new nor strange, but a genuine Jewish possession, the recognition of which by the Jews did not mean an abandonment of their nationality in the Babylonian melting pot, but rather a strengthening and final solidification of their nationality.

This task was well calculated to sharpen the wits, to develop the art of interpretation and hair-splitting, which from that time on was developed to such perfection, particularly among the Jews. And this it was that placed its peculiar mark on the historical literature of the Jews.

And now begins a process which has taken place quite frequently, and which Marx has analyzed in his investigation of the views of the natural condition of man as held in the Eighteenth Century. Marx speaks of this process as follows:

"The individual and isolated hunter and fisher who forms the starting point with Smith and Ricardo, belongs to the insipid illusions of the Eighteenth Century. They are Robinsonades, which do not by any means represent, as students of the history of civilization imagine, a reaction against over-refinement and a return to a misunderstood natural life. They are no more based on such a naturalism than is Rousseau's *Contrat Social,* which makes naturally independent individuals come in contact and have intercourse by contract. They are the fiction and only the æsthetic fiction of the small and great Robinsonades. They are, moreover, the anticipation of 'bourgeois society,' which had been in course of development since the Sixteenth Century and made gigantic strides towards maturity in the Eighteenth. In this society of free competition the individual appears free from the bonds of nature, etc., which in former epochs of history made him a part of a definite, limited human conglomeration. To the prophets of the Eighteenth Century, on whose shoulders Smith and Ricardo are still standing, this Eighteenth Century individual, constituting the joint product of the dissolution of the feudal form of society and of the new forces of production which had developed since the Sixteenth Century, appears as an ideal whose existence belongs to the past; not as a result of history, but as its

starting point. Since that individual appeared to be in conform-
ity with nature and corresponded to their conception of human
nature, he was regarded not as a product of history, but of nature.
This illusion is characteristic of every new epoch." [26]

Such was the illusion suffered by the thinkers who developed
the notions of monotheism and of priestly domination among the
Jews, during and after the period of Exile. This thought did not
appear to them to have been produced by an historical development, but as a condition given from the start, not as "an historical
result", but as the "initial point of history". History itself was
now conceived in a like sense and the more easily adapted to the
new conditions since it was largely a mere oral tradition and for
the most part not based on documentary evidence. The faith in
a single God and the control of Israel by the priests of Jehovah
was now made the starting point of Israel's history; polytheism
and fetishism, which could not be entirely denied, were represented as a later deviation from the faith of the fathers, and not
as this primitive faith itself, which they really were.

And this conception had the great advantage of possessing an
uncommonly consoling appeal, as did also the race's proclaiming
itself God's chosen people. The assumption that Jehovah had
been only the ancestral God of Israel made it necessary to interpret the defeats of this people as so many defeats of its God, who
thus turned out to be the weaker in combats with other gods;
there was therefore every reason to doubt Jehovah and his priests.
But the case became quite different once there was no other god
than Jehovah, if Jehovah had chosen the Israelites before all
other peoples and they had rewarded him with ingratitude and
defection. All the misfortunes of Israel and Judea now appeared
as so many righteous punishments for its sins, for its neglect of
Jehovah's priests, thus becoming evidences not of God's weakness,
but of his anger, for he will not be scoffed at in vain. But a
natural corollary of this notion was to the effect that God would
again have mercy on his people, would rescue and redeem it as
soon as it again was imbued with the proper faith in him and in

[26] Marx, *Introduction to the Critique of Political Economy*, printed with *A
Contribution to the Critique of Political Economy*, Chicago, 1913, pp. 265-267.

his priests and prophets.   If the national life was not to die out, such a faith became the more necessary as the position of the little community, the "worm Jacob, and ye men of Israel" (Isaiah xli, 14), became more hopeless among hostile communities of superior power.

Only a supernatural, superhuman, divine power, a savior, a Messiah sent by God, could now save and liberate Judea and finally elevate it to be a master over the peoples now maltreating it.   The faith in the Messiah arises simultaneously with monotheism, and is intimately connected with it.   For this very reason, the Messiah is not imagined as a god, but as a human sent by God.   For it was his function to erect an earthly kingdom, not a kingdom of God, for Jewish thought had not yet reached this stage of abstraction, but a kingdom of the Jews.   In fact, Cyrus, who released the Jews from Babylon and sent them back to Jerusalem was already greeted as the anointed of Jehovah, Messiah, Christ.   (Isaiah xlv, 1.)

This transformation of Jewish thought, which received its strongest stimulus during the Exile, but which surely did not achieve its final form in that period, cannot possibly have taken place in a single instant or by peaceful means.   We cannot afford to forget that this transformation was expressing itself in powerful polemics in the style of the prophets, in profound doubts and broodings after the fashion of the Book of Job, and finally in historical presentations in the style of the various components of the Five Books of Moses, which were set down at that time.

Not until long after the Exile did this revolutionary period come to an end.   Certain definite dogmatical, ecclesiastical, legal and historical views came out victorious, and were accepted as correct by the priesthood, which had obtained control of the people, as well as by the masses of the people themselves.   Certain writings which were in accord with these views were declared to be very ancient and holy and transmitted as such to posterity. But it was felt to be necessary to introduce some unity into the various ingredients of this literature, which was still full of contradictions, uniting within itself in a most motley fashion elements old and new, rightly understood and not understood at all, genuine and fabricated; this purpose was achieved by means of exhaustive "editings", cuts and interpolations. In spite of all this "editorial work", we fortunately still have in its result, the Old Testament, enough of the original substance to enable us to recognize in it at least a trace—among all the profusion of luxuriant forgeries—of the character of the ancient pre-exile Hebrew people, that Hebrew people of whom the modern Jews are not only a continuation, but also a perfect opposite.

b. The Jewish Diaspora

In the year 538 B.C. the Babylonian Jews were permitted by Cyrus to return to Jerusalem, but we have already seen that by no means all took advantage of this permission. How could all have lived in Jerusalem? The city was devastated and much time would be needed for making it habitable, fortifying it, and rebuilding the Temple of Jehovah. But even then it would not offer all the Jews an opportunity for making their living. Probably it was as true then as now that the peasant has a predilection for moving cityward, while the transition from urban to agricultural life is as difficult as it is rare.

The Jews probably had hardly acquired any industrial skill in Babylon; possibly they had lived there too short a time. Judea did not attain any national independence, remained dependent on foreign conquerors, first on the Persians, then, beginning with Alexander the Great, on the Greeks, and finally, after a short interregnum of independence and of very varied and destructive revolutions, it came under the control of the Romans. All the conditions were as a rule lacking for the existence of a warlike monarchy, acquiring wealth by subjecting and plundering weaker neighbors.

While agriculture, industry, military service, did not offer very large fields for the Jews after the Exile, the majority of them had no other means of livelihood than trade, which had already been the case in Babylon. They embraced this opportunity the more readily since they had been in possession of the necessary mental qualifications and equipment for centuries.

But it was just in this period beginning with the Babylonian captivity that great changes were taking place in politics and trade which had disastrous effects on the commercial status of Palestine. Peasant agriculture and also handicraft are extremely conservative occupations. Progress rarely takes place in them, progress rarely even interests them, while the goad of competition is lacking—always the case in primitive conditions—and while the normal course of events, when there are no crop failures, pestilences, wars and similar mass misfortunes, afford every workingman who operates in the traditional manner, his daily bread, while that which is new and untried may be the occasion for failures and losses.

Technical advances in peasant agriculture and in handicraft therefore usually do not arise directly from these sources, but from trade, which brings new products and new processes from abroad, which gives cause for thought and finally produces new profitable cultivations and new methods.

Trade is far less conservative, being freed from the start from local and professional limitations, and being by nature critical of home traditions, because it is capable of comparing them and measuring them by the standard of what has been attained in other places and under other conditions. Furthermore, the merchant succumbs to the pressure of competition more readily than does the farmer or the artisan, for he meets competitors of the most various nations in the great centers of trade. He is therefore forced to be always on the lookout for something new, particularly to work for an improvement in the means of traffic, and for an extension of the circle of his commercial relations. As long as agriculture and industry are not conducted with the use of capital and not built up on a scientific basis, trade is the only revolutionary element in economy; maritime commerce has a particularly powerful effect in this direction. Maritime navigation makes it possible to cover greater distances and to secure contact between more varied peoples than is the case with trade by land. For the ocean at first keeps the races further apart than does the land, thus making the evolution of each people more independent of the others and more peculiar. But with the development of maritime navigation, bringing about contact between peoples hitherto separated, there is frequently a meeting between more divergent extremes than are brought together in trade by land. But navigation also makes higher demands in the form of technical skill; maritime commerce develops much later than land trade, for a much more thorough control of nature is presupposed in the construction of a seaworthy ship than in the process of taming a camel or an ass. On the other hand, it is precisely the great profits of sea-trade, which are attainable only on the basis of a high degree of ability in shipbuilding, which constitute one of the most powerful impulses to develop this ability. The technical skill of ancient times probably did not develop so far, or achieve such triumphs in any other field, as in the field of ship construction.

Sea-trade does not serve as an impediment to land-trade; on the contrary, it encourages trade by land. The prosperity of a seaport town usually requires the presence of a *hinterland* furnishing the commodities to be loaded on ships in the seaport, and which purchases the commodities brought to port by the ships. The seaport must seek to develop its trade by land together with its trade by sea, but the latter continues to gain in importance more and more, it becomes the decisive factor, while the former remains dependent on it. If the routes of sea-trade change, those of the trade by land must also change. Phœnicia, lying between the old centers of civilization on the Nile and the Euphrates, and participating in their commerce, furnished the first navigators who made great voyages in the Mediterranean. This country had as good an access to the Mediterranean as did the land of the Egyptians. But the latter invited its population chiefly to agriculture, the production of which, owing to the inundations of the Nile, was inexhaustible, not to navigation. Egypt lacked the necessary wood for the construction of ships, but it also lacked the stimulus of necessity which is the only impulse that can tempt man at an early stage to expose himself to the dangers of the open sea. Great as was the development of river navigation among the Egyptians, their ocean navigation remained a coastwise navigation with short courses. They developed agriculture and industry, particularly weaving, and their commercial traffic prospered. But they did not travel abroad as traders; they waited for foreigners to bring their wares to them. The desert and the sea remained hostile elements in their eyes.

The Phœnicians, on the other hand, lived in a strip of land along the coast, which literally forced them into the sea, as this strip lay along the foot of a rocky chain of mountains which afforded but slight opportunities for agriculture, thus making it necessary to supplement its insufficient yield by catches of fish, and which also furnished excellent wood for shipbuilding. These were the conditions that forced the Phœnicians to take to the sea. And the fact that they were placed between regions with very highly developed industries later stimulated them to expand their fishing expeditions into expeditions for commercial operations by sea. They thus became the bearers of Indian, Arabian, Babylonian and Egyptian products, particularly textile goods and spices, to the West, whence they brought in return products of another kind, particularly metals.

But in the course of time they encountered serious competitors in the Greeks, the inhabitants of island and coast regions whose farm lands were almost as niggardly as those of Phœnicia, with the result that the Greeks also were forced to undertake fisheries and navigation. These grew to larger and larger proportions and became more and more dangerous to the Phœnicians. At first the Greeks sought to avoid the Phœnicians and to obtain new routes to the Orient. They penetrated into the Black Sea, from whose seaports they established a trade with India by way of Central Asia. Simultaneously they attempted to establish relations with Egypt and to open up that country to their maritime commerce. Just before the period of the Babylonian captivity of the Jews, the Ionians and Karians succeeded in this attempt. Beginning with the time of Psammetikh (663 B.C.) they had a firm foothold in Egypt, almost inundating it with their merchants. Under Amasis (569-525 B.C.) they were already given a territory along the western arm of the Nile, on which to establish their own seaport after their own fashion, which was to be called Naukratis. This was to serve as the sole center for the trade with

Greece.   Soon thereafter Egypt succumbed to the Persians (525 B.C.), as Babylonia had succumbed before.   But the position of the Greeks in Egypt was not altered by this circumstance.   On the other hand, foreigners were now given full rights to trade with all Egypt; and the Greeks profited most by this arrangement. As soon as the Persian régime weakened, the warlike spirit of the former nomadic people becoming enervated owing to life in the large cities, the Egyptians rose in rebellion and attempted to regain their independence, in which attempt they were for a time successful (404-342 B.C.).   This also could not have been done without the assistance of the Greeks, who had meanwhile become strong enough to force back the mighty Persians on land and sea, and not only the Persians, but also their subjects, the Phœnicians.   Under Alexander of Macedonia the Greek community begins, in 334 B.C., to take the offensive against the Persian Empire, annexes it, and puts an end to the glory of the Phœnician cities, which had long been declining.

The trade of Palestine had gone down more rapidly than that of Phœnicia, and world traffic had deserted the routes of Palestine, not only the exports of India, but also those of Babylonia, Arabia, Ethiopia and Egypt.   Palestine, being the buffer between Egypt and Syria, remained the theater on which the *wars* between the lords of Syria and those of Egypt were most likely to be fought, but the *trade* between these two regions now went by sea, to the neglect of the land route.   Palestine simply retained all the disadvantages of its intermediate position, losing all the advantages. While the majority of the Jews were more and more forced into trade as an occupation, the possibility of their practicing trade in their own country was progressively decreasing.   Since trade, therefore, did not come to them, they were forced to seek it abroad by trading with such nations as had not developed a commercial class of their own, but waited for merchants to come to them.   There were quite a number of such races.   Where agriculture supported the majority of the population, where it was not necessary to supplement it by means of nomadic cattle-breeding or fisheries, and where the aristocracy satisfied its desire for expansion by accumulating latifundia at home and waging war abroad, it was generally preferred to wait for traders to come to the country instead of setting out to secure foreign commodities abroad. This had been the practice of the Egyptians, and was to be the practice of Rome. In both cases the traders were foreigners, particularly Greeks and Jews. The greatest prosperity encountered by such traders was in countries of the above mentioned type.

The Diaspora, the dispersal of the Jews outside of their home, therefore begins just in the time following the Babylonian Exile; in other words, in the time when the Jews had been permitted to return to their own home. This dispersal was not the consequence of an act of violence, like the destruction of Jerusalem, but of an imperceptible transformation then in process, namely, the shifting of the routes of commerce. And as the routes of world trade have never again favored Palestine since then, that country is avoided even now by the majority of the Jews, even when an opportunity to settle in the land of their fathers is offered them. Zionism will alter nothing in this condition unless it possesses the power of shifting the center of world trade to Palestine.

The greatest gathering of Jews took place in cities where there was most commercial activity and the greatest accumulations of riches, namely in Alexandria and later in Rome. The Jews increased in these places, not only in numbers, but also in wealth and power. Their powerful national feeling also cemented them strongly together, which was a factor of all the greater importance since in the days of the general and increasing social disintegration which was characteristic of the centuries immediately preceding Christ, the social bonds were universally dissolving and disappearing. And as it was possible to find Jews in all the commercial centers of the entire world of Hellenic and Roman civilization as it existed at that time, the bonds of their kinship extended throughout this area, constituting an International which gave assistance to each of its members, no matter what country he came from. If we consider in addition the commercial abilities which they had acquired in the course of many centuries, and which since their exile they had been developing under pressure in a single direction, we shall understand this increase in their power and wealth.

Mommsen says of Alexandria that it "was almost as much a city of the Jews as of the Greeks; the Alexandrian Jews must have been at least equal to those of Jerusalem in number, wealth, intelligence, and organization. In the First Imperial Era it was estimated that there were a million Jews to eight million Egyptians, and their influence was probably greater than would be represented by this ratio. . . . They, and they only, were permitted to form a community within the community as it were, and while other non-burgesses were ruled by the authorities of the burgess-body, they were permitted to a certain extent to govern themselves.

" 'The Jews,' says Strabo, 'have a national head (ἐθνάρχης) of their own in Alexandria who presides over the people and decides processes and disposes of contracts and arrangements as if he were ruling an independent community.' This was done because the Jews declared that such specific jurisdiction was a requirement of their nationality, or, what is equivalent to the same thing, their religion. Further, the usual national regulations paid attention to an extensive degree to the national and religious scruples of the Jews, and wherever possible granted the necessary exemptions. The fact that they lived together strengthened this peculiar position; for example, in Alexandria, of the five quarters of the city, two were inhabited chiefly by Jews." [27]

Some of the Jews of Alexandria became not only wealthy but also attained high repute and influence among the rulers of the world.

For instance, the Supreme Customs Lessee on the Arabian side of the Nile, the Alabarch Alexander, had an enormous influence. Agrippa, who later became King of Judea, borrowed two hundred thousand drachmas from him under the reign of Tiberius. Alexander gave him five talents in cash and an order for the payment of the balance in Dikæarchia.[28] This shows how

[27] Mommsen, *The Provinces of the Roman Empire*, London, 1886, vol. ii, pp. 163-165.
[28] Josephus, *Antiquities of the Jews*, xviii, 6, 3.

close were the commercial relations between the Jews of Alexandria and those in Italy. There was an important Jewish community in Dikæarchia, or Puteoli, near Naples. Josephus further reports concerning the same Alexandrian Jew: "He, Emperor Claudius, again liberated the Alabarch Alexander Lysimachus, his *good old friend*, who had been a trustee for his mother Antonia and had been imprisoned by Caius in a fit of rage. Alexander's son Marcus later married Berenice, daughter of King Agrippa." [29]

What was true of Alexandria is also true of Antioch: "The Jews were granted a certain independence as a community, and a privileged position, not only in the capital of Egypt, but also in that of Syria, and the position occupied by these two cities as centers of the Jewish Diaspora has not been the least of the elements contributing to their development." [30]

We can trace back the presence of Jews in Rome to the Second Century B.C. In 139 B.C. the Roman Prætor for Foreigners exiled Jews who had admitted Italic proselytes to the celebration of their Sabbath. Perhaps these Jews were members of an embassy sent out by Simon Maccabeus to gain the favor of the Romans, and who were making use of this opportunity to carry on propaganda for their religion. Soon thereafter we find Jews domiciled in Rome, and the Jewish community there became quite strong when Pompey conquered Jerusalem in 63 B.C. He brought a large number of Jewish prisoners of war to Rome, who continued living there as slaves or freedmen. This community became very influential. About the year 60 Cicero complained that their power was being felt even on the Forum. This power continued to increase under Caesar, and is described by Mommsen in the following words:

"How numerous even in Rome the Jewish population was already before Caesar's time, and how closely at the same time the Jews even then kept together as fellow-countrymen, is shown by the remark of an author of this period, that it was dangerous for a governor to offend the Jews of his province, because he

[29] *Antiquities*, xix, 5, 1.
[30] Mommsen, *The Provinces of the Roman Empire*, London, 1886, vol. ii, p. 127.

might then certainly reckon on being hissed after his return by the populace of the capital. Even at this time the predominant business of the Jews was trade; the Jewish trader moved everywhere with the conquering Roman merchant then, in the same way as he afterwards accompanied the Genoese and the Venetian, and capital flowed in on all hands to the Jewish, by the side of the Roman, merchants. At this period, too, we encounter the peculiar antipathy of the Occidentals towards this so thoroughly Oriental race and their foreign opinions and customs. This Judaism, although not the most pleasing feature in the nowhere pleasing picture of the mixture of nations which then prevailed, was nevertheless a historical element developing itself in the natural course of things, which the statesman could neither ignore nor combat, and which Caesar on the contrary, just like his predecessor Alexander, with correct discernment of the circumstances, fostered as far as possible. While Alexander, by laying the foundation of Alexandrian Judaism, did not much less for the nation than its own David by planning the Temple of Jerusalem, Caesar also advanced the interests of the Jews in Alexandria and in Rome by special favors and privileges, and protected in particular their peculiar worship against the Roman as well as against the Greek local priests. The two great men of course did not contemplate placing the Jewish nationality on an equal footing with the Hellenic or Italo-Hellenic. But the Jew who has not like the Occidental received the Pandora's gift of political organization, and stands substantially in a relation of indifference to the state; who, moreover, is as reluctant to give up the essence of his national idiosyncrasy, as he is ready to clothe it with any nationality at pleasure and to adapt himself up to a certain degree to foreign habits—the Jew was for this very reason as it were made for a state, which was to be built on the ruins of a hundred living polities and to be endowed with a somewhat abstract and, from the outset, toned-down nationality. Even in the ancient world Judaism was an effective leaven of cosmopolitanism and of national decomposition, and to that extent a specially privileged member in the Caesarian state, the polity of which was strictly speaking nothing but a citizenship of the world, and the nationality of which was at bottom nothing but humanity." [31]

Mommsen here succeeds in giving shelter within a single sentence to three distinct varieties of professorial historical wisdom. In the first place, there is the conception that the monarchs make history, that a few decrees of Alexander the Great created the Jews in Alexandria, not the alteration of the commercial routes which had already brought a large Jewish colony to Egypt and continued to develop and strengthen it after Alexander's death. Or shall we believe that the entire world trade of Egypt, which lasted for many centuries, was created by the Macedonian conqueror, as the result of a momentary whim during his temporary stay in that country?

This superstitious respect for royal decrees is immediately followed by the superstition of race. The races of the West are equipped by nature with the "Pandora's gift" of political organization, which is lacking to the Jews from birth. Nature apparently is represented as creating political inclinations from its own resources, before any such thing as politics exists, and then distributing them capriciously among the various "races", whatever that may mean. This mystical caprice of nature is here all the more comic in its effect when we recall that the Jews up to the time of their exile possessed and applied just as large a proportion of the "Pandora's gift" of political organization as did all the other races at their stage in civilization. Only the pressure of external circumstances deprived them of a State and thus of the material necessary for political organization.

In addition to these monarchic and anthropological conceptions of history, Mommsen provides us with a third conception, which represents the generals and organizers of states as influenced by mental processes similar to those hatched by German professors in their studies. The unscrupulous embezzler and soldier of fortune, Julius Caesar, is represented as desiring to create an abstract nationality of world citizenship and humanity, and as having recognized and therefore favored the Jews as the most useful means for attaining this end!

[31] Mommsen, *History of Rome*, New York, 1895, vol. v, pp. 418, 419.

Even if Caesar had pretended to be acting in this spirit, one should not feel entirely obliged to consider such an expression as in accord with his real thoughts; we are just as unwilling to take seriously the phrases of Napoleon III. The liberal professors of the period in which Mommsen's *History of Rome* was written would permit themselves to be easily deceived by Napoleonic turns of phrase, but this tendency did not constitute a political virtue. But Caesar never even said a word to suggest any such idea. The Caesars never used any phrases except those that were current at the time, that could be used for demagogic purposes, among gullible proletarians or gullible professors. The fact that Caesar not only tolerated the Jews but also favored them could be explained more simply, though not quite so magnificently, by his eternal debts and his eternal lust for money. Money had become the decisive power in the State. Because the Jews had money and had become useful to him, and not because their national characteristics might be of value in the creation of an "abstract, prepared nationality" Caesar protected them and allowed them privileges.

The Jews were appreciative of this favor; they deeply mourned his death.

"In the great public mourning he was also lamented by the foreign inhabitants (of Rome), by each nation according to its fashion, *particularly the Jews,* who went so far as to visit the mortuary chamber several nights in succession." [32]

Augustus also appreciated the importance of the Jews.

"The communities of Asia Minor under Augustus made the attempt to draw upon their Jewish fellow-citizens uniformly in the levy, and no longer to allow them the observance of the Sabbath; but Agrippa decided against them and maintained the *status quo* in favor of the Jews, or rather, perhaps, now for the first time legalized the exemption of the Jews from military service and their Sabbath privilege, that had been previously conceded according to circumstances only by individual governors or communities of the Greek provinces. Augustus further directed the governors of Asia not to apply the rigorous imperial laws respect-

[32] Suetonius, *Julius Caesar*, chap. lxxxiv.

ing unions and assemblies against the Jews. . . . Augustus showed himself favorably inclined to the Jewish colony in the suburb of Rome on the other side of the Tiber, and permitted those who had neglected to collect his largesses because of the Sabbath, to receive their quota subsequently." [33]

The Jews in Rome must have been very numerous at that time. More than eight thousand (only men?) of their congregation took part in a Jewish delegation to Augustus in the year 3 B.C.! Very recently, numerous Jewish burial places have again been discovered in Rome.

Furthermore, while trade was their chief occupation, not all the Jews living abroad were traders. Where many lived together, they also employed Jewish artisans; Jewish physicians are mentioned in inscriptions at Ephesus and Venosa.[34] Josephus even tells us of a Jewish court actor at Rome: "In Dikæarchia, or Puteoli, as the Italians call it, I made the acquaintance of the actor (μιμολόγος) Aliturus, who was of Jewish descent and a great favorite with Nero. I became acquainted through him with the Empress Poppæa." [35]

c. The Jewish Propaganda

Up to their exile, the people of Israel had not multiplied at an unusual rate, not more than other races. But from that time on it increased to a remarkable extent. The promise of Jehovah, alleged to have been already given to Abraham, now was fulfilled: "that in blessing I will bless thee, and in multiplying, I will multiply thy seed as the stars of the heaven, and as the sand which is upon the sea shore; and thy seed shall possess the gate of his enemies; and in thy seed shall all the nations of the earth be blessed." [36]

This promise, like practically all the other promises of the Bible, was not fabricated until the condition prophesied in it had already been realized—like the prophecies to which certain divinely favored heroes give utterance in modern historical dramas.

[33] Mommsen, *The Provinces of the Roman Empire*, 1886, vol. ii, pp. 171-172.
[34] Schürer, *Geschichte des jüdischen Volkes*, vol. iii, p. 90.
[35] Josephus, *Autobiography*.
[36] Genesis xxii, 17, 18.

Jehovah's promise to Abraham could not have been written until after the Exile, for the statement had no meaning before that period; but then it was beautifully appropriate. The Jews indeed did increase in numbers, establishing themselves in all the important cities of the Mediterranean world, "possessing the gates of their enemies", everywhere stimulating their trade and "blessing all the nations of the earth".

The geographer Strabo, who wrote about the time of the birth of Christ, says of the Jews: "This race has already come into every city and it is difficult to find a single spot of the inhabited earth which has not received this nation and is not ruled (financially) by it."

This rapid increase in the Jewish population should probably be attributed in part to their great fruitfulness. But even this fruitfulness may not be taken as a special *racial* trait—in that case it would have attracted attention from the earliest times—but rather a special trait of the *class* now chiefly represented by the Jews, the trading class.

Not only every form of society, but each class within the given society has its special law of population. The modern wage proletariat, for example, increases rapidly, by reason of the fact that the proletarians, female as well as male, become economically independent at an early age and have an opportunity to secure jobs for their children while still young; furthermore, the proletarian has no possessions to be divided, which might tempt him to limit the number of his children.

The law governing the increase in the population of settled farmers is variable. Wherever they find free soil, as is always the case when they are invading new country, hitherto occupied by hunters or shepherds, they multiply with great rapidity, for the conditions of their existence are much more favorable for the bringing up of their children than are, for example, the conditions of nomadic hunters with uncertain sources of food and the lack of all nourishment in the form of milk aside from mother's milk, a condition which forces the mothers to nurse their children for a number of years. The farmer produces an abundance of nourishment at regular intervals and the cattle raised by him also produce milk in plenty, more than the cattle of the nomad shepherds, which use up much of their strength in the search for pasture.

But the available land for agriculture is limited, and the limitations imposed by private property may become greater than those imposed by nature. And besides, the technical development of agriculture is for the most part very slow. Sooner or later therefore a nation of farmers will reach a point at which it no longer finds any new soil for the establishment of new homes and families. This forces the peasant, unless his excess posterity can be accommodated in another calling, for instance, military service or urban industry, to impose artificial limits upon the number of his children. Peasants faced by this situation are the ideals of the Malthusians.

But mere private property in land may have the same effect, even when not all the arable land has been tilled. The possession of land is now a source of power; the more land one owns, the more power and wealth one has in society. It now becomes the desire of landed proprietors to increase their possessions in land, and as the area of the country is fixed and not capable of expansion, real property can only be increased by combining already existing parcels. Inheritance laws may encourage or retard this process; they may encourage it by marriage, if both parties inherit land, which is then thrown together; they may retard it whenever a piece of land must be divided among several heirs. Therefore a point will be reached by the great landed proprietor, as well as by the peasant proprietor, at which he either will limit the number of his children, in order to maintain his property as large as possible, or disinherit all the children but one. Wherever the division of inheritance among all the children remains the rule, private property in land will sooner or later lead to a limitation of the number of children of land-owners, and under certain circumstances to a considerable decrease in this number. This is one of the reasons why the Roman Empire decreased in population, for the Empire was based essentially on agriculture.

In strong contrast with this was the fertility of the Jewish families. The Jews had just ceased to be a people chiefly en-

gaged in agriculture. The great majority of them were traders
and capitalists. But capital differs from land in that it may be
increased. When trade is flourishing it may increase more rapidly than the posterity of the traders; the latter may therefore be
increasing quite rapidly, while the wealth of each is still increasing. But it was just in the centuries beginning with the Exile
and extending into the early portion of the Imperial Era that a
notable increase in trade took place. The exploitation of the
workers engaged in agriculture—slaves, tenants, peasants—rapidly increased, while the area of this exploitation was extending.
The exploitation of the mines continued to increase until the supply of slaves ran low. This finally led, as we have seen, to the
decline of agriculture, to a depopulation of the provinces, and in
the long run to a weakening of the military power, involving also
a cessation of the supply of slaves, which was based on continuous successful wars, and therefore again to a decline in mining.
But it was a long time before these consequences made themselves felt, the accumulation of wealth in a few hands, and the
luxury of the rich increasing, while the population as a whole became impoverished. But trade then was chiefly a trade in luxuries. Transportation methods were as yet but little developed;
cheap consignments of great bulk were only beginning to be
possible. The trade which carried grain from Egypt to Italy
achieved some importance, but in general, articles of luxury remained the chief object of trade. While modern trade is concerned chiefly with the production and consumption of great
masses, it was formerly concerned rather with the arrogance and
extravagance of a small number of exploiters. While trade today
depends on the increase of the consumption of the masses, it
formerly depended on an increase in exploitation and wasteful-
ness. It never found more favorable conditions for the latter
than in the period beginning with the foundation of the Persian
Empire and ending with the time of the first Caesars. While the
shifting commercial routes imposed great hardship on Palestine,
it immensely stimulated trade in general from the Euphrates and
the Nile, to the Danube and the Rhine, from India to Britain.

Nations whose economic basis was that of agriculture might go down and lose in population; but a nation of merchants necessarily flourished and had no occasion to impose the slightest limit upon its natural increase in population.   Nor was there any external pressure serving to keep down this increase.

But no matter how high may be our estimate of the natural fruitfulness of the Jewish people, this fruitfulness alone would not be a sufficient explanation of their rapid increase.   This factor was greatly enhanced by the strength of the *propaganda* of Judaism.

The spectacle of a nation increasing its numbers by means of religious propaganda is as extraordinary as is the historical situation of the Jews itself.

Like other nations, the Israelites were kept together at first by ties of blood.   Under the kings, the gentile constitution replaced the territorial organization, the state and its districts. This tie ceased to be effective when the Jews were dragged into exile; the return to Jerusalem restored this tie only for a small fraction of the nation.   The greater and ever increasing section of the nation was living outside of the Jewish national state, abroad, not only temporarily as do the merchants of other nations, but permanently.   But this led to the loss of an additional bond of nationality, namely, the *common language*.   The Jews living abroad had to speak the foreign tongue, and if several generations had already been living abroad, the younger generations finally would be able to speak only the language of their native country, forgetting their mother tongue.   Greek particularly became very popular among them.   Already in the Third Century B.C., the sacred writings of the Jews were translated into Greek, probably for the reason that but few of the Alexandrian Jews still understood Hebrew, and possibly also for purposes of propaganda among the Greeks.   Greek became the language of the new Jewish literature, and even the language of the Jewish people living in Italy.   "The different (Jewish) communities in Rome had burial grounds in common, five of which are known. The inscriptions are *mainly in Greek,* some written in an almost

unintelligible jargon; some are in Latin, none in Hebrew." [37]
The Jews were not able to maintain the use of Hebrew even in
Palestine, where they adopted the language of the population sur-
rounding them, which was Aramaic.

Several centuries before the destruction of Jerusalem by the
Romans, Hebrew already ceased to be a living tongue. It no
longer served as a means of communication between the members
of the nation, but only as a means of access to the sacred writings
of antiquity, which were not really so many centuries or so many
thousands of years old as they were alleged to be, having been
recently pieced together from old remnants and new fabrications.

Their religion, alleged to have been revealed to the primitive
fathers of Israel, but actually constructed during and after the
period of exile, became, with their commercial activity, the strongest bond among the Jews, the only trait distinguishing them from
other nations.

But the single God of this religion was no longer one of many
ancestral gods as he had once been; he was now the sole God of
the world, a God of all men, whose commandments applied to all
men.   The Jews differed from all the others merely by the fact
that they had recognized him while the others in their blindness
had failed to do so.   The recognition of this God was now the
mark of Judaism: he who recognized him and his commandments
was among God's chosen, was a Jew.   Monotheism therefore
created the logical possibility of extending the limits of Judaism
by propagating this idea.   This possibility would perhaps not
have been utilized if it had not coincided with the tendency to expansion on the part of the Jews.   Their small numbers had
brought the deepest humiliation upon them; yet they had not been
destroyed.   They had survived the worst tribulations, had again
found a firm foothold, and were beginning to attain power and
wealth among the most varied surroundings.   This circumstance
inspired them with the proud confidence that they were really
the chosen people, really destined to rule the other nations.   But
great as was their faith in their God and in the Messiah whom

[37] Friedländer, *Roman Life and Manners under the Early Empire,* vol. iii,
p. 178.

their God would send, they nevertheless could not fail to recognize how hopeless was their situation as long as they remained so tiny a nation among the millions of pagans whose overwhelming superiority in numbers necessarily became the more evident to them as the circle of their commercial relations broadened. The stronger their desire for elevation and strength, the more diligently were they obliged to increase the number of their people, to find adherents among the foreign nations. We therefore find among the Jews in the centuries immediately preceding the destruction of Jerusalem a powerful tendency to expansion.

In the case of the inhabitants of the Jewish state, the simplest way of realizing this expansion was by means of conversion by force. It was not an unusual thing to conquer a people; whenever the Jews succeeded in this they attempted to force their religion upon it. This was done in the age of the Maccabees and their successors, extending approximately from 165 to 63 B.C., when the downfall of the Syrian Empire afforded the Jewish people a certain elbow-room for a time, which they utilized not only to shake off the Syrian yoke, but also to expand their own territory. Galilee, which had not been Jewish before, was conquered at this period, as Schürer has shown.[38] Idumea and the land to the east of the Jordan were subjected, and a foothold was even gained on the coast, in Jaffa. Such a policy of conquest was not unusual; but it was quite unusual for such a policy to develop into one of *religious* expansion. The inhabitants of the newly conquered regions had to accept as their own the God who was worshiped in the Temple at Jerusalem, had to make pilgrimages to Jerusalem to worship him, had to pay temple taxes to Jerusalem, had to become distinct from other nations by the practice of circumcision and the observance of the peculiar Jewish ritual laws.

Such a procedure was absolutely unknown in the ancient world, in which the conqueror usually allowed full religious and moral freedom to the conquered and demanded from the latter only his tribute in wealth and blood.

This form of Jewish expansion was possible only for a time,

[38] *Geschichte des jüdischen Volkes*, vol. ii, p. 5.

however, while the power of the Syrians was too slight, and that of the Romans not yet close enough to menace the military progress of Judea. Even before Pompey had occupied Jerusalem (63 B.C.) the advance of the Jews in Palestine had already come to a standstill. The expansion of the Jewish religious community by means of force was then effectively stopped by the superior power of the Romans.

From this time on the Jews resorted with all the more energy to the other method of increasing the numbers of their believers, that of peaceful *propaganda*. The latter was also an exceptional phenomenon in its day. Earlier than Christianity, Judaism developed the same degree of proselytizing zeal as the former, and met with considerable success. It was quite natural, although of course not very logical, that the Christians should censure the Jews for this zeal which they themselves were developing in such active proportions for their own religion:

"But woe unto you, scribes and Pharisees, hypocrites!" The Gospel lays these words in the mouth of Jesus, "for ye compass sea and land to make one proselyte, and when he is made ye make him twofold more the child of hell than yourselves". (Matthew xxiii, 15.)

Such were the Christian tones in which the zeal of competition expressed itself.

Material interest alone must have led a number of adherents from "pagan" surroundings to the Jews. To be members of so widely ramified and prosperous a commercial organization was a prospect that must have been enticing to not a few. No matter where a Jew came, he could count on energetic support and encouragement at the hands of his fellow-believers.

Other causes also contributed to the strength of the Jews in propaganda. We have seen above how a certain favorable attitude toward ethical monotheism is bred by a certain stage in the development of town life. But the monotheism of the philosophers was in opposition to the traditional religion, or at least outside its sphere. This monotheism demanded independence of thought. But the same social development that favored the monotheistic idea also led, as we have seen, to a disintegration of state and society, to an increasing isolation of the individual, to a rising need for a firm authority; in the attitude towards life, it therefore led not to philosophy, which makes the individual dependent on himself, but to religion, which approaches the individual as a finished and fixed product of some superhuman authority.

Only two of the nations of ancient civilization, the Persians and the Jews, owing to special conditions, had come to monotheism not as a philosophy but as a religion. The religions of both made considerable advances among the nations of the Hellenic world and later of the Roman Empire. But owing to their sad position as a people, the Jews were moved to a great zeal in proselytizing, and in Alexandria they came into close contact with Greek philosophy.

The Jews were thus enabled to offer the most acceptable pabulum to the minds of the declining ancient world, which doubted their own traditional gods, but did not have sufficient energy to create a view of life without a god or with one god only, the more since the Jews combined with their belief in a single primitive ethical force also a belief in the coming of the Redeemer for whom the entire world was then longing.

Among the many religions that met in the Roman Empire, the Jewish religion was that which best answered the thought and the wants of the epoch; it was superior not to the philosophy of the "pagans", but to their religions—it is hardly to be wondered at that the Jews felt proudly superior to the latter, and that the number of their adherents should grow rapidly. "All men," said the Alexandrian Jew Philo, "are being conquered by Judaism and admonished to virtue; barbarians, Hellenes, dwellers on continents and islands, the nations of the East and of the West, Europeans, Asiatics, the races of the earth." He expected that Judaism would become the religion of the world; and this was in the time of Christ.[39]

We have already pointed out that as early as 139 B.C. Jews were deported from Rome because they had made proselytes in Italy. It is reported from Antioch that the majority of the

[39] Compare the Book of Tobit, xiv, 6, 7.

Jewish congregation in that town consisted of converted Jews, not of Jews by birth. Conditions must have been similar in many other places. This fact alone shows the absurdity of the effort to explain the traits of the Jews on the basis of their race.

Even kings became converted to Judaism: Izates, king of the district of Adiabene in Assyria, was induced to embrace Judaism by several women who had been converted to that faith, which had been taken also by his mother Helena. Zeal caused him to go so far as to be circumcised, although even his Jewish teacher had counseled against this, as unnecessarily endangering his status. The king's brothers also became Jews; this was in the time of Tiberius and Claudius.

Beautiful Jewesses brought quite a number of other kings into the arms of Judaism.

Thus, King Aziz, of Emesa, was converted to Judaism in order to marry Drusilla, the sister of Agrippa II. This lady later rewarded his devotion rather shabbily by deserting her royal lord for a Roman Procurator named Felix. Her sister Berenice, for whose sake King Polemon had himself circumcised, did no better. In fact Polemon became disgusted, because of his wife's lewdness, not only with the wife, but also with her religion. But Madame Berenice, being accustomed to changes of men, was not at a loss for consolation. At first she had married a Marcus, and after his death her uncle Herod. After he too had died she lived with her brother Agrippa, until her marriage with the above-mentioned Polemon. Finally, however, she was advanced to the dignity of mistress of the Emperor Titus.

While this lady was faithless to her people, there were many others who embraced Judaism, which had a certain fascination for them. Among them was Nero's wife, Poppæa Sabina, of whom we are told that she became a zealous Jewess, which did not, however, improve her moral conduct.

Josephus relates of the inhabitants of the city of Damascus that they had intended, on the occasion of the Jewish insurrection under Nero, to wipe out the Jews who lived in the city. "They were afraid only of their wives, for *almost every one of these was of the Jewish faith.* They therefore kept their plan secret from the latter, and it was successful. They murdered 10,000 Jews in a single hour." [40]

The forms by which conversion to Judaism was declared varied considerably. The most zealous of the new converts accepted it in its entirety. Their admission was based on three requirements; in the first place, circumcision; second, an immersion in order to purify them from pagan sinfulness; finally, a sacrifice. Women were, of course, exempt from the first requirement.

But not all converts could bring themselves to obey all the rules of Jewish law without exception. We have seen that Judaism was full of contradictions, that it included on the one hand a highly enlightened international monotheism, and on the other an extremely narrow-minded tribal monotheism, thus uniting pure ethics with a timid retention of traditional customs, and therefore embracing not only ideas which appeared extremely modern and sublime to the people of that age, but also conceptions which must have seemed very strange and even repulsive, particularly to a Hellene or a Roman, and which therefore made social intercourse between the members of the Jewish community and non-Jews infinitely difficult. Among these were, for example, the dietary laws, the circumcision, and the strict observance of the Sabbath, the latter often going to ridiculous extremes.

We learn from Juvenal that the fireless cooker, now considered an extremely modern invention in housekeeping, was already known to the ancient Jews. On the eve of the Sabbath they placed their victuals in baskets filled with hay, in order to keep them warm. Such a basket is said to have been lacking in no Jewish household. This is an indication of the inconveniences involved in a strict observance of the Sabbath. But this observance was sometimes carried so far as to become disastrous to the Jews. Pious Jewish warriors, who were attacked by the enemy on the Sabbath, would neither defend themselves nor take to flight, but consented to be cut down without resistance, in order not to transgress God's commandments.

Not many were capable of such fanaticism and faith in God.

[40] *Jewish War*, ii, 20, 2.

But even a less stringent enforcement of the Jewish law was not to everyone's taste. We therefore find, together with those who entered the Jewish congregation and accepted all the consequences of the Jewish law, a number who took part in the Jewish divine service and attended the synagogues, but rejected the Jewish regulations. Outside of Palestine there were even many among the Jews themselves who did not set great store by these rules. They contented themselves in many cases with worshiping the true God and believing in the coming of the Messiah, dispensing with circumcision and were satisfied to have the newly won friend of the congregation cleanse himself of his sins by immersion (baptism). These "pious" (*sebomenoi*) comrades of Judaism probably constituted the majority of those pagans who embraced the faith. They probably also constituted the most important recruiting ground for the Christian congregation when the latter began to operate outside of Jerusalem.

d. Hatred of the Jews

Great as was the propaganda power of Judaism, it evidently did not have quite the same effect on all classes. Many must have been repelled by Judaism, particularly the great landed proprietors, whose permanent habit of domicile and whose local narrow-mindedness were most opposed to the restlessness and the international character of the merchant. Furthermore, the merchant made a portion of his profit at the expense of the landowner, for the merchant would try to reduce as far as possible the price of the product sold by the landowner, and to screw up as high as possible the prices of those products purchased from him by the landowner. The great landowners have always been on excellent terms with usurious capital; we have seen that they derive much of their strength from usury at an early period. But the landowners were, as a rule, hostile to trade.

However, the industrial employees working for the export trade were in a relation of hostility to the merchant, similar to that of the domestic workers today toward their jobbers.

This opposition to trade took the form chiefly of an opposition to the Jews, who so firmly clung to their nationality and who, the

less their language served to distinguish them from their surroundings, remained the more firmly attached to the traditional
national customs, which were now most intimately fused with the
national bond, religion, and which made the Jews the objects of
such intense interest to the mass of the population outside of
Palestine.   While these peculiarities in most cases called forth
only the derision of the mob, like everything that is foreign, they
were regarded with hostility whenever they were felt to represent
a class living on exploitation, which is the case with all merchants,
and which at the same time was cemented together in a close
international organization as opposed to the remainder of the
population, and was increasing in wealth and privileges while
the rest of the population were becoming visibly poorer and endowed with less and less rights.

We may learn from Tacitus what was the impression made by
Judaism on other peoples; he says:

"New religious customs were introduced by Moses, which are
opposed to those of other mortals.   Among them everything is
profane that to us is holy; and everything is permitted among
them that is abhorrent to us."   Among such usages he mentions
the abstinence from pork, the frequent fasts, the Sabbath.

"They defend these religious customs, whatever may have been
their origin, on the ground of their great antiquity.   Other repulsive and abhorrent customs came into force by reason of their
wickedness; for thus they brought it about that the worst persons
became faithless to the religion of their fathers and brought them
contributions and gifts: thus the wealth of the Jews increased.
Which is also due to the fact that among themselves the most
stringent honesty and a most solicitous charity prevail, combined
with a hateful hostility to all others.   They segregate themselves
from the latter in their meals, they refrain from cohabiting with
women of other faiths, but among themselves there is nothing
that is not permitted.   They introduced circumcision as a means
of distinguishing themselves from others.   Those joining their
ranks also accept circumcision, and are filled with nothing but
contempt for the gods, renunciation of their fatherland, disre-
spect for parents, children and brothers, and they are constantly

attempting to increase their numbers, and to kill one's posterity appears to them as a crime. The souls of those killed in battle, or executed because of their religion, are considered by them as immortal; thence their tendency to beget children and their contempt for death."

Tacitus then discusses their rejection of all worship of images and concludes: "The customs of the Jews are senseless and sordid (*Judæorum mos absurdus sordidusque*)." [41]

The satirists derided the Jews; jokes about Jews always found an eager public.

In his Fourteenth Satire, Juvenal depicts the effects of a parent's example on the children. A father who has a tendency toward Judaism sets a bad example for his children:

"You will find men whose fate it is to have a father that keeps holy the Sabbath. Such people pray only to the clouds and to a god in Heaven. They believe that the flesh of pigs is not different from human flesh, because their father did not eat pigs' flesh. Soon they part with their foreskins and despise the laws of the Romans. But they learn, and obey, and honor the Jewish laws, everything, in short, that Moses handed down in his secret scrolls. They will not show the way to one who has lost it except to worshipers of the same faith, they will lead only the circumcised (*verpos*) to the spring for which the thirsty languish. Such is the influence of a father for whom every seventh day was a day of rest (*ignavus*), on which he refrained from any expression of life." [42]

With the increase of the general social misery, the hostility to the Jews also increased.

This hostility was at that early day already the simplest and least heroic method of expressing dissatisfaction with the decline of state and society. It was not an easy matter to attack the aristocrats and owners of latifundia, the usurers and generals, or even the despots on the throne; but the Jews were almost defenseless as far as the state power was concerned, in spite of their privileges.

In the early days of the Imperial Era, when the impoverish-

---

[41] *Histories*, v, 5.   [42] *Satires*, xiv, 96-105.

ment of the peasantry had already progressed very far, and a very numerous rabble was accumulating in the cities, eager for plunder, regular pogroms were occasionally resorted to.

Mommsen has an excellent description of one of these pogroms, which took place under the Emperor Gaius Caligula (37-41 A.D.), in other words, at about the time in which Christ is said to have died.

"A grandson of Herod I and the beautiful Mariamne, named Herod Agrippa, after the protector and friend of his grandfather, and who was probably the most worthless and good-for-nothing of the numerous sons of princes living in Rome, but who nevertheless, or perhaps for that very reason, was the favorite and the childhood friend of the new emperor, and who had until then been known only for his lewdness and his debts, had received as a present from his protector whom he was so fortunate as to notify first of the death of Tiberius, one of the vacant petty Jewish principalities, with the royal title into the bargain. Herod Agrippa in the year 38 A.D., on his journey to his new kingdom, arrived at the city of Alexandria, where he had tried a few months before, having run away from the payment of his due notes, to borrow money from Jewish bankers. When he appeared in public in Alexandria in his royal garments, and with his splendidly equipped halberdiers, he naturally inspired the non-Jewish inhabitants of this great city—fond as it was of ridicule and of scandal—and far from friendly to the Jews, to indulge in a parody on the situation, nor did the matter stop there. It culminated in a furious hunting-out of the Jews. Those dwellings of the Jews which were not close together were robbed and burned, Jewish ships in port were plundered, Jews found in non-Jewish quarters were maltreated and slain. But it was impossible to effect anything by violence against the purely Jewish quarters of the city. The leaders of the persecution then hit upon the plan of consecrating the synagogues, to which they were devoting most of their attention, unless they had already been destroyed, as temples of the new ruler and to set up images of the latter in all of them, in the chief synagogue a statue on a quadriga. Everybody, including also the Jews and the government, knew that Emperor

Gaius considered himself seriously—as seriously as his confused spirit would permit—to be a true god in the flesh. The Governor Avilius Flaccus, an able man and an excellent administrator under Tiberius, but now handicapped by the disfavor in which he stood with the new emperor, and fearing to be recalled and indicted at any moment, did not disdain to utilize this occasion for his re-habilitation. He not only issued an edict forbidding the offering of resistance to the erection of these statues in the synagogues, but even entered into the spirit of the pogrom. He ordered that the Sabbath be abolished, he declared further in his edicts that these tolerated strangers had taken possession without permission of the best portions of the city; they were now assigned to a single one of the five quarters, and all other houses belonging to Jews were handed over to the rabble, while their former in-habitants lay without shelter on the strand in great numbers. No supplication was even listened to; thirty-eight members of the Council of Elders, which ruled the Jewish community at the time instead of the *Ethnarch*, were flogged in the open Circus before the entire population. Four hundred houses lay in ruins; trade and traffic were at a standstill; the factories were closed. No one could give assistance but the emperor. Two Alexandrian delegations appeared before him, that of the Jews led by the above-mentioned Philo, a scholar of the Neo-Judaic tendency, with more gentleness than valor in his heart, but who nevertheless bravely interceded for his people in this difficult moment; that of the anti-Jews led by Apion, also an Alexandrian scholar and writer, the 'world's clapper' (*cymbalum mundi*), as Emperor Tiberius was wont to call him, full of great words and greater lies, of the most impudent ignorance and unquestioning faith in himself, with knowledge if not of men, at least of their baseness, a celebrated master of eloquence as well as of demagogy, quick-witted, sharp, shameless, and unconditionally loyal. The result of the transaction might have been expected in advance; the emperor admitted the two parties while he was going through the grounds of his gardens, but instead of giving the supplicants a hearing, he put derisive questions to them, which were greeted by the anti-Jews in defiance of all etiquette with loud laughter, ànd since he was in good humor he contented himself with an expression of his regret that these people, otherwise good fellows, should be so unhappily constituted as not to be able to grasp his innate divine nature, which he no doubt meant seriously. Apion thus had the best of the argument, and in all places where the anti-Jews felt so disposed the synagogues were transformed into temples to Gaius." [43]

Is there anyone who is not reminded by this description of present-day conditions in Russia? [44] And the similarity is not limited to the pogroms. We cannot mention Gaius, the insane beast on the imperial throne, without thinking of the high-born protectors of the pogroms in Russia. These rascals are not even original in their methods!

In Rome itself the available military power was too great, and the emperors were too strongly opposed to any popular movement, to permit any such scenes to take place in that city, but since the imperial power had been solidified, and the Caesars no longer needed the Jews, they oppressed them. In view of the distrust which the Caesars had for all organizations, even the most innocent ones, this international religious organization must have impressed them very unfavorably.

Persecutions of the Jews already began under Tiberius. Josephus describes their cause as follows: "In Rome there was a Jew, an exceedingly godless man, who had been accused of many offenses in his native country, and had become a fugitive to escape the penalty. This man set himself up to be a teacher of the Mosaic Law, and together with three confederates persuaded Fulvia, an aristocratic lady who had accepted the Jewish faith, and had put herself under his instruction, to forward a present consisting of gold and purple to the Temple in Jerusalem. Having received this present from the lady they used it for themselves, for no other had been their purpose. Saturninus, Fulvia's husband, complained of this to his friend, the Emperor Tiberius, at her request, and Tiberius immediately ordered all Jews to be

[43] *The Provinces of the Roman Empire,* vol. ii, pp. 191-194.
[44] Kautsky was writing in 1908.—TRANSLATOR.

banished from Rome. Four thousand Jews were made soldiers and sent to Sardinia." [45]

This story is typical of the tendency of distinguished ladies in Roman court society to embrace Judaism. If this incident served as the occasion for such severe measures against the entire Jewry of Rome, it surely could not have been the real reason for them. It would have been sufficient to punish the guilty, unless strong hostility was felt for the entire Jewish community. No less hostile was Gaius Caligula, as we have seen above. Under Claudius (41-54 A.D.) the Jews were again driven out of Rome because, as Suetonius (*Claudius,* chap. xxv) reports, they aroused disturbances under the leadership of a certain Chrestos. The latter was not a Jew by birth, but a Greek converted to Judaism. This incident again serves as an illustration both of the hatred for the Jews as well as of the strength of the Jewish propaganda.

e. *Jerusalem*

It is manifest that such an attitude toward the Jews on the part of the ruling classes as well as of the people themselves must have made the Jews look longingly toward Jerusalem and its country environment, the only corner of the earth in which they were at least in a measure masters of their own houses, in which the entire population consisted of Jews, the only corner whence the promised great empire of the Jews was to emanate, and where the longed-for Messiah would establish the dominion of Judaism. And this, in spite of the increasing impossibility of finding sufficient means of subsistence in their home country.

Jerusalem remained the center, remained the capital of Judaism, growing with the growth of the latter. It again became a wealthy city, a city of about 200,000 inhabitants, but it no longer based its greatness and its wealth on the warlike power or the trade of the peoples of Palestine, as it had under David and Solomon, but only on the Temple of Jehovah. Every Jew, no matter where he might live, had to contribute to its maintenance, for which purpose he was obliged to pay annually a Temple tax of one double drachma, which was sent to Jerusalem.

[45] *Antiquities,* xviii, 3, 8.

In addition, the sanctuary received many other extraordinary gifts. Not every such gift was made away with like the valuable consideration which the four Jewish swindlers took from Fulvia, according to Josephus. But besides this, each pious Jew was obliged at least once in his life to make a pilgrimage to the place in which his God dwelt and which was the only place where the God received these offerings. The synagogues of the Jews in the various cities outside of Jerusalem were only places of gathering and prayer, as well as schools, but not temples in which offerings might be made to Jehovah.

The Temple taxes and the pilgrims necessarily brought immense sums of money to Jerusalem and kept a large number of persons profitably occupied. Directly or indirectly, not only the priests of the Temple and the scribes lived on the worship of Jehovah, but even the shopkeepers and money changers, the artisans, the farmers, peasants, the cattle-breeders, the fishermen of Judea and Galilee, who found an excellent market in Jerusalem for their wheat and honey, for their lambs. and kids, as well as for the fish that were caught on the seacoast and in Lake Gennesareth, and sent dried or salted to Jerusalem. When Jesus found buyers and sellers in the Temple, money-changers and pigeon-dealers, this was fully in accord with the task that had devolved upon the Temple for Jerusalem.

What had been represented in Jewish literature as the condition of the oldest ancestors, was actually true of the period in which this literature was produced: the entire Jewish population of Palestine now lived literally on the worship of Jehovah, and was threatened with destruction as soon as this worship should subside, or even assume different forms. There was no lack of attempts to establish other places for the worship of Jehovah, outside of Jerusalem.

Thus a certain Onias, the son of a Jewish high priest, erected a temple to Jehovah in Egypt under Ptolemy Philometor (173-146 B.C.), with the assistance of the king, who expected that the Egyptian Jews would be his more faithful subjects if they had a temple of their own in his country.

But the new temple did not attain any significance; possibly just for the reason that its object was to secure the Jews of Egypt as faithful subjects. In Egypt they continued to remain strangers, a tolerated minority: how could their Messiah come from Egypt, who was to bring independence and national greatness to their people? But the faith in the Messiah was one of the strongest motive forces in the worship of Jehovah.

Far more inconvenient was a competitive temple not far from Jerusalem on Mt. Garrizim near Sikhem, which had been built by the Samaritan sect, as Josephus reports, in the time of Alexander the Great—according to Schürer, a century earlier—and where the sect carried on its worship of Jehovah. It is not surprising that the most acute hostility arose between these two competitors. But the old established business was too rich and enjoyed too high a reputation to be much injured by the younger enterprise. In spite of all the propaganda of the Samaritans, they did not increase as rapidly as did the Jews, who considered that their Lord dwelt in Jerusalem.

But the more the monopoly at Jerusalem was menaced, the more seriously did its inhabitants watch over the "purity" of their worship, and the more fanatically did they oppose any effort to alter anything about it, or to go so far as impose an alteration upon it by force. Thence the religious fanaticism and the religious intolerance of the Jews of Jerusalem, which are in such curious contrast with the religious liberality of the other nations of that time. The other nations regarded their gods as means of explaining incomprehensible phenomena, also as a means of consolation and aid in situations in which human strength seemed insufficient. But the Jews of Palestine regarded their God as the means by which they lived. They all now had the attitude toward God which is usually the attitude of his priests only. Priestly fanaticism in Palestine became a fanaticism of the entire population.

But although this population was united in defense of the worship of Jehovah, although it opposed as one man anyone who would dare violate it, the class distinctions nevertheless made themselves felt; not even Jerusalem was spared them. Every class sought to please Jehovah and to protect his Temple in some other way. And every class was waiting, in its own fashion, for the Messiah that was to come.

f. The Sadducees

Josephus reports in the Eighth Chapter of the Second Book of his *History of the Jewish War*, that there are three intellectual currents among the Jews; the Pharisees, the Sadducees, and the Essenes. Concerning the former two he goes on to say:

"As for the two other sects, it is believed that the *Pharisees* interpret the law the more severely. They were the first who formed a sect that believed that everything is determined by Fate and by God. In their opinion it may indeed depend on man whether he performs good or evil, but Fate has its influence on man's actions. They believe, concerning the soul of man, that it is immortal, and that the souls of the good will enter into new bodies, while those of the wicked will be tormented by eternal suffering.

"The other sect is that of the *Sadducees*. They deny that Fate has any influence at all and declare that God may not be blamed for the good or evil actions of the individual; man alone is responsible for these, as he may perform good actions and refrain from evil actions, in accordance with his own free will. They also deny that souls are immortal and that there is to be any reward or punishment after death.

"The Pharisees are charitable and try to live in concord with the masses of the people. The Sadducees, on the other hand, are cruel even to each other, and severe both with regard to their fellow-countrymen as well as toward strangers."

These sects are here represented as embodying certain religious views. But although Jewish history has thus far been studied almost exclusively by theologians to whom religion is everything while class oppositions count for nothing, even these historians have discovered that the contrast between the Sadducees and the Pharisees was not at bottom a religious one, but a class opposition, a hostility that can be compared with that between the nobility and the Third Estate before the French Revolution.

The Sadducees were the representatives of the priestly nobility, which had gained control of the Jewish State, and exercised this control, first under Persian domination, later under that of the successors of Alexander the Great. This priesthood was absolute master of the Temple. Through its control of the Temple it ruled Jerusalem and all of Judaism besides. To the priesthood came all the taxes that were paid to the Temple, and they were by no means inconsiderable. Up to the banishment, of course, the receipts of the priesthood had been modest and irregular, but from this time on they increased tremendously. We have already mentioned the double drachma tax (or the half-shekel, equivalent to about forty cents in American money) which every male Jew, rich or poor, who was over two years of age, had to pay annually to the Temple; we have also mentioned the presents flowing into the Temple. We shall give only a few examples to indicate the amounts received by the Temple. Mithridates on one occasion confiscated eight hundred talents on the Island of Kos, which were destined for the Temple.[46]

Cicero says in the oration delivered in 59 B.C. in defense of Flaccus, who had been Governor of the Province of Asia two years before: "Since the money of the Jews passes out of Italy and all the provinces each year in order to be forwarded to Jerusalem, Flaccus ordered that no money should be forwarded (to Jerusalem) from the province of Asia (Western Asia Minor)." Cicero further relates that Flaccus confiscated funds that had been gathered in various towns in Asia Minor, destined for the Temple; in Appamea alone he confiscated one hundred pounds of gold.

In addition, there were the sacrifices. Formerly those making offerings had themselves consumed the sacrifices in a merry feast, in which the priest might only participate. But after the Exile the share of those making sacrifices is limited more and more, while that of the priests increases. Having been a contribution to a merry banquet, consumed by the givers themselves in pleasant company, to be a delight not only to God but also to man, this gift becomes a mere tax in kind, demanded by God for him-

[46] Josephus, *Antiquities*, xiv, 7; one talent—$1,100.

self, *i.e.*, for his priests. And the amount of these taxes increased more and more. Not only did the offerings in animals and other foodstuffs now belong more and more exclusively to the priests but there were added the payment of the tithes (the tenth part) of all agricultural products, as well as the payment of the first-born of every animal. The first-born of "clean" animals, cattle, sheep, goats, in other words, such animals as were eaten, was to be paid in kind in the House of God. "Unclean" animals, horses, asses, camels, could be replaced by money, as was also the case with the first-born human male. The charge for the latter was five shekels.

This gives us a good idea of how much the Jewish priesthood obtained from the people, and these quantities were increased later; thus the third part of a shekel was soon raised to half a shekel, as indicated in Nehemiah x, 32-39:

"Also we made ordinances for us, to charge ourselves yearly with the third part of a shekel for the service of the house of our God. . . . And we cast the lots among the priests, the Levites, and the people, for the wood-offering, to bring it to the house of our God, after the houses of our fathers, at times appointed year by year, to burn upon the altar of the Lord our God, as it is written in the law: and to bring the firstfruits of our ground, and the firstfruits of all fruit of all trees, year by year, unto the house of the Lord: also the firstborn of our sons, and of our cattle, as it is written in the law, and the firstlings of our herds and of our flocks, to bring to the house of our God, unto the priests that minister in the house of our God: and that we should bring the firstfruits of our dough, and our offerings, and the fruit of all manner of trees, of wine and of oil, unto the priests, to the chambers of the house of our God: and the tithes of our ground unto the Levites, that the same Levites might have the tithes in all the cities of our tillage. And the priest the son of Aaron shall be with the Levites, when the Levites take tithes: and the Levites shall bring up the tithe of the tithes unto the house of our God, to the chambers, into the treasure house. For the children of Israel and the children of Levi shall bring the offering of the corn, of the new wine, and the oil, unto the chambers, where are the vessels of the sanctuary, and the priests that minister, and the porters, and the singers: and we will not forsake the house of our God."

It is evident that this temple was not exactly comparable to a church edifice. It included immense storehouses, in which there were great stores of natural products, and also of gold and silver. Accordingly it had to be strongly fortified and well guarded. Like the pagan temples it was considered to be a place in which money and property were particularly well safeguarded. Like them, therefore, it was very often used even by private persons as a place in which to deposit their treasures. Jehovah probably did not undertake without recompense to carry out this function of a bank of deposit.

However that may be, it is certain that the wealth of the Jerusalem priesthood increased tremendously.

Marcus Crassus, Caesar's fellow-conspirator, whose acquaintance we have already made, took advantage of this condition when undertaking his predatory expedition against the Parthians. On his journey, he called at Jerusalem and pocketed the treasures of the Jewish Temple.

"When Crassus was about to set forth against the Parthians, he came to Judea and took all the money (χρήματα) from the Temple, which Pompey had left intact, two thousand talents, as well as all the (uncoined) gold, amounting to eight thousand talents. In addition, he robbed a bar of gold weighing three hundred minæ; but a mina with us weighs two and one-half pounds." [47]

This amounts to about twelve million dollars altogether; and yet the Temple was soon filled with gold again.

Membership in the priesthood was limited to certain families. They constituted an aristocracy by birth, among whom this office was hereditary. According to Josephus, who refers to Hecatæus (*Polemic against Apion*, I, 22), "there are fifteen hundred Jewish priests, who receive tithes and administer the community."

Among this priesthood a division gradually ensued between a higher and a lower aristocracy. Certain families managed to

[47] Josephus, *Antiquities*, xiv, 7.

arrogate the entire authority of government permanently to themselves, and thus increased their wealth, which in turn meant a further increase of influence. They constituted a firmly coherent clique which always appointed the High Priest out of its own ranks. They consolidated their power by hiring mercenaries and defending their authority against the other priests, whom they succeeded in relegating to a lower position.

Thus Josephus reports: "About this time King Agrippa bestowed the High Priesthood on Ishmael, Phabi's son. But the High Priests came into conflict with the priests and elders of the people in Jerusalem. Each of them surrounded himself with a gang of the most lawless and troublesome persons, becoming their leader. They occasionally had wordy conflicts, in which they vituperated each other and threw stones at each other. No one was able to stop them, their actions were of such violence that it seemed there was no authority in the town at all. The High Priests finally became so audacious that they did not hesitate to send their soldiers into the granaries, in order to take away the tithes belonging to the priests, so that a few impoverished priests starved to death." [48]

Of course conditions did not become as bad as this until the last stages of the Jewish community had been reached.

But from its very beginning, the priestly aristocracy had exalted itself above the masses of the people and become imbued with views and inclinations opposed to those of the people, particularly those of the Jewish population of Palestine. This became particularly apparent in their foreign policy.

We have seen that Palestine, owing to its geographical position, was constantly subject to foreign rule or at least to the danger of foreign rule. There were two ways in which this condition could have been resisted or at least attenuated: diplomacy, or insurrection by force.

While the Persian Empire still existed, neither of these methods gave promise of any success, but the situation became quite different after Alexander had destroyed this empire. The new form of state which he put in its place disintegrated after his death

[48] Josephus, *Jewish Antiquities,* xx, 8, 8, cf. also 9, 2.

and again we find a Syrian-Babylonian Empire struggling against an Egyptian Empire for dominion over Israel. But now both were ruled by Greek dynasties, one by the Seleukides, the other by the Ptolemies, and both became more and more imbued with the Greek spirit.

It seemed futile to attempt to defeat either of these powers by military means; but it was all the more possible to make gains through astute diplomacy, by joining forces with the stronger and thus achieving a privileged position as a portion of the latter's empire. But owing to the hatred for foreigners and a rejection of the superior Greek civilization and its instruments of power, this was not done; furthermore, it would have been necessary to absorb this civilization.

The aristocracy at Jerusalem was being impelled in the direction of accepting the Greek culture, owing to their better knowledge of things foreign, which was an advantage given them by their social position as compared with the mass of the population; but their wealth also impelled them in this direction. The reproductive arts, as well as the arts of enjoyment, had not flourished in Palestine; but the Greeks had brought these arts to a level that was above anything achieved in any country at that time or for many, many centuries thereafter. The ruling classes of all nations, even of victorious Rome, were borrowing the forms of splendor and of the enjoyment of life from Greece. The Greek forms were adopted by all exploiting classes in the ancient world, just as the French forms were adopted in the Eighteenth Century by all European exploiters.

As the exploitation of the Jews by their aristocracy increased, and with the rising wealth of the latter, this aristocracy became more eager for Hellenic culture.

Thus, the First Book of the Maccabees laments concerning the period of Antiochus Epiphanes (175-164 B.C.):

"In those days worthless persons originated in Israel; these persuaded many, by saying: Why not let us fraternize with the nations that are round about! for much misery has befallen us since we have cut ourselves off from them! Such speech pleased them well, and some of the people declared themselves ready to go to the king, who gave them authority to introduce the customs of the pagans. Therefore, they built at Jerusalem a gymnasium (in other words, an arena in which naked wrestlers appeared) according to the custom of the pagans, restored their prepuces and thus became traitors to the sacred covenant, and also united themselves with the pagans, and sold themselves to do evil."

So evil were these wicked persons, who made themselves artificial foreskins, that they even denied their Jewish names, replacing them by Greek names. A High Priest named Jesus called himself Jason, another High Priest named Eliochim called himself Alkimos; a Menassah renamed himself Menelaus.

But the masses of the Jewish people were offended by this encouragement of foreign Hellenic ways. We have several times pointed out how slight was the development of industry and art in Judea. The advance of the Hellenic influence meant the introduction of foreign products to replace domestic products. But the Hellene always came as an oppressor and exploiter, whether he was king of Syria or king of Egypt. Judea, already drained dry by its aristocracy, naturally felt the tributes to be a greater burden that had now to be paid to the foreign monarchs and their officials. And as a rule the aristocrats managed to shield themselves by having themselves appointed as representatives and tax collectors for the foreign masters; furthermore, they were able to enrich themselves by applying usurious practices to those oppressed by the taxes. But the people felt only the burden of foreign rule.

This had already taken place under Persian rule, as is very neatly described in an account given by the Jew Nehemiah, who had been appointed by King Artaxerxes to be his governor in Judea (445 B.C.). He gives us the following record of his own activities:

"And there was a great cry of the people and of their wives against their brethren the Jews. For there were that said: We, our sons, and our daughters, are many: therefore we take up corn for them, that we may eat, and live. Some also there were that said: We have mortgaged our lands, vineyards, houses, that we may buy corn, because of the dearth. There were also that said: We have borrowed money for the king's tribute, and that upon our lands and vineyards. Yet now our flesh is as the flesh of our brethren, our children as their children, and, lo, we bring into bondage our sons and our daughters to be servants, and some of our daughters are brought into bondage already: neither is it in our power to redeem them; for other men have our lands and vineyards.

"And I was very angry when I heard their cry and these words. Then I consulted with myself and I rebuked the nobles, and the rulers, and said unto them: Ye execute usury, everyone of his brother. And I set a great assembly against them. And I said unto them: We after our ability have redeemed our brethren the Jews, which were sold unto the heathen; and will ye even sell your brethren? or shall they be sold unto us. Then held they their peace and found nothing to answer. Also I said: It is not good that ye do; ought ye not to walk in the fear of our God because of the reproach of the heathen our enemies? I likewise, and my brethren, and my servants, might exact of them money and grain: I pray you, let us leave off this usury. Restore, I pray you, to them, even this day, their lands, their vineyards, their oliveyards, and their houses, also the hundredth part of the money, and of the corn, the wine, and the oil, that ye exact of them. Then said they: We will restore them, and will require nothing of them: so will we do as thou sayest. Then I called the priests and took an oath of them, that they should do according to this promise. Also I shook my lap and said: So God shake out every man from his house, and from his labor, that performeth not this promise, even thus be he shaken out, and emptied. And all the congregation said, Amen, and praised the Lord. And the people did according to this promise.

"Moreover, in the time that I was appointed to be their Governor in the land of Judah, from the twentieth year even unto the two and thirtieth year of Artaxerxes the King, that is, twelve years, I and my brethren have not eaten the bread of the governor. But the former governors that had been before me were chargeable unto the people, and had taken of them bread and wine, besides forty shekels of silver; yea, even their servants bare rule over the people: but so did not I, because of the fear of God. Yea, also I continued in the work of this wall (*the city walls of Jerusalem*), neither bought we new land: and all my servants were gathered thither unto the work. Moreover, there were at my table an hundred and fifty of the Jews and rulers, besides those that came unto us from among the heathen that are about us. Now that which was prepared for me daily was one ox and six choice sheep; also fowls were prepared for me, and once in ten days store of all sorts of wine; yet for all this required not I the bread of the governor, because the bondage was heavy upon this people. Think upon me, my God, for good, according to all that I have done for this people." [49]

Such self-praise is not unusual in ancient documents, particularly in the Orient. But it would be going too far if we should always assume that the official in question had really deserved as well of his people as his boastful story would go to show. But one thing is clearly shown by such tales, namely: the manner in which governors and nobles as a rule exploited and oppressed the people. Nehemiah would have had no reason for boasting of his actions if he had not regarded them as exceptional. No one will boastfully declare that he has not stolen silver teaspoons unless such thefts are the regular thing in the society of which he is a part.

Under the Syrian and Egyptian kings the taxes of Palestine were farmed out. The tax farmer as a rule was the High Priest. But he occasionally met with competitors of his own class, and then there was always a row among the dignified priesthood.

Therefore, the mass of the people in Judea had much more cause to oppose the foreign rule than did the aristocracy which benefited by it. Their rage against foreigners was further stimulated by their ignorance of the true alignment of forces. The mass of the Jews in Palestine did not know how immensely superior was the opponent's strength. For all these reasons they scorned diplomacy and demanded that the yoke of foreign rule be cast off by force. But they did not go beyond this; they did not speak of the yoke of the aristocracy. The latter also was a

[49] Nehemiah v, 1-19.

heavy burden to the people, but after all, both in Jerusalem and in the surrounding country, the people gained their entire livelihood by reason of the Temple, by reason of the significance of its worship and its priesthood. Therefore, the entire fury caused by their wretchedness was necessarily concentrated on the foreign exploiters alone. Democracy was transformed to chauvinism.

Owing to a fortunate turn of events, an insurrection of this little people against its mighty conquerors was crowned with success on one occasion. This event occurred at the time, as we have already pointed out, when the empire of the Seleukides was profoundly disorganized owing to internal warfare, and was engaged in a process of complete disintegration, like that of the Ptolemies, while both empires were fighting each other furiously, and paving the way for their complete subjection by the new rulers of the East as well as the West, the Romans.

Like every decaying system, this system increased its oppressive measures, which naturally produced resistance. The attitude of Jewish patriotism became more and more rebellious, and its center and leadership was found in the organization of the *Asidæans*.

Probably the Book of Daniel is one of the products of Asidæan activity; it was written about this time (between 167 and 164 B.C.), a pamphlet prophesying to the oppressed that Israel would soon arise and make itself free. Israel would be its own savior, its own Messiah. This is the beginning of the series of messianic propaganda pamphlets which proclaimed the defeat of foreign rule and the victory of the Jews, their liberation and rule over the nations of the earth.

But in the Book of Daniel, this thought is still expressed in a democratic form. The Messiah is still represented as the people itself; as "the people of the saints of the most High." "And the kingdom and dominion, and the greatness of the kingdom under the whole Heaven shall be given to the people of the saints of the most High, whose kingdom is an everlasting kingdom, and all dominions shall serve and obey him." [50]

This messianic prophecy soon appeared to have been splendidly fulfilled. The guerilla warfare against the oppressors was assum-

[50] Daniel, vii, 27.

ing larger and larger dimensions, until fortunate chieftains of the house of the Hasmonæans, including in the first place Judas Maccabæus, succeeded in proving their mettle in the conflicts in the open fields with the Syrian troops, and finally in conquering Jerusalem, which was being held by the Syrians. Judea became free and even extended its boundaries. After Judas Maccabeus had fallen (160 B.C.), his brother Simon had courage enough to achieve a task which has been since achieved by many a general of democracy who, after having conquered freedom for his people by successful warfare, has snatched away this freedom and placed the crown on his own head. Or rather, Simon permitted the people to place the crown upon him. A great gathering of the priests and the people decided that he should be High Priest, supreme war lord, and Prince of the people (*archiereus, strategos* and *ethnarches,* 141 B.C.). Thus Simon became the founder of the Hasmonæan dynasty. He probably felt how insecure the newly won independence was, for he immediately hastened to seek foreign support. In the year 139 we find a delegation, sent by him, in Rome, for the purpose of requesting the Romans to guarantee the Jewish territory. This was the delegation to which we have already referred, a few members of which were deported for their proselytic activities; but the delegation attained its purpose.

But Simon did not imagine that his rule would be of short duration, until the new friends of Judea came out as its most dangerous enemies, who were ultimately destined to destroy the Jewish State forever. So long as civil wars raged among the various Roman leaders, the fate of Judea still had its ups and downs. Pompey conquered Jerusalem in 63 B.C., taking many prisoners of war, whom he sent to Rome as slaves; he restricted the Jewish territory to Judea, Galilee, Peræa, and imposed a tax upon the Jews. Crassus plundered the Temple in 54 B.C.; after his defeat, the Jews rebelled against the Romans in Galilee, and were put down, many of the prisoners being sold as slaves. Caesar, in his turn, treated the Jews better, made them his friends. The civil wars after Caesar's death devastated Judea also and imposed heavy burdens upon it. After the victory of

Augustus, the latter again, like Caesar, showed himself favorable
to the Jews, but Judea remained dependent on the Romans, was
again occupied by Roman troops, came under the supervision of
Rome and finally under direct administration by Roman officials,
and we have already seen how these gay fellows disported themselves in the provinces, which they drained completely dry.
Therefore the hatred for the Romans grew apace, particularly
among the masses of the population. The puppet kings and
priestly aristocrats who ruled them tried to gain the favor of the
new Roman masters, as they had tried to ingratiate themselves
with the Greek masters before the Maccabæan insurrection,
though many of them must have hated the strangers bitterly at
the bottom of their hearts. But their party, that of the *Sadducees,* was capable of offering less and less resistance to the
democratic patriotic party, that of the *Pharisees.*

Josephus reports concerning so early a period as the year
100 B.C., in his *Antiquities*: "The rich were on the side of the
Sadducees, but the mass of the people clung to the Pharisees"
(xiii, 10, 6), and he also informs us concerning Herod's period
(the time of Christ):

"The sect of the Sadducees has but few adherents, but they
are the most distinguished people of the country. However,
affairs of state are not conducted according to their views. As
soon as they attain public office, they must willy-nilly act in
accordance with the views of the Pharisees, for otherwise the
common people would not tolerate them." (*Antiquities* xviii, 1.4.)

The Pharisees were gradually becoming the mental rulers of
the Jewish people, taking the place of their priestly aristocracy.

g. The Pharisees

We have already made the acquaintance, in the Maccabæan
conflicts, of the pious ones, the Asidæans. A few decades later
under John Hyrcanus (135-104 B.C.), the bearers of this doctrine
appear under the name of Pharisees; the bearers of the opposite
doctrine now for the first time take the name of Sadducees.

The origin of the latter name is not clear; perhaps the word
is derived from the priest Zadok, after whom the priesthood were

called the race of Zadokides. The Pharisees (*perushim*) really are *those segregated*, but called themselves "comrades" (*chaberim*) or confederates.

Josephus on one occasion tells us there were 6,000 of them, which was quite a political organization for such a small country. He reports from the time of Herod (37-4 B.C.):

"But there then existed people among the Jews who were proud of their strict observance of the law of their fathers, and who believed that God had a special affection for them. These people were called Pharisees. They had great power and were best able to oppose the king, but they were wise enough to wait for an opportunity which would seem favorable for such an insurrection. When the entire Jewish people took an oath to be faithful to the emperor (Augustus) and to obey the king (Herod), these men refused to take the oath, and there were more than 6,000 of them." [51]

Herod, the cruel tyrant who was ever ready to resort to the death penalty, did not dare punish severely this refusal to take the oath of subjection, which is a sign of his respect for the influence of the Pharisees on the masses of the people.

The Pharisees became the spiritual masters of the masses; among the Pharisees, the "scribes," or *literati*, who are always mentioned together with them in the New Testament, the rabbis (*rabbi* = my lord, *monsieur*), were the dominant group.

The class of the intellectuals was originally the priestly caste, among the Jews as well as everywhere else in the Orient. But this class in Judea suffered the fate of every aristocracy. With its increase in wealth went an increase in its neglect of the functions on which its privileged position was based. They may hardly be said to have done more than carry out the perfunctory ceremonials of worship that were assigned to them. They neglected more and more their scientific, literary, legislative, and judicial activities, with the result that the latter fell almost entirely into the hands of educated elements rising from the people.

The judicial and legislative activities attained particular im-

[51] *Antiquities*, xvii, 2, 4.

portance. Legislative gatherings are unknown to the nations of the ancient Orient. All their law takes the form of precedent, of ancient law. To be sure, the social development may continue, may produce new conditions, and new problems, requiring new legal formulation; but the feeling that the law remains ever the same, that it is from God, is so deeply rooted in the popular mind that the new laws are more readily accepted when they assume the form of the habitual law, the traditional law, existing from time immemorial, and seeming new only for the reason that they have been in disuse.

The simplest means at the disposal of the ruling classes for making new law look like old law is that of forging documents.

The priesthood of Judea, as we have already seen in several cases, made extensive use of this practice. This was not difficult in a country in which the masses felt that a single ruling class served as experts and preservers of the religious traditions. But in the countries in which a new class of persons with literary education was arising by the side of the ancient priesthood, it became quite difficult for either of these classes to try to represent any innovation as a work created by Moses or some other authority in ancient times. For now the competing class was keeping a sharp eye on the practices of such forgers.

There is an uninterrupted effort on the part of the rabbis throughout the two centuries preceding the destruction of Jerusalem by the Romans to cut a breach in the canon of sacred writings laid down by the priesthood, and to increase it by the addition of new literary productions which were to be represented as ancient, and therefore entitled to the same respect as the earlier writings; but this effort met with no success.

In his *Polemic against Apion* (i, 7 and 8), Josephus examines the plausibility of the Jewish writings: "For not every man has the right to write as he pleases, for that right belongs only to the prophets who have faithfully recorded the things of the past under the inspiration of God, as well as the events of their own time. For this reason we do not possess thousands of writings, contradicting and denying each other, but only twenty-two books, which record that which has happened since the beginning of the world, and are rightly considered to be of divine origin"; namely, the five books of Moses, thirteen books of Prophets, embracing the period from the death of Moses until Artaxerxes, and four books of Psalms and Proverbs.

"From the time of Artaxerxes to the present day, to be sure, everything is also recorded, *but it is not so trustworthy.* . . . The high respect that we have for our scriptures is shown by the fact that for a long time no one has dared add anything or subtract anything, or alter anything."

No doubt this was the case in the days of Josephus. As it became more difficult to alter the existing law as set down in the literature enumerated above, the innovators were forced more and more to resort to an *interpretation* of the law in order to adapt it to the new conditions. The sacred writings of the Jews were well suited for this practice, since they were not a unified whole but constituted the literary precipitations of the most varied periods and social conditions. They embraced legends of the primitive Bedouin period, as well as the highly cultured metropolitan wisdom of Babylon, the whole having been edited under priestly editorship in the post-Babylonian period, an editorship that was often extremely crude and tactless, permitting outright contradictions to pass unquestioned. A body of "law" of this kind would permit anything to be proved, if the manipulator possessed the necessary acuteness and the necessary power of memory to learn all the passages of the law by heart and keep them constantly at the tip of his tongue, and such indeed was the nature of the rabbinical wisdom. They did not make it their task to study life, but to imbue their scholars with a precise knowledge of the sacred scriptures, to mobilize to the highest degree their powers of repartee and subtlety in the interpretation of these writings. Of course, they remained unconsciously under the influence of the life that was surging about them, but the further the development of the pedantic rabbinical wisdom progressed, the more it ceased to be a means of understanding life, and thus of mastering life; it became, on the one hand, the art of outwitting all comers, including God himself, by a nimble juristic pettifogging, a superficial cleverness, and, on the other hand, the art of consoling and edifying oneself in any situation of life by means of a pious quotation. It has made no contribution to our knowledge of the world; in fact, its ignorance of the world was constantly increasing. This became fully apparent in the struggles which finally brought about the destruction of Jerusalem.

The wise and sophisticated Sadducees were well acquainted with the alignment of power in their day. They knew that it was impossible to offer serious resistance to the Romans. The Pharisees, on the other hand, tried all the more vigorously to shake off the Roman yoke, the more heavily the latter weighed down upon Judea and drove the people to despair. The Maccabæan insurrection had given a splendid example of how a people should and could defend its liberties against a tyrant.

The hopes for the coming of the Messiah, which had given strong support to that insurrection, and which in turn had been much strengthened by its success, became stronger with the growing desire to shake off the Roman yoke. To be sure, the Romans were more formidable opponents than the decaying Syrian Empire, and the confidence in the ability of the nations to act for themselves had decreased throughout the ancient world since the days of the Maccabæans. What were called civil wars were in reality the struggles of certain successful generals to achieve world power. Thus the conception of the Messiah was no longer the conception of a Jewish people liberating itself, but that of a powerful hero, full of miraculous energy, sent out by God to rescue and redeem the tormented nation of the chosen and saintly from their trials and tribulations.

Even the most enthusiastic Pharisees did not consider it possible to defeat their oppressors without the aid of such a miraculous general. But they did not build their hopes on him alone. They probably pointed to the constant increase in the numbers of their adherents in the Empire, particularly among the neighboring peoples, to their numerical strength in Alexandria, Babylonia, Damascus, and Antioch. Would not the latter come to the aid of their oppressed motherland if it should rebel? And if a single city, like Rome, had succeeded in conquering world power, why should the great and proud Jerusalem not be able to do the same?

The basis of the Revelation of St. John is a Jewish propaganda document after the fashion of the Book of Daniel. It was probably written in the time when Vespasian, and later Titus, were besieging Jerusalem. The Revelation prophesied a duel between Rome and Jerusalem. Behold Rome, the "woman sitting upon seven hills", "Babylon (*i.e.*, Rome), the great, the mother of harlots and abominations of the earth", "with whom the kings of the earth have committed fornication", and "the merchants of the earth are waxed rich through the abundance of her delicacies" (xvii and xviii). This city will fall, judgment will be pronounced over it, "and the merchants of the earth will weep and mourn over her, for no man buyeth their merchandise any more", its place will be taken by the holy city of Jerusalem, and "the nations of them that are saved shall walk in the light of it; and the kings of the earth do bring their glory and honor into it" (xxi, 24). As a matter of fact, Jerusalem was a city that might yet appear in the minds of simple-minded persons, unacquainted with the power of Rome, as a dangerous rival to the mistress of the world on the Tiber.

Josephus reports that the priests had once counted the number of persons found in Jerusalem on the occasion of the Easter Festival. "The priests counted 256,500 Easter lambs. But there were not less than ten persons at table feasting on each lamb. But sometimes there were as many as twenty such persons to a single lamb. But if we count ten persons only to each lamb, we shall arrive at the figure of 2,700,000 persons," not counting the impure and the unbelievers, who were not permitted to take part in the Easter Festival.[52]

Although Josephus here refers to an actual count, his information seems nevertheless to be incredible, even if we assume that these 2,700,000 persons included numerous country people from the surrounding districts, who did not require either foodstuffs or shelter in Jerusalem. Large consignments of foodstuffs from great distances were at that time possible only by means

[52] *Jewish War*, vi, 9, 3.

of ships. The great cities of that day all lay on navigable rivers or on the seacoast. But there was no possibility of any transportation reaching Jerusalem by water, since both the sea and the River Jordan were far away, and the latter, besides, is not navigable. Such immense numbers of people could not even have been provided with sufficient drinking water in Jerusalem. We know that the city depended in part on supplies of rainwater kept in cisterns.

Similarly, it is impossible to believe Josephus' statement found in the same passage, that 1,100,000 Jews perished in Jerusalem during the siege preceding the destruction of the city.

Tacitus gives a far smaller number.[53] The besieged population, including all ages and both sexes, amounted, according to him, to 600,000. As there were many among the besieged who did not ordinarily live in the city, it may perhaps be reasonable to assign about one-half of the above figure as its usual population during the few decades immediately preceding its destruction. Even if we take only one-third of this figure of 600,000, the population is a rather large one for a city of that time. But Josephus' figures show how this number was inflated in the imagination of the Jewish people.

But, however great and strong Jerusalem might have been, it had no possibility of obtaining a victory without assistance from the outside, and the Jews were counting on such assistance; but they forgot that the Jewish population outside of Palestine was a purely urban population; in fact, a population of *large* cities, and furthermore constituting a minority everywhere. But at that time, as well as in later periods, only the peasant was capable of enduring lengthy military service. The masses in the large cities, consisting of tradesmen, workers in domestic industries, and a *Lumpenproletariat*, could not form an army that could hold its own in the open field against trained troops. There is no doubt that at the time of the last great insurrection of Jerusalem there were also Jewish disturbances outside of Palestine, but they nowhere attained the proportions of a real aid to Jerusalem.

Unless a Messiah would really operate miracles, all Jewish

[53] *Histories,* v. 13.

insurrections seemed hopeless. The more rebellious the situation in Judea, the more fervently was the hope of the Messiah cherished in Pharisaic circles. Of course the Sadducees were rather skeptical of these hopes, as well as of the doctrine of the *resurrection,* which was intimately connected with the hopes of a coming Messiah.

As in all the rest of their mythology, the notions of the Israelites concerning the condition of man after death had originally contained nothing that would have distinguished them from other nations on the same level of culture. The fact that deceased persons would appear in dreams led to the assumption that the deceased still continued to live a personal life, but it was an incorporeal, shadow-like existence. Possibly it was the burial of the deceased in a dark vault which gave rise to the view that this shadowy existence was connected with a gloomy subterranean location. And a healthy love of life and life's pleasures, finally, could not imagine that the end of life would not also be the end of all joy and pleasure, that the shadowy existence of the dead could be anything but a joyless and gloomy one.

We find these views originally among the ancient Israelites, as well as, for example, among the ancient Greeks. The latters' Hades corresponded to the Israelites' Sheol, a place of the most intense darkness, far down in the earth, which was well guarded so that those who had died and descended into it could never again return. If the shade of Achilles laments in Homer the fact that a living day-worker is better off than a dead prince, the preacher Solomon (in Ecclesiastes, a document written in the time of the Maccabæans) still declares: "A living dog is better than a dead lion," and continues, "The dead know not anything, neither have they any more a reward; for the memory of them is forgotten, also their love and their hatred, and their envy is now perished; neither have they any more a portion forever in anything that is done under the sun."

The dead therefore may not expect any reward; whether they were godless or righteous, they are all visited with the same fate in the lower world. Joy and pleasure may be had only in life.

"For to him that is joined to all the living there is hope. Go thy way, eat thy bread with joy, and drink thy wine with a merry heart for God now accepteth thy works. Let thy garments be always white and let thy head lack no ointment. Live joyfully with the wife whom thou lovest all the days of the life of thy vanity, which he hath given thee under the sun, all the days of thy vanity: for that is thy portion in this life, and in thy labor which thou takest under the sun. Whatsoever thy hand findeth to do, do it with thy might; for there is no work, nor device, nor knowledge, nor wisdom, in the grave, whither thou goest." (Ecclesiastes ix, 4-10.)

Here we still have a purely "Hellenic" joy of life, but also a purely "pagan" view of death. Such were the ancient Jewish conceptions, as preserved by the Sadducees. Conceptions of an opposite kind were already arising at the time of Ecclesiastes (the "Preacher").

This joy of life was fully in accord with the popular feeling in the period of a healthy, prosperous peasantry. After their downfall, the aristocracy might still find joy in reality, pleasure in life, might even raise these joys to the pitch of voluptuousness, but the lower classes were losing them more and more, as their existence became more wretched. However, they had not descended so far as to doubt every possibility of improving the actual conditions. The more miserable the latter became, the more ardently did they cherish the hope of *revolution,* which would provide them with a better life and thus with more of its joy. The Messiah meant revolution, which of course came to be based more and more on superhuman powers, on miracles, as the actual alignment of forces gradually shifted to the disadvantage of the exploited and tormented masses. As the belief in miracles and the faith in the miraculous power of the Messiah who was to come increased, the mass of the sufferings and sacrifices demanded by the struggle against oppression increased in the same measure, also the number of martyrs who succumbed in this conflict. Was it possible to believe that they all had hoped and waited in vain, that the splendid life which the victory of the Messiah would bring to his chosen should be cut off from his most devoted and valorous champions? Should they who had renounced all pleasure in the cause of the saints and the elect, who had even sacrificed life itself, receive no reward for these sacrifices? Should they lead a gloomy, shadowy existence in Sheol, while their victorious comrades in Jerusalem ruled the world and enjoyed all its pleasures? If the Messiah was credited with sufficient strength to conquer Rome, he could probably also conquer death; awakenings from the dead were then not considered impossible.

Thus the view gradually took shape that the champions of Judaism who had fallen in battle would rise from their graves with full bodily vigor, and would begin a new life of pleasure and enjoyment. This was not a belief in the immortality of the soul, but in a reanimation of the body, which was to enjoy very real pleasures in the victorious city of Jerusalem. An extensive consumption of wine was a prominent feature in these hopes. But the pleasures of love were also not forgotten. Josephus tells us of a eunuch of Herod, whom the Pharisees won to their cause by promising him that the Messiah who was to come would give him the power to practice cohabitation and beget children.[54]

But if the Messiah was to be strong enough to reward his faithful it was natural also to assign him a similar power in matters of punishment. As a matter of fact, while the thought that the martyrs would remain unrewarded was intolerable, it was just as intolerable for those battling for Judaism to believe that all their persecutors who died happy were now exempt from punishment, since they were leading the same unfeeling existence in the underworld as were the shades of the righteous. Therefore the bodies of these wicked persons were also to be awakened by the Messiah and assigned to frightful torment.

The original conception by no means involved a reawakening of all the dead. The resurrection was to represent the final outcome of the struggle for the independence and the world dominion of Jerusalem, and was therefore only concerned with those dead who had fought on either side in this conflict. Thus we read in the Book of Daniel concerning the day of Judaism's victory:

"And *many* of them that sleep in the dust of the earth shall

[54] *Antiquities*, xvii, 2, 4.

awake, some to everlasting life, and some to shame and everlasting contempt" (xii, 2).

The so-called Revelation of St. John, as we have already observed, is a work belonging to the same class. In the Christian
version that has been handed down, Revelation distinguishes
between two resurrections. The first does not apply to all men,
but only to the martyrs, in our traditional version, of course to
the Christian martyrs, who shall be awakened to a thousand years
of life in this world: "The souls of them that were beheaded for
the witness of Jesus, and for the word of God, and which had not
worshiped the beast, neither his image, neither had received his
mark upon their foreheads, or in their hands; and they lived and
reigned with Christ a thousand years. But *the rest of the dead
lived not again* until the thousand years were finished" (xx, 4, 5).

The belief in resurrection was a doctrine of battle. Born from
the fanaticism of a long and savage struggle with an enemy of
superior power, and incomprehensible, except on this basis, this
belief was quite capable of continuing to cherish and give strength
to such fanaticism.

But in the non-Jewish world this belief encountered the wish
of man for immortality, entirely independent of the demands of
battle, the product rather of fatigue and resignation. It is to
this that the philosophical conceptions of the immortality of the
soul found in the Platonic and Pythagorean doctrines owe their
wide dissemination. But the hope of resurrection preached by
the Pharisees had a far more immediate and vivid effect on the
masses of men in those days, who had faith in miracles, but no
training in abstract thought. They gladly accepted this hope,
which they translated from the Jewish environment into their own
quite different language.

Judaism owed the success of its propaganda up to the time of
the destruction of Jerusalem in large measure to the belief in the
resurrection. But the destruction of this city destroyed the
majority of those who had firmly expected the Messiah to come
at an early date, while it shook the foundations of the faith in
his early approach, among the other Jews.

The messianic expectation ceased to be a motive power of

practical politics in Judaism; it became a pious wish and a melancholy longing. Simultaneously, however, the Pharisaic belief in the resurrection lost its foothold in Jewish thought. This belief, together with the belief in the Messiah, was maintained only in the Christian congregation, which thus took over from the Pharisees a portion of their best propaganda.

But the Christian congregation drew even more energy from the proletarian elements in Judaism than from bourgeois democracy, if we may so term it.

h. The Zealots

The Pharisees were the representatives of the mass of the people as opposed to the priestly aristocracy. But these masses resembled the "Third Estate" in France before the revolution of 1789 in that they also were composed of very different elements with very different interests, with varying degrees of fighting spirit and fighting ability.

This is true even of the Jews outside of Palestine. While these Jews constituted an exclusively urban population, living chiefly by trade and financial transactions, tax-farming and the like, it would nevertheless be a serious mistake to assume that they consisted only of rich merchants and bankers. We have already pointed out that trade is far more insecure than the occupation of the peasant or the artisan. This was even more the case then than now, for navigation was less perfected and piracy flourished on a large scale. And how many persons were ruined by the civil wars!

But there must have been many Jews who had been rich and were now poor, and many who had never succeeded in getting rich. While trade was the occupation that afforded them the best prospects under the given conditions, this does not mean that every individual had the available capital necessary for trade on a large scale. The trade practiced by most of the Jews must have remained a petty peddling or shopkeeping.

In addition, they probably practised such handicrafts as did not require great skill or exceptionally good taste. Where large numbers of Jews were living together, the peculiarities of their manners and customs alone must have produced a demand for many artisans of their own faith. When we read that there were a million Jews among the eight million inhabitants of Egypt, it is impossible to assume that all these Jews lived by trade; and we actually find mention of Jewish industries in Alexandria as well as Jewish artisans in other cities.

In many cities, particularly in Rome, the Jews must have been rather fully represented among the slaves also, and therefore among the freedmen. Their repeated unsuccessful struggles and attempted insurrections furnished an ever-renewed supply of fresh prisoners of war, who were sold into slavery.

From all these classes, some of whom were already quite close to the proletariat, there was recruited a sediment of *Lumpenproletariat,* which at some points became very numerous. Thus, for example, the Jewish beggars seem to have attracted special attention among the Roman proletarians. Martial gives us a description of the life of the streets in the capital: together with the artisans working in the street, the processions of the priests, the jugglers and peddlers, he also mentions the Jewish boy sent out by his mother to beg. Juvenal in his Third Satire speaks of the Grove of Egeria, "now leased to the Jews, whose entire household utensils consist of a basket and a bundle of hay. For every tree is now forced to yield us a profit. The forest is now owned by beggars, the muses have been driven out." [55]

Of course this is an evidence from the period after the destruction of Jerusalem, from the reign of Domitian, who had driven the Jews out of Rome and permitted them to sojourn in this grove on payment of a head tax. At any rate, it indicates the presence of a large number of Jewish beggars in Rome.

The *schnorrer* was already a noteworthy phenomenon in Judaism at that early day.

The *Lumpenproletariat* was, of course, a very unstable element.

The principal goal of the pilgrimages of the Jewish beggars was surely Jerusalem. There they felt themselves at home, there they had no reason to fear that they would be derided or maltreated by a hostile or at least unsympathetic population. There

[55] Juvenal, *Satires,* iii, 13-16.

the wealthy pilgrims from the most varied parts of the world assembled in great masses; there their religious impulses and simultaneously also their generosity reached the largest proportions.

In the time of Christ there was not a single large city that did not possess a numerous *Lumpenproletariat*. But after Rome, Jerusalem probably contained the largest proletariat of this description, at least relatively; for in both cities this rabble was recruited from the whole empire. The artisans of the period were as yet in close contact with this proletariat; they were as a rule merely domestic workers, and even today domestic workers are counted among the proletarians. It was not an unusual thing for them to consort with beggars and burden-bearers.

Wherever such penniless classes of the population congregated in great numbers, they became particularly aggressive. Unlike the possessing classes, they have nothing to lose; their social position is intolerable, and they have nothing to gain by waiting. They are emboldened by the consciousness of number. Furthermore, the military power could not easily employ its strength in the narrow and winding streets of those days. Little as the city proletarians were fitted for military service in the open field, unsatisfactory as their conduct usually was in such situations, they nevertheless were equal to the requirements of street battle. Events both in Alexandria and Jerusalem have shown the correctness of this observation.

In Jerusalem, this proletariat was inspired with quite a different fighting spirit from that of the possessing and intellectual classes which furnished the recruits of the Pharisees. Of course, in normal times the proletarians consented to be led by the Pharisees, but as the oppositions between Jerusalem and Rome were sharpened, as the decisive moment came nearer and nearer, the Pharisees became more and more cautious and timid, and thus frequently came into conflict with the advancing proletarians.

The latter found a powerful support in the country population of Galilee. The petty peasants and shepherds were being exploited to the utmost by the pressure of taxation and usury, and were thrown into servitude or expropriated, as they were everywhere in the Empire. Some of them probably came to Jerusalem, increasing the strength of the proletariat there. But as in other regions of the Empire, the more energetic elements among those expropriated and driven to desperation resorted to violent insurrection, to banditry. The proximity of the desert, still a home for Bedouin customs and habits, facilitated this struggle by offering numerous hiding places known only to those acquainted with the country. And Galilee itself, with its irregular soil and many caves, offered conditions that were not less favorable to the trade of the bandit. The flag under which these robbers fought was the hope in the Messiah. Just as today, in Russia, the revolution is taken as a pretext by every robber in executing his "expropriations", and as, on the other hand, the desire to advance the revolution makes a bandit of many a simple-minded, aggressive revolutionary,[56] so also was the case in Galilee. Bandit chieftains declared themselves to be the Messiah or at least his forerunner, and enthusiasts who felt themselves called to be the prophet or the Messiah, became bandit chieftains.

The bandits of Galilee and the proletarians of Jerusalem were in close coöperation with each other, supporting each other, and finally constituting a common party opposed to the Pharisees, namely the party of the Zealots, or those full of zeal. The contrast between these two groups shows many points of similarity with the contrast between the Girondists and the Jacobins.

The connection between the proletarians of Jerusalem and the armed bands of Galilee, and their eagerness for action, become particularly apparent in the time of Christ.

During Herod's last illness (4 B.C.), the people of Jerusalem already rebelled in mighty tumult against the innovations Herod had undertaken; above all, their fury was aroused by a golden eagle which Herod had caused to be set on the roof of his temple. This riot was put down by force of arms. But after Herod's death the people again rose at Easter, and this time with such energy that it was only after considerable bloodshed that the troops of Archelaus, Herod's son, succeeded in putting down the insurrection; 3,000 Jews were slain. But even this did not dis-

[56] The reader will recall that Kautsky wrote these words in 1908.—TRANSLATOR.

courage the aggressive spirit of the masses in Jerusalem. When Archelaus traveled to Rome in order to have himself declared king, the people again rebelled, but now the Romans intervened. Varus, who later fell in battle against the Cherusci, was then governor of Syria. He hastened to Jerusalem, put down the rebellion, and then returned to Antioch, leaving a legion behind in Jerusalem in charge of the Procurator Sabinus. The latter, relying upon his military strength, oppressed the Jews to the utmost and plundered and robbed as much as he could. This was the last straw. At Pentecost many persons gathered in Jerusalem, including a large number of Galileans. They were strong enough to encircle and besiege the Roman legion, together with the mercenaries recruited by Herod, who continued to operate after his death. The Romans attempted to make sorties in vain, although many Jews were killed in these efforts. The besiegers did not recede, and succeeded even in enticing some of Herod's troops to join their number.

Meanwhile rebellion broke out in the country districts. The brigands of Galilee now found many adherents and formed regular armies. Their leaders had themselves proclaimed kings of the Jews, in other words Messiahs. Among them, *Judas* was particularly prominent, whose father Ezechias had already been a famous robber and been executed as such (47 B.C.). In Peræa a former slave of Herod, *Simon*, gathered another band, while a third was commanded by the shepherd *Athronges*.

The Romans had great difficulty in putting down this insurrection, which made it necessary for Varus to come with two legions and numerous auxiliary forces to the aid of those besieged in Jerusalem. There began an unspeakable slaughtering and plundering; *two thousand* of those captured were crucified, many others sold into slavery.

This was at the time commonly assigned to the birth of Christ.

There now was peace for a few years, but only a few years. In 6 A.D., Judea was placed directly under Roman rule. The first measure taken by the Romans was the recording of a census, for the purpose of assessing taxes. This resulted in a new attempt at insurrection by Judas, the Galilean, probably the same

Judas who had been so prominent in the insurrection ten years before. He joined forces with the Pharisee Sadduk, who was instructed to arouse the people of Jerusalem. This attempt had no important results, but it led to a breach between the lower classes of the population and the rebellious Galileans on the one hand, and the Pharisees on the other. In the insurrection of 4 B.C. they had all still acted together. Now the Pharisees felt they had enough, and refused to work with the others. The party of Zealots was therefore formed in opposition to them. From this time on the fires of insurrection were never completely extinguished in Judea and Galilee until the destruction of Jerusalem. Josephus describes this situation from his own Pharisaic point of view:

"Thereupon Judas, a Gaulanite, from the city of Gamala, with the aid of Sadduk, a Pharisee, aroused the people to rebellion by making them believe that they would become slaves if they should submit to the census of their property, and that they ought to defend their liberties. They pointed out that they would thus not only preserve their possessions, but would attain a far greater good fortune, for their boldness would bring them great honor and fame. God would not aid them in this ambition unless they adopted energetic measures and shunned no efforts to carry them out. The people were glad to hear this and became thoroughly inspired to bold deeds.

"It is impossible to dwell too long on the amount of evil these two men produced among the people. There was no misfortune which was not due to them. They fomented one war after the other. They were constantly resorting to violence; anyone who expressed himself against such violence had to pay for it with his life. Bandits harried the land. The most distinguished persons were killed allegedly in order that liberty might be preserved. In reality it was done for greed and owing to the desire to rob their possessions. Thereupon many uprisings and general bloodshed ensued, since on the one hand the people of the country were themselves warring against each other, each party seeking to overthrow the other, while on the other hand external foes were cutting them down. Finally, famine was added to all this, which removed all barriers to destruction and plunged the cities into extreme wretchedness, until finally the Temple of God was reduced to ashes by the enemies. Thus their innovations and alterations of old habits redounded to the destruction of the rebels themselves. In this manner, Judas and Sadduk, who introduced a fourth doctrine and found many adherents, not only disturbed the state in their day, but also through this new doctrine, that had never been heard of before, gave rise to all the ills that came to pass later. . . . The young people who became attached to this doctrine have brought about our ruin." (*Antiquities,* xviii, I, I.)

At the end of the same chapter, Josephus speaks far more respectfully of the same Zealots whom he denounces so emphatically at its opening. His words now are:

"The fourth of these doctrines (the other three being those of the Pharisees, Sadducees, and Essenes) was introduced by Judas, the Galilean. His adherents agreed in all respects with the Pharisees, except that they showed a stubborn love for liberty, and declared that God alone should be recognized as Lord and prince. They prefer to suffer the most terrible tortures, and to see their own friends and relatives tortured, rather than call any human being their master. But I shall not dwell on this subject at length, because it is too well known what obstinacy they have shown in these things. I am not afraid that I shall not be believed, but rather that I shall not find words in order to express sufficiently the heroism and steadfastness with which they bear the worst tortures. This madness infected the entire people as a contagious disease, when the governor Gessius Florus (64-66 A.D.) abused his authority over them to such an extent as to drive them in desperation to secede from the Romans."

As the Roman yoke became more oppressive and the desperation of the Jewish masses increased, they escaped more and more from the influence of the Pharisees and were attracted by Zealotism, while the latter was simultaneously developing by-products of a peculiar kind.

One of these was that of rapturous ecstasy. Knowledge was

not the strong point of the ancient proletarian, not even a desire
for knowledge. Dependent on social forces more than any other
stratum of the population, forces that he did not understand, that
seemed uncanny to him; driven to desperation more than any
other class, grasping at every straw, he was particularly inclined
to believe in miracles; the messianic prophecy took a particularly strong hold on him, and he was left more than any other
class in complete ignorance of all actual conditions, a condition
in which he expected the impossible would happen.

Every madman that had proclaimed himself Messiah and promised to liberate the people through the miracles he would perform, found numerous adherents. One such was the Prophet
Theudas, under the governorship of Fadus (beginning in 44
A.D.), who led a host with him to the Jordan, where they were
scattered by Fadus' cavalry. Theudas himself was captured and
beheaded.

Under the Procurator Felix (52-60 A.D.), these ecstatic practices became even more prevalent:

"There was a band of evil men, who did not indeed murder,
but who had godless thoughts, and who made the city (Jerusalem) restless and insecure as much as murderers themselves
could have done. For they were seductive deceivers, who under
the pretext of divine revelation preached innovations of every
sort, and incited the people to insurrection. They enticed them
into the desert and pretended that God would permit them to
behold a token of liberty. As Felix assumed this to be the beginning of the rebellion, he sent soldiers against them, cavalry as
well as infantry, and had a great number slain."

"Still greater misfortune was brought upon the Jews by a false
prophet from Egypt (*i.e.*, an Egyptian Jew, *K.*). He was a sorcerer and succeeded in having himself accepted as a prophet because of his witchcraft. He misled about thirty thousand persons,
who became his adherents; he led them out of the desert to the
so-called Mount of Olives, in order to penetrate into Jerusalem
from that point, overpowering the Roman garrison, and conquering the authority over the people. As soon as Felix obtained
news of his plan, he set out to meet him, together with the Roman

soldiers, and all the people that were ready to fight for the common weal, and gave battle to him. The Egyptian escaped together with a few others. Most of them were captured, the rest hid in the country.

"Hardly had this rebellion been put down when again, as if from a diseased and infected body, a new pestilence broke forth. A few wizards and murderers joined forces and gained many adherents. They summoned everyone to seize his liberty, and threatened with death those that would henceforth continue to be subject and obedient to the Roman authority, saying of them: One must free, even against their wills, those that were willing to bow their heads under the yoke of servitude.

"They passed through the entire Jewish land, plundered the houses of the rich, slaying them that dwelled therein, set fire to the villages and harried the land so terribly that they were an oppression to the entire Jewish people, and this ruinous pestilence spread day by day." [57]

Within Jerusalem open rebellion against the Roman military power was not an easy matter. Here the most embittered enemies of the ruling system resorted to assassination. Under Governor Felix, in whose governorship the robbers and prophets became more numerous, a Terrorist sect was also formed. As explosive materials had then not yet been invented, the favorite weapon of the Terrorists was a curved dagger concealed under their cloaks; this dagger (*sica*) gave them their name (*Sicarians*).

The desperate turmoil brought about by all these advocates of the cause of the people was only the inevitable answer to the shameless fury of their oppressors. Let the reader simply learn what Josephus, who witnessed all these things, tells concerning the actions of the last two governors who ruled over Judea before the destruction of Jerusalem:

"*Festus* became governor (60-62). He made serious attempts to combat the robbers who plagued the Jewish land, seized and slew many of them. His successor *Albinus* (62-64) unfortunately did not follow his example. There was no crime and no vice too monstrous for him to commit. He not only embezzled

[57] Josephus, *Jewish War*, ii, 13, 4-6.

public funds while administering the state, but even attacked the private property of his subjects, appropriating it to himself by force. He oppressed the people with large and unreasonable taxes. The robbers whom the authorities of the towns as well as his predecessors had thrown into prison were released by him on payment of a piece of money, and only those that could not pay were criminals and remained in prison. The audacity of the rebels at Jerusalem was thus increased. The rich were able to gain such great favor with Albinus by means of presents and gifts, that he closed his eyes to their gathering a retinue about them. But the masses of the people, who do not love peace, began to attach themselves to them, because Albinus favored them. Therefore each evildoer surrounded himself with a band in which he himself was prominent as the supreme rascal, who had all good citizens plundered and robbed by his mercenaries. Those robbed kept their silence, and those not yet robbed even flattered the hangman-like scoundrel, for fear of otherwise incurring similar treatment. No man dared complain, for the oppression was too great. Thus the germ of the destruction of our city was planted.

"Although Albinus carried on in a shameful and malicious manner, he was far outdone by his successor Gessius Florus (64-66), with the result that Albinus, in a comparison between the two, would seem to have been the better. For Albinus carried on his misdeeds secretly and was able to cloak everything under a fair appearance, but his successor did all publicly as if he would seek his fame by maltreating our people. He robbed, he plundered, he imposed penalties, and acted not as if he had been sent to be governor, but to be a hangman to torture the Jews. Where clemency was in place, he applied cruelty; besides, he was impudent and deceitful, and no man could have invented more devices to mislead the people than he. It was not sufficient for him to bleed private individuals and gain profit at their expense. He plundered whole cities and ruined the entire nation. He omitted only to proclaim publicly that one might rob and steal as one liked provided only *he* obtained his share. Thus it came to pass that the whole land became desolate, since many left their native country and went to foreign parts." [58]

Does this not sound like a report concerning the brutalities of Russian *chinovniks?*

Finally the great insurrection came under Florus, in which the whole people rose with all its might against its tormentors. Jerusalem rebelled when Florus proposed to plunder the Temple, in May, 66 A.D. Or rather, the lower classes in the population of Jerusalem rebelled. The majority of the wealthy, Pharisees as well as Sadducees, feared this rebellion and desired peace. The rebellion against the Romans also meant the beginning of civil war. The war party was victorious; the peace party succumbed in street fights; and the Roman garrison in Jerusalem was forced to leave the city and was cut to pieces while doing so.

So great was the fighting zeal of the insurgents, that they succeeded in putting to flight a relief army of 30,000 men which arrived under the leadership of the Syrian Legate Cestius Gallus.

In all Palestine and far beyond its limits, the Jews rose in rebellion. The uprising of the Jews in Alexandria required the raising of all the military forces the Romans had in Egypt.

Of course it was out of the question for the Jews to defeat Rome; they were too weak; their population was too exclusively urban in character. But they might nevertheless have succeeded in wresting a certain consideration for Judea from the Romans for a time at least, if the rebels had immediately and energetically taken the offensive, and pursued the advantages they had gained. Conditions would soon have become favorable to them. In the second year of the Jewish War, the soldiers in the western portion of the Empire rebelled against Nero; the combats between the various legions continued until after his death (June 9, 68 A.D.); Vespasian, Commander-in-Chief of the army that was to repacify Judea, paid far more attention to events in the West, which involved the control of the Empire, than to the little local war into which he had been drawn.

But the sole slight opportunity that offered itself to the rebels was neglected. The reader will recall that it was the lower classes

[58] *Jewish War,* ii, 14, 1, 2.

that had declared war on the Romans and defeated the Jewish peace party. But the wealthy and the intellectuals still had enough power to gain control of the conduct of the war against the Romans, with the result that this war was not waged with a whole heart, with the object of defeating the enemy, but merely for the purpose of coming to terms with him. Of course, this upper class did not remain at the helm for long; the rebels finally noticed how lukewarmly their leaders fought, and the Zealots now succeeded in gaining control of the military authority.

"The unfortunate course of events was ascribed by the fanatical people's party—and rightly so—to the lack of energy displayed in the previous conduct of the war. The men of the people therefore put everything at stake in order to gain control of the situation themselves and drive out the former leaders. As the latter did not voluntarily relinquish their position, a terrible, bloody civil war ensued in Jerusalem in the winter of 67-68, with atrocities that may be paralleled only in the first French Revolution." [59]

In fact, any observer of these events cannot escape drawing comparisons with the French Revolution. But while the Reign of Terror in France was used as a means of saving the Revolution, and enabling it to advance successfully against the armies of all Europe, such an outcome was precluded in advance, owing to the nature of the case, in Jerusalem. The Reign of Terror established by the lower classes came too late in Jerusalem to gain even a short respite for the Jewish State, for the latter's days were numbered. The resort to terror resulted only in prolonging the conflict, increasing its sufferings, and aggravating the rage of the final victor to worse atrocities. But it did result in leaving to the world a monument of endurance, heroism, and devotion, which stands alone and is all the more impressive in the mire of universal cowardice and self-seeking of the times.

Not the entire Jewish population of Jerusalem continued for three years, until September, 70 A.D., to fight the hopeless battle against the superior enemy in the bravest, most obstinate and most brilliant manner, covering every inch of ground with

[59] Schürer, *Geschichte des jüdischen Volkes,* vol. i, p. 617.

corpses, before it yielded, exhausted by famine and disease, and was consumed in the burning ruins. The priests, the scribes, the merchants, had for the most part found safety early in the siege. It was the petty artisans and shopkeepers as well as the proletarians of Jerusalem that became the heroes of their nation, together with the proletarianized peasants of Galilee who had cut their way through to Jerusalem.

This was the atmosphere in which the Christian congregation originated. It does not at all present the smiling picture sketched for us by Renan in his *Life of Jesus,* when he describes its environment; for Renan based his picture not on a contemplation of the social conditions of the time but on the picturesque impressions received by the modern tourist in Galilee. That is why Renan finds it possible to say in his novel concerning Jesus (the *Life of Jesus*), that this beautiful country in the time of Jesus "overflowed with abundance, joy and comfort," so that "any history of the origin of Christianity must take the form of a lovely idyll."

Not more pleasant, I should say, than the lovely month of May in Paris in 1871.

i. The Essenes

But we must admit that in the midst of the terrible picture of woe and blood which is afforded by the history of Judea in the age of Christ, there is one phase which makes the impression of a peaceful ideal. It is the order of the Essenes or Essæans,[60] which arose, according to Josephus, about the year 150 B.C. and continued in existence up to the destruction of Jerusalem, whereupon it disappears from history.

Like the Zealots, the Essenes were of proletarian origin, but quite different in character. The Zealots developed no theory of society peculiar to them; they differed from the Pharisees not by the end they pursued, but by their means, by the ruthlessness and violence with which they fought to attain this end. Once

---

[60] Josephus writes "Essenes," Philo "Essæans." The word is a Græcization of the Syrian *Khasi* (Hebrew *Khasid*), "pious." The plural of the word has two forms: *Khasen, Khasuya.*

the goal was attained, once Jerusalem had taken Rome's place as mistress of the world, receiving all the treasures now falling to Rome, all distress would cease for all classes. Nationalism seemed even to the proletarians to make Socialism unnecessary. The proletarian character expressed itself in the Zealots only in the energy and fanaticism of their patriotism.

But not all the proletarians were willing to wait for the Messiah to bring about the new Jerusalem that would rule the world. Many sought to improve their situation at once, and as politics did not seem to offer any immediate remedy, they set about the question of an economic organization. Probably the Essenes owed their origin to this attitude; tradition tells us nothing on the subject.

But the nature of their organization is clear; it was an outspoken form of *communism*. At the time of Josephus there were four thousand Essenes, living in houses of the order in various villages and country towns of Judea.

"There they live together," Philo says of them, "organized into corporations, free unions, boarding clubs (κατὰ θάσους, ἑταιρίας καὶ συσσίτια ποιούμενοι), and are regularly occupied in various tasks for the community.

"For none of them wishes to have any property of his own, either a house, or a slave, or land, or herds, or anything else productive of wealth. But rather, by joining together everything without exception, they all have a common profit from it.

"The money which they acquire by various kinds of labor, they entrust to an elected trustee, who receives it and buys with it that which is necessary, providing them with abundant food and everything required for living."

We might therefore assume that everyone was producing for himself or working for wages.

Josephus describes their life as follows:

"Thereupon (after morning prayer) they are dismissed by their overseers and each proceeds to his work which he has learned, and after all have worked diligently to the fifth hour (counting from sunrise, therefore, to 11 A.M.), they gather in a certain place, gird themselves with linen cloths, and wash their bodies with cold water. After this cleansing they enter their dining-hall, to which none is admitted who is not of their sect. They enter it as clean and pure as if it were a temple. After they have been seated in silence, the baker comes and places every man's bread before him, and the cook likewise places before each a bowl of food; then the priest comes and blesses their food. And it is not permitted to touch the food until prayer is over. After the meal has been eaten, they similarly give thanks, thus having praised God both at the beginning and at the conclusion of their meal as the giver of all sustenance. Thereupon they again lay aside their garments, as a sacred robe, and again go about their work until evening. They partake of their supper just as they did of their dinner, and if there are guests (probably members of the order from other towns, for outsiders were not admitted to the dining-hall, *K*.), they permit the latter to sit at table with them. There is never shouting nor any disturbance to dese-crate the house, and if they talk to each other, one speaks after the other, not all at once, so that persons outside of their house regard the quiet pervading the building as an awe-inspiring mys-tery. The cause for their silent life is their constant moderation; they neither eat nor drink more than is required for the preser-vation of life.

"As a rule they perform no labor except under the instructions of their overseers, but they may give free expression to their feel-ings of compassion and charity; whenever distress requires it, each may give aid to those that need it and deserve it, and also give food to the poor. But they may not give anything to friends and relatives without previously notifying their overseer or trustee."

Communism among them was pushed to the utmost degree, extending even to matters of clothing. Philo informs us:

"Not only their food, but also their clothing is common to all. There are thick cloaks for winter time, and light raiment for summer time, each being permitted to use them at his discretion. For what is the possession of one, belongs to all, while the pos-session of all belongs to everyone."

They disapproved of slavery. Agriculture was their principal occupation, but they also worked as artisans.   They forbade only the production of articles of luxury and tools of war, as well as all commerce.

The basis of their entire communistic system was a community of *consumption*, not of social *production*.   To be sure, even the latter is suggested, but we also read of tasks performed by the individual and yielding money to him, either in the form of wages, or as a return for the goods sold, but these are tasks performed outside the social organism.   On the other hand, all members of the order have their dwelling and meals in common; it is this that serves chiefly to hold them together.   This is a communism of the common *household,* which requires a giving up of the isolated household, of the isolated family, and therefore also of the individual marriage.

As a matter of fact we find in all organizations based on a communism of consumption, on a common household, that they encounter difficulties owing to monogamy, and that they therefore seek to abolish it.   There are two methods by which this may be done—these represent the opposite poles in sexual relations, which appear diametrically opposed to each other, namely, extreme chastity and extreme "wickedness".   And yet these two methods are equally likely to be followed in communistic organizations.   From the time of the Essenes, in all the Christian communistic sects, down to the sectarian communistic colonies in the United States in our day, we may trace this tendency to reject marriage, and this inclination to favor either austere celibacy or a community of wives.

This would be inconceivable if this communism and its mental superstructure were based on mere ideological considerations; but it is easy to explain on the basis of its economic conditions.

The majority of the Essenes disapproved of touching a woman at all.

"They despised marriage, but adopted strange children, if they were still young and might still be taught, keeping them as their own, and instructing them in their customs and manners.   They do not wish to abolish or prohibit marriage and the propagation of man.   But they say that one must be on one's guard because of the unchastity of women, as no woman is satisfied with one man alone." Thus Josephus in the Eighth Chapter of the Second Book of his *History of the Jewish War,* from which we take the above quotations concerning the Essenes. In the Eighteenth Book of his *Antiquities of the Jews,* Chapter I, he also says on this subject:

"They take no wives and keep no slaves. They imagine that the latter is not just, and that the former gives rise to discord."

In both cases, Josephus assigns only practical considerations as the reason for the hostility to marriage, not an ascetic impulse; and Josephus knew them from his own observation; he had made common cause, in succession, with the Sadducees, the Essenes, and the Pharisees, finally remaining with the latter.

Josephus is therefore best able to inform us as to the reason for the Essenes' opposition to women, which does not mean that these considerations were necessarily the final reason for this opposition. We must always distinguish between the arguments advanced by man as the causes for his actions, and the psychological motives that actually condition these actions. Few persons are clearly conscious of these motives. Our historians love to accept the arguments handed down to them as the true motives for historical actions and conditions. They condemn a seeking for the true motives as an arbitrary "construction," *i.e.,* they wish our historical knowledge to attain no higher levels than those achieved in the times from which their sources date. The entire vast body of material that has been accumulated since those times, enabling us to isolate the essential and typical elements in the most varied historical phenomena from the non-essential and accidental elements, and to discover the true motives of men that lie behind their supposed motives—we are to regard all this material as non-existent!

He who knows the history of communism will at once understand that it was not the nature of women, but the nature of the communistic household, that disgusted the Essenes with marriage. Where many males and females lived together in a common household, temptations to adultery and to conjugal disagreements owing to jealousy were too many. Unless one would relinquish this sort of household, one was necessarily obliged to renounce either the dwelling together of men and women, or monogamy. Not all the Essenes did the former. Josephus reports in the Eighth Chapter of the Second Book of the *Jewish War*, which we have so often cited:

"There is also another variety of Essenes, who completely resemble the former in their mode of life, their customs and regulations, but differ from them only in regard to marriage, for they say that those who refrain from conjugal cohabitation deprive life of its most important function (μέρος); propagation must decrease constantly, and the human race rapidly die out, if all should think as they. These Essenes have the custom of trying out their wives for three years (δοκιμάζοντες). If after three purifications the women show that they are fit to bear children, the Essenes marry them. As soon as a woman is pregnant, her husband will no longer sleep with her. The purpose of this practice is to show that they enter into marriage not for the pleasures of the flesh, but only in order to have children."

This passage is not entirely clear. At any rate it goes to show that these marriages of the Essenes were different from the common marriages. The "trials" of the women seem capable of no other construction, however, than the assumption of a sort of community of wives.

Of the ideological superstructure that arose on these social bases, one thought deserves particular mention, namely, that of lack of freedom of the will, which was maintained by the Essenes in opposition to the Sadducees, who believed in freedom of the will, and to the Pharisees, who took an intermediate position.

"While the Pharisees maintain that everything proceeds in accordance with Fate, they nevertheless do not abolish man's free will, but declare that it has pleased God to bring about a sort of mixture between the decision of Fate and that of men, who wish to do good or evil." [61]

"The Essenes, on the other hand, ascribe everything to Fate. They believe nothing can befall man unless it has been ordained by Fate. But the Sadducees do not consider Fate at all. They

[61] Josephus, *Antiquities*, xviii, 1, 3.

say there is no such thing, and that it does not govern the destinies of men. They ascribe everything to man's free will, with the result that he has himself to thank if good befalls him, while he must ascribe adverse events to his own folly." [62]

These different attitudes seem to be the result of philosophy alone. But the reader already knows that each of these tendencies represents a different class, and if we read history carefully, we shall find that the ruling classes are often inclined to accept the idea of freedom of the will, while the oppressed classes, on the other hand, more often favor the idea of an unfree will.

And this is very easy to understand. The ruling classes feel themselves free to act or refrain from action, as they please. This is the result not only of their position of power, but also of the small number of their members. The necessary operation of natural laws becomes apparent only in mass phenomena, in which the various deviations from the normal mutually counteract each other. The smaller the number of individuals under observation, the greater the predominance of personal and accidental elements over universal and typical elements. In the case of a monarch, the latter seem to be entirely absent.

Therefore the rulers do not find it difficult to consider themselves as superior to social influences, which, so long as they had not been recognized, appear to men as mysterious powers, as Fate, Destiny. The ruling classes also feel themselves impelled to ascribe freedom of the will not only to themselves, but also to those ruled by them. The misery of the exploited man appears to them as due to his own fault; each of his transgressions appears as a base misdeed, arising merely from a personal joy in evil, and demanding severe punishment.

The assumption of freedom of the will makes it easy for the ruling classes to discharge their functions as judges and guardians of the oppressed classes with a feeling of moral superiority and indignation which must surely serve to enhance their energy.

But the great mass of the poor and oppressed must feel at every step that they are the slaves of circumstances, of Fate, the decisions of which may be inscrutable to them, but which at any

[62] *Antiquities,* xiii, 5, 9.

rate is stronger than they.   Their own bodies have been made to feel the absurdity of the proverb declaimed at them by the fortunate ones: "Each man is the architect of his own fortune." They try in vain to escape from the conditions that oppress them. They constantly feel the pressure of these conditions, and from their vast numbers they learn that it is not only the individual among them who fares thus, but that all of them are dragging the same chain.   And they also appreciate quite well that not only their actions and the results of their actions, but that even their feelings and ideas and volitions are entirely dependent on the conditions surrounding them.

It may seem amusing that the Pharisees because of their socially intermediate position simultaneously accepted freedom of the will and also the necessity of natural law.   Yet, the great philosopher Kant did precisely the same thing two thousand years after their time.

The rest of the ideological superstructure based on the Essenian constitution of society does not require further treatment here, although the historian usually gives most of his attention to just this point.   For these ideas give him an opportunity to institute profound investigations as to the origin of Essenism in Parseeism, or Buddhism, or Pythagoreanism, or in some other "-ism."

The question as to the true roots of Essenism cannot be solved thus.   Social institutions within a nation always rise from its real needs, not through mere imitation of external models.   There is no doubt we may learn from foreign countries, or from antiquity, but we accept from them only so much as can be used, so much as may accord with our own needs.   Roman law, for example, found a ready welcome in Germany after the Renaissance for the sole reason that it admirably answered the requirements of certain powerful and rising classes, namely, the absolute monarchy and the merchants.   One naturally saves oneself the pains of inventing a new tool if a finished tool is ready to hand.   But the fact that a tool is of foreign origin will not explain why an application is found for it; such an application can only be explained by the actual needs among the nation itself.

Furthermore, all the influences that might have been exerted on Essenism by Parseeism, by Buddhism, or by Pythagoreanism are of very dubious nature. There is no evidence anywhere of a direct influence of any of these elements on the Essenes. And the similarities between them can be explained only by the fact that they all arose under approximately the same conditions, which in each of them exerted pressure in the direction of the same attempts at solution.

The most reasonable of these connections is probably that between the Pythagoreans and the Essenes. Even Josephus says (*Antiquities*, xv, 10, 4) that the Essenes had a mode of life that was quite similar to the Pythagorean. But we might well ask whether it was the Essenes that learned from the Pythagoreans or the Pythagoreans from them. Of course, Josephus' claim (*Polemic against Apion*, i, 22) that Pythagoras himself had accepted Jewish ideas and published them as his own is an exaggeration probably based on forgery, for the purpose of glorifying the Jews. As a matter of fact, we know hardly anything definite about Pythagoras; only a long time after his death do we begin to have fairly plentiful data concerning him, and the latter become the more numerous and the more definite—also the more implausible—as the lapse of time since his death increases. We pointed out at the outset that Pythagoras fared as Jesus did; he became an ideal figure to whom all those qualities were ascribed that were demanded of a pattern of morality; he also became a wonder-worker and prophet, who gave evidence of his divine mission by the most extraordinary performances. Precisely because nothing definite was known of him, one could ascribe to him whatever actions or words one thought best. Also, the regulation of life alleged to have been introduced by Pythagoras, which was very similar to that of the Essenes, with its community of goods, is probably of later origin, perhaps not much older than the Essenian.

This Pythagoreanism probably had its origin in Alexandria.[63]

---

[63] On this subject, as well as on the Pythagoreans in general, consult Zeller, *Philosophic der Griechen,* vols. i and iii. A translation in 2 vols. appeared in London in 1881.—TRANSLATOR.

Some contact with Judaism was very natural under the circumstances; it is quite possible that Pythagorean views passed into Palestine. The opposite process is also possible. Finally, it is no less possible that both systems were drawing from a common source, from the practice of the Egyptians, for in Egypt the rather high stage of social evolution had come comparatively early to take the step of establishing monastic institutions.

If the ancient culture of Egypt, and its protracted process of disintegration, had produced earlier than any other portions of the Roman Empire an aversion to the pleasures of life and to private property, and a desire to flee from the world, this desire could not anywhere be more conveniently carried out than in Egypt, where the desert began in close proximity with the seats of civilization. In any other part of the Empire, he who fled from the great city found private property even in the country, and this was the most oppressive of all the forms of private property, it was landed property; otherwise it was necessary for such a man to retire to the wilderness, many miles remote from civilization, which could be rendered habitable only by the most strenuous labor, and a form of labor for which the dweller in great cities was least fitted.

In the Egyptian desert, as in all other deserts, there was no private property of the soil. Yet it was not hard to live in the desert. Its climate required no great expenditure for buildings, clothing, fuel, protection against the inclemency of the weather. And the desert was so close to the city that the hermit could at any time easily be supplied with the needs of life by his friends, in fact he might even secure such materials himself with the effort of an hour's walk.

Egypt therefore began at an early age to develop a sort of monk-like hermit system. Then Neo-Pythagoreanism arose in Alexandria, and finally, in the Fourth Century of our era, the Christian monastery originated in the same city. But the Alexandrian Jews also developed a peculiar order of monks, that of the *Therapeutæ*. Philo's book *On the Life of Wisdom,* in which he tells us about them, has been declared a forgery, but the suspicion seems to be baseless in this case.

According to this report they renounced all possessions as does the sage, dividing them among their relatives and friends, deserted their brothers, children, wives, friends, parents, their native city, and found their true home in an association with others of like mind. These associations are found in many parts of Egypt, particularly near Alexandria. Here each of them lives by himself in a simple cell close to the cells of the others, but spends his time in meditative piety. Their nutrition is very simple, consisting of bread, salt and water. On the Sabbath all gather, men and women, in a general dining-hall, in which the sexes, however, are separated by a partition, to sing and hear pious discourses. They condemn the eating of meat, the drinking of wine, and slavery, but we hear nothing of work in their system; they probably live on the alms of their friends and well-wishers.

It is quite possible that Alexandrian Jews brought the notions of the Therapeutæ to Palestine, and thus exercised an influence on the Essenes, and yet the two are essentially different. The Therapeutæ lived in contemplative idleness on the labor of others; the Essenes labored diligently and acquired enough not only to enable them to live on it, but even to give to the needy of their surplus. Both condemned private property, but the Therapeutæ had no idea of what could be done with the goods of this world. Labor was as hateful to them as enjoyment; they did without articles of production and consumption and distributed their possessions to friends and relatives. The Essenes worked, for which they needed tools; therefore their members did not distribute their possessions to their friends, but collected them for the common use.

Working, they must also remain efficient, must take sufficient nourishment. Austere asceticism is impossible for those who work.

The difference between the Therapeutæ on the one hand—particularly the Neo-Pythagoreans—who for the most part merely babbled about asceticism and unworldliness, and a surrender of property, and the Essenes on the other hand, is indicative of the contrast between the Jews of Palestine and the rest of the civilization of ancient Rome at the time when Christianity arose.

In Essenism we meet with the same vigor that we have encountered in Zealotism, and which so greatly elevates the Jews of that era above the cowardly querulousness of the other civilized peoples, who fled enjoyment and temptation because they feared the struggle, even their communistic tendencies assuming a cowardly and ascetic character.

The thing that made Essenism possible was the Jewish vitality, but not this alone; other factors are also responsible for making this phenomenon appear among the Jews rather than elsewhere.

In the last century before Christ, we find that the widespread poverty is accompanied by an increased desire on the part of the proletarians and their friends to remedy the evil by their organizations. Common meals, the last remnant of the original communism, also serve as the beginning of the later communism.

But among the Jews the need for union and mutual aid was particularly great. Fellow-countrymen living abroad will always stand more closely together than at home, and there was no one more homeless, more constantly in foreign lands than the Jew outside of Judea. Therefore, the Jews among themselves were characterized by a charity which was just as striking as their exclusiveness with regard to non-Jews. Tacitus mentions in the same breath their hatred toward all other nations, and their ever-ready charity to each other.[64]

They seem to have clung with particular obstinacy to their organizations having common meals. It would otherwise be impossible to explain why Caesar, who forbade all organizations that were not of great age, should make an exception in favor of Jewish organizations.

"While he made the establishment of all other independent organizations holding property of their own depend on the consent of the Senate, he placed nothing in the way of the formation of Jewish organizations with common meals and property of their own. In view of the widespread desire for fellowship which then characterized the organizations so much feared and persecuted by the state, this favoring of the Jewish religious organizations caused a large number of pagans to apply for admis-

[64] *Histories*, v, 5.

sion to the Jewish community, which was granted them without difficulty." [65]

It was natural for such an association, if proletarian, to assume a purely communistic character. But it was difficult for the organization in a large city to do more than provide common meals from the common provisions. Nor was there much need for more; clothing was not an important item among the proletarians in Southern Europe; it was an adornment rather than a protection from the weather. The proletarians of the city could always find a nook to sleep in. Furthermore, their occupations usually scattered them to the various parts of the city, where these consisted in begging, stealing, peddling, bearing burdens, etc.

The common meal of the organization—to which each member contributed his part and which each member attended, whether he happened to be in a position to make a contribution or not— was the most important bond cementing the organization, the most important means of protecting the individual member against the vicissitudes of life, only too fatal to those who had no property.

But it was not the same in the city as in the country. In the city, the household and occupation are closely connected. Common meals also require a common dwelling and a common management. Large agricultural establishments were nothing unusual at the time; run either by slaves or as large communistic families, household brotherhoods, they are a peculiarity of this stage of society.

But Palestine was the only region in which the Jews still had a peasantry; the latter, as we have seen, was in close and constant contact with the large city of Jerusalem and its proletariat. It was therefore not difficult for communistic tendencies, more natural to the Jewish proletariat than to any other at that period, to pass into the country districts and there attain the development which is characteristic of the Essenes.

The economic basis of the Essenian organization was the peas-

[65] O. Holtzmann, *Das Ende des jüdischen Staatswesens und die Entstehung des Christentums,* 1888, p. 460.

ant economy. "They are all engaged in agriculture," is Josephus' somewhat exaggerated statement (*Antiquities*, xviii, 1, 5).

But such an organization could only maintain itself in the provinces while tolerated by the state. A producing coöperative organization cannot exist as a secret society, particularly in the country.

Essenism was therefore bound up with the existence of Jewish freedom. The destruction of the latter meant that of the former also. And it was not capable of existing in a large city, outside of a free Palestine, as a secret society.

The large city of Jerusalem was nevertheless destined to develop a form of organization that turned out to be more adaptable than any other to the needs of the urban proletariat throughout the Empire, finally even more adaptable than any other to the needs of the Empire itself.

This organization, born from Judaism, extended over the entire Empire and absorbed all the elements of the new attitude towards life, which arose from the social transformation and disintegration of that era.

We have now to consider this organization, which is the *Christian Congregation*.

Part Four

THE BEGINNING OF
CHRISTIANITY

I. THE PRIMITIVE CHRISTIAN CONGREGATION

a. *The Proletarian Character of the Congregation*

WE have seen that the purely nationalistic character of democratic Zealotism did not correspond to the needs of many proletarian elements in Jerusalem. But the flight from the great city into the open country, which had been the effort of the Essenes, did not suit everyone's taste. Then, as now, it was easy to escape from the country, difficult to escape from the city. The proletarian who had become accustomed to city life no longer felt at home when in the country. The rich, in their country villas, perhaps found a pleasant change from the turmoil of the great city; but the return to the country in the case of the proletarian meant hard work in the fields, which he had not learned to do, and to which he was not equal.

The mass of the proletarians necessarily preferred, in Jerusalem as well as in other large cities, to remain in the city. Essenism did not offer them what they needed. Certainly not to those among them who belonged to the *Lumpenproletariat* and had become accustomed to live as social parasites.

By the side of the Zealots and the Essenes, there necessarily was built up a third proletarian tendency, uniting the Zealotic and Essenian tendencies in one movement. The expression of this tendency was the congregation of the Messiah.

It is generally recognized that the Christian congregation originally embraced proletarian elements almost exclusively, and was a proletarian organization. And this was true for a long time after the earliest beginnings.

Saint Paul in his First Letter to the Corinthians points out that neither culture nor property was represented in the congregation.

"For ye see your calling, brethren, how that not many wise men after the flesh, not many mighty, not many noble, are called;

but God hath chosen the foolish things of the world to confound the wise; and God hath chosen the weak things of the world to confound the things which are mighty; and base things of the world and things which are despised, hath God chosen." [1]

A good outline of the proletarian character of the primitive Christian congregation is given by Friedländer in his *Roman Life and Manners under the Early Empire*, from which we have already quoted several times:

"However numerous the causes that contributed to the spread of the Gospel, it is certain that before the middle or end of the Second Century it had only a few isolated followers among the upper classes. Not only did their philosophical training, and a general education intimately connected with polytheism, offer the strongest resistance, but, in addition, the Christian profession of faith led to the most dangerous conflicts with the existing order of things; and, lastly, the renunciation of all earthly interests was naturally most difficult for those who possessed honor, wealth and influence. The poor and lowly, says Lactantius, are more ready to believe than the rich, whose hostility was no doubt in many ways aroused against the socialistic tendencies of Christianity. On the other hand, in the lower strata of society the spread of Christianity, assisted to a remarkable extent by the dispersion of the Jews, must have been very rapid, especially in Rome; as early as the year 64 the number of Christians there must have been considerable."

But this expansion was for a long time limited to certain localities.

"Statements quite accidentally preserved show that up to 98 some 42, up to 180 some 74, up to 325 more than 550, places contained Christian communities."

"But in the Roman Empire the Christians not only formed a small minority as late as in the Third Century, but this minority, at least up to the beginning of the century, was drawn almost exclusively from the lowest classes of society. It was a joke amongst the heathen that the Christians could only convert the simple-minded, only slaves, women and children; that they were

[1] I Corinthians, i, 26 *ff.*

rude, uneducated, and boorish; that the members of their communities were chiefly people of no account, artisans and old women. The Christians themselves did not dispute this. Jerome says: the community of Christ is recruited, not from the Lyceum and the Academy, but from the lowest rabble (*de vili plebecula*). It is expressly attested by Christian writers that, even up to the middle of the Third Century, the new faith counted but few adherents amongst the higher classes. Eusebius says that the peace which the Church enjoyed, under Commodus (180-192 A.D.), contributed greatly to its propagation, 'so that several persons in Rome, distinguished for their birth and wealth, turned to salvation with their entire household and family'. Origen, in the reign of Alexander Severus (222-235 A.D.), says that 'at the present day rich men and many high dignitaries, as well as delicate and nobly born ladies, receive the Christian messengers of the word'; that is to say, Christianity then obtained successes of which it had not previously been able to boast. . . . Consequently, from the time of Commodus onwards, the spread of Christianity amongst the upper classes is variously and expressly attested, whereas the reverse is the case in regard to the preceding period. . . . The only persons of rank in the time before Commodus, whose conversion to Christianity seems probable, are the Consul Flavius Clemens, executed in the year 95 A.D., and his wife (or sister), Flavia Domitilla, who was banished to Pontia." [2]

This proletarian character of early Christianity is not the least of the reasons for our being so poorly informed on this early phase. Its first advocates may have been very eloquent persons, but they were not versed in reading and writing. These arts were far stranger to the habits of the masses of the people of those days than they are now. For a number of generations the Christian teaching of the history of its congregation was limited to oral transmission, the handings down of feverishly excited, incredibly credulous persons, reports of events that had been witnessed only by a small circle, if they ever really took place at all; and which therefore could not be investigated by the mass of the population, and certainly not by its critical and unprejudiced

[2] *Roman Life and Manners under the Early Empire,* vol. iii, pp. 205-208.

elements. Only when more educated persons, of a higher social level, turned to Christianity, was a beginning made in the written fixation of its traditions, but even in this case the purpose was not historical so much as controversial, to defend certain views and demands.

Much courage or much prejudice is required, not to mention a complete ignorance of the conditions of historical reliability, to pretend to be able to give a record of the career and even the speeches of certain personages with absolute certainty, on the basis of literary documents produced in the above manner and full of impossibilities and outright contradictions. We have already shown in our Introduction that it is impossible to say anything definite of the alleged founder of the Christian congregation. After what has just been said, we may add that it is really not necessary to know anything about him. All the modes of thought which are commonly designated, in praise or condemnation, as characteristically Christian, have already been shown to be products in part of the Roman-Hellenic, and in part of the Jewish tradition. There is not a single Christian thought that requires the assumption of a sublime prophet and superman to explain its origin, not one thought that cannot be pointed out before the time of Jesus in "pagan" or Jewish literature.

Slight as is the importance, however, as far as our historical understanding is concerned, of being fully informed concerning the personality of Jesus and his apostles, it is nevertheless very important to have definite information concerning the nature of the primitive Christian congregation.

Fortunately this is by no means impossible. No matter how fantastically adorned or how full of absolute inventions the speeches and acts of the persons may be who were honored by the Christians as their champions and teachers, there is no doubt that the first Christian authors wrote in the spirit of the Christian congregations in which and for which they were working. They were simply transmitting traditions from an earlier day which they might, to be sure, alter as to detail, but whose fundamental character was nevertheless so definite that they would have encountered active opposition had they attempted to alter these traditions in any very striking manner. They might attempt to weaken or reinterpret the spirit that prevailed in the beginnings of the Christian congregation; but conjure it away completely they could not. Such attempted dilutions can still be proved, and they become bolder and bolder as the Christian congregation loses more and more of its primitive proletarian character and accepts educated as well as wealthy and respected personages as members. But precisely these attempts enable us to recognize clearly this original proletarian character.

The knowledge we have thus gained finds a support in the evolution of later Christian sects, which are well known from their very beginnings and which clearly reflect in their later history the evolution of the Christian congregation after the Second Century, as we now know it. We may therefore assume that this sequence of events constituted a natural law, and that the beginnings, well known to us, of the later sects, furnish an analogy to the unknown beginnings of Christianity. To be sure, such an argument by analogy does not constitute evidence in itself alone, but it may very well give support to a hypothesis that has been formed in another way.

Both these elements, the analogy of the later sects, as well as the actually preserved remnants of the earliest traditions of primitive Christian life, are equally definite as evidences of tendencies which we might reasonably have expected in advance, knowing the proletarian character of the congregation.

b. Class Hatred

In the first place, there is a savage class hatred against the rich.

This class hatred is clearly apparent in the Gospel of Saint Luke, which was written early in the Second Century, particularly in the story of Lazarus, which we find in this Gospel alone (xvi, 19 ff.). In this passage, the rich man goes to Hell and the poor man into Abraham's bosom, not because the former is a sinner and the latter a righteous man; of this we are told nothing. The rich man is condemned for the simple reason that he is a rich man. Abraham calls to him: "Remember that thou in thy life-time receivedst thy good things and likewise Lazarus evil things;

but now he is comforted and thou art tormented." It was the desire for revenge on the part of the oppressed which rejoiced in this depiction of the future state. The same Gospel has Jesus say: "How hardly shall they that have riches enter into the Kingdom (Βασιλείαν) of God, for it is easier for a camel to go through a needle's eye than for a rich man to enter into the Kingdom of God (xvii, 24, 25)." Here also the rich man is condemned because of his wealth, not because of his sinfulness.

Similarly in the Sermon on the Mount (Luke vi, 20 ff.): "Blessed be ye poor (πτωχοί *are those so poor that they must beg*): for yours is the kingdom of God. Blessed are ye that hunger now: for ye shall be filled; blessed are ye that weep now: for ye shall laugh . . . but woe unto you that are rich: for ye have received your consolation; woe unto you that are full! for ye shall hunger. Woe unto you that laugh now! for ye shall mourn and weep."

The reader will observe that to be rich and enjoy one's wealth is regarded as a crime, worthy of the most cruel punishment.

The same spirit is still breathed by the Epistle of Saint James to the Twelve Tribes of the Diaspora, dating from the middle of the Second Century:

"Go to now, ye rich men, weep and howl for your miseries that shall come upon you. Your riches are corrupted and your garments are moth-eaten; your gold and silver is cankered, and the rust of them shall be a witness against you and shall eat your flesh as it were fire. Ye have heaped treasure together for the last days. Behold, the hire of the laborers who have reaped down your fields, which is of you kept back by fraud, crieth: and the cries of them which have reaped are entered into the ears of the Lord of sabaoth. Ye have lived in pleasure on the earth and been wanton; ye have nourished your hearts as in a day of slaughter. Ye have condemned and killed the just and he doth not resist you. Be patient, therefore, brethren, unto the coming of the Lord." (v. 1 ff.).

Saint James even fumes against the rich in his own ranks, against those who have joined the Christian congregation:

"Let the brother of low degree rejoice in that he is exalted:

But the rich in that he is made low, because as the flower of the grass he shall pass away. For the sun is no sooner risen with a burning heat but he withereth the grass and the flower thereof falleth and the grace of the fashion of it perisheth; so also shall the rich man fade away in his ways. . . . Hearken my beloved brethren. Hath not God chosen the poor of this world rich in faith, and heirs of the kingdom which he hath promised to them that love him? But ye have despised the poor. Do not rich men oppress you and draw you before the judgment seats? Do they not blaspheme that worthy name by which ye are called?" [3]

Few are the occasions on which the class hatred of the modern proletariat has assumed such fanatical forms as that of the Christian proletariat. In the short moments in which the proletariat of our epoch has hitherto held power it has never heaped vengeance on the rich. To be sure, it feels itself far stronger today than the proletariat of nascent Christianity ever felt. But he who knows himself to be strong is always more inclined to be magnanimous than he who is weak. It is a sign of the lacking confidence of the bourgeoisie in its own strength that they always wreak such terrible vengeance on an uprisen proletariat.

The Gospel of Saint Matthew is younger by a few decades than that of Saint Luke. In the meantime, wealthy and cultured persons had begun to seek contact with Christianity, and many a Christian propagandist began to feel the need of putting the Christian doctrine more amiably in order to attract these people. The "fire-eating" primitive Christian manner was no longer available. But this older attitude had struck too deep a root to be merely set aside, and an effort was made therefore simply to "revise" it in an opportunistic sense. It is this revisionistic spirit that has made the Gospel of Saint Matthew "the gospel of contradictions",[4] but also the "favorite gospel of the Church". In this Gospel, the Church found "the audacious and revolutionary character of the primitive Christian enthusiasm and Socialism so modified into the appropriate golden mean of an ecclesiastical opportunism, that it no longer seemed a menace to the existence

[3] James i, 9-11; ii, 5-7.
[4] Pfleiderer, *Primitive Christianity*, vol. ii, pp. 378, 380.

of an organized church that had made its peace with human society".

Of course, the various writers who successively collaborated in producing the Gospel of Saint Mark omitted all the unfavorable parts which they possibly could omit, such as the story of Lazarus, the condemnation of the inheritance dispute, which also leads to a tirade against the rich (Saint Luke xii, 13 *ff.*). But the Sermon on the Mount had probably become too popular and too well known to make it feasible to treat this episode in the same way. The Sermon was therefore bowdlerized. Matthew has Jesus say: "Blessed are the poor *in spirit* for theirs is the Kingdom of *Heaven.* . . . Blessed are they who are hungry and thirsty *for justice,* for they shall have their fill."

Of course, this astute revisionism has wiped out every trace of class hatred. It is now the poor in spirit that shall be blessed. It is uncertain what manner of persons are meant by this expression, whether idiots, or such who are beggars only in their own imaginations and not in reality, in other words, those who continue to possess while maintaining that their heart is not attached to their possessions. Probably it is the latter who are meant, but at any rate the condemnation of wealth, which was once expressed by declaring the beggar blessed, is no longer present. It is amusing to find that the hungry have now been transformed into those hungry for justice, who are fed with the prospect that they shall have their fill of justice. The Greek word here translated by "have their fill" (χορτάζω) was used mostly of animals, being applied to humans only in a contemptuous or ludicrous sense, to designate a base mode of stuffing one's belly. The fact that the word occurs in the Sermon on the Mount also is a suggestion of the proletarian origin of Christianity, the expression having probably been current in the circles from which it was drawn, to indicate a full appeasement of bodily hunger. But it becomes ridiculous when applied to the satisfaction of a hunger for justice.

The counterpart of these beatitudes, namely, the cursing of the rich man, is not found in Matthew at all. Even the most ingenious distortion could not have devised a form that would have made them acceptable to the wealthy classes whose conversion was desired, and therefore this portion had to go.

But however much certain influential circles of the Christian congregation, as it became more and more opportunistic, may have sought to obliterate its proletarian character, the proletariat and its class hatred were not eliminated thereby, and scattered thinkers arose from time to time to express this hatred.   The reader will find a good collection of passages from the writings of Saint Clement, Bishop Asterius, Lactantius, Basilius the Great, Saint Gregory of Nyssa, Saint Ambrose, Saint John Chrysostom, Saint Jerome, Saint Augustine, etc., almost all of them writing in the Fourth Century, when Christianity was already a state religion, in the little book of Paul Pflüger, *The Socialism of the Fathers of the Church*.[5]   All of them give vent to the sharpest denunciations of the rich, placing them on the same level with thieves and bandits.

c. Communism

In view of this outspoken proletarian character of the congregation, it is natural that it should aim to achieve a communistic organization.   In fact, so much is definitely declared.   We read in the Acts of the Apostles: "And they continued stedfastly in the apostles' doctrine and fellowship (κοινωμία) and in breaking of bread and in prayers. . . . And all that believed were together and had all things common; and sold their possessions and goods and parted them to all men, as every man had need" (ii, 42, 44).

"And the multitude of them that believed were of one heart and of one soul: neither said any of them that aught of the things which he possessed was his own; but they had all things common. . . . Neither was there any among them that lacked: for as many as were possessors of lands or of houses sold them and brought the prices of the things that were sold, and laid them down at the apostles' feet: a distribution was made unto every man as he had need" (iv, 32-34).

It will be remembered that Ananias and Sapphira, who had

[5] *Der Sozialismus der Kirchenväter.*

attempted to withhold some of their money from the congregation, were punished for this offense by death by divine intervention.

Saint John Chrysostom (the longer word means "mouth of gold", because of his fiery eloquence), an undaunted critic of his period (347-407 A.D.), added to the above quoted presentation of primitive Christian communism a discussion of its advantages, which has a very realistic economic sound, far removed from ecstatic asceticism. We find this passage in the eleventh of his *Homilies* (sermons) on the Acts of the Apostles. His words are as follows:

"Grace was among them, because none suffered lack, for the reason that they gave so generously that none remained poor. For they did not give one part and retain another part for themselves; nor did they give everything as if it were their own property. They abolished inequality and lived in great abundance; and they did this in the most praiseworthy manner. They did not dare to place alms into the hands of the needy, nor did they give largesses with arrogant condescension, but they laid them at the feet of the apostles and made them the masters and distributors of the gifts. Each man took his needs then from the supply of the community, not from the private property of individuals. This prevented the givers from acquiring a vain self-complacency.

"If we should do this today, we should live much more happily, rich as well as poor. And the poor would not gain more happiness thereby than the rich. . . . For the givers not only did not become poor but they made the poor rich also.

"Let us picture the thing to ourselves thus: All give that which they have to the common fund. Let no one be disturbed by this prospect, either the rich man or the poor man. Do you know how much money would thus be accumulated? I suppose—for it cannot be determined with absolute certainty—that if each man should give up all his money, his fields, his lands, his houses (not to mention the slaves, for we may assume that the first Christians had none, having most probably liberated them), I suppose a mass of about a million pounds of gold could be raised, perhaps even twice or thrice as much. For, let us see, how many persons does our city (Constantinople) contain? How many Christians? Are there not fully one hundred thousand? And how many pagans and Jews? How many thousands of pounds of gold could thus be raised? And how many poor have we? I do not believe that there are more than fifty thousand. How much would be required in order to feed them every day? If they should dine at a common table, the costs could not be very great. What shall we set about to do with our gigantic treasury? Do you believe that it could ever be exhausted? And will not the blessing of God be poured out upon us a thousand times more abundantly than before? Shall we not make a heaven of the earth? If this experiment turned out so brilliantly successful in the case of three thousand or five thousand persons (the first Christians) and none of them suffered any lack, how much better must be the outcome in the case of so great a number as now? Will not each newcomer add something of his own?

"The dividing up of lands causes greater expenditures and therefore produces poverty. Just consider a house with a man and wife and ten children. She weaves, he tries to make a living on the market-place; will it be cheaper for them to live together in one house or to live separately? Of course it will be more expensive to live separately. If the ten sons separate, they will need ten houses, ten tables, ten servants, and everything else tenfold in the same manner. And how is it with the mass of slaves? Are they not fed together at one table in order to save expense? Splitting up always leads to extravagance; joining together always leads to a husbanding of resources. Thus people live now in monasteries and so the faithful ones lived. Who then died of hunger? Who was not richly satisfied? And yet people fear this condition more than they would fear a leap into the boundless sea. Why should we not at least make an effort and go about the thing bravely! How great would be our blessing thereby! For if in those days, when the number of the faithful was so small, only from three to five thousand, if at that time when the whole world was hostile to us, where we met with consolation nowhere, our predecessors set about the task so resolutely, how much more confidence should we have, now that there are faithful everywhere by the grace of God! Who would then still wish to remain a pagan? No one, I think. We should draw all to us and make all incline toward us." [6]

The first Christians were not capable of making such a clear and calm statement of the case. But their short observations, exclamations, demands, imprecations, clearly indicate in every case the uniformly communistic character of the first stage of the Christian congregation.

In the Gospel of Saint John which, it must be admitted, was not written until the middle of the Second Century, the communistic fellowship of Jesus with his apostles is taken for granted. They all had but one purse between them and this purse was carried by Judas Iscariot. John, who in this case as in all others attempts to outdo his predecessors, increases the abhorrence in which the betrayer Judas must be held by branding him as an embezzler of the common fund. John describes the incident of Mary's anointing the feet of Jesus with precious ointment.

"Then saith one of his disciples, Judas Iscariot, Simon's son, which should betray him, Why was not this ointment sold for three hundred pence and given to the poor? This he said, not that he cared for the poor, but because he was a thief and had the bag and bare what was put therein." [7]

At the last supper, Jesus says to Judas: "That thou doest, do quickly."

"Now no man at the table knew for what intent he spake thus unto him. For some of them thought, because Judas had the bag, that Jesus had said unto him, Buy those things that we have need of against the feast; or, that he should give something to the poor." [8]

Jesus in the Gospels repeatedly demands of his disciples that each shall give away everything he possesses.

"So likewise, whosoever he be of you that forsaketh not all that he hath, he cannot be my disciple." [9]

"Sell that ye have, and give alms." (Luke xii, 33.).

---

[6] S.P.N. Joanni Chrysostomi opera omnia quæ exstant, Paris, 1859, Ed. Migne, vol. ix, pp. 96-98.   [7] John xii, 4-7.
[8] John xiii, 27-29.   [9] Luke xiv, 33.

"And a certain ruler (ἄρχων) asked him (Jesus), saying, Good Master, what shall I do to inherit eternal life? And Jesus said unto him, Why callest thou me good? none is good save one, that is, God. Thou knowest the commandments. Do not commit adultery, Do not kill, Do not steal, Do not bear false witness, Honor thy father and thy mother. And he said, All these things have I kept from my youth up. Now when Jesus heard these things, he said unto him, Yet lackest thou one thing: sell all that thou hast, and distribute unto the poor, and thou shalt have treasure in Heaven; and come, follow me. And when he heard this he was very sorrowful; for he was very rich." [10]

This incident impels Jesus to utter the parable of the camel, for which it will be easier to pass through the needle's eye, than for a rich man to enter the Kingdom of God. The Kingdom of Heaven is represented as accessible only to those who share their wealth with the poor.

The Gospel attributed to Saint Mark presents the matter in exactly the same light.

But the revisionistic Saint Matthew here again dilutes the original severity of the demand, by putting it only in a hypothetical form. Matthew has Jesus say to the rich youth: "If thou wilt be perfect, go and sell that thou hast, and give to the poor" (xix, 21).

What Jesus was originally represented as demanding of every one of his adherents, of every member of his congregation, became in time a demand to be made only of those who laid claim to perfection.

This sequence of events is quite natural in an organization that was at first purely proletarian and later admitted more and more elements that were wealthy.

Nevertheless, there are a number of theologians who deny the communistic character of primitive Christianity. They allege that the report in the Acts of the Apostles on this subject is of later origin; as was so often the case in antiquity, it is alleged that the writer here also had placed the ideal condition of which he dreamed, back into the past. But these theologians forget

[10] Luke xviii, 18-23.

that the communistic character of primitive Christianity was very inconvenient for the official Church of the later centuries, which was more or less accommodating in its attitude toward the rich. If this picture of primitive Christianity depended on a later fabrication, the champions of the opportunist tendency would not have hesitated to protest against it and would have seen to it that the books containing such pictures should be stricken from the canon of books recognized by the Church. The Church has never tolerated forgeries except when it was fully in accord with its policy to do so, and surely this would not apply to communism. If communism has been officially admitted to be the most basic demand of the primitive congregation, surely such recognition has been given only for the reason that it was impossible to do otherwise, tradition in this matter having struck too deep a root and being too generally disseminated.

d.   The Objections to Communism

The objections of those who would deny the existence of communism in the primitive congregation are by no means convincing. We find all these objections recapitulated by a critic who opposes the picture I drew of primitive Christianity in my *Forerunners of Socialism.*

This critic, A. K., a Doctor of Theology, published his objections in an article in *Die Neue Zeit,* concerning the *So-called Primitive Christian Communism.*[11]

It is pointed out to us, first of all, that "The Sermons of the Nazarene did not aim at an economic revolution." But where does A. K. get this information? The Acts of the Apostles seem to him an uncertain source on which to base the description of organizations whose origin he assigns to the period *after* the alleged death of Christ; the Gospels, which are some of them younger than the Acts of the Apostles, he considers as absolutely sure sources even for the *speeches* of Christ!

As a matter of fact, the same truth is applicable to the Gospels as to the Acts of the Apostles. What we may learn from them

[11] *Der sogenannte urchristliche Kommunismus. Die Neue Zeit,* vol. xxvi, No. 2, p. 482.

is the character of those that wrote them, in addition they may also contain some reminiscences, but reminiscences of *organizations* are more tenacious than reminiscences of *speeches*, and cannot be so easily distorted. Furthermore, as we have seen, we can very well ascertain in the communicated speeches concerning Christ a quality that very definitely indicates the communism of the primitive congregation.

The specific teachings of Jesus, of which we know nothing definite at all, cannot be used to prove anything against the assumption of the early communism. Furthermore, A. K. makes every effort to have us believe that the practical communism of the Essenes, which was developing under the very eyes of the proletarians of Jerusalem, had had no influence on them at all. But the communistic *theories* of the Greek philosophers and poets had exerted the most profound influence on the uneducated proletarians of the Christian congregations outside of Jerusalem and had imbued them with communistic ideals, the realization of which, in accordance with the habits of the time, they had placed in the past; in other words, in the period of the primitive congregation in Jerusalem.

In other words, we are told that the *educated* succeeded *later* in imbuing the proletarians with a communism, the *practical observation* of which had *earlier* left them untouched. We should certainly need the strongest proofs to make this view seem plausible to us. All that we have in the form of evidence is opposed to it. As the influence of the educated classes upon Christianity increases, Christianity departs more and more from communism, as we have already seen from Matthew, and as we shall later learn in tracing the evolution of the congregation.

A. K.'s ideas of the Essenes are entirely erroneous. He says of the communistic Christian congregation of Jerusalem:

"The fact that this single communistic experiment should happen to be made by an association consisting of *Jews* should arouse our suspicion. Down to the very beginning of our era, the Jews never made any such social experiments; never before then was there such a thing as a Jewish communism. But communism, both theoretical and practical, was nothing new to the Hellenes."

Our critic does not reveal the source in which he discovers the practical communism of the Hellenes in the time of Christ. But it is almost incredible to hear him say that he finds less communism among the Jews than among the Hellenes, when as an actual fact the communism of the former is far superior to the communistic visions of the latter, owing to its having been actually carried out. And A. K. evidently has not the slightest suspicion of the fact that the Essenes are mentioned a hundred and fifty years *before Christ,* but seems to think that they did not arise until the time of Christ!

Yet, these same Essenes who are represented as having had no influence on the practices of the Jerusalem congregation, are alleged to have produced the communist *legend* which was admitted to the Acts of the Apostles in the Second Century after Christ. The Essenes, who disappear from sight with the destruction of Jerusalem, probably because they were dragged down in the general destruction of the Jewish community, are represented as having imbued the Hellenic proletarians with legends concerning the origin of the Christian congregation, and caused them to adopt the idea of a communistic past, at a time when the hostility between Judaism and Christianity had already assumed the sharpest forms, while it is also claimed that at the time when the Jewish proletarians founded an organization in Jerusalem which necessarily must have had close personal and practical contact with the Essenian movement, the latter had not the slightest influence on that organization!

It is quite possible that Essenian legends and views were among the elements included in early Christian literature. But it is far more probable that in that early state of the Christian congregation, in which it was as yet producing no literature, its organization was under the influence of Essenian models. And this could only have been an influence in the sense of the actual carrying out of communism, and not in the sense of merely imagining an alleged communistic past, corresponding to no reality.

This entire artificial construction, the creation of modern theologians, and accepted by A. K., which would deny the

Essenian influence at a time when there really was such an influence, and then ascribe a decisive function to it at a time when it had ceased, merely shows how ingenious many a theological brain can become in the service of the task of liberating the early Church from the "indecent odor" of communism.

But all the above are not decisive reasons for A. K. He knows a "chief reason," hitherto "never appreciated: The opponents of the Christians have accused them of all possible offenses, but not of having been communists. And yet these opponents would not have relinquished the opportunity of making such an accusation if there had been any foundation for it." I fear the world will continue to ignore this "chief reason". For A. K. cannot deny that the communistic character of Christianity is distinctly emphasized in a number of passages in the Acts of the Apostles, as well as in the Gospels. He merely maintains that these passages are purely legendary in character. But there is no denying that they are there and that they express genuine Christian tendencies. If the opponents of Christianity nevertheless did not emphasize the communism of Christianity, this cannot be due to the fact that they found no support for such an accusation. For they accused the Christians of other things, such as infanticide, incest, etc., for which there was not the slightest evidence in the Christian literature. It is hard to believe, therefore, that they would have refrained from making accusations for which they could offer proof in the Christian writings of even the earliest periods of Christian literature.

We must seek the reason for this elsewhere than in the absence of communism in early Christianity.

The true reason is that the attitude toward communism in those days was quite different from that of today.

Today, communism in the early Christian sense, in other words, *dividing up*, has become incompatible with the progress of production, with the existence of society. Today, economic needs unconditionally demand just the opposite of a dividing up, namely, they demand a concentration of wealth in a few spots, either in the hands of private individuals, as is the case today, or in the hands of society, of the state, of the municipalities, perhaps also in those of coöperative organizations, as in the Socialist scheme of things.

But in the days of Christianity the case was quite different. Aside from mining, industry was almost altogether of a petty kind. In agriculture, it is true, there were cases of extensive large-scale establishments, but this large-scale enterprise, manned by slaves, was not technically superior to the petty establishment, and could only maintain itself where it permitted of a ruthless destructive exploitation of resources with the aid of the labor of cheap slaves. Large-scale production had not become the basis of the entire mode of production that it is today.

Therefore, the concentration of wealth in a few hands then meant anything else but an enhancement of the productivity of labor, and certainly not a basis for the process of production and therefore of the social welfare.

The concentration of wealth in a few hands did not mean a development of the productive forces, but merely an accumulation of articles of consumption in such volume that the individual could not possibly consume them himself, with the result that he had no other recourse but to share them with others.

And the rich did this on a large scale, and partly voluntarily. *Generosity* was considered one of the most distinguished virtues in the Roman imperial era. It was a means of gaining adherents and friends and therefore a means of increasing one's power.

"Slaves, on their manumission, generally received a donation more or less generous. Martial instances one of 10,000,000 (sesterces). The families, too, of dependents and clients received gratuities and protection. And a freedman of Cotta Messalinus, a friend of Tiberius, celebrates on his tombstone in the Via Appia, how his patron often gave him sums amounting to the knightly census (400,000 sesterces), educated his children, provided paternally for his sons, conferred a military tribunate on his son Cottanus, and paid the expenses of that tombstone." [12]

There were very many such cases. But, where democracy prevailed, there was also an involuntary sharing of possessions in

[12] Friedländer, *Roman Life and Manners under the Early Empire,* vol. i, pp. 114, 115.

addition to the voluntary one. Anyone desiring an office had to purchase it by generous gifts to the people; the latter, wherever they had power, in addition imposed high taxes on the rich, in order to live on the yield of these taxes, while citizens were recompensed from the revenues of the state for their participation in the popular assemblies and even for their attendance at public spectacles, or regaled at the public expense at great public tables, or given food from the public stores.

There was nothing offensive in the eyes of the masses in the thought that the rich existed in order that they might share their property with others, nothing that contradicted the general views. It was rather an idea fully in accord with these views.

The masses were not repelled by such actions, but rather flattered by them. The opponents of the Christians would have been fools to have emphasized just this phase. Let the reader merely note the respect with which such conservative writers as Josephus and Philo speak of the communism of the Essenes; they do not find this communism repulsive or ridiculous but quite sublime.

A. K.'s "principal objection" to the assumption of a primitive Christian communism, namely, that the Christians were not accused of this practice by their opponents, is therefore merely a proof that A. K. sees the past with the eyes of modern capitalistic society and not with its own eyes.

In addition to these objections, which are based on no proofs at all and therefore are mere imaginings, A. K. now mobilizes a number of strictures which are based on facts related in the Acts of the Apostles. Curiously enough, our critic, who is so skeptical with regard to the delineations, in primitive Christian literature, of conditions of long standing, now accepts every mention of a single occurrence at its face value. It is the same case as if he should declare the descriptions of social conditions in the heroic age which are found in the Odyssey to be inventions, but should accept Polyphemus and Circe as historical characters who actually performed the deeds ascribed to them.

But even these individual facts do not militate against the assumption of communism in the early congregation.

In the first place, A. K. says the congregation at Jerusalem had a membership of five thousand, and asks: How could so great a number, with their wives and children, constitute a single family?

No one has claimed that they constituted a single family or that they ate at a single table. And it would be difficult even to assert that the primitive congregation really did have a membership of five thousand, as is reported in the Acts of the Apostles (iv, 4). Statistics were not the strong point of ancient literature and certainly not of oriental literature; exaggeration as a means of producing an effect was much in favor.

The number five thousand was often assigned in order to indicate a very great quantity. Thus, the Gospels very precisely state that the number of persons fed by Jesus with five loaves of bread was five thousand men "without women and children" (Matthew xiv, 21). Will my critic also insist on the correctness of the number in this case?

But we have every reason to believe that the assignment of a membership of five thousand to the primitive congregation was a little boastful.

Soon after the death of Jesus, according to the Acts of the Apostles, Peter delivers an eloquent revival speech, and at once *three thousand* persons have themselves baptized (ii, 41). His further propaganda brings it about that "many become believers" and now the number *five thousand* is given (iv, 4). Now what was the actual size of the congregation at the time of the death of Jesus? Immediately after his death the congregation met and "there were about one hundred and twenty persons all together" (i, 15).

Surely this indicates that the congregation at first was very small, in spite of the most diligent agitation on the part of Jesus and his apostles. And now we are to believe that suddenly, after his death, the congregation is increased from hardly more than a hundred to five thousand, by delivering a few speeches? If we must accept any definite number, the latter is probably much farther from the truth than the former.

Five thousand organized members would have been a band quite noticeable in Jerusalem, and Josephus would surely have given them some attention. The congregation must actually have been very insignificant, since none of its contemporaries mentions it. Furthermore, A. K. raises the objection that the report concerning the communism of the congregation states, after describing the congregation:

"And Joses, who by the apostles was surnamed Barnabas (which is, being interpreted, the Son of Consolation), a Levite and of the country of Cyprus, having land, sold it and brought the money and laid it at the apostles' feet. But a certain man named Ananias, with Sapphira, his wife, sold a possession, and kept back a part of the price, his wife also being privy to it, and brought a certain part and laid it at the apostles' feet." We are told that this is a testimony against communism, for A. K. thinks that Barnabas would not have been singled out for mention if the members had sold their possessions and brought the money to the apostles.

A. K. forgets that Barnabas is here contrasted with Ananias as a model of proper conduct; surely nothing could more clearly express the demand of communism. Was it necessary for the Acts of the Apostles to mention *every* man that sold his possessions? We do not know why it was just Barnabas that received mention, but to maintain that his mention is equivalent to a statement that *he only* had made an actual practice of communism, is putting too low an estimate on the intelligence of the authors of Acts. The example of Barnabas is mentioned in direct connection with the fact that all who owned anything sold it. If Barnabas is given special mention, the reason may have been that he was a favorite of the authors of Acts, for they singled him out for attention again and again. But another reason may be that his name happened to have been handed down together with that of Ananias. Or perhaps these two were the only members of the original congregation who had anything worth selling, while all the rest were proletarians.

The third fact adduced is the following: we read in the Acts of the Apostles (vi, 1 ff.):

"And in those days when the number of the disciples was multiplied there arose a murmuring of the congregations against the Hebrews, because their widows were neglected in the daily ministration."

"Would this be possible if communism were actually in practice?" A. K. indignantly asks.

But no one maintains that communism encountered no difficulties in carrying it out, or indeed, that it was not possible to encounter such difficulties! And the report further states, not that communism was now given up, but that its organization was improved by the introduction of a division of labor. The apostles were now occupied only with propaganda while a committee of seven members was elected to take charge of the economic functions of the congregation.

The whole story is quite compatible with an assumption that communism was practiced, but becomes entirely ridiculous if we accept our critic's view, borrowed by him from Holtzmann, to the effect that the Christians were distinguished from their Jewish fellow-citizens not by their social organization, but only by their faith in the "recently executed Nazarene".

Why should there have been any objection to the mode of division, unless a division had been resorted to?

Furthermore: "In Chapter xii (Acts of the Apostles) we read, as a direct contradiction to the reported existence of communism, that a certain Maria, a member of the society, was living in a house of her own."

This is true, but how does A. K. know that Maria had any right to *sell* this house? Perhaps her husband was still alive and had not joined the congregation? But even if she had a right to sell her house, the congregation would not necessarily have demanded that it be sold. This house was the meeting place of the members; Maria had placed it at the disposal of the congregation. It was used by the congregation, though legally it belonged to Maria. The fact that the congregation needed meeting places, that it was not a legal personage that might itself acquire such premises, and that therefore individual members went through the form of such ownership, certainly does not speak against the assumption of communism. We have no right to assume that the primitive Christian communism was so pedantically stupid in applying its regulations as to force its members to sell even those houses which it wished to make use of, handing in the proceeds for distribution.

The last objection raised seems to be the fact that communism is reported only in the case of the congregation of Jerusalem while no mention of it is made in connection with the other Christian congregations. We shall have occasion to refer to this point in tracing the later history of the Christian congregation. We shall then see whether, and to what extent, and for how long, communism was successfully carried out; but that is another question. We have already indicated that difficulties were encountered in large cities, which did not exist in the case of agricultural communities, for instance among the Essenes.

We are concerned now only with the original communistic tendencies of Christianity. We have not the slightest cause for doubt as to these. We have in their favor the testimony of the New Testament, the proletarian character of the congregation, and the strongly communistic tendency of the proletarian section of the Jews during the two centuries preceding the destruction of Jerusalem, which was very clearly expressed in Essenism.

All the arguments against the communistic tendency are based on misunderstandings, subterfuges and ingenious sophistries, for which there is not the slightest material support.

e. Contempt for Labor

The communism to which primitive Christianity aspired was— in accordance with the conditions of the times—a communism in articles of consumption, a communism in the distribution and joint consumption of such materials. As applied to agriculture this communism might also lead to a communism in production, in joint organized labor. In the large city, the manner of earning a living, whether by labor or by begging, necessarily dispersed the proletarians, owing to the conditions of production in those days. Communism in the large city could not signify in its goal anything but the highest possible stage of that bleeding of the rich by the poor which had been so masterfully developed in earlier centuries wherever the proletariat had attained political power, as in Athens and in Rome. The joint activities to which it aspired could at most be equivalent to a joint consumption of the foodstuffs and other materials thus obtained—a communism equivalent to a common household, to a family organization. In fact, Chrysostom, as we have seen, makes the case for communism from this point of view only. Who is to *produce* the wealth that is to be consumed in common, is not one of his concerns, and we find the same condition in primitive Christianity. The Gospels cite remarks by Jesus on all possible subjects, but not on labor. Or rather, when he does speak of labor, he does so in the most disdainful terms. Thus we read in Luke (xii, 22 *ff*.):

"Take no thought for your life, what ye shall eat; neither for the body, what ye shall put on. The life is more than meat and the body is more than raiment. Consider the ravens: for they neither sow nor reap; which neither have storehouses nor barn; and God feedeth them: How much better are ye than the fowls? And which of you with taking thought can add to his stature one cubit? If ye then be not able to do that thing which is least why take ye thought for the rest. Consider the lilies how they grow: they toil not, they spin not; and yet I say unto you, that Solomon in all his glory was not arrayed like one of these. If then God so clothed the grass which is today in the field and tomorrow is cast into the oven; how much more will he clothe you, O ye of little faith? And seek not ye what ye shall eat, or what ye shall drink, neither be ye of doubtful mind. For all these things do the nations of the world seek after: and your Father knoweth that ye have need of these things. But rather seek ye the Kingdom of God; and all these things shall be added unto you. Fear not, little flock; for it is your Father's good pleasure to give you the kingdom. Sell that ye have, and give alms."

This by no means is to be understood as an exhortation to the Christian to be ascetic and therefore ignore matters of eating and drinking, because of the necessity of turning his mind to his soul's welfare. No, the Christians are to strive for the Kingdom of God; in other words, for their own rule, and then they will have everything they need. We shall have further occasion to observe how earthly was their conception of this "Kingdom of God".

f. The Destruction of the Family

Whenever communism is based not upon a community of production but upon a community of consumption, and pursues the goal of transforming the entire community into a new family, it necessarily finds the presence of the traditional family ties to be a disturbing element. We have already seen this in the case of the Essenes, and now we are to observe a repetition in the case of Christianity, which often expresses its hostility to the family in a very emphatic manner. Thus the Gospel ascribed to Mark tells us (iii, 31 ff.):

"There came then his (Jesus's) brethren and his mother, and standing without, sent unto him, calling him. And the multitude sat about him, and they said unto him, Behold, thy mother and thy brethren without seek for thee. And he answered them, saying, Who is my mother, or my brethren? And he looked round about on them which sat about him, and said, Behold my mother and my brethren! For whosoever shall do the will of God, the same is my brother, and my sister, and mother." Luke is particularly emphatic on this point; we read (ix, 59 ff.):

"And he said unto another, Follow me. But he said, Lord, suffer me first to go and bury my father. Jesus said unto him, Let the dead bury their dead: but go thou and preach the kingdom of God. And another also said, Lord, I will follow thee; but let me first go bid them farewell, which are at home at my house. And Jesus said unto him, No man, having put his hand to the plough, and looking back, is fit for the kingdom of God."

While the above is an evidence that the greatest ruthlessness was demanded with regard to the family, we find in another passage in Luke a distinct expression of hatred against the family (xiv, 26):

"If any man come to me, and hate not his father, and mother, and wife, and children, and brethren, and sisters, yea, and his own life also, he cannot be my disciple."

In this connection Matthew again is found to be the opportunistic revisionist. Matthew renders the above sentence in the following manner (x, 37):

"He that loveth father or mother more than me is not worthy of me; and he that loveth son or daughter more than me is not worthy of me." This already represents a considerable attenuation of the hatred toward the family. Closely connected with this hatred of the family is the renunciation of marriage, which was as inexorably demanded by Christianity as by Essenism. But the two systems are again found to be similar in the fact that both develop the two possible forms of the unmarried state: celibacy, or a renunciation of all conjugal life; and the irregular, extra-marital sexual relations that have also been designated under the name "community of wives."

There is a very noteworthy passage in Campanella's *City of the Sun*, in which a critic maintains: "Saint Clement the Roman says that by the arrangements of the Apostles even their wives had to be owned in common, and praises Plato and Socrates for having also maintained that things should be so arranged. But the Glosses interpret this as meaning a common obedience to all, but not a community of the bed. And Tertullian confirms these Glosses and states that the first Christians owned everything in common except their wives, who, however, had shown common obedience to all."

This "common obedience" is an interesting parallel to the blessedness of those who are "poor in spirit".

A peculiar state of sexual relations is suggested by a passage in the *Doctrines of the Twelve Apostles*, one of the oldest literary products of Christianity, which gives an idea of its institutions in the Second Century; here we read (xi, 11):

"But every prophet, tried and true, who acts with regard to the earthly mystery of the Church, but does not teach others to do that which he himself does, let him not be judged by you, for he has a judgment in God; such was the conduct of the ancient (Christian) prophets."

Harnack observes that the obscure words, "the earthly mystery of the church" signify the married state, and that the object of these lines was to counteract the suspicion felt by the congregation toward such prophets as entered into peculiar conjugal relations. Harnack surmises that the reference here is to persons who lived in marriage as eunuchs, or lived with their wives as sisters. Is it possible that such continence could really have given offense? We may hardly assume so. It would be very interesting if we could learn that these prophets, while no longer preaching an extra-marital sexual practice, nevertheless still "resembled the old prophets", in other words, the first teachers of Christianity, in that they actually practised such relations.

Harnack himself quotes the following passage as a "good illustration of conduct with regard to the earthly mystery of the church", from the *Letter on Virginity* (1, 10), wrongly ascribed to Saint Clement:

"Many shameless persons live together with virgins under the pretext of piety and thus incur danger, or they roam about with them alone on the paths and in wildernesses, on ways that are full of dangers, vexation, pitfalls, and ditches. . . . Others eat and drink with them, lie together with them at table, with virgins and consecrated women (*sacratis*), with luxurious revelry and much shamefulness; such things should not come to pass among the faithful and least of all among those who have chosen the office of virginity."

In the First Epistle of Saint Paul to the Corinthians, the apostles, who are bound to celibacy, claim the right to roam about the world with female comrades. Paul cries to his hearers:

"Am I not free? . . . Have we not power to lead about a sister (ἀδελφήν), a wife [13] (γυναῖκα), as well as other apostles and as the brethren of the Lord and Cephas (Peter)?" [14]

A moment before Paul had advised against marriage.

---

[13] Luther translates thus: To lead about a sister as my wife; Weizsäcker, "To lead about as my married wife." Γυνή means *woman*, as a sexual creature, the female of animals, even a concubine, and therefore also a wife. It is impossible that a legally married wife should here be meant by the Apostle's defense of his "freedom."

[14] I Corinthians ix, 1, 5.

This roaming about of the apostle with a young lady is an important element in the *Acts of Saint Paul,* a romance which is said by Tertullian to have been written by a presbyter in Asia Minor in the Second Century, according to the latter's own admission. Yet "these Acts were for a long time a favorite book of edification,"[15] a sign that the facts communicated in them must have been considered by many pious Christians as not at all offensive but rather quite edifying. The most remarkable part of this book is the "pretty legend of Thekla, . . . which constitutes an excellent depiction of the atmosphere of the Christianity of the Second Century."[15]

This legend tells us that Thekla, the betrothed of an aristocratic youth of Icarium, had heard one of the apostle's orations and had at once become enthusiastic for him. The narration gives us an interesting personal description of the apostle: short in stature, bald, with crooked legs, projecting knees, large eyes, eyebrows meeting over the nose, a rather long nose, full of charm, having the appearance now of a man and now of an angel. Unfortunately, we are not told which of the above corporal assets is to be classed as aiding to make up his angelic appearance.

In short, the magic power of his speech makes a profound impression on the beautiful Thekla and she renounces her betrothed. The latter denounces Paul before the governor as a man who by his speeches induces women and maidens to refrain from marriage. Paul is thrown into prison but Thekla finds her way to his cell and is found there with him. The governor thereupon condemns Paul to be banished from the city and Thekla to be burned at the stake. She is saved by a miracle: the burning pyre is extinguished by a cloudburst, which also confuses and disperses the spectators.

Thekla, now free, follows after Paul, whom she finds on the highway. He takes her by the hand and wanders to Antioch with her, where they meet an aristocrat, who at once falls in love with Thekla and is willing to take her from Paul and indemnify him richly for his consent. Paul replies that she be-

---

[15] Pfleiderer, *Primitive Christianity,* vol. iii, pp. 245, 246.

longs not to him and he knows her not, which is a very feeble sort of answer for a proud apostle to make. But Thekla makes up for this weakness by the energy with which she defends herself against the aristocratic voluptuary, who attempts to take possession of her by force. For this offense she is thrown to the wild animals in the circus, but they will do her no injury, with the result that she is once more freed. She now clothes herself as a man, cuts off her hair and again follows after Paul, who instructs her to teach the word of God and probably also bestows upon her the right to baptize, if we may infer this from an observation of Tertullian.

The original form of this story evidently contained much that was offensive in the eyes of the later Church; "but as the Acts were found to be otherwise edifying and entertaining, the device of a clerical editing was resorted to, which eliminated the most objectionable elements, without entirely removing all traces of the original character of the work" (Pfleiderer, *op. cit.*, vol. iii, p. 256). But though many such writings may have been lost, we still have a sufficient number of indications that point to the existence of peculiar sexual relations, which deviated considerably from the traditional forms, gave much offense, and therefore required energetic defense on the part of the apostles; the later Church, which had to bear the responsibility for these conditions, tried as far as possible to suppress the record of them.

We need hardly point out that the unmarried state is likely to lead to extra-conjugal sexual relations, except in the case of fanatical ascetics.

The fact that the Christians expected their future state, which was to begin with the resurrection, to be characterized by a cessation of marriage, is also clearly indicated by the following passage in which Jesus answers the delicate question: If a woman has had seven husbands in succession, to which of them will she belong after the resurrection:

"And Jesus answering said unto them: The children of this world (αἰῶνος) marry, and are given in marriage: But they which shall be accounted worthy to obtain that world, and the resurrection from the dead, neither marry nor are given in marriage:

Neither can they die any more: for they are equal unto the angels; and are children of God, being the children of the resurrection" (Luke xx, 34-36).

This must not be interpreted as signifying that men would be pure spirits in the primitive Christian state of the future, without fleshly needs. Their physical character and their delight in material enjoyments is expressly emphasized, as we shall still have occasion to learn. There is no doubt that Jesus is here saying that all existing marriages will be dissolved in the state of the future, so that the question as to which of the seven husbands is the proper one loses its point.

But we must not consider the act of the Roman Bishop Callistus (217-222), who permitted maidens and widows of senatorial station to enter into extra-conjugal relations even with slaves, to be an evidence of hostility to marriage. This consent was not the product of a communism whose hostility to the family had been exaggerated to the highest point, but rather the product of an opportunistic revisionism which gladly made exceptional concessions in order to obtain wealthy and powerful supporters.

But this revisionism was repeatedly opposed by the revival of communistic tendencies in the Christian Church, and these were very frequently connected with a denunciation of marriage, by resorting to celibacy, or with the practice of a so-called community of wives, frequently found among the Manicheans and Gnostics.

The most vigorous of these tendencies was that represented by the Carpocratians.

"Epiphanes (the son of Carpocrates) taught that divine justice had bestowed everything upon its creatures for equal possession and enjoyment. The mine and thine were not introduced into the world until human laws became operative, and with them theft and adultery and all other sins; for does not the Apostle say: 'For by the law is the knowledge of sin' (Romans iii, 20), and 'Nay, I had not known sin, but by the law' (vii, 7). Since God himself had implanted in men the powerful sexual impulse in order to maintain the race, any prohibition of sexual lust is absurd, and prohibition of lusting after one's neighbor's wife is doubly absurd, since thereby what is common is made a private possession. The Gnostics therefore consider monogamy to be as much a transgression of the community of wives required by divine justice as the private ownership of property is a violation of the community of goods. . . . Saint Clement concludes his sketch of these libertine Gnostics (Carpocratians and Nicolaites, a special division of the Simonians) with the observation that all these heresies may be classified according to two tendencies: either they teach a moral indifferentism or an exaggerated sanctimonious continence." [16]

These were indeed the two alternatives which a consistent communism of the household might follow. We have already indicated that these two extremes may meet, that they take their origin from the same economic root, irreconcilable though they may appear to be in philosophy.

With the dissolving, or at least the loosening, of the traditional family ties, there necessarily resulted a change in the position of woman. Once she ceased to be bound to the narrow family activities, once she cast them off, she was enabled to devote her mind and her interests to other thoughts, outside the family sphere. According to her temperament, constitution, and social station, she might in some cases free herself not only from the family ties, but also from all ethical considerations, from all respect for social commandments, from all virtue and modesty. This was usually the case with the aristocratic ladies of imperial Rome, who were enabled by their great wealth and by their artificial childlessness to refrain from doing any work in the family.

On the other hand, the abolition of the family by a communism of the household produced in the proletarian women a great strengthening of the ethical feelings, which were now transferred from the narrow circle of the family to the much wider circle of the Christian congregation; their unselfish solicitude for the daily satisfaction of the needs of husbands and children became a solicitude for the liberation of the human race from all its wretchedness.

We therefore find in the early Christian congregation not only

[16] Pfleiderer, *Primitive Christianity*, vol. iii, p. 160.

prophets, but also prophetesses. For instance, the Acts of the Apostles tell us of the "evangelist" Philippos; "and the same man had four daughters, virgins, which did prophesy" (xxi, 9).

The story of Thekla, whom Paul commissions to teach and perhaps even to baptize, also indicates that the presence of female teachers of the divine word was not at all unusual in the Christian congregation.

In the First Epistle to the Corinthians (chap. xi), Paul expressly recognizes the right of women to act as prophets. He asks of them only that they should be veiled when discharging this duty in order not to arouse the lust of the angels! To be sure, chapter xiv says:

"Let your women keep silence in the churches, for it is not permitted unto them to speak; but they are commanded to be under obedience as also saith the law. And if they will learn anything, let them ask their husbands at home, for it is a shame for women to speak in the church" (34, 35).

But modern biblical critics consider this passage to be a later interpolation. Similarly, the entire First Epistle of Saint Paul to Timothy (as well as the Second, and that addressed to Titus) is a forgery dating from the Second Century. These writings already attempt to force woman back into the narrow confines of the family; concerning her we read: "Notwithstanding she shall be saved in childbearing" (ii, 15).

This was by no means the view of the early Christian congregation; its conceptions of marriage, the family, the position of woman, are fully in accord with what we may logically infer from the forms of communism that were then realizable in practice, and furnish an additional proof that communism dominated the philosophy of primitive Christianity.

II. THE CHRISTIAN IDEA OF THE MESSIAH

a. The Coming of the Kingdom of God

THE title of this chapter is actually a pleonasm; we know that "Christus" is simply the Greek translation of "Messiah." The "Christian Idea of the Messiah" therefore means nothing more nor less, if we take it etymologically, than the messianic idea of the Messiah.

But historically, Christianity does not include all those who believed in the Messiah; it includes only a specific class of these believers, a class whose messianic expectations differed but little at first from those of the rest of the Jewish people.

In the first place, the Christian congregation in Jerusalem, like all the rest of the Jews, expected that the Messiah would come within a short but not precisely fixed time. While the Gospels preserved to us were written at a time when most of the Christians no longer had such sanguine hopes—the Gospels show us quite clearly that the expectations of Christ's contemporaries had been completely disappointed—they nevertheless still preserve certain remnants of such a hope, remnants which they received from the oral and written sources with which they worked.

According to Mark (i, 14, 15), "After that John was put in prison, Jesus came unto Galilee, preaching the gospel of the Kingdom of God and saying, the time is fulfilled and the *kingdom of God is at hand.*"

The disciples ask Jesus what is the token by which they shall recognize the coming of the Messiah. He tells them all these tokens: earthquakes, pestilence, the disasters of war, eclipses of the sun, etc., and then informs them that the Son of Man will come with great power and magnificence to redeem his faithful, adding:

"Verily I say unto you, this generation shall not pass away till all be fulfilled" (Luke xxi, 32).

Mark's report is similar (xiii, 30). Again he has Jesus say in chapter ix:

"Verily I say unto you, that there be some of them that stand here which shall not taste of death until they have seen the kingdom of God come with power."

Finally, Matthew has Jesus promise his disciples:

"But he that endureth to the end shall be saved, but when they persecute you in this city, flee ye into another, for verily I say unto you, ye shall not have gone over the cities of Israel until the Son of man be come" (x, 22, 23).

Paul's statement in his First Epistle to the Thessalonians (iv, 13 *ff.*) is similar:

"But I would not have you to be ignorant, brethren, concerning them which are asleep, that ye sorrow not, even as others which have no hope. For if we believe that Jesus died and rose again, even so them also which sleep in Jesus will God bring with him. For this we say unto you by the word of the Lord, that we which are alive and remain unto the coming of the Lord shall not prevent them which are asleep. For the Lord himself shall descend from Heaven, with a shout, with the voice of the archangel and with the trump of God: and the dead in Christ shall rise first: *then we which are alive and remain* shall be caught up together with them in the clouds to meet the Lord in the air: and so shall we ever be with the Lord."

It was therefore not at all necessary that one should have died in order to enter the kingdom of God. The living might count upon beholding its coming; and it was conceived as a kingdom in which both those who were alive at the time, as well as those resurrected from the dead, would enjoy life in a full corporeal sense. We still have traces of this belief in the Gospels, although the later conception of the Church dropped the idea of an earthly state of the future and substituted the heavenly state for it.

Thus Jesus promises (Matthew xix, 28 *ff.*): "Verily I say unto you, that ye which have followed me in the regeneration when the Son of man shall sit in the throne of his glory, ye also shall sit upon twelve thrones, judging the twelve tribes of Israel. And everyone that hath forsaken houses, or brethren, or sisters, or father, or mother, or wife, or children, or lands, for my name's sake, shall receive an hundredfold and shall inherit everlasting life."

In other words, the reward for having dissolved the family and given away one's property will be a real enjoyment of earthly pleasures in the state of the future. It is particularly the pleasures of the table that are meant.

Jesus threatens them that will not follow him, with exclusion from his society on the day after the great catastrophe:

"There shall be weeping and gnashing of teeth when ye shall see Abraham, Isaac and Jacob and all the prophets in the kingdom of God and you yourselves thrust out, and they shall come from the east, and from the west, and from the north, and from the south, and shall *sit down* in the kingdom of God" (Luke xiii, 28, 29: compare also Matthew viii, 11, 12).

But he promises the apostles:

"And I appoint unto you a kingdom, as my Father hath appointed unto me; that ye may eat and drink at my table in my kingdom, and sit on thrones judging the twelve tribes of Israel" (Luke xxii, 29, 30).

Disputes even arose among the apostles as to precedence at table in the state of the future. James and John demand the places at the master's right and left, which causes much anger among the remaining ten apostles (Mark x, 35 *ff*.).

Jesus tells a Pharisee, at whose house he is dining, not to invite his friends and relatives to dine, but the poor, the crippled, the lame, the blind: "And thou shalt be blessed; for they cannot recompense thee: for thou shalt be recompensed at the resurrection of the just." We are immediately made to understand the nature of this blessedness: "And when one of them that sat at meat with him heard these things, he said unto him: Blessed is he that shall *eat bread* in the kingdom of God" (Luke xiv, 15).

But there will also be beverages to accompany the food. At the last supper Jesus announces: "But I say unto you, I will not drink henceforth of this fruit of the vine until that day when I drink it anew with you in my Father's kingdom" (Matthew xxvi, 29).

The resurrection of Jesus is considered as a harbinger of the resurrection of his disciples; but the Gospels expressly emphasize the bodily presence of Jesus after the resurrection.

He meets two of his disciples after his resurrection at the village of Emmaus, has supper with them, and then disappears.

"And they rose up the same hour, and returned to Jerusalem, and found the eleven gathered together, and them that were with them, saying: The Lord is risen indeed, and hath appeared to Simon. And they told what things were done in the way, and how he was known of them in breaking of bread. And as they thus spake, Jesus himself stood in the midst of them, and saith unto them, Peace be unto you. But they were terrified and affrighted and supposed that they had seen a spirit. And he said unto them: Why are ye troubled? and why do thoughts arise in your hearts? Behold my hands and my feet, that it is I myself: handle me, and see; for a spirit hath not flesh and bones, as ye see me have. And when he had thus spoken, he showed them his hands and his feet. And while they yet believed not for joy, and wondered, he said unto them: Have ye here any meat? And they gave him a piece of a broiled fish and of an honeycomb. And he took it and did eat before them" (Luke xxiv, 33 ff.).

In the Gospel of Saint John, Jesus gives evidence not only of his existence in the flesh after his resurrection, but also of a very healthy appetite. John reports that Jesus appeared to his disciples in a room the doors of which were locked and was "handled" by the doubting Thomas, and then goes on to say:

"After these things Jesus showed himself again to the disciples at the Sea of Tiberias; and on this wise showed he himself. There were together Simon Peter and Thomas called Didymus and Nathaniel of Cana in Galilee and the sons of Zebedee, and two other of his disciples. Simon Peter saith unto them, I go afishing. They say unto him, We also go with thee. They went forth and entered into a ship immediately; and that night they caught nothing. But when the morning was now come Jesus stood on the shore: but the disciples knew not that it was Jesus. Then Jesus saith unto them: Children, have ye any meat? They answered him, No. And he said unto them, Cast the net on the right side of the ship and ye shall find. They cast therefore and now they were not able to draw it for the multitude of fishes. Therefore that disciple whom Jesus loved saith unto Peter: It is the Lord. . . . As soon as they were come to land, they saw a fire of coals there, and fish laid thereon, and bread. . . . Jesus saith unto them: Come and dine. . . . This is now the third time that Jesus showed himself to his disciples, after that he was risen from the dead" (John xxi).

The third time was probably the last. Perhaps it was after the strengthening by this fish breakfast that Jesus rose to Heaven in the imagination of the Evangelist, from whence he should return as the Messiah.

While the Christians firmly maintained the bodily presence of the resurrected, they nevertheless had to assume that this body was of a different nature than the former body, if only for the sake of the life eternal. In a period which was so ignorant and so gullible as that of primitive Christianity, it is no source for surprise to find the most exaggerated notions flourishing on this subject in Christian as well as in Jewish minds.

In Paul's First Epistle to the Corinthians, we find the view expressed that those of his comrades who will live to see the state of the future, as well as those that will be resurrected for the purpose, will both have a new and higher type of bodily existence:

"Behold, I show you a mystery; we shall not all sleep (*until the Messiah comes*), but we shall be changed, in a moment, in the twinkling of an eye, at the last trump; for the trumpet shall sound and the dead shall be raised incorruptible, and we (*the living*) shall be changed" (xv, 51, 52).

The Revelation of Saint John even speaks of two resurrections, the first of which is to occur after the overthrow of Rome:

"And I saw thrones and they sat upon them, and judgment was given unto them: and I saw the souls of them that were beheaded for the witness of Jesus and for the word of God. . . . And they lived and reigned with Christ a thousand years, but the rest of the dead lived not again until the thousand years were finished. This is the first resurrection. Blessed and holy is he that hath part in the first resurrection. On such the second death hath no power, but they shall be priests of God and of Christ and shall reign with Him a thousand years" (xx, 4-6).

But then there arises a rebellion of the nations of the earth against these holy men. The rebels are cast into a lake of fire and brimstone, and the dead, all of whom are now resurrected, are judged, the unrighteous being cast into the lake of fire, while the righteous shall no longer know death and shall rejoice in life in the new Jerusalem, to which the nations of the earth shall bring their splendors and their treasures.

The reader will observe that Jewish nationalism here still peers through in the most naïve manner. As a matter of fact, as we have already had occasion to observe, the pattern for the Christian Revelation of Saint John is of Jewish origin, having been composed in the period of the siege of Jerusalem.

Even after the fall of Jerusalem there were still Jewish Apocalypses which similarly expressed their messianic hopes; examples of these are Baruch and the Fourth Book of Ezra.

Baruch announces that the Messiah will gather the peoples and bestow life upon them that submit to the descendants of Jacob and destroy the others who have oppressed Israel. Then the Messiah will seat himself on his throne and everlasting joy will prevail; nature will grant all gifts most generously, particularly wine. The dead shall be resurrected and men shall be organized quite differently. The righteous shall no longer be fatigued with labor, their bodies shall shine in splendor, but the unrighteous shall be even more ugly than before and shall be handed over to torture.

The author of the Fourth Book of Ezra expounds similar thoughts. The Messiah will come, will live for four hundred years, and then die together with all the rest of mankind. Thereupon there will follow a universal resurrection and a judgment in which the righteous shall have peace and sevenfold joy.

We see how slight is the difference in all these points between the messianic hopes of the early Christians and those of the Jewish population as a whole. The Fourth Book of Ezra, with numerous later adornments, also attracted great attention in the

Christian Church, and has been admitted to a number of Protestant translations of the Bible.

b. The Ancestry of Jesus

The early Christian conception of the Messiah coincided so completely with the Jewish conception at that time that the Gospels still lay the greatest stress on making Jesus appear as the descendant of David. For the Messiah, according to the Jewish notion, was to be of royal race. He is spoken of again and again as the "son of David" or the "son of God", which amounts to the same thing in Hebrew. Thus the Second Book of Samuel (vii, 14) has God say to David: "I will be his (*your descendant's*) father and he shall be my son."

And the King says in the Second Psalm:

"The Lord hath said unto me: Thou art my Son; this day have I begotten thee."

It was therefore necessary to prove by means of a long ancestral tree that Joseph, the father of Jesus, was a descendant of David, and to cause Jesus, the Nazarene, to be born in Bethlehem, the city of David. In order to make this seem plausible, the most remarkable assertions were mobilized. We have already referred to the account given by Luke (ii, 1 *ff*.).

"And it came to pass in those days that there went out a decree from Caesar Augustus that all the world should be taxed. (And this taxing was first made when Cyrenius was governor of Syria.) And all went to be taxed, everyone into his own city. And Joseph also went up from Galilee, out of the city of Nazareth, into Judea, into the city of David which is called Bethlehem; (because he was of the house and lineage of David:) to be taxed with Mary his espoused wife, being great with child."

The author or authors of the Gospel of Saint Luke had a suspicion that something was wrong and in their ignorance set down the baldest nonsense. Augustus never ordered a universal imperial census. The reference is evidently to the census that was carried out by Quirinius in the year 7 A.D. in Judea, which had just become a Roman province. This was the first census of this kind in Judea.

This mistake, however, is comparatively unimportant. But what are we to say of the notion that a general imperial census, or even a mere provincial census would require everyone to travel to his native town to be registered! Even today, in the age of railroads, such a regulation would produce an immense migration, the immensity of which would be exceeded only by its idiocy. As a matter of fact, the Roman census never required anyone to report except in his *place of domicile,* and only the men had to report in person.

But the pious end would not have been served if the good Joseph had traveled alone to the city of David. The taking of the census is therefore also made to require each head of a family to travel to his ancestral home with child and bag and baggage in order that Joseph might be represented as dragging his wife thither in spite of the advanced stage of her pregnancy.

But all this labor of love was lost. In fact, it even became a source of serious embarrassment for Christian thought, when the congregation began to outgrow the Jewish milieu. The pagans had no particular interest in David, and to be a descendant of David was no recommendation in their eyes. The Hellenistic and Roman mode of thought was much inclined to take the Fatherhood of God seriously, while to the Jews it had been merely a symbol of royal descent. It was nothing unusual among the Greeks and Romans, as we have seen, to represent a great man as the son of Apollo or some other god.

But Christian thought, in these efforts to give the Messiah prestige in the eyes of the pagans, encountered a little difficulty: namely, monotheism, which it had borrowed from the Jews. The fact of a god's having begotten a son is nothing out of the way in polytheism; you simply have one god more to deal with. But to have God beget another god, and yet have God remain a unit— this is not so easy to explain. And the matter was not simplified by isolating the creative power emanating from the godhead in the form of a special Holy Ghost. The task now was to accommodate these three persons under a single conception that would embrace them all. This was a task which brought to grief even the most extravagant imagination and the most ingenious quibbling. Therefore the Trinity became one of the mysteries that must simply be believed without being understood; a mystery that had to be believed for the very reason of its absurdity.

There is no religion without its contradictions. No religion ever was born from a single brain as the result of a purely logical process: each religion is the product of manifold social influences, often extending through centuries, and reflecting the most varied historical situations. But it would be difficult to find any other religion so rich in contradictions and unreasonable assumptions as is the Christian, because hardly any other religion arose out of such strikingly different elements: Christianity was handed down by Judaism to the Romans, by proletarians to world rulers, by a communistic organization to an organization formed for the exploitation of all classes.

Yet, the union of father and son in a single person was not the only difficulty arising from the image of the Messiah, for Christian thought, as soon as it came under the influence of a non-Jewish environment.

What was to be done with Joseph's paternity? It was no longer possible to have Mary conceive Jesus from her husband. And as God had cohabited with her not as a human being but in the form of a spirit, she must have remained a virgin. This meant relinquishing Jesus's descent from David. But so great is the power of tradition in religion that in spite of all this the beautifully devised ancestral tree of Joseph and the designation of Jesus as the son of David continued to be faithfully handed down. But to poor Joseph was now assigned the ungrateful task of living together with a Virgin without violating her virginity, and also, without even being in any way offended by her pregnancy.

c. Jesus as a Rebel

Although the Christians of later days could not bear to relinquish entirely the royal ancestry of their Messiah, in spite of his divine origin, they took all the greater pains to eliminate another characteristic of his Jewish birth, namely, his *rebellious spirit*.

Christianity in the Second Century was more and more dominated by a passive obedience, which was quite different from the nature of the Judaism of the preceding century. We have already learned the rebellious character of those strata of the Jewish people that were waiting for the Messiah, particularly the proletarians of Jerusalem and the roving bands of Galilee, the very elements from which Christianity took its origin. We must therefore assume at the outset that Christianity was characterized by violence in its beginnings. This assumption becomes a certainty when we discover traces of this condition in the Gospels, in spite of the fact that their later editors were most solicitously ambitious to eliminate any element that might give offense to those in power.

Gentle and submissive though Jesus may appear as a rule, he occasionally delivers himself of a statement of an entirely different kind, a statement forcing us to assume that—whether he actually existed or was merely an ideal figure of men's visions—he was, in the original tradition, a rebel who was crucified as an unsuccessful leader of an insurrection. Even the manner is noteworthy in which he occasionally speaks of legally righteous persons:

"I came not to call the righteous (δικαίους) but the sinners" (Mark ii, 17).

Luther translates: "I came not to call the righteous but sinners to *repentance*." Perhaps this was the variant in the manuscript he used. Certainly, Christians must have learned rather early how dangerous it would be to admit that Jesus summoned to him particularly those elements who were opposed to the laws. Saint Luke therefore added to the "calling": *to remorse* (εἰς μετάνοιαν), which addition may also be found in many manuscripts of Saint Mark. But in altering the "summoning to himself" or "calling" (καλέω) to the words "calling to repentance" they robbed this sentence of any meaning at all. Who would think of calling the "righteous", as Luther translates the δικαίους, to repentance? Besides, such an alteration would contradict the context, for Jesus makes use of the word because he has been accused of *eating* in the company of persons who are despised, and of associating with them, not of conjuring them to alter their conduct of life. No one would have objected to his calling sinners "to repentance".

Bruno Bauer rightly remarks in his discussion of this passage:
"In its original form this dictum is not even concerned with the
question of whether the sinners actually will do penance, accept
the call and *earn* their right to the Kingdom of Heaven by obedience to him who preaches penance. *Being* sinners, they have
privileges transcending those of the righteous. *Being* sinners,
they are summoned to blessedness, *given unconditionally favorable treatment*. The Kingdom of Heaven is *created* for the sinners and the call that goes out to them merely installs them in
their *property rights,* inhering in them as sinners." [1]

This passage suggests a contempt for the traditional laws, and
the words in which Jesus announces the coming of the Messiah
are suggestive of violence: the existing Roman Empire will perish
in an orgy of murder. And it appears the saints are not to play
a passive rôle in this process.

Jesus declares:

"I am come to send fire on the earth; and what will I, if it be
already kindled? But I have a baptism to be baptized with and
how am I straitened till it be accomplished! Suppose ye that I
am come to give peace on earth? I tell you, Nay, but rather
division: For from henceforth there shall be five in one house
divided, three against two, and two against three" (Luke xii, 49).
And in Matthew we read the plain words:

"Think not that I am come to send peace on earth: I came
not to send peace, but a sword" (x, 34).

Having arrived at Jerusalem at the time of the Passover, he
drives out the merchants and bankers from the Temple, the doing
of which is inconceivable without the active assistance of a considerable body of people whom he has aroused.

Not long after, at the Last Supper, immediately before the
catastrophe, Jesus says to his disciples:

"Now, he who has a purse, let him take it and also a pocket,
and he who has it not, let him sell his cloak, and buy a sword.
For I say unto you it must now be fulfilled in me what is written,
namely: And he will be counted among the lawless (ἀνόμων).
For what is written of me shall be fulfilled. They said, however:

[1] *Kritik der Evangelien und Geschichte ihres Ursprungs,* 1851, p. 248.

Lord, here are two swords. And he said to them, That is sufficient."

Immediately thereafter, on the Mount of Olives, the conflict takes place with the armed power of the state. Jesus is about to be arrested.

"And, behold, one of them which were with Jesus stretched out his hand, and drew his sword, and struck a servant of the high priest's, and smote off his ear."

But in this Gospel, Jesus is represented as being opposed to all bloodshed, consents peaceably to be chained, and is thereupon executed, while his companions remain absolutely unmolested.

In the form in which we have it, this story is a most remarkable one, full of contradictory statements that must originally have been quite different.

Jesus calls for swords as if the hour for action had come; his faithful set out armed with swords—and at the very moment when they encounter the enemy and draw their swords, Jesus suddenly declares that he is opposed in principle to all use of force—of course this statement is particularly sharp in the case of Matthew:

"Put up again thy sword into his place: for all them that take the sword shall perish with the sword. Thinkest thou that I cannot now pray to my Father and he shall presently give me more than twelve legions of angels? But how then shall the scriptures be fulfilled, that thus it must be?"

But if Jesus was opposed on principle to any use of force, why did he call for swords? Why did he permit his friends to bear arms when they went about with him? We can only understand this contradiction by assuming that the Christian tradition in its original form must have contained a report of a carefully planned *coup d'état*, in which Jesus was captured, a *coup d'état* for which the time had seemed to be ripe after he had successfully driven the bankers and sellers out of the Temple. The later editors did not dare to throw out this report, deeply rooted in tradition, in its entirety. They mutilated it by making the use of force appear to be an act undertaken by the apostles against the will of Jesus.

It is perhaps not unimportant to recall that this collision took place on the Mount of Olives.   This was the indicated starting point for any *coup d'état* against Jerusalem.

Let us record, for instance, the report in Josephus concerning the unsuccessful insurrection led by an Egyptian Jew in the time of the Procurator Felix (52-60 A.D.).[2]

This man came from the desert to the Mount of Olives with thirty thousand men in order to attack the city of Jerusalem, drive out the Roman garrison and seize power.   Felix gave battle to the Egyptian and scattered his adherents; the Egyptian himself appears to have escaped.

Josephus's history swarms with similar events.   They are indicative of the mood of the Jewish population in the time of Christ.   An attempted insurrection by the Galilean prophet Jesus would be not at all in contradiction with this mood.

If we are to regard his enterprise as an attempt of this kind, we can also understand Judas's treason, which is woven in with the report we are now discussing.

According to the version that has been preserved, Judas betrayed Jesus by means of a kiss, thus designating him to the detectives as the man to be arrested.   But this operation would have no meaning at all.   Jesus was well known in Jerusalem, according to the Gospels; he preached publicly every day; he was received by the masses with open arms; and yet we are suddenly to believe that it was necessary for Judas to point him out, in order that he might be distinguished from his adherents. A somewhat parallel situation would be to behold the Berlin police paying a stool-pigeon in order that he might point out to them who Bebel is.

But the matter becomes entirely different, if we are dealing with a carefully elaborated *coup d'état*.   Such a situation would involve something worth betraying, a secret worth buying.   If the report of the *coup d'état* that had been planned must be eliminated from the story, the tale of Judas's treason also becomes pointless.   But as this act of treason was apparently too well known among the comrades, and their hatred of the betrayer too great, it was impossible for the evangelist to eliminate this event entirely.   But

[2] See Pages 302-303 of this book.

he was now obliged to construct a new act of treason out of his own imagination, in which he did not meet with much success.

Not less unhappily invented than the present version of Judas's treason is that of the capture of Jesus. It is just he that is arrested, although he is represented as preaching the use of peaceful methods, while the apostles who have drawn their swords and used them are not at all molested. In fact, Peter, who has "smitten off" Malchus's ear, walks after the policemen and takes a seat in the high priest's yard and converses peaceably with them. Just imagine a man in Berlin opposing by force the arrest of a comrade, discharging a revolver in this situation, thus injuring a policeman, and then walking along quietly, chatting amiably with the police, and then sitting down with them in the station-house to warm up and drink a glass of beer with them!

It would have been impossible to invent more stupid situations. But it is precisely this awkwardness that must show us that an effort is being made to conceal something that must be eliminated at any price. A natural action, one easily understood, a hand-to-hand conflict ending in a defeat because of Judas's treason, and in the capture of the leader, becomes an absolutely senseless and incomprehensible process, which has come to pass only "that the scriptures might be fulfilled."

The execution of Jesus, which is easy to understand if he was a rebel, now becomes a completely incomprehensible act of senseless malice, which even succeeds in gaining its point in opposition to the Roman governor, who would liberate Jesus. This is an accumulation of unreasonable situations that can only be explained by the need felt by the later editors to whitewash the real event.

Even the Essenes, who were peaceable and opposed to all conflict, were carried away at the time by the general wave of patriotism. We find Essenes among the Jewish generals in the last great war against the Romans. Thus, Josephus reports of the beginning of the war:

"The Jews had chosen three mighty generals, who were endowed not only with bodily strength and bravery, but also with intelligence and wisdom, Niger of Peræa, Sylas of Babylon, and *John, the Essenian.*" [3]

The assumption that the execution of Jesus was due to the fact that he was a rebel is therefore not only the sole assumption which can make the indications in the Gospel clear, but it is also completely in accordance with the character of the epoch and of the locality. From the time to which Jesus's death is commonly assigned, up to the destruction of Jerusalem, there was no end of restlessness in that city. Street fights were a very common thing, as well as executions of individual insurgents. Such a street fight waged by a little group of proletarians, followed by the crucifixion of its ringleader, who was a native of Galilee, always a rebellious province, might very well indeed have made a profound impression on all the participants who survived, while history itself might perhaps not have taken the trouble to record such an every-day event.

In view of the rebellious agitation in which the entire Jewish race was living at that period, it was natural for the sect which had brought about this attempted insurrection to emphasize it for purposes of propaganda, thus giving it a firm place in tradition and naturally also somewhat exaggerating and adorning such details as the personality of the hero.

But the situation changed when Jerusalem had been destroyed. With the destruction of the Jewish community, the last remnants of the democratic opposition that had still maintained themselves in the Roman Empire were also destroyed. At about this time the civil wars in the Roman Empire itself cease.

In the two centuries lying between the Maccabæans and the destruction of Jerusalem by Titus, the eastern basin of the Mediterranean had been in a constant state of unrest, one government after another collapsed, one nation after another lost its independence or its dominant position. But the power which directly or indirectly was behind all these convulsions, namely, the Roman State, was at the same period torn by the most gigantic disasters, from the Gracchi to Vespasian, which emanated more and more from the armies and their leaders. At this epoch, in which the

[3] *The Jewish Wars,* iii, 2, 1.

expectation of the Messiah was developed and solidified, no political organism seemed more than provisional, while political revolution seemed that which was inevitable, that which was to be expected. This period ended under Vespasian. Under his reign, the military monarchy finally achieved the financial arrangement that was needed by the Imperator in order to preclude in advance any activity of a possible rival in wooing the favor of the soldiers and thus for a long period to stop military rebellions at their source.

From this time on we have the "Golden Era" of the Empire, a general condition of internal peace lasting more than a century, from Vespasian (69 A.D.) to Commodus (180 A.D.). While for the two preceding centuries unrest had been the rule, quiet was the watchword of this century. Political revolution, formerly a natural thing, now became most unnatural. Submission to the imperial power, patient obedience, now seemed not only a commandment of wisdom to the cowardly but became more and more deep-rooted as a moral obligation.

This naturally had its effect on the Christian congregation. The latter no longer had any use for the rebellious Messiah, who had been acceptable to Jewish thought. Even the moral feeling of the congregation rebelled against this rebellious Messiah. But as the congregation had become accustomed to regard Jesus as its God, as the incorporation of all the virtues, the transformation did not involve a relinquishment of the rebellious Jesus and the substitution of an ideal image of another personality, more adapted to the new conditions, but simply meant a gradual elimination of all rebellious elements from the image of the Jesus God, thus transforming the aggressively rebellious Jesus gradually into a passive figure, who had been murdered not because of an insurrection but simply because of his infinite goodness and sanctity, and the viciousness and malice of treacherous enviers.

Fortunately the retouching was done so unskillfully that traces of the original pigments may still be detected, permitting us to make inferences as to the entire picture. It is precisely because these remnants do not harmonize with the later retouching that we can the more surely infer that the former are genuine, and represent the actual original report.

In this respect, as well as in the others already discussed, the image of the Messiah in the first Christian congregation fully corresponded with the original Jewish image. Only the later Christian congregation began to introduce divergences. But there are two points in which the image of the Messiah in the Christian congregation differs at the very outset from the Jewish Messiah.

d.   The Resurrection of the Crucified

There was no lack of Messiahs at the time of Jesus, particularly in Galilee, where prophets and leaders of bands arose at every moment, revealing themselves as redeemers and the anointed of the Lord. But when such a redeemer had succumbed to the Roman power, been taken captive, been crucified or killed, his messianic rôle was ended, and he was naturally regarded as a false prophet and a false Messiah. The true prophet was still to come.

But the Christian congregation stood by its champion. For them also the Messiah in all his glory was still to come. But the Messiah still to come was none other than he who had already been, namely, the Crucified, who had arisen three days after his death and, having appeared to his adherents, ascended heavenward.

This conception was peculiar to the Christian congregation. What was its origin?

According to the primitive Christian conception it was the miracle of the resurrection of Christ on the third day after his crucifixion which proved his divine character and caused expectations to be formed of his return from heaven. Our present-day theologians have not advanced beyond this point. Of course the "liberal spirits" among them no longer take the resurrection literally. For the latter, Jesus did not really arise from the dead, but his disciples believed they saw him in their ecstatic raptures after his death, and therefore inferred that he was of divine origin:

"Therefore, we will have to regard the first appearance of Christ which Peter experienced in the same way as that of Paul who saw the celestial light-appearance of Christ in a sudden ecstatic vision on the way to Damascus—a physical experience, in no way an incomprehensible miracle, but psychologically conceivable according to many analogous experiences in all ages. . . . Following other analogies, it is also easy to understand that this experience of inspired vision did not confine itself to Peter, but repeated itself soon for the other disciples and, finally, for assemblages of believers. . . . The historical basis of the disciples' belief in the resurrection we find in the ecstatic visionary experiences emanating from an individual and soon convincing all; in these experiences they believed that they saw the crucified master alive and raised to heavenly glory. At home in the world of the miraculous, the imagination wove the garment to clothe that which was moving and suffusing the soul. At bottom, the moving force of the resurrection of Jesus in their faith was nothing more than the ineffaceable impression which one person had made upon them; their love and their confidence in him were stronger than death. This miracle of love and not a miracle of omnipotence was the foundation of the resurrection-belief in the early-congregation. Therefore it did not stop at passing emotions, but the newly awakened, inspired belief compelled action; the disciples recognized their life-task. They were to proclaim to their compatriots that Jesus of Nazareth, whom they had delivered up to their enemies, was the Messiah; that God had shown it the more by the resurrection of Jesus and his ascension to heaven, and that Jesus would soon return to take up his messianic government of earth." [4]

The above exposition would have us accept the dissemination of the Christian congregation's faith in the Messiah, and with it the entire enormous historical phenomenon of Christianity, as consequences of an accidental hallucination of a single mortal.

It is by no means impossible that one of the apostles may have had a vision of the Crucified; nor is it impossible that there were many persons who believed in this vision, as the epoch was one that was quite credulous and the Jewish people were profoundly impressed with the faith in the resurrection. Awakenings from

[4] O. Pfleiderer, *Christian Origins*, New York, B. W. Huebsch, 1906, pp. 137-139.

the dead were by no means considered inconceivable. Let us add a few examples to those we have already given.

In Matthew, Jesus prescribes to the Apostles their activities:

"Heal the sick, cleanse the lepers, *raise* the dead, cast out devils" (x, 8). The raising of the dead is here included in the most matter-of-fact way in an enumeration of the daily duties of the apostles, together with the healing of the sick. An admonishing addition warns them against accepting pay for this work. Jesus, or rather the author of the Gospel, considered raisings from the dead for a fee, in other words, conducted as a business, to be quite within the realm of possibility.

Quite characteristic is the story of the resurrection as reported in Matthew. The tomb of Jesus is guarded by soldiers, so that the apostles may not steal the corpse and spread the report that he has risen. But the stone is rolled from the opening of the grave to the accompaniment of flashes of lightning and earthquakes, and Jesus arises.

"Now when they were going, behold, some of the watch came into the city, and showed unto the chief priests all the things that were done. And when they were assembled with the elders, and had taken counsel, they gave large money unto the soldiers, saying: Say ye, his disciples came by night, and stole him away while we slept. And if this come to the governor's ears, we will persuade him, and clear you. So they took the money and did as they were taught: and this saying is commonly reported among the Jews until this day." (xxviii, 11 *ff.*)

These Christians therefore imagined that the resurrection of a man dead and buried for three days would not make so profound an impression upon eye-witnesses as to render it necessary to give more than a generous bribe in order to impose silence upon them, and even to induce them to spread a report that was the opposite of the truth.

We may readily believe that authors who held views like those expressed here by the evangelist were capable of accepting the fable of the resurrection without the slightest hesitation.

But this does not dispose of the entire question. This gullibility, this firm faith in the possibility of the resurrection, was not a characteristic peculiar to the Christian congregation, as the latter shared it with the entire Jewish population at the time, at least that portion of the Jewish population which was expecting a Messiah. Why did only the Christian congregation have a vision of the resurrection of its Messiah? Why not also the adherents of one of the other Messiahs who suffered a martyr's death in that era?

Our theologians will reply that we must explain this by means of the particularly profound impression made by the personality of Jesus, an impression that none of the other Messiahs had been capable of making. But in contradiction to this statement is the fact that Jesus's activities, which according to all indications lasted but a short time, left no traces in the masses, with the result that not a single contemporary recorded them. But other Messiahs continued fighting for a long time against the Romans and temporarily achieved great successes against the latter, successes that have been recorded in history; was it possible that these Messiahs made less of an impression than Jesus? But let us assume that Jesus, while incapable of fascinating the masses, was nevertheless able to leave behind ineradicable impressions among a few of his adherents, owing to the power of his personality. This would at most explain why the faith in Jesus continued among his personal friends, and not why it attained the force of propaganda among persons who had not known him, and whom his personality could not influence. If it was only the personal impression made by Jesus that produced the faith in his resurrection and his divine mission, this faith would necessarily become weaker as personal recollection of him died away, and the number of people who had been in personal contact with him decreased.

Posterity has no laurels for dramatic performers,[5] and in this respect the comedian and the clergyman have much in common. What is true of the actor is also true of the preacher, if he is *only* a preacher, and operates only through his personality, leaving no writings behind that may survive his personal life. His ser-

---

[5] *"Dem Mimen flicht die Nachwelt keine Kränze."*—Schiller, Prologue to *Wallensteins Lager.*

mons may be ever so profoundly effective, may elevate ever so powerfully, they cannot produce the same impression on those that do not hear them, on those who obtain them only by hearsay. And his personality will not have any effect on such persons at all; their imagination will not be stimulated by him. No one can leave behind a memory of his personality beyond the circle of those who have been in personal contact with him, unless he has produced a creation which is capable of making an impression quite apart from his person, be it an *artistic creation,* an edifice, a reproduction, a musical composition, a work of literature; or a *scientific achievement,* a methodically arranged collection of data, a theory, an invention, a discovery; or, finally, a *political* or *social institution* or *organization* of some kind or other, produced by him or at least with his distinguished coöperation.

As long as such a product endures and has its effect, an interest in the personality of the creator will also endure. In fact, while such a creation may have been practically ignored during the lifetime of its producer, it will grow after his death and begin to achieve significance, as is the case with many discoveries, inventions and organizations; it is quite possible that the interest in its creator may only begin after his death, and may continue increasing more and more. The less attention was paid to him when alive, the less actually known about his person, the more will this ignorance stimulate the imagination, if his creation is a mighty one, the more will this personality be surrounded by a halo of anecdotes and legends. In fact, man's love of causal relations, which seeks in every social event—and at one time also in every natural event—an active personality behind it, this love of causal relations is strong enough to cause the invention of the originator of any work that has become of great importance, or at least an association of this work with some name that has been handed down, in case the actual originator has been forgotten, or, as is so frequently the case, if it is the product of the coöperation of so many talents, none of which completely overshadows the others—as to make it impossible from the start to name a specific originator.

It is not in his *personality,* but in the *creation* that is connected with his name, that we must seek the reason why the messianic activity of Jesus did not have the fate of the similar activities of Judas and Theudas and the other Messiahs of that time. Ecstatic faith in the personality of the prophet, and the love of miracles, rapture, the faith in the resurrection—all these we find among the adherents of the other Messiahs as well as among the adherents of Jesus. We may not seek the cause for the differentiation of one of them in that which all have in common. While it may be natural for theologians, even the most liberal, to assume that though all the miracles may be abandoned that are told of Jesus, Jesus himself remains a miracle, a superman, such as the world has never seen—we are forced to deny even this miracle. The only point of difference between Jesus and the other Messiahs is in the fact that the latter left nothing behind them in which their personality might be preserved, while Jesus bequeathed an organization with elements that were excellently calculated to hold together his adherents and attract increasing numbers of new adherents.

The other Messiahs had merely gathered together bands for the purpose of insurrection; the bands dispersed after the failure of the insurrection. If Jesus had done no more than this, his name would have disappeared without a trace after his crucifixion. But Jesus was not merely a rebel, he was also a representative and champion, perhaps even the founder of an organization which survived him and continued to increase in numbers and in strength.

To be sure, the traditional assumption is that the congregation of Christ was not organized until after his death by the Apostles. But nothing obliges us to accept this assumption, which is, moreover, very implausible. For this assumption takes for granted no less a condition than that immediately after Jesus's death his adherents introduced into his doctrine an entirely new element, hitherto ignored and not desired by him, and that those who had remained unorganized until that time proceeded to take the step of organization, to which their teacher had been opposed, at the very moment when they had suffered a defeat that was strong enough to have destroyed even a well-knit organization.

To judge by the analogy of other similar organizations with whose beginnings we are better acquainted, we should rather assume that communistic beneficiary organizations of the proletarians of Jerusalem, imbued with hopes for the coming of the Messiah, had existed even before the time of Jesus, and that a bold agitator and rebel named Jesus, coming from Galilee, merely became their most prominent champion and martyr.

According to John, the Twelve Apostles had a common treasury while Jesus was still alive. But Jesus also demands that all his other disciples surrender all their property.

Nor do we read anywhere in the Acts of the Apostles that the Apostles and the congregation were not organized until after the death of Jesus. We find them already organized at this time, and holding their membership meetings and discharging their functions. The first mention of communism in the Acts of the Apostles is the following:

"And they continued stedfastly (ἦσαν δὲ προσκαρτεροῦντες) in the Apostles' doctrine and fellowship, and in breaking of bread, and in prayers" (ii, 42). In other words, they continued to take their meals together as before, also continuing other communistic practices. If these practices had not been introduced until after the death of Jesus, this wording could not have been used.

It was the organization of the congregation that served as a bond to hold together Jesus's adherents after his death, and as a means of keeping alive the memory of their crucified champion, who according to tradition had announced himself to be the Messiah. With the increase of the organization, as it grew more and more powerful, its martyr necessarily occupied the imagination of its members more and more, and they necessarily became more and more averse to regarding the crucified Messiah as a wrong Messiah, more and more impelled to recognize him as the true Messiah in spite of his death, as the Messiah who would come again in all his splendor; it became more natural for them to believe in his resurrection, and the belief in the messianic character and in the resurrection of the Crucified became the characteristic mark of the organization, distinguishing it from

other believers in the Messiah. If the faith in the resurrection
of the Messiah had arisen from *personal* impressions, it would
necessarily have become fainter and fainter in the course of time,
being more and more obliterated by other impressions, and would
finally disappear altogether with the death of those who had
known Jesus. But if the faith in the resurrection of the Crucified
was a result of the influence of his *organization*, then this faith
would become all the more solid and enthusiastic with the increase in the organization, the less it positively knew concerning
the person of Jesus, the less the imagination of his worshipers
was fettered by definite details.

It was not the faith in the resurrection of the Crucified which
created the Christian congregation and gave it its strength, but,
on the contrary, it was the vigor and strength of the congregation
that created the belief in the continued life of the Messiah.

There was nothing in the belief in the resurrection of the
Messiah that had been crucified, which would be in contradiction
with the Jewish philosophy of life. We have seen how thoroughly
that philosophy was permeated with the belief in the resurrection;
but we must not overlook the fact that the entire messianic
literature of the Jews was shot through with the thought that
the future glory could be obtained only at the price of the
suffering and death of the righteous, a thought which was a
natural consequence of the trials and tribulations to which the
Jews were then exposed.

The faith in the crucified Messiah gave every indication, therefore, of becoming simply one of the numerous variations of the
messianic prophecy among the Jews of that day; it might never
have amounted to more than that. But it was saved from this
fate—and from the resulting oblivion—by the fact that the
foundation on which it rested was a foundation that necessarily
involved the development of an opposition to the Jews. This
foundation, which was the life and vigor of the communistic
organization of the proletariat, was closely connected with the
peculiar quality of the messianic expectations of the communistic
proletarians in Jerusalem.

e. The International Redeemer

The messianic expectations of the rest of the Jews were purely national in character, including those of the Zealots. They involved: a subjection of the other nations under Jewish world dominion, which was to replace Roman world rule; the taking of revenge against the nations that were oppressing and maltreating the Jews. But the messianic expectations of the Christian congregation were quite different. This congregation also was filled with Jewish patriotism and hostility to the Romans; the throwing off of the foreign yoke was the necessary preliminary to any liberation, but the adherents of the Christian congregation did not content themselves with that. They did not plan to throw off only the yoke of foreign rulers, but of *all* rulers, including those at home. They summoned to themselves only the weary and heavy-laden; the day of judgment was to be a day of revenge on all the rich and powerful.

The passion which animated them was not race hatred but class hatred; this characteristic was the germ of their separation from the rest of the Jews, who were unified by a national spirit. But this element also was a germ of *rapprochement* to the rest of the world, the non-Jewish world. The national theory of the Messiah remained limited to the Jewish world, being rejected by the rest of the world, whose subjection was a portion of this idea.

Class hatred against the rich as well as proletarian solidarity were thoughts that were by no means acceptable to Jewish proletarians only. A messianic hope that involved a redemption of the poor must necessarily have found a willing ear among the poor of all nations. Only the social Messiah, not the national Messiah, could transcend the bounds of Judaism. Only such a Messiah could victoriously survive the terrible catastrophe that befell the Jewish community, culminating in the destruction of Jerusalem.

On the other hand, a communistic organization could not maintain itself in the Roman Empire, except in a region where this organization was strengthened by the faith in the coming of the Messiah and in his saving of those that were oppressed and maltreated. Practically, these communistic organizations, as we shall learn later, were based on an association for mutual aid. The need for such organizations had become universal in the Roman Empire beginning with the First Century of our era, and was the more vividly felt as the general poverty was increasing and as the last remnants of the traditional primitive communism were dissolving. But a suspicious despotism was putting down all forms of organizations; we have seen that Trajan was afraid even of the volunteer fire organizations. Caesar had still spared the Jewish organizations, but later these also lost their privileged position.

The mutual aid organizations could not continue to exist except as secret bodies. But would anyone consent to risk his life for the profit of mere aids in illness? Or who would risk his life through a feeling of solidarity with his comrades at a time when almost all public spirit had been extinguished? Whatever was left of such public spirit, or of devotion to the common weal, did not anywhere encounter a great, elevating idea like that of a messianic renewal of the world, which means, of society. And the more selfish among the proletarians, those that joined the mutual aid associations for the sake of personal advantage, were reassured as to the endangering of their persons by the idea of a personal resurrection with a subsequent rich reward; an idea which would not have been necessary in order to keep up the morale of the persecuted in an age whose conditions goaded the social instincts and feelings to the utmost, so that the individual felt himself irresistibly forced to obey them, even to the point of endangering his own advantage, his own life. The idea of a personal resurrection was, on the other hand, indispensable in the conduct of a dangerous struggle against powerful forces, in an age in which all the social instincts and feelings had been depressed to an extremely low point by the progressive social dissolution, not only among the ruling classes, but also among the oppressed and exploited.

Only in the *communistic* form of the Christian congregation, in that of the *crucified* Messiah, could the idea of the Messiah strike root outside of Judaism. Only through faith in the *Messiah* and in the *resurrection* could the communistic organization maintain and extend itself in the Roman Empire as a secret body. But when united, these two factors—communism and the faith in the Messiah—became irresistible. What the Jews had vainly hoped for from their Messiah of royal lineage was accomplished by the crucified Messiah who had issued forth from the proletariat: he subjected Rome, he brought the Caesars to their knees, conquered the world. But he did not conquer the world for the proletariat. In its victorious course, the proletarian, communistic, beneficial organization became transformed into the most tremendous instrument of domination and exploitation in the world. This dialectic process is not an entirely new one. The crucified Messiah was neither the first nor the last conqueror who finally turned the armies that had won his victories, to fight their own people, utilizing them for their subjection and enslavement.

Caesar and Napoleon also had their origins in democratic victories.

III. JEWISH CHRISTIANS AND PAGAN CHRISTIANS

a. The Agitation Among the Pagans

THE first communistic congregation of the Messiah was formed in Jerusalem; we have not the slightest reason to doubt the statement to this effect in the Acts of the Apostles. But congregations soon arose in other cities having a Jewish proletariat. Between Jerusalem and the other portions of the Empire, particularly its eastern half, there was of course a very active traffic, if only because of the many hundreds of thousands, perhaps millions of pilgrims, who annually made pilgrimages to that city. And numerous propertyless beggars without family or home were ceaselessly traveling from place to place, as is still the case in eastern Europe, staying at each place until the local charity was exhausted. Such is the meaning of the instructions given by Jesus to his apostles:

"Carry neither purse, nor scrip, nor shoes: and salute no man by the way. And into whatsoever house ye enter, first say: Peace be to this house. And if the son of peace be there, your peace shall rest upon it: if not, it shall turn to you again. And in the same house remain, eating and drinking such things as they give: for the laborer is worthy of his hire. Go not from house to house. And into whatsoever city ye enter, and they receive you, eat such things as are set before you: and heal the sick that are therein, and say unto them: The kingdom of God is come nigh unto you. But into whatsoever city ye enter, and they receive you not, go your ways, out into the streets of the same, and say: Even the very dust of your city, which cleaveth on us, we do wipe off against you: notwithstanding be ye sure of this, that the kingdom of God is come nigh unto you. But I say unto you, that it shall be more tolerable on that day for Sodom, than for that city" (Luke x, 4-13).

The final threat which the evangelist puts in Jesus's mouth is typical of the spitefulness of the beggar who has been deceived in his expectations of alms. He would most like to be requited by seeing the entire city go up in flames. But in this case the Messiah is to play the incendiary for him.

All the propertyless agitators of the new organization who thus wandered about were considered apostles, not only the twelve whose names have been handed down as installed by Jesus to be proclaimers of his word. The already mentioned *Didache* (the teaching of the twelve apostles) still speaks in the middle of the Second Century of apostles who are active in the congregation.

Such traveling "beggars and conspirators," who held themselves to be full of the holy spirit, brought the principles of the new proletarian organization, the "joyous message" of the evangel [1] from Jerusalem to the neighboring Jewish communities and ultimately as far as Rome. But as soon as the Gospel left the soil of Palestine, it entered an entirely different social environment, which placed an entirely different stamp upon it.

Together with the members of the Jewish community, the Apostles found another group, in close contact with these members, the associates of the Jews, the "god-fearing" pagans (σεβόμενοι), who worshiped the Jewish God, attended the synagogues, but were unable to go so far as to accept all the Jewish customs. At most they would subject themselves to the ceremony of immersion or baptism; but they would have nothing to do with the circumcision or with the dietary laws, the observance of the Sabbath, and other externals which would have cut them off entirely from their "pagan" surroundings.

The social content of the Gospel must have found ready acceptance in the proletarian strata of such "god-fearing pagans." It is they who transplanted it into other non-Jewish proletarian groups, which offered a favorable soil for the doctrine of the crucified Messiah, at least to the extent that it promised a social transformation and immediately organized institutions for the giving of aid. But these classes had no sympathy for all the

---

[1] *Evangel* (gospel) is derived from εὐ, *good, bringing good fortune,* and αγγέλλω, angello, *to announce, report.*

specifically Jewish customs; in fact, regarded them with aversion and contempt.

The more the new teaching spread in the Jewish communities outside of Palestine, the more evident it necessarily became that it would gain immensely in propaganda power if it should slough off its Jewish peculiarities, cease to be national, and become exclusively social in nature.

The man who first recognized this condition and advocated it energetically is called Saul, a Jew of whom tradition says that he did not come from Palestine, but from the Jewish congregation of a Greek city, Tarsus, in Cilicia. A fiery spirit, he first threw himself with all his strength into an advocacy of Phariseeism, and as a Pharisee he fought the Christian congregation, which was closely related to Zealotism, until, according to the tale, he was suddenly convinced of the error of his ways by a vision, with the result that he went to the opposite extreme. He joined the Christian congregation, but immediately appeared in it as one in favor of the overthrow of the established views, since he demanded that the new doctrine be propagated among non-Jews, and that it be made unnecessary for the latter to accept Judaism.

The fact that he altered his Hebrew name of Saul into the Latin Paul is typical of his tendencies. Such changes of name were frequently undertaken by Jews who wished to play a rôle in non-Jewish circles. If Manasse should change his name to Menelaus, why should not Saul call himself Paul?

The historically correct portion of the story of Paul can probably not be determined at this date with any certainty. As in all matters concerning personal histories, the New Testament here again is a very unreliable source, full of contradictions and impossible tales of miracles. But the personal acts of Paul are a subsidiary matter. The important point is his opposition in principle to the former views of the Christian congregation. This opposition arose from the nature of the case; it was unavoidable, and no matter how much the Acts of the Apostles may exaggerate individual events, the fact of the conflict between these two tendencies within the congregation has not been concealed from us. The Acts of the Apostles itself is a polemic product, the result

JEWISH AND PAGAN CHRISTIANS 385

of this conflict, written for the purpose of winning friends for
the Pauline position, and also of hushing up the opposition between the two tendencies.

At first the new tendency probably was very modest, demanding
only tolerance in certain points which the mother congregation
could have afforded to overlook.

At least that is what seems probable from the report in the
Acts of the Apostles, which, we must admit, however, painted the
situation in rather rosy colors and pretended that peace reigned
where actually a savage struggle was in progress.[2]

Thus, Acts relate, for example, from the time of Paul's propaganda activity in Syria:

"And certain men which came down from Judea taught the
brethren, and said: Except ye be circumcised after the manner
of Moses, ye cannot be saved. When therefore Paul and Barnabas had no small dissension and disputation with them, they
determined that Paul and Barnabas, and certain other of them,
should go up to Jerusalem unto the apostles and elders about this
question. And being brought on their way by the church, they
passed through Phenice and Samaria, declaring the conversion of
the Gentiles: and they caused great joy unto all the brethren.
And when they were come to Jerusalem, they were received of
the church, and of the apostles and elders, and they declared all
things that God had done with them. But there rose up certain
of the sect of the Pharisees which believed, saying: That it was
needful to circumcise them, and to command them to keep the
law of Moses" (Acts of the Apostles xv, 1-5).

The Apostles and Elders, in other words, the executive committee of the party, now assemble; Peter as well as James deliver
conciliatory speeches, and it is finally resolved to send Judas
Barsabas and Silas, likewise members of the executive committee,
to Syria, for the purpose of proclaiming to the brethren there
(Acts of the Apostles xv, 28, 29):

"For it seemed good to the Holy Ghost, and to us, to lay upon
you no greater burden than these necessary things; that ye

[2] Cf. Bruno Bauer, *Die Apostelgeschichte, eine Ausgleichung des Paulinis-
mus und des Judentums innerhalb der christlichen Kirche,* 1850.

abstain from meats offered to idols, and from blood, and from things strangled, and from fornication." The executive committee thus renounced the circumcision of the pagan proselytes, but the charitable practices might not be neglected: "Only they would that we should remember the poor; the same which I also was forward to do." Such is the Apostle's report in his Epistle to the Galatians (ii, 10).

The system of aids was dear to the hearts both of the Jewish Christians and the pagan Christians, and did not constitute a subject of dispute between them. Therefore it is so little mentioned in their literature, which was concerned almost exclusively with polemic aims. But it would be wrong to assume from these infrequent mentions that this charitable activity played no part in primitive Christianity. It is true it did not play a part in the latter's internal disagreements.

These disagreements went on in spite of all efforts at conciliation.

In the above quoted Epistle of Saint Paul to the Galatians, we already find the advocates of circumcision accused of acting from opportunistic considerations:

"As many as desire to make a fair show in the flesh, they constrain you to be circumcised; only lest they should suffer persecution for the cross of Christ" (vi, 12).

After the above-mentioned congress at Jerusalem, the Acts of the Apostles describe Paul as undertaking an agitational tour through Greece, the object of which is again propaganda among the pagans. After his return to Jerusalem, he reports to his comrades concerning the success of his mission.

"And when they heard it, they glorified the Lord, and said unto him: Thou seest, brother, how many thousands of Jews there are which believe; and they are all zealous of the law: and they are informed of thee, that thou teachest all the Jews which are among the Gentiles to forsake Moses, saying that they ought not to circumcise their children, neither to walk after the customs" (Acts of the Apostles, xxi, 20-21).

Paul is now requested to clear himself of this charge and to give evidence that he is still a pious Jew. He declares he is

ready to do this, but is prevented from carrying out his intention
by a sudden attack made on him by the Jews, who wish to kill
him as a traitor to their nation. The Roman authorities place
him under a kind of protective arrest and finally send him to
Rome, where he is enabled to carry on his agitation absolutely
unmolested, which was far from being the case in Jerusalem:
"Preaching the kingdom of God and teaching those things which
concern the Lord Jesus Christ, with all confidence, no man forbidding him" (Acts xxviii, 31).

b. The Opposition between Jews and Christians

It was natural that the pagan Christians should proclaim their
standpoint more emphatically when their numbers increased. The
opposition therefore was bound to become sharper and sharper.

The longer this opposition endured, the more numerous the
surfaces of friction, the more hostile was necessarily the attitude
of these two tendencies toward each other. This condition was
further sharpened by the aggravation of the contrast between
the Jews and the nations in whose midst they lived, in the decades
just preceding the destruction of Jerusalem. It was precisely the
proletarian element in Judaism, particularly in Jerusalem, that
approached the non-Jewish nations, especially the Romans, with
a more and more fanatical hatred. The Roman was the worst
oppressor and exploiter, the worst enemy, and the Hellene was
his ally. Every point by which the Jews were distinguished from
them was now emphasized more than ever before. All those who
laid the greatest stress on propaganda among the Jews were
necessarily impelled, from considerations based on the success of
their agitation, to place greater emphasis on Jewish characteristics, to cling to all the Jewish laws, to which they were furthermore inclined, owing to the influences of their environment.

But in the same measure as the fanatical hatred of the Jews
for the nationalities of their oppressors increased, the repulsion
and contempt which the masses felt for the Jews also increased.
Again this led many of the pagan Christians and their agitators
not only to demand for themselves exemption from the Jewish

laws, but also to speak more and more disparagingly of these laws. The contrast between the Jewish Christians and the pagan Christians became more and more, in the case of the latter, a hostility to Judaism itself. Yet, the belief in the Messiah, including also the crucified Messiah, was far too intimately interwoven with Judaism to enable the pagan Christians to deny the latter outright. They took over from Judaism all the messianic prophecies and other supports for the faith in the Messiah, and nevertheless were simultaneously becoming more and more hostile towards Judaism. This added a new contradiction to the many contradictions already found in Christianity.

We have already seen how great was the emphasis placed by the Gospels on Jesus's descent from David, and how they make the most peculiar combinations in order to have the Galilean born in Jerusalem. Again and again they quote passages from the sacred scriptures of the Jews, in order to prove by them Jesus's messianic mission. And they even represent Jesus himself as protesting against any accusation that he wished to abolish the Jewish law. "Think not that I am come to destroy the law, or the prophets: I am not come to destroy but to fulfill. For verily I say unto you: Till heaven and earth pass, one jot or one tittle shall in no wise pass from the law until all be fulfilled" (Matthew v, 17; cf. Luke xvi, 16).

Jesus commands his disciples as follows:

"Go not into the way of the Gentiles and into any city of the Samaritans enter ye not: But go rather to the lost sheep of the house of Israel" (Matthew x, 6).

This is an outright prohibition against propaganda outside of Judaism. Jesus expressed himself similarly, though more gently, to a Phœnician woman in Matthew (a Greek woman, born in Syro-Phœnicia, in Mark). She called out to him:

"Have mercy on me, O Lord, thou son of David; my daughter is grievously vexed with a devil. But he answered her not a word. And his disciples came and besought him, saying: Send her away; for she crieth after us. But he answered and said: *I am not sent but unto the lost sheep of the house of Israel.* Then

came she and worshiped him, saying: Lord, help me.   But he
answered and said: It is not meet to take the people's bread and
to cast it to dogs, and she said: Truth, Lord, yet the dogs eat of
the crumbs which fall from their masters' table.   Then Jesus
answered and said unto her: O woman, great is thy faith: be it
unto thee even as thou wilt.   And her daughter was made whole
from that very hour" (Matthew xv, 21 ff.; cf. Mark vii, 27).

In this case Jesus consents to listen to reason.   But at first he
shows himself to be very ungracious toward the Greek woman,
for the reason that she is not a Jewess, although she calls upon
him as the son of David in terms suggesting a Jewish faith in the
Messiah.

Quite Jewish is the thought behind Jesus's promise to his
Apostles that they shall sit in his state of the future upon twelve
thrones, judging the twelve tribes of Israel.   This promise could
have charms only for a Jew, and only for a Jew in Judea.   It
completely lost its point in the propaganda among the pagans.

But while the Gospels took over such impressive traces of the
Jewish faith in the Messiah, they often placed them in immediate
juxtaposition with outbursts of that hostility to the Jews with
which their authors and editors were filled.   Jesus again and
again delivers sermons against everything that is dear to the
pious Jew, the fasts, the dietary laws, the observance of the
Sabbath.   He exalts the pagans over the Jews:

"Therefore say I unto you: The kingdom of God shall be
taken from you, and given to a nation bringing forth the fruits
thereof" (Matthew xxi, 43).

Jesus even goes so far as to curse the Jews outright:

"Then began he to upbraid the cities wherein most of his
mighty works were done, because they repented not: Woe unto
thee, Chorazin! woe unto thee, Bethsaida! for if the mighty
works, which were done in you had been done in Tyre and Sidon,
they would have repented long ago in sackcloth and ashes.   But
I say unto you: It shall be more tolerable for Tyre and Sidon at
the day of judgment, than for you.   And thou, Capernaum,
which art exalted into heaven, shalt be brought down to hell: for

if the mighty works, which have been done in thee, had been done in Sodom, it would have remained until this day. But I say unto you, that it shall be more tolerable for the land of Sodom in the day of judgment, than for thee" (Matthew xi, 20-24).

These words are an evidence of distinct hatred of the Jews. We no longer hear one sect of Judaism reviling another sect of the same nation. Here the Jewish nation as such is branded as morally inferior, is represented as unusually malicious and stubborn.

We also find this thought expressed in the prophecies laid into the mouth of Jesus concerning the destruction of Jerusalem, which of course were only fabricated after this event had come to pass. The Jewish War, which so astonishingly revealed the strength of the Jews and the danger they embodied for their enemies, this savage outburst of wild despair, exaggerated the hostility between Jews and pagans to the utmost degree, and had about the same effect therefore as the June Battle and the Paris Commune had in the Nineteenth Century on the class hatred between the proletariat and the bourgeoisie. This also deepened the chasm between Jewish Christianity and pagan Christianity, but in addition it deprived the former more and more of its entire basis. The destruction of Jerusalem took the ground from under the feet of any independent class movement on the part of the Jewish proletariat. Such a movement must be based on the independence of the nation. After the destruction of Jerusalem, Jews existed only in foreign countries, among enemies, by whom they were all, rich and poor, equally hated and persecuted, and against whom they all had to hold firmly together. The charity of the wealthy toward their poor fellow-countrymen therefore reached a very high point precisely among the Jews; in many cases the feeling of national solidarity overpowered class hostilities. The Jewish phase of Christianity therefore actually lost its propaganda strength. Christianity from that time on became more and more exclusively a pagan Christianity, it was no longer a political party within Judaism, but a political party outside of Judaism, even hostile to Judaism. A Christian attitude and an anti-Semitic attitude gradually became identical conceptions.

But with the downfall of the Jewish community, the national Jewish hope for the Messiah lost the soil from which it grew. It was possible for it to continue to live for a few decades, to make a few more spasmodic motions before its death, but as an effective factor in political and social development it had received its death-blow in the destruction of the Jewish capital.

But this was not true of the hopes of the Messiah among the pagan Christians, who had been completely divorced from the Jewish nation and were untouched by its tribulations. The idea of the Messiah now retained its living force only in the form of the *crucified Messiah*, in other words, the non-Jewish Messiah, the Messiah translated into Greek, the *Christ*.

In fact, the Christians went so far as to transform the gruesome event which signified the *bankruptcy* of the Jewish hope for the Messiah into a *triumph* of their Christ. Jerusalem now begins to appear as the enemy of Christ, the destruction of Jerusalem is Christ's revenge on the Jews, a fearful evidence of his victorious power. Luke tells of Jesus's entrance into Jerusalem:

"And when he was come near, he beheld the city, and wept over it, saying: If thou hadst known, even thou, at least in this thy day, the things which belong unto thy peace! But now they are hid from thine eyes. For the days shall come upon thee, that thine enemies shall cast a trench about thee, and compass thee round, and keep thee in on every side, and shall lay thee even with the ground, and thy children within thee; and they shall not leave in thee one stone upon another; because thou knewest not the time of thy visitation" (Luke xix, 41-44).

And immediately thereafter Jesus again says that the days of the destruction of Jerusalem, bringing annihilation even to the pregnant and nursing mothers, will be "days of revenge" (ἐκδικήσεως, Luke xxi, 22).

The September murders of the French Revolution, which were not committed for the purpose of wreaking *vengeance* on infants, but in order to repel a cruel enemy, seem relatively gentle when compared with this judgment of the Good Shepherd.

But the destruction of Jerusalem also had other consequences for Christian thought. We have already pointed out how Christianity, which until then had been characterized by violence, now achieved its peaceful character. It was only among the Jews that we still find a vigorous democracy in the early beginnings of the Imperial Era. The other nations of the Empire had become cowardly and unfit for warfare, even their proletarians. The destruction of Jerusalem destroyed the last reservoir of popular energy in the Empire. All rebellion now became hopeless. Christianity now became pagan Christianity only; this made it submissive, even servile.

But the rulers of the Empire were the Romans. It was necessary for all the other elements of the Empire to ingratiate themselves with the Romans. While the first Christians had been Jewish patriots and enemies of all foreign rule and exploitation, the pagan Christians supplemented their hatred of the Jews with a worship of Romanism and of the imperial authority. We find this expressed even in the Gospels, in the well-known story of the provocateurs sent by the "scribes and Pharisees" to Jesus in order to provoke him to treasonable utterance:

"And they watched him, and sent forth spies (ἐγκαθέτους), which should feign themselves just men,[3] that they might take hold of his words, so that they might deliver him unto the power and authority of the governor. And they asked him, saying, Master, we know that thou seest and teachest rightly, neither acceptest thou the person of any, but teachest the way of God truly: Is it lawful for us to give tribute unto Caesar or no? But he perceived their craftiness, and said unto them, Why tempt ye me? Show me a penny. Whose image and superscription hath it? They answered and said, Caesar's. And he said unto them: Render therefore unto Caesar the things which be Caesar's, and unto God the things which be God's" (Luke xx, 20-25).

Jesus here expounds a remarkable theory of money and taxation: The coin belongs to him whose image and superscription

---

[3] *i.e.,* members of Jesus's group.

it bears; in paying taxes, we are therefore only returning his
money to the emperor.

The same spirit pervades the writings of the champions of
propaganda among pagan Christians. Thus we read in the
Epistle of Paul to the Romans (xiii, 1-7):

"Let every soul be subject unto the higher powers. For there
is no power but of God: the powers that be are ordained of God.
Whosoever therefore resisteth the power, resisteth the ordinance
of God: and they that resist shall receive to themselves damnation. . . . For he beareth not the sword in vain; for he is the
minister of God, the revenger to execute wrath upon him that
doeth evil. Wherefore ye must needs be subject not only for
wrath but also for conscience sake. For for this cause pay ye
tribute also: for they are God's ministers, attending continually
upon this very thing. Render therefore to all their dues: tribute
to whom tribute is due; custom to whom custom; fear to whom
fear; honor to whom honor."

How far removed we are now from the Jesus who summoned
his disciples to buy swords and who preached hatred of the rich
and powerful; how far removed from the Christianity which in
Saint John's Revelation curses Rome and the kings allied with it
most roundly: "Babylon, the great (Rome) the habitation of
devils, and the hold of every foul spirit, and a cage of every unclean and hateful bird. For all nations have drunk of the wine of
the wrath of her fornication, and the kings of the earth have committed fornication with her, and the merchants of the earth are
waxed rich through the abundance of her delicacies. . . . The
kings of the earth, who have committed fornication and lived
deliciously with her, shall bewail her and lament for her, when
they shall see the smoke of her burning," etc.! (xviii, 2, 3, 9).

The fundamental note in the Acts of the Apostles is the
emphasis on the hostility felt by the Jews for the teaching of
the crucified Messiah, and also the emphasis on a certain alleged
receptivity of the Romans for this teaching. What the Christians either desired or imagined to be the case after the fall of
Jerusalem is represented as having been the case in that city.

The Christian propaganda, according to the Acts of the Apostles, is again and again suppressed by the Jews in Jerusalem; the Jews persecute and stone the Christians wherever they can, while the Roman authorities protect the Christians. We have seen that Paul was said to have been seriously menaced in Jerusalem while he was permitted to preach unmolested in Rome. Freedom in Rome, suppression by force in Jerusalem!

But the most striking evidence of a hatred for the Jews and flattery for the Romans appears in the story of Christ's Passion, the tale of the sufferings and death of Christ. Here we can distinctly observe how the content of this story was transformed into its precise opposite under the influence of the new tendencies.

As the story of the Passion is the most important part of the historical outline given by the Gospels, the only part in which we can pretend that we are dealing with history, and as it is very typical of the primitive Christian mode of writing history, this story deserves our special consideration.

IV. THE STORY OF CHRIST'S PASSION

THERE are indeed few things that may be pointed out in the Gospels with a certain degree of plausibility as actual facts in the life of Christ: his birth and his death; two facts which indeed, if they can be proved, would show that Jesus actually lived and was not merely a mythical figure, but which throw no light whatever upon the most important elements in a historical personality: namely, the *activities* in which this person engages between birth and death. The hodge-podge of moral maxims and miraculous deeds which is offered by the Gospels as a report on these activities is so full of impossible and obviously fabricated material, and has so little that can be borne out by other evidence, that it cannot be used as a source.

Not much different is the case with the testimony as to the birth and death of Christ. Yet we have here a few indications that an actual nucleus of fact lies hidden under the mass of fabrications. We may infer the existence of some such basic facts if only from the circumstance that these stories contain communications that were extremely embarrassing for Christianity, which Christianity had surely not invented, but which were obviously too well known and accepted among its adherents to have enabled the authors of the Gospels to substitute their own inventions for them, which they often did without hesitation in other cases.

One of these facts is the Galilean origin of Jesus, which was very inconvenient in view of his claims to be a Messiah of the line of David. For the Messiah had to come from the city of David. We have seen what peculiar subterfuges were required in order to connect the Galilean with this city. If Jesus had been merely a product of the imagination of some congregation with an exaggerated messianic vision, such a congregation would never have thought of making a Galilean of him. We may therefore at least accept his Galilean origin, and with it his existence, as extremely probable. Also, we may accept his death on the cross. We have seen that the Gospels still contain passages which permit us to assume that Jesus had planned an insurrection by the use of force, and had been crucified for this attempt. This also is such an embarrassing situation that it can hardly be based on invention. It is too sharply in contrast with the spirit prevailing in Christianity at the time when it was beginning to reflect on its past and to record the history of its origin. Not—be it remembered—for historical purposes, but for polemical and propaganda purposes.

The death of the Messiah himself by crucifixion was an idea so foreign to Jewish thought, which always represented the Messiah with the splendor of a victorious hero, that only a real event, the martyrdom of the champion of the good cause, producing an ineffaceable impression on his adherents, could have created the proper soil for the idea of the crucified Messiah.

When the pagan Christians accepted the tradition of this crucifixion, they soon discovered that it had a drawback: tradition declared that the Romans had crucified Jesus as a Jewish Messiah, a king of the Jews, in other words, a champion of Jewish independence, a traitor to Roman rule. After the fall of Jerusalem this tradition became doubly embarrassing. Christianity was now in open opposition to the Jews, and wished to be on good terms with the Roman authorities. It was now important to distort the tradition in such a manner as to shift the blame for the crucifixion of Christ from the shoulders of the Romans to those of the Jews, and to cleanse Christ not only from every appearance of the use of force, but also from every expression of any pro-Jewish, anti-Roman ideas.

But as the evangelists were just as ignorant as the great mass of the lower classes in those days, they produced the most remarkable mixtures of colors in their retouching of the original picture.

Probably nowhere in the Gospels can we find more contradictions and absurdities than in the portion which for nearly two thousand years has always made the profoundest impression on the Christian world and stimulated its imagination most powerfully. Probably no other subject has been so frequently painted as the sufferings and the death of Christ. And yet this tale will bear no sober investigation, and is an aggregation of the most inartistic and crude devices.

It was only the power of habit which caused even the finest spirits of Christendom to remain obtuse to the incredible interpolations made by the authors of the Gospels, so that the elemental pathos involved in the crucifixion of Jesus, as well as in any martyrdom for a great cause, had its effect in spite of this mass of detail and imparted a brighter halo even to the ridiculous and absurd elements of the story.

The story of the Passion begins with Jesus's entrance into Jerusalem. This is a king's triumphal procession.[1] The population comes out to greet him, some spread their clothes before him on the road, others chop down branches from the trees, in order to strew them on his path, and all shout to him with jubilation: "Hosanna (*Help us!*); blessed is he that cometh in the name of the Lord: blessed be the kingdom of our father David, that cometh in the name of the Lord" (Mark xi, 9).

Kings were received thus among the Jews (cf. Kings ix, 13, speaking of Jehu). The common people are attached to Jesus; only the aristocracy and bourgeoisie, "the high priests and scribes", are hostile to him. Jesus conducts himself as a dictator. He has sufficient strength to drive the sellers and bankers out of the Temple, without encountering the slightest resistance. He appears to have absolute control of this citadel of Judaism.

---

[1] As an amusing curiosity, let us here call attention to the "literary miracle accomplished by Matthew by having Jesus seated *simultaneously* on *two* animals as he rides into the city." (Bruno Bauer, *Kritik der Evangelien,* vol. iii, p. 114.) The traditional translations gloss over this miracle. Thus, Luther translates:
"And brought the ass, and the colt, and put on them their clothes, and they set him thereon" (Matthew xxi, 7).
But in the original we read: "And they brought the ass (*female*) and the colt and laid their clothes upon *both* (ἐπ ἀυτῶν) and set him upon *both*" (ἐπάνω ἀυτῶν).
And in spite of all the liberties formerly taken by skilled literary artists, this stuff was rewritten century after century by one copyist after another, a proof of the thoughtlessness and simplicity of the compilers of the Gospels.

Of course this is a slight exaggeration on the part of the evangelist. If Jesus had ever possessed such great strength, it would not have failed to attract considerable notice. An author like Josephus, who relates the most insignificant details, surely would have had something to say on the subject. Besides, even the proletarian elements in Jerusalem, the Zealots, for instance, were never strong enough to govern the city without opposition. They encountered resistance again and again. If Jesus had been attempting to enter Jerusalem and purify the temple against the opposition of the Sadducees and Pharisees, it would have been necessary for him first to fight a victorious battle in the streets. Such street battles between the various Jewish factions were every-day events in Jerusalem at that time.

It is worthy of note, however, in the tale of his entrance, that the population is represented as greeting Jesus as the bringer of "the kingdom of our father David", in other words, as the restorer of the Jewish kingdom. This shows Jesus not only in the light of an opponent of the ruling class among the Jews, but also as opposing the ruling classes of the Romans. This hostility is surely not the product of a Christian imagination, but of the Jewish reality.

There now follow in the report of the Gospels the events that we have already treated: the order that the disciples obtain arms, the treason of Judas, the armed conflict on the Mount of Olives. We have already seen that these are remnants of an ancient tradition that later were no longer felt to be appropriate and were retouched to make them more peaceful and submissive in tone.

Jesus is taken prisoner, led to the high priest's palace and there tried:

"And the chief priests, and all the council sought for witnesses against Jesus to put him to death; and found none. For many bare false witness against him, but their witness agreed not together. . . . And the high priest stood up in the midst, and asked Jesus, saying: Answerest thou nothing? What is it which these witness against thee? But he held his peace and answered nothing. Again the high priest asked him, and said unto him: Art thou the Christ, the Son of the Blessed? And Jesus said: I am: and ye shall see the Son of man sitting on the right hand of power, and coming in the clouds of heaven. Then the high priest rent his clothes, and saith, What need we any further witnesses? ye have heard the blasphemy: what think ye? and they all condemned him to be guilty of death" (Mark xiv, 55, 56, 60-64).

Truly a remarkable form of court procedure! The court assembles immediately after the arrest of the prisoner, the same night, and not in the courthouse, which was probably on the Mount of the Temple,[2] but in the palace of the high priest! What would we think in Germany of the reliability of an account of a trial for high treason, with the court reported as sitting in the Royal Palace in Berlin! False witnesses now appear against Jesus, but in spite of the fact that no one cross-examines them, and that Jesus makes no reply to their accusations, they can adduce nothing to incriminate him. Jesus is the first to incriminate himself by declaring that he is the Messiah. Wherefore all this apparatus of false witnesses if this admission is sufficient to condemn Jesus? Their object is solely to demonstrate the wickedness of the Jews. The death sentence is immediately imposed. This is a violation of the prescribed forms, on which the Jews at that time laid very careful stress. Only a sentence of acquittal could be pronounced by the court without delay; a condemnation could only be pronounced on the day following the trial.

But did the council at that time have the right to impose sentence of death at all? The Sanhedrin says: "Forty years before the destruction of the Temple Israel was deprived of the right to pronounce judgment of life and death."

We find this confirmed in the fact that the council does not execute the punishment of Jesus, but hands him over, after having tried him, to be tried again by Pilate, this time under the accusation of high treason against the Romans, the accusation that Jesus had intended to make himself king of the Jews

[2] Schürer, *Geschichte des jüdischen Volkes,* vol. ii, p. 211.

and thus free Judea from the Roman rule. An excellent indict-
ment to be drawn by a court of Jewish patriots!

It is quite possible, however, that the council had the right
to pronounce sentences of death which required the approval
of the Procurator for their execution.

Now what course does the trial take before the Roman
potentate?

"And Pilate asked him: Art thou the King of the Jews? And
he answering said unto him: Thou sayest it. And the chief
priests accused him of many things: but he answered nothing.
And Pilate asked him again, saying: Answerest thou nothing?
Behold how many things they witness against thee. But Jesus
yet answered nothing; so that Pilate marveled. Now at that
feast he released unto them one prisoner, whomsoever they desired and there was one named Barabbas, which lay bound with
them that had made insurrection with him, who had committed
murder in the insurrection. And the multitude crying aloud
began to desire him to do as he had ever done unto them. But
Pilate answered them, saying: Will ye that I release unto you
the King of the Jews? For he knew that the chief priests had
delivered him for envy. But the chief priests moved the people,
that he should rather release Barabbas unto them. And Pilate
answered and said again unto them: What will ye then that I
shall do unto him whom ye call the King of the Jews? And
they cried out again: Crucify him. Then Pilate said unto
them: Why, what evil hath he done? And they cried out the
more exceedingly: Crucify him. And so Pilate, willing to content
the people, released Barabbas unto them, and delivered Jesus,
when he had scourged him, to be crucified" (Mark xv, 2-15).

In Matthew, Pilate goes so far as to wash his hands in the
presence of the multitude and to declare: "I am innocent of the
blood of this just person: see ye to it. Then answered all the
people, and said: his blood be on us, and on our children"
(Matthew xxvii, 24, 25).

Luke does not tell us that the council condemned Jesus to
death; the council simply denounced Jesus to Pilate.

"And the whole multitude of them arose, and led him unto

Pilate, and they began to accuse him, saying, We found this fellow perverting the nation, and forbidding to give tribute to Cæsar, saying that he himself is Christ a King. And Pilate asked him, saying, Art thou the King of the Jews? And he answered him and said: Thou sayest it. Then said Pilate to the chief priests and to the people: I find no fault in this man. And they were the more fierce, saying, He stirreth up the people, teaching throughout all Jewry, beginning from Galilee to this place" (Luke xxiii, 1-5).

Luke is probably closest to the truth. Jesus is here accused of treason in the presence of Pilate and with courageous pride he does not deny his guilt. When asked by Pilate whether he is the king of Jews, in other words, their leader in the struggle for independence, Jesus declares: "Thou hast said it." The Gospel of Saint John is aware how awkward it would be to retain this remnant of Jewish patriotism, and therefore has Jesus reply: "My kingdom is not of this world," meaning: if it had been of this world, my subordinates would have fought. The Gospel of Saint John is the youngest; it therefore took a long time for the Christian writers to make up their minds thus to distort the original facts.

The case for Pilate was very clear. As a representative of the Roman power, he was merely doing his duty in having the rebel Jesus executed.

But the great mass of the Jews had not the slightest cause to be indignant at a man who wished to have nothing to do with Roman rule and summoned them to refuse to pay taxes to the emperor. If Jesus really did so, he was acting in full accord with the spirit of Zealotism, then dominant in the Jerusalem population.

It therefore follows from the nature of the case, if we assume the accusation in the Gospel to be true, that the Jews sympathized with Jesus, while Pilate was obliged to condemn him.

But what is the record in the Gospels? Pilate finds not the slightest guilt in Jesus, although the latter admits such guilt himself. The governor again and again declares the innocence of the accused, and asks what evil this man has done.

This alone would be peculiar. But still more peculiar is the fact that although Pilate does not recognize Jesus's guilt, he yet does not acquit him.

Now it sometimes came to pass that the Procurator found a political case too complicated to judge it himself. But it is unheard of that one of the emperor's officials should seek a solution of the difficulty by asking the *masses of the people* what was to be done with the accused. If he preferred not to pronounce condemnation in cases of high treason, he would have to send the accused to Rome, to the emperor. The Procurator Antonius Felix (52-60 A.D.), for example, acted thus. He enticed the head of the Jerusalem Zealots, the bandit chieftain Eleazar, who had harried the land for twenty years, to come to him, by promising him safe-conduct, then took him prisoner and sent him to Rome, besides crucifying many of his adherents.

Pilate might thus have sent Jesus to Rome. But Matthew assigns a most ridiculous rôle to Pilate: a Roman judge, a representative of the Emperor Tiberius, lord of life and death, begs a popular gathering in Jerusalem to permit him to acquit a prisoner, and on their deciding negatively, replies: "Well, slay him, I am innocent of this blood!"   But no quality could more violently contradict that of the historical Pilate than the clemency suggested in the Gospels. Agrippa I, in a letter to Philo, calls Pilate "an inexorable and ruthlessly severe character," and accuses him of "corruption, bribery, violence, theft, manhandling, insults, *continuous executions without sentence,* endless and intolerable cruelties."

His severity and ruthlessness produced such terrible conditions that even the Central Government at Rome became disgusted and recalled him (36 A.D.).

And we are asked to believe that this man was exceptionally just and kind in the case of the proletarian seditionist Jesus, besides showing a degree of consideration for the wishes of the people that was of fatal outcome for the accused!

The evangelists were too ignorant to notice these difficulties. But they must have felt that they were assigning a peculiar rôle to the Roman governor. Therefore they looked for a cause that would make this rôle more plausible: they report that Pilate was accustomed to release a prisoner at Easter at the request of the Jews, and that when he offered to release Jesus they replied: "No, we should rather have the murderer Barabbas!"

In the first place, it is peculiar that no such custom is mentioned anywhere except in the Gospels; such a custom would be contrary to the Roman practice, which did not give governors the right of pardon. And it is contrary to any orderly legal practice to assign the right of pardon to an accidental mob rather than to a responsible body. Only theologians could accept such legal conditions at their face value. But even disregarding this, even if we accept the right of pardon so peculiarly assigned to the Jewish mob that happens to be circulating in front of the Procurator's house, we must nevertheless ask what is the relation between this practice and the present case?

Jesus has not even been legally sentenced. Pontius Pilate is faced with the question: Is Jesus guilty of high treason or not? Shall I sentence him or not? And he answers with the question: Will you make use of your right of pardon in his favor or not? Pilate, instead of pronouncing judgment, appeals for pardon! If he considers Jesus innocent, has he not the right to acquit him?

Now follows a new absurdity. The Jews are supposed to have the right to pardon; how do they exercise this right? Do they content themselves with asking that Barabbas be freed? No, they also demand that Jesus be crucified! The evangelists apparently infer that the right to pardon one implies the right to condemn the other.

This insane judicial practice is paralleled by a not less insane political practice.

The evangelists depict for us a mob that hates Jesus to such an extent that it would rather pardon a murderer than him; the reader will please remember, a *murderer*—no more worthy object of clemency was available—and is not satisfied until Jesus is led off to crucifixion.

Remember that this is the same mob that only yesterday hailed him as a king with cries of hosanna, spread garments before his

steps and greeted him jubilantly, without the slightest contradicting voice. And it was just this devotion on the part of the mob
that constituted—according to the Gospels—the cause for the
desire on the part of the aristocrats to take Jesus's life, also
preventing them from attempting to arrest him by daylight,
making them choose the night instead. And now this same mob
appears to be just as unanimous in its wild, fanatical hatred
against him, against the man who is accused of a crime that
would make him worthy of the highest respect in the eyes of
any Jewish patriot: the attempt to free the Jewish community
from foreign rule.

Has anything happened to justify this astonishing mental
transformation? The most powerful motives would be needed
as an explanation of such a change. The evangelists merely
utter a few incoherent and ridiculous phrases, if anything at
all. Luke and John assign no motives; Mark says: "The high
priests incited the multitude against Jesus"; Matthew: "They
persuaded the multitude." These turns of phrase merely show
that the Christian writers had lost even the last remnant of their
political sense and political knowledge.

Even the most brainless mob cannot be talked into fanatical
hatred without some motive. This motive may be foolish or base,
but there must be a motive. The Jewish mob in the Gospels
exceeds the most infamous and idiotic stage villain in its stupid
villainy. For without the slightest reason, without the slightest
cause, it clamors for the blood of him whom it venerated but
yesterday.

The matter becomes still more stupid when we consider the
political conditions of the time. Distinguishing itself from almost
all the other portions of the Roman Empire, the Jewish community had a particularly active political life, presenting the
highest extremes of all social and political oppositions. The
political parties were well organized, were by no means mobs
beyond control. The lower classes of Jerusalem had been completely imbued with Zealotism, and were in constant sharp clash
with the Sadducees and Pharisees, and filled with the most savage

hatred against the Romans. Their best allies were the rebellious Galileans.

Even if the Sadducees and Pharisees succeeded in "inciting" certain of the people against Jesus, they could not possibly have brought about a unanimous popular demonstration, but at most a bloody street-battle. There is nothing more ridiculous than the notion that the Zealots would dash with savage cries, not against the Romans and aristocrats, but against the accused rebel whose execution they force from the jelly-fish Roman governor, in spite of the governor's strange infatuation for the traitor.

No one ever invented anything more outrageously childish. But with this effort to represent the bloody tyrant Pilate as an innocent lamb, and to make the native depravity of the Jews responsible for the crucifixion of the harmless and peaceful Messiah, the genius of the evangelists is completely exhausted. The stream of their invention runs dry for a bit and the original story again peeps through at least for a moment: After being condemned, Jesus is derided and maltreated—but not by the Jews—by the soldiers of the same Pilate who has just declared him innocent. Pilate now has his soldiers not only crucify Jesus, but first has him scourged and derided as King of the Jews; a crown of thorns is put upon his head, a purple mantle folded about him, the soldiers bend the knee before him, and then they again beat him upon the head and spit on him. Finally they place upon his cross the inscription, "Jesus, King of the Jews".

This again brings out the original nature of the *dénouement*. Again the Romans appear as Jesus's bitter enemies, and the cause of their derision as well as of their hatred is his high treason, his claim to be King of the Jews, his effort to shake off the Roman yoke.

Unfortunately, the simple truth does not continue to hold the floor for long.

Jesus dies, and it is now necessary to furnish proof, in the form of a number of violent theatrical effects, that a god has passed away:

"Jesus, when he had cried again with a loud voice, yielded up the ghost. And behold, the veil of the temple was rent in twain from the top to the bottom; and the earth did quake, and the rocks rent; and the graves were opened, and many bodies of the saints which slept arose, and came out of the graves after his resurrection, and went into the holy city, and appeared unto many" (Matthew xxvii, 50-53).

The evangelists do not report what the resurrected "saints" accomplish in and after their joint outing to Jerusalem, whether they remain alive or duly lay themselves down again in their graves. In any case, one would expect that such an extraordinary event would have made a profound impression on all eye-witnesses and convinced everyone of the divinity of Jesus, but the Jews still remain obstinate; again it is only the Romans who recognize the divinity.

"Now when the centurion, and they that were with him, watching Jesus, saw the earthquake and those things that were done, they feared greatly, saying, 'Truly, this was the Son of God' " (Matthew xxvii, 54).

But the high priests and Pharisees on the other hand still declare Jesus to be an impostor (xxvii, 63), and when he is resurrected from the dead the only effect is that the Roman eye-witnesses become richer by the bribe we have already mentioned, in payment for their declaring the miracle to be an imposture.

Thus, at the end of the story of the Passion, Jewish bribery transforms the honest Roman soldiers into tools of Jewish treachery and baseness, which had shown devilish hatred in fighting the sublimest divine clemency.

In this entire tale the tendency of servility toward the Romans and hatred for the Jews is laid on so thick and expressed in such an accumulation of monstrosities that one would think it could not have had the slightest influence on intelligent persons, and yet we know that this device worked very well. This tale, enhanced by the halo of divinity, ennobled by the martyrdom of the proud proclaimer of a high mission, was for many centuries one of the best means of arousing hatred and contempt for the Jews, even in the most benevolent minds of Christendom; for Judaism was nothing to them, and they kept aloof from it; they branded the Jews as the scum of humanity, as a race endowed by nature with the most wicked malice and obstinacy, that must be kept away from all human society, held down with an iron hand.

But it would have been impossible ever to secure a general acceptance of this attitude toward the Jews, if it had not arisen at a time of a universal hatred and persecution of the Jews.

Arising at a time when the Jews were outlawed, it has immensely aggravated this condition, prolonged its duration, widened its sphere.

What we know as the story of the Passion of our Lord Jesus Christ is in reality only an incident in the history of the sufferings of the Jewish people.

V. THE EVOLUTION OF THE ORGANIZATION
OF THE CONGREGATION

a. Proletarians and Slaves

WE have seen that several ingredients of Christianity, monotheism, messianism, belief in the resurrection, the Essenian communism, arose among the Jews, and that a part of the lower classes of this people found the most satisfactory expression of its desires and aspirations in a combination of these elements. We have also seen that the whole social organism of the Roman Empire was permeated with conditions rendering it—particularly its proletarian sections—more and more susceptible to these new tendencies of Jewish origin, but that these tendencies, when subjected to the influence of a non-Jewish environment, not only were severed from Judaism, but even assumed a hostile attitude toward the latter. These tendencies now became fused with the movements of the dying Græco-Roman world, which transformed the vigorous national spirit prevailing among the Jews down to the destruction of Jerusalem into its precise opposite, diluting the Jewish movement in a helpless resignation, an abject servility, a longing for death.

Simultaneously with the change in the realm of thought, the organization of the congregation also was profoundly altered.

At first it had been inspired with a vigorous but hazy communism, a condemnation of all private property, a desire for a new and better social order in which all class differences should be eliminated by a division of property.

Probably the Christian congregation was at first chiefly a fighting organization, if we are correct in our assumption that the various otherwise inexplicable references to violence in the Gospels are the remnants of the original tradition. This trait would also be in full accord with the historical position of the Jewish nation at that time.

It would be inconceivable to assume that a proletarian sect —above all—should remain untouched by the general revolutionary current.

At any rate, the first Christian organizations among the Jews were saturated with the desire for revolution, for the coming of the Messiah, for social upheaval. Attention to the present moment, the practical detail work in other words, was probably neglected.

But this condition changed after the destruction of Jerusalem. The elements that had given the messianic congregation its rebellious character had been defeated. And the congregation of the Messiah became more and more an anti-Jewish congregation, within the non-Jewish proletariat, which had neither the ability nor the desire for struggle. But as the congregation became older, it became more and more clear that it could no longer count on the fulfillment of the prophecy still contained in the Gospels, to the effect that the contemporaries of Jesus would live to see the great change. Faith in the coming of the "Kingdom of God" on earth gradually disappeared. The Kingdom of God, which was to descend from Heaven, was now more and more transferred *to* Heaven; the resurrection of the flesh was transformed into the immortality of the soul, which was alone destined to experience all the joys of Heaven or the pangs of Hell.

As the messianic expectations of the future assumed more and more this unworldly form, becoming politically conservative or indifferent, the practical interest in the present day necessarily became more and more prominent.

But with the decrease in revolutionary enthusiasm, practical communism itself underwent certain changes.

Originally it had resulted from an energetic but vague desire for the abolition of all private property, a desire to remedy the poverty of the comrades by pooling all possessions.

But we have already pointed out that in contrast to the Essenes, the Christian congregations were originally merely urban, even chiefly metropolitan congregations, and that this constituted an obstacle to the full and permanent development of their communism.

Among the Essenes, as well as among the Christians, communism had originally been a communism of consumption, of ownership in commodities. But consumption and production are today still closely related in country districts, and this was then far more the case. Production meant production for private consumption, not for sale; agriculture, cattle-breeding, the household, all were closely related. Large-scale production in agriculture was quite feasible at the time and already superior to petty production, inasmuch as it permitted a more perfect division of labor and a fuller utilization of the various tools and structures. Of course, this was more than neutralized by the disadvantages of slave labor. But while operation by slaves was then by far the most common form of large-scale agriculture, it was not the only possible form. We already find large establishments operated by numerous peasant families, at the very beginning of agricultural evolution. The Essenes probably established family coöperative agricultural enterprises on a large scale wherever the Essenes constituted great semi-monastic settlements in the wilderness, resembling the settlement by the Dead Sea of which Pliny reports (*Natural History*, Book v), where they "lived in the society of the palms".

But the form of production is in the last analysis always the decisive factor in every social structure. Only such societies as are based on the mode of production may have strength and endurance.

While social or coöperative agriculture was possible at the time when Christianity originated, none of the necessary prerequisites for coöperative urban industry was, however, present. Workers in urban industries were either slaves or free domestic workers. Large establishments with free workers, resembling the large peasant family, were hardly known. Slaves, domestic workers, burden-bearers, also peddlers, small shopkeepers, the *Lumpenproletariat*, these were the lower classes of the urban population of those times among whom communistic tendencies might arise. But these classes present no element that might have expanded the common possession of commodities into a common faculty of production. The common element remained a community of consumption only. And this community in turn was essentially nothing more than the taking of common meals. Clothing and habitations in the cradle of Christianity, also in southern and central Italy, were not of great importance. Even such a thoroughgoing communism as that of the Essenes did not go far in establishing a community of clothing. In the matter of clothing, private property seems indeed inevitable. A community in dwellings was all the harder to attain in a large city since the workshops of the various comrades were scattered in all directions, and since real estate speculation in the early Christian era made the prices of houses in large cities very high. The absence of transportation facilities herded the population of large cities in a small space and made the owners of this space the absolute masters of its inhabitants, who were frightfully mulcted. Houses were built as high in the air as the art of masonry then permitted; in Rome they were seven stories or more in height; rents reached fabulous figures. Real estate profiteering was therefore a favorite form of investment for the capitalist of the time. In the triumvirate which bought out the Roman Republic, particularly Crassus had gained his wealth by such speculations.

The proletarians of the large city could not compete in this field; this alone made it impossible for them to resort to community dwellings. Furthermore, in view of the suspicious character of the emperors, the Christian congregation could not exist except as a secret society. Community dwellings would have rendered its discovery an easy matter.

Therefore the Christian communism could not have any permanent general form for most of the members except as expressed in the common meals.

The gospels also describe the "Kingdom of God", the state of the future, almost exclusively as a common repast; no other joy is expected; this bliss evidently was foremost in the minds of the early Christians.

Important though this form of practical communism may have been for the free proletarians, it meant very little to the slaves, who usually were a part of the family of their master and were fed at his table, frugally enough, to be sure. Only a few slaves lived outside of their master's home, for instance, those who kept a shop in town for the sale of the products of their master's country estate.

For the slaves the hope in the coming Messiah, the prospect of a kingdom of general bliss, necessarily was most attractive, much more so than practical communism, which could be realized only in forms that had little meaning for them so long as they were slaves.

We do not know the attitude of the first Christians with regard to slavery.   The Essenes condemned it, as we have seen.   Philo reports:

"Among them none is a slave, but all are free, mutually working for each other.   They consider slave-holding to be not only unjust and a violation of piety, but also godless, a transgression of the natural law, which has created all equal . . . as brothers."

Probably the proletarians of the Jerusalem congregation of the Messiah were of the same mind.

But the prospects of social revolution disappeared with the destruction of Jerusalem.   The spokesmen of the Christian congregation, who were so solicitously concerned not to give rise to any suspicion of hostility to the dominant powers, necessarily attempted also to pacify the rebellious slaves whom they might count in their ranks.

Thus, for example, the author of the Epistle of Paul to the Colossians—in the extant form an "editing" or fabrication dating from the Second Century—adjures the slaves as follows:

"Servants, obey in all things your masters according to the flesh; not with eye service as men pleasers; but in singleness of heart, fearing God" (iii, 22).

The author of the First Epistle of Saint Peter—probably composed in the time of Trajan—uses even plainer terms:

"Servants, be subject to your masters with all fear; not only to the good and gentle, but also to the froward.[1]   For this is thankworthy, if a man for conscience toward God endure grief, suffering wrongfully.   For what glory is it, if, when ye be buf-

[1] Σκολιοις, which implies *injustice, treachery, malice*. Luther very mildly translates: *die wunderlichen.*

feted for your faults, ye shall take it patiently? But if when ye do well and suffer for it, ye take it patiently, this is acceptable with God" (I Peter ii, 18-20).

The incipient Christian opportunism of the Second Century even found it proper for Christian masters to keep slaves who were their brethren in the congregation, as is proved by Paul's First Epistle to Timothy:

"Let as many servants as are under the yoke count their own masters worthy of all honor, that the name of God and his doctrine be not blasphemed. And they that have believing masters, let them not despise them, because they are brethren; but *rather do them service*, because they are faithful and beloved, partakers of the benefit" (ἀγαπητοί). [2] (vi, 1, 2.)

Nothing could be more erroneous than the assumption that Christianity abolished slavery; on the contrary, it provided slavery with a new support. In antiquity, the slave was kept in his place by *fear*. It was reserved for Christianity to exalt the blind obedience of the slave to a *moral duty*, cheerfully performed.

Christianity, at least after it ceased to be revolutionary, no longer offered the slave a hope for freedom, and its practical communism also rarely involved advantages for the slave. The sole element that might still attract the latter was "equality before God," in other words, within the congregation, where each comrade had equal rights, where the slave might sit beside his master at the common repast, if the latter also was a member of the congregation.

Callistus, the Christian slave of a Christian freedman, even became bishop of Rome (217-222 A.D.).

But even this form of equality was no longer of much significance. The reader should recall how close the status of the free proletariat was to that of the slaves, from whose number it drew many of its members, and that on the other hand the slaves of the imperial family attained high positions in the state and were often flattered even by aristocrats.

If Christianity, in spite of all its communism and all its prole-

[2] The common meals.

tarian sentiment, was unable to abolish slavery even in its own ranks, slavery must have had powerful roots in "pagan" antiquity, although the latter on the whole was opposed to it, and although ethics as a rule is closely bound up with the mode of production. The all-embracing love of one's neighbor, the fraternity, the equality of all before God, as proclaimed in the congregation of the Messiah, were no more incompatible with slavery than were the Rights of Man, as proclaimed in the Declaration of Independence of the United States of America. Christianity from the start was chiefly a religion of the free proletariat, but in spite of all the *rapprochement* between the latter and the slaves in antiquity, there remained a difference of interests between the two classes.

The free proletarians constituted a majority in the Christian congregation from the outset, preventing the interests of the slaves from finding a full expression in the congregation. This in turn necessarily made the congregation less attractive to slaves than to free proletarians, thus strengthening the latters' majority.

Economic evolution was working in the same direction. Precisely at the time when the revolutionary tendencies in the Christian congregation received their death-blow, namely, at the time of the fall of Jerusalem, a new era begins for the Roman Empire, an era of universal peace, domestic peace, but also in great measure international peace, since the Roman Empire had lost its power of expansion. But war, civil war as well as imperialistic war, had been the means of obtaining cheap slaves; this condition now ceased. The slave became rare and costly; slave operation no longer paid; in agriculture it was replaced by the *coloni*, in urban industry by the labor of free workers. More and more the slave ceased to be a producer of necessary products and became a producer of luxuries. Personal services to the great and powerful now became the chief function of slavery. The spirit of the slave now became more and more synonymous with the spirit of the lackey. The days of Spartacus were gone.

The opposition between the slaves and the free proletarians necessarily was sharpened by a decrease in the number of slaves, proceeding simultaneously with an increase in the number of free proletarians in the large cities. Both these tendencies caused the slave element in the Christian congregation to be relegated still further to the background. It is not surprising that Christianity finally lost all interest in the slaves.

This evolution is easy to understand if we regard Christianity as the precipitation of certain class interests; but it cannot be understood if we consider Christianity merely as an ideological structure. For the logical development of its fundamental notions necessarily would have led to the abolition of slavery; but logic has never operated in universal history when class interests have decreed otherwise.

b. The Decline of Communism

The recognition of slavery, as well as the increasing tendency to limit the community of goods to the common meals, were not the only obstacles encountered by the Christian congregation in its effort to carry out its communistic ambitions.

These aspirations demanded that every member of the congregation sell all his possessions and place the proceeds at the disposal of the congregation for distribution to its members.

It is plain at the outset that such a practice could not be carried out on a large scale. Its necessary presupposition was that at least one-half of society should remain unbelievers, otherwise there would have been no one to buy the possessions of the believers. Nor could anyone have been found to sell to the believers the foodstuffs they needed, in return for the proceeds of these sales.

If the believers intended to live not on production but by division, a sufficient number of unbelievers was necessary, who would produce for the believers. But even in the latter case, the system was doomed as soon as all the believers had sold their property, distributed and consumed it. Of course the Messiah would descend from the clouds before then and remedy all the evils "of the flesh".

But this test never had time to be applied.

The number of the members who had anything worth selling and dividing was very small in the early stages of the congregation. They could not live on that. They could obtain a permanent income only by having each member deliver his daily *earnings* to the congregation. If the members were not mere beggars or burden-bearers, they needed some *property* if they would earn anything, property in the *means of production* for weavers, potters, or smiths, or in *stock of goods,* in the case of shopkeepers or peddlers.

Under the given circumstances, the congregation could not arrange special workshops to produce for its own needs, as did the Essenes; it could not isolate itself from the realm of commodity production and individual production; therefore, in spite of all its communistic aspirations, it had to accept private property in the means of production and stocks of commodities.

But having recognized production by the individual, the recognition of the individual household, connected with such production, had to follow; also that of the single family, and monogamy, in spite of all their common meals.

Again the practical outcome of the communistic tendencies is found to be the common meals. But it was not their only result. The proletarians had succeeded in uniting in order to reduce their misery by their united efforts. When they encountered obstacles in the execution of a perfect communism, they found themselves all the more obliged to expand their charity work, which would give assistance to the individual in cases of extraordinary distress.

The Christian congregations were closely connected with each other. A member arriving from another town was given work by the congregation if he wished to stay; if he wished to travel further, he was given an expense mite.

If a member became ill, the congregation took charge of him. When he died, it buried him at its own expense and looked after his widow and children; if he was imprisoned, which happened often enough, it was again the congregation that brought him consolation and aid.

The Christian proletarian organization thus created a sphere of duties about equivalent to the system of insurances in a modern nation. In the Gospels, it is the observance of this mutual insurance system that entitles one to the life eternal. When the Messiah comes, he will divide men into those that are to share in the splendor of the state of the future and the life eternal and those destined to eternal damnation. To the former, the sheep, the King will say:

"Come, ye blessed of my Father, inherit the kingdom prepared for you from the foundation of the world: For I was an hungered, and ye gave me meat: I was thirsty and ye gave me drink: I was a stranger, and ye took me in: naked, and ye clothed me: I was sick and ye visited me: I was in prison, and ye came unto me." The righteous will then reply that they have done no such thing for the King. "And the King will answer and say unto them: Verily I say unto you, Inasmuch as ye have done it unto one of the least of these my brethren, ye have done it unto me" (Matthew xxv, 34, 40).

Their common meals and their mutual charity were in any case the securest bond within the Christian congregation, permanently holding the masses together.

But precisely this practice of charity was developing a force destined to weaken and burst asunder the original communistic aspirations.

As the expectation of the coming of the Messiah in all his glory dwindled, as the congregation became more and more convinced that it was necessary to acquire property in order to carry out its program of assistance, the proletarian class character of the Christian propaganda was violated. More and more effort was directed to the recruiting of wealthy members whose money could be put to use.

The more money the congregation needed, the more diligently did its agitators work in order to prove to wealthy patrons the vanity of all the treasures of this world, their worthlessness compared to the bliss of eternal life, which was attainable by the rich only if they parted with their possessions. And their preaching in that time of general dispiritedness, particularly among the wealthy classes, was not without effect. How many wealthy persons there were who, after a dissipated youth, were filled with disgust with all enjoyments and all means of enjoyment. Having exhausted all the sensations to be bought with money, one sensation still remained: that of poverty.

Down into the Middle Ages we still find a frequent recurrence of the case of wealthy persons who give all their possessions to the poor and lead the life of beggars themselves, in most cases after having fully enjoyed all the pleasures of the world, to the point of complete nausea.

But such persons were not so numerous as to make these windfalls as frequent as the congregation required. With the increasing distress in the empire, with the multiplication of the *Lumpenproletariat* in the congregation, who either could not or would not earn their bread by toil, it became more imperative to recruit rich persons in order to pay the expenses of the congregation.

It was easier to get a rich man to leave his money for the charity purposes of the congregation at his death than to make him donate it during his lifetime. Childless families were very common; family ties were very weak; the desire to make bequests to relatives often very slight. On the other hand, the interest in one's own personality had been developed to a high point, involving a desire for a continued life after death, for a happy life, of course.

The Christian doctrine was well adapted to the satisfaction of this desire, and a convenient way of attaining eternal bliss without serious privations in this life was open to the rich if they did not give away their property until death, when it was no longer of use to them. The bequest of their property, now quite useless, might purchase them eternal salvation.

The Christian agitators therefore captured the young and passionate aristocrats through their disgust with the life they had led; they captured exhausted old rich men through their fear of death and the pangs of Hell awaiting them. A stealthy manipulation of inheritances has never since ceased to be a favorite method of Christian agitators, for gorging the strong stomach of the Church with more and more food.

But in the first few centuries of the congregation's life, the supply of rich bequests was probably not large, particularly since the congregation, being a secret organization, was not a legal personage and could therefore not inherit directly.

Efforts were therefore made to recruit rich persons while they were still alive for the support of the congregation, even if such persons were not ready to carry out strictly the Lord's commandment to distribute among the poor all they possessed. We have seen that generosity was a common trait among the wealthy of that day before the accumulation of capital played an important part in the mode of production. This generosity redounded to the advantage of the congregation, constituting a permanent source of its income, whenever it was possible to awaken the interest and the sympathy of the wealthy for the congregation. The more the congregation ceased to be a fighting organization, the more its charity phase was emphasized, the stronger became the tendencies within the congregation to soften the original proletarian hatred against the rich and to enable the latter to feel at home in the congregation, even though they remained rich and clung to their possessions.

The congregation's view of life—rejection of the ancient gods, monotheism, the belief in resurrection, the hope for the Messiah—these things, as we have seen, were in accord with the general tendencies of the times, making the Christian doctrine sympathetic even to the upper classes.

On the other hand, the rich, faced with the increasing distress of the masses, were seeking for methods of decreasing this distress, as their charity foundations go to show. For this distress menaced all society. This fact also made the Christian organizations more sympathetic in their eyes.

Finally, the desire for popularity also played a part in the support given the Christian congregations, at least in places where these congregations acquired an influence over a considerable portion of the population.

Therefore the Christian congregation might very well become attractive even to such rich persons as had not become unworldly and despairing, as were not driven to promise a bequest of their property by fear of death or the pangs of eternal damnation.

But to make the rich feel at home in the congregation, its char-

acter had to be changed fundamentally; class hatred of the rich
had to be abandoned.

The proletarian fighting spirits in the congregation were hurt
by this effort to attract the rich and make concessions to them,
as we learn from the General Epistle of James to the twelve tribes
of the Diaspora, dating from the middle of the Second Century
and mentioned before in this book.   James admonishes the members: "For if there come unto your assembly a man with a gold
ring, in goodly apparel, and there come in also a poor man in
vile raiment; and ye have respect to him that weareth the
gay clothing, and say unto him, Sit thou here in a good place;
and say to the poor, Stand thou there, or sit here under my foot-
stool: are ye not then partial in yourselves and are become judges
of evil thoughts? . . . But ye have despised the poor. . . . But
if ye have respect to persons, ye commit sin" (ii, 2-9).

And then he attacks those who would require only a theoretical
acceptance of doctrine by the rich, and not that they give their
money:

"What doth it profit, my brethren, though a man say he hath
faith, and have not works? can faith save him?   If a brother or
sister be naked, and destitute of daily food, and one of you say
unto them, Depart in peace, be ye warmed and filled; notwithstanding ye give them not those things which are needful to the
body; what doth it profit?   Even so faith, if it hath not works, is
dead, being alone" (ii, 14-17).

The foundation of the organization was of course not altered
by this consideration for the rich; that foundation remained
theoretically and practically unchanged.   But the duty to give
all one owned was replaced by a voluntary self-imposed tax, often
amounting to but a small gift.

Somewhat younger than the Epistle of James is the *Apolo-
geticus* of Tertullian (probably about 150-160 A.D.).   This document also describes the organization of the congregation:

"Even if there does exist a sort of common fund, it is not made
up of fees, as though we contracted for our worship.   Each of us
puts in a small amount one day a month, or whenever he pleases;
and only if he pleases and if he is able, for there is no compulsion

in the matter, everyone contributing of his own free will. These monies are, as it were, the deposits of piety. They are expended upon no banquets or drinking-bouts or useless eating-houses, but on feeding and burying poor people, on behalf of boys and girls who have neither parents nor money, in support of old folk unable now to go about, as well as for people who are shipwrecked, or who may be in the mines or exiled in islands or in prison—so long as their distress is for the sake of God's fellowship, and they themselves entitled to maintenance by their confession."

Tertullian goes on: "We who feel ourselves united heart and soul, have no difficulties about community of goods; with us all is common, except our wives; the community ceases there, where alone others practice it."[3]

Communism was therefore retained theoretically, and in practice only the severer of its applications seemed to be softened. But imperceptibly the entire character of the congregation, originally adapted solely to proletarian conditions, was changing because of the increased consideration for the rich. Those elements who favored the recruiting of rich members had to combat not only the class hatred of the congregation, but also to alter its internal operations in many ways.

Although communism had been much weakened, the common meals still remained the firm bond uniting all the members. The charitable arrangements were applicable only in isolated cases of distress, to which all members were, however, exposed. But the common meal satisfied the daily needs of every member. This meal was attended by the entire congregation; it was the center around which the entire life of the congregation revolved.

But the common meal had no significance as a meal, in the case of the wealthy members. They had better food and drink at their own homes. The simple, often coarse meal surely offended their fastidious palates. They came to these meals for the purpose of participating in the congregational life, obtaining influence in it, not to fill their stomachs. That which meant the sat-

---

[3] Quoted in Harnack, *The Expansion of Christianity in the First Three Centuries*, London and New York, 1904-6, vol. i, pp. 189-190. *Cf.* Pfleiderer, *Primitive Christianity*, vol. iv, p. 479.

isfaction of a physical need for the others, meant for them only the satisfaction of a spiritual need; sharing the bread and wine was a purely symbolic performance. As the number of the wealthy increased in the congregation, there was also an increase in the number of those participants in the common meals who were concerned only in the gathering and its symbols, not in eating and drinking. Therefore, in the Second Century, the actual common meals for the poorer members were detached from the purely symbolic meals intended for the entire congregation, and in the Fourth Century, after the Church had become the dominant power in the State, meals of the former kind were eliminated from the meeting houses of the congregation, the churches. They fell more and more into disuse, being abolished in the course of the following centuries. The most prominent feature of practical communism thus disappeared entirely from the Christian congregation, and its place was taken exclusively by the charity work, the solicitude for the poor and weak, which has been retained to this day, on a considerably less extensive scale, however.

There remained nothing in the congregation that might offend the rich; it had ceased to be a proletarian institution. The rich, who originally had been entirely excluded from the "Kingdom of God", unless they gave their possessions to the poor, might now play the same rôle in this Kingdom as in the "World of the Devil", and they have made abundant use of this privilege.

Not only were the old class contrasts again revived in the Christian congregation, but a new dominant class arose in the latter, a new bureaucracy with a new head, the bishop, whose acquaintance we shall make very soon.

It was the Christian *congregation*, not Christian communism, to which the Roman emperors finally bent the knee. The victory of Christianity was not a dictatorship of the proletariat, but a dictatorship of the masters it had raised in its own congregation.

The champions and martyrs of the early congregations, who had surrendered their possessions, their labors, their lives, for the liberation of the poor and miserable, had merely laid the foundations for a new mode of tyranny and exploitation.

c. Apostles, Prophets and Teachers

Originally the congregation had no officers and no distinctions between its members. All members, male or female, might set up as teachers and agitators, if they felt that they had the stuff in them. Each spoke out frankly, "according to his lights", or as it was phrased in those days, as the Holy Ghost moved him. Most of them also, of course, continued their own trades, but quite a number, who had gained particular prestige, sold their possessions and devoted themselves entirely to agitation as apostles or prophets. A new class distinction was the result.

Two classes now arose within the Christian congregation: the ordinary members, whose practical communism was applied only to the common meals and the general welfare arrangements of the congregation: assigning jobs, giving aid to widows and orphans, as well as to prisoners; sickness insurance, death benefits.

But those who carried out communism completely were considered to be "holy" or "perfect" ones; these renounced property and monogamy, giving all their possessions to the congregation.

This was a fine gesture and gave these radical elements, as their very names indicate, great prestige in the congregation; and they were animated by a feeling of superiority over the other comrades and conducted themselves as a dominant élite.

Thus the radical form of communism was the one that produced a new aristocracy.

Like every other aristocracy, the latter did not content itself with claiming the right to command the rest of the community, but also attempted to exploit the community.

After all, how should the "holy" live, having given away all the means of production and stores of goods that they owned? They could only resort to occasional labor, such as carrying parcels or running errands and the like, or to mendicancy.

The most natural thing to do was to gain a livelihood by begging from their comrades and from the congregations themselves, who could not permit a worthy man or a worthy woman to starve, particularly if this meritorious member possessed the gift of propaganda; this gift then required no knowledge that was difficult to acquire, but merely temperament, a nimble wit and readiness in repartee.

We already find Paul upbraiding the Corinthians and reminding them that the congregation is obliged to relieve him and all other apostles of manual labor, and also to support them:

"Am I not an apostle? am I not free? have I not seen Jesus Christ our Lord? . . . Have we not power to lead about a sister, a wife, as well as other apostles, and as the brethren of the Lord, and Cephas? Or I only and Barnabas, have we not power to forbear working? . . . Who feedeth a flock, and eateth not of the milk of the flock? . . . For it is written in the Law of Moses, Thou shalt not muzzle the mouth of the ox that treadeth out the corn. Doth God take care for oxen? Or saith he it altogether for our sakes?"

God's threshing ox means *us*: this is the significance of Paul's words. Of course this passage does not refer to oxen who are threshing empty straw. The apostle continues:

"If we have sown unto you spiritual things, is it a great thing if we shall reap your carnal things? If others be partakers of this power over you, are not we rather?" (I Corinthians ix, 7-12).

The last sentence, we may remark in passing, also indicates the communistic character of the first Christian congregations.

After this plea for the good things of life for the apostles, Paul states that he is not speaking for himself, but for others; he asks nothing from the Corinthians. But he permits other congregations to support him: "I robbed other churches, taking wages of them (ὀψώνιον), to do you service . . . for that which was lacking to me the brethren which came from Macedonia supplied" (II Corinthians xi, 8).

But this does not alter the fact that Paul emphasizes the congregation's duty to look after its "holy", who do not recognize the obligation to work.

The effect this Christian communism made on the minds of non-believers is apparent from the story of Peregrinus Proteus, written in 165 A.D., by Lucian. The scoffer Lucian is of course not an unprejudiced observer; he reports much malicious gossip of a very improbable variety, relating for instance that Peregrinus had left his native city, Parium on the Hellespont, because he had murdered his own father. Since no accusation was ever made for this offense in court, the matter is at least quite doubtful.

But after we have applied the necessary restrictions to Lucian's report, enough still remains that is of great value because it not only shows how the Christian congregation impressed the pagans, but also affords glimpses of the actual life of the former.

After Lucian has made a number of most malicious statements about Peregrinus, he tells how the latter became a voluntary exile after he had murdered his father, and drifted around in the world:

"At this time he also became acquainted with the admirable wisdom of the Christians by intercourse with their priests and scribes in Palestine. They soon appeared mere children in comparison with him; he became their prophet, the spokesman at their banquets (θιασάρχης), head of the synagogue (Lucian apparently draws no distinction between Jews and Christians, K.), all in one person; he commented a number of writings and explained them to them, a number he wrote himself, in short, they took him for a God, made him their legislator and appointed him their head. Of course, they still venerate that great man who was crucified in Palestine, for having introduced this new religion (τελετήν).[4] For this reason Peregrinus was then arrested and thrown into prison, which gave him considerable prestige for the rest of his life, besides imparting to him his lying habits and his desire for fame, which became his dominant passions.

"As he lay in prison, the Christians, believing this to be a great

---

[4] This sentence is contrary to the thought, and other objections may also be raised against it; particularly the words "of course" (γοῦν). Furthermore, Suidas, a lexicographer of the Tenth Century, expressly states that Lucian had "calumniated Christ himself" in his biography of Peregrinus. But no such passage can be found in the variants that have been preserved. It seems reasonable to seek such a passage in the above sentence, and to assume that this was the place in which Lucian jeered at Christ, which scandalized pious souls, and induced them to transform the passage into its opposite while copying it. As a matter of fact, a number of students assume that this sentence in its present form is a Christian distortion.

misfortune, left no stone unturned to help him escape. Finding this to be impossible, they lavished every possible care and solicitude upon him. From early in the morning you could see old women, widows and orphans, sitting outside the jail while their Elders bribed the wardens and spent the night with him. Many articles of food were brought to him, they exchanged their holy legends, and the dear Peregrinus, as he was still called, was a new Socrates in their eyes. Certain representatives of the Christian congregations even came from the Asiatic towns in order to support him, to assist him in court, and to console him. In such cases, in which their brotherhood is involved, they show an incredible zeal, in short, they spare no wealth. Peregrinus also received much money from them because of h's imprisonment, and gained not a little thereby.

"For these sad wretches live in the conviction that they will be altogether immortal and live forever, wherefore they despise death and often seek it voluntarily. Furthermore, their first legislator persuaded them that they had all become brothers since they had foresworn the Hellenic gods, and worshiped that crucified teacher (σοφιστήν) of theirs and lived by his laws; therefore they esteem all things as equally unimportant, considering them common possessions (κοινα ήγοῦνται), without having any good reason for this view. If they are visited by a clever impostor, capable of utilizing this situation, he will soon become very rich, because of his ability to hoodwink these simple folk."

Of course all this may not be taken literally; it is probably no more, true than the tales of the treasures accumulated by Socialistic agitators from the pennies of the workers. The Christian congregation had first to become richer than it was, before anyone could become rich on it. But it is probably true that at that time it took good care of its agitators and organizers and that unscrupulous fellows took advantage of this condition. And we must also note what this implies with regard to communism in the congregation.

Lucian then tells us that the Government of Syria liberated Peregrinus because the latter seemed so insignificant. Peregrinus thereupon returned to his native town, where he found his patri-

mony considerably reduced.   However, he still had a large sum
of money, considered immense by his adherents, and estimated
even by Lucian, who is by no means favorably disposed, at 15
talents ($17,000).   This sum he gave to the population of his
native town, according to Lucian, in order to free himself from
the accusation of patricide:

"He spoke in the Popular Assembly of the Parians: he already
had long hair, wore a dirty cloak, had a bag slung around him, a
staff in his hand, and made in general a very theatrical impression.
He appeared before them in this raiment and declared the entire
property left him by his father to be the property of the people.
When the people heard this, poor fellows whose mouths were
watering for a division, they at once shouted that he alone was a
friend of wisdom and of the nation, he alone a successor of
Diogenes and Krates.   But the mouths of his enemies were sealed,
and anyone who would have recalled the incident of the murder
would have been slain immediately.

"He now set forth a homeless wanderer for the second time,
the Christians supplying him plentifully with traveling money
and following him everywhere, permitting him to suffer no want.
He thus made his way for some time." [5]

But finally he was excluded from the congregation, for the
alleged reason that he had eaten forbidden foods.   He was thus
deprived of his means of subsistence, and attempted to regain
his property, in which he was unsuccessful.   A cynical and ascetic
mendicant philsopher, he now wandered through Egypt, Italy,
Greece, finally putting an end to his life in Olympia, after the
games, in the presence of an audience invited for this spectacle,
by the theatrical method of leaping into a burning pyre at midnight, by the light of the moon.

It is evident that the age in which Christianity arose was productive of singular creatures.   But it would be doing an injustice
to a man like Peregrinus to consider them as swindlers only; his
voluntary death alone is an evidence to the contrary.   Suicide
as an advertising stunt certainly requires not only a boundless

[5] Lucian, *The Death of Peregrinus,* 11-16.

vanity and love of sensation, but also a bit of contempt for the world and disgust with life, or else it must be laid to insanity altogether.

If Peregrinus Proteus, as depicted by Lucian, is not the real Peregrinus Proteus, but a caricature, the caricature is a brilliant one. The essence of caricature is not a mere distortion of appearances, but a one-sided emphasis and exaggeration of the characteristic and determining elements. The true caricaturist may not be a mere grotesque clown; he must see through things and recognize essential and significant elements in them.

Thus Lucian has emphasized those phases of Peregrinus that were to become important for the entire class of the "holy and perfect" whose representative he was. They might have been impelled by the most varied, sometimes sublime, sometimes idiotic motives, appearing very unselfish to themselves, while behind their entire attitude to the congregation there was already the exploiting tendency observed by Lucian. The enrichment of the impoverished "holy" by the communism of the congregation may in his days have still been an exaggeration; it was soon to become a reality, a reality that finally left far behind it the crudest exaggerations of the scoffer of its early stage.

Lucian lays most emphasis on the "wealth" acquired by the prophets; another pagan, a contemporary of Lucian, stresses their insanity.

Celsus describes "how they prophesy in Phœnicia and Palestine":

"There are many who, although they are without reputation or name, carry on at the slightest provocation, with the greatest ease, within and without the sacred places, as if they were seized with prophetic ecstasy; others, roaming about as beggars, and visiting the cities and military camps, offer the same spectacle. Each of them has the words at the tip of his tongue and uses them instantly: 'I am God', or 'God's son', or 'God's spirit'. 'I am come because the destruction of the world is already approaching, and you humans are going to destruction because of your unrighteousness. But I will save you, and you will soon behold me coming again with heavenly power! Blessed is he who now honors me! I shall consign all others to the eternal fire, the cities as well as the countries and their peoples. Those who will not recognize now the dooms impending over them, will soon change their minds in vain and lament! But those who have believed in me, them will I preserve forever!' To these grandiloquent threats they add curious, half idiotic and absolutely incoherent words whose sense may not be understood by any man, however intelligent, so obscure and empty are they; but the first simpleton or mountebank that hears them can explain them as he may like . . . these alleged prophets whom I have more than once heard with my own ears have admitted their weaknesses to me, after I convinced them, and confessed that they had themselves invented all their inscrutable words." [6]

Here again we are dealing with the amiable combination of swindler and prophet, but again we should be going too far if we should designate the entire business as an imposture. It merely indicates a general condition of the population which offered a good field of activity for impostors, but which also must have given rise to real cases of exaggerated and ecstatic feelings in minds easily aroused.

Apostles as well as prophets probably were alike in this respect. But they differed in one important respect: the apostles had no permanent place of domicile; they wandered about homeless, whence their name (ἀπόστολος, *messenger, traveler, seafarer*); the prophets, on the other hand, were the "local celebrities". The apostle class must have developed first. While a congregation was still small, it could not permanently support an agitator. As soon as its means for supporting him were exhausted, he had to go elsewhere. And while the number of congregations was small, the important task was that of founding new congregations in cities as yet without them. The extension of the organization into new fields, hitherto untouched, and the maintenance of a connection between them, was the great task of these traveling agitators, the apostles. They are particularly responsible for the international character of the Christian organization, which con-

[6] Cited by Harnack in his edition of the *Doctrine of the Twelve Apostles* (*Die Lehre der Zwölf Apostel*), p. 130 *ff.*

tributed so much to its permanence. A local organization could be destroyed, as it had no outside support. But it was hardly possible, with the resources then at the disposal of the state authority, to persecute all the Christian congregations in all parts of the Empire. There always remained a few who could supply material aid to the persecuted, and in which the persecuted could seek refuge. This was due above all to the apostles who were constantly on the move, and whose number must at times have been considerable.

Local agitators, concerned entirely with organizational work, could not arise until certain congregations had attained such size that their means permitted them to maintain such agitators permanently.

The larger the number of cities containing Christian congregations, and the larger the membership of the latter, the more did the prophets flourish, and the smaller was the field of activity of the apostles, who had operated chiefly in the cities as yet containing no congregations or only small ones. The prestige of the apostles necessarily declined. But there must have been a sort of opposition between them and the prophets. For the means of the congregations were limited. The more the apostles took for themselves, the less was left for the prophets. The latter therefore necessarily strove to diminish the already declining prestige of the apostles, to restrict the gifts allotted to them, and, on the other hand, to raise their own prestige and formulate definite claims on the gifts of the believers.

These efforts are clearly apparent in the *Doctrine* (Didache) *of the Twelve Apostles,* already several times cited, a document written between 135 and 170 A.D. We read in this document:

"Every apostle that comes to you shall be received as the Master. But he must stay not longer than one day, at most two days. *But if he remains for three days, he is a false prophet.* And when the apostle leaves you, he shall *receive nothing* except so much bread as he needs on his journey to his next stop. *But if he demands money, he is a false prophet.*

"Do not tempt nor test any prophet who speaks in the spirit; for every sin will be forgiven, but this sin will not be forgiven.

But not every man speaking in the spirit is a prophet, but only if he has the deportment of the master, therefore the prophet and the false prophet may be distinguished by their conduct. And no prophet who, impelled by God's spirit, orders a meal (Harnack says: *for the poor*), will partake of it unless he be a false prophet. But every prophet that teaches the truth is a false prophet if he does not practice what he preaches. And every prophet, tried and true, who acts with respect to the earthly mysteries of the church, but does not teach others to do all that he does himself, let him not be judged by you; for he has his judgment with God. The ancient (Christian) prophets acted thus always."

The fact that this passage probably contains a reference to free love, which was to be permitted to the prophets if they did not require the congregation to emulate their example, we have already seen.

We read further:

"But he who says in the spirit: Give me money or some other thing, heed him not; but if he requests gifts for other sufferers, no one shall judge him.

"But every man who comes in the name of the Lord (in other words, every comrade, *K*.), let him be admitted; but you shall test him and distinguish the true and the false, for you must have understanding. If the newcomer is a transient visitor, help him, but he shall not stay longer than two or three days with you at most. If he wishes to settle among you, let him work and eat, if he is an artisan. But if he knows no trade, see to it to the best of your knowledge that no Christian shall live idle among you. If he will not accept this condition, he is one who is drawing profit from Christ. Avoid such."

It was therefore already considered necessary to see to it that the congregation was not overrun and exploited by beggars from other places. But this was to apply only to common beggars:

"But every true prophet that wishes to settle among you is worthy of his nourishment. Likewise, a true teacher, like any worker, is worth his nourishment. All the first fruits of thy wine-presses and threshing floors, of thy cattle and sheep, thou shalt take and give them to the prophets, for they are your high priests. But if you have no prophet, give them to the poor. When thou makest dough, take the first piece of it and give in accordance with the commandment. Likewise, when thou openest a vessel of wine or oil, take the first outflow and give it to the prophets. But of money and clothing and other possessions, take a share according to your judgment and give in accordance with the commandment."

The apostles are treated very shabbily in these regulations. It is not yet possible to suppress them altogether, but the congregation in which they present themselves is to dispatch them as quickly as possible. While an ordinary transient comrade may claim entertainment by the congregation for two or three days, the unhappy apostle gets only one or two days. Money he may not ask for at all.

The prophet, on the other hand, is "worthy of his nourishment"! He must be supported from the treasury of the congregation. But besides this, believers are obliged to deliver to him all the first fruits of wine, bread, oil and cloth, even of their money income.

This accords very well with the description given by Lucian just at the time when the *Didache* was written, of the prosperous life of Peregrinus, who also had declared himself a prophet.

While the prophets were thus displacing the apostles, they were themselves encountering a new competition in the *teachers*, whose importance when the *Didache* was written was still quite small, for they are only mentioned in passing.

In addition to these three elements, there were also others active in the congregation that are not mentioned in the *Didache*. Paul mentions them all in his First Epistle to the Corinthians (xii, 28):

"And God hath set some in the church, first apostles, secondly prophets, thirdly teachers, after that miracles, then gifts of healings, helps, governments, diversities of tongues."

Of these, the gifts of *helps* and *governments* became quite important, but not those of quackery and healing, which probably did not take, in the congregation, any forms that distinguished them from those generally current at the time. The rise of the teachers is connected with the admission of wealthy and cultured elements to the congregation. The apostles and prophets were ignorant people who kept on talking, without ever studying the subjects of their remarks. The cultured probably merely turned up their noses at this. Soon persons were found among the number of the latter who, attracted either by the charitable nature of the congregation, or by its power, or possibly by the general character of the Christian doctrine, attempted to raise the latter to a higher stage of what was then known as science, which, to be sure, no longer amounted to much. These persons became teachers. It is they who first sought to fill Christianity with the spirit of Seneca or of Philo, of which it had previously not had too much.

But they were regarded with envy and dislike by the body of the congregations, probably also by most of the apostles and prophets; the relation was perhaps not dissimilar to that between the "horny hand of toil" and the "intellectuals". Nevertheless, the teachers would undoubtedly have secured more and more prestige with the increase of the wealthy and cultured elements in the congregations, and would ultimately have done away with the prophets and apostles.

But before matters reached this point, all three categories were absorbed by a power that was beginning to exceed them all in strength, but which the *Didache* only mentions in passing: the *Bishop*.

d.   The Bishop

The beginnings of the Christian congregations were not unlike the circumstances attending every new proletarian organization. Its founders, the apostles, had to conduct all the work of the congregation themselves, propaganda as well as organization and administration. But with the growth of the congregation, the need for a division of labor became felt, the necessity to assign certain functions to definite functionaries.

First, the administration of the *income* and *expenses* of the congregation was made a separate congregational office.

Propaganda might be carried on by any member as he thought best. Even those who were exclusively concerned with propaganda had, in the Second Century, as we have just seen, not yet been intrusted with this task by the congregation. Apostles and prophets were self-appointed to their callings, or, as it seemed to them, they followed God's voice alone. The prestige enjoyed in the congregation by the individual propagandist, whether apostle or prophet, as well as the amount of his income, depended on the impression made by him, in other words, on his personality.

On the other hand, the maintenance of party discipline, if we may call it so, was a matter for the congregation itself, so long as it was small and all the members knew each other. The congregation itself decided on the admission of new members; it was immaterial who should conduct the initial ceremony, which was that of immersion. The congregation itself decided on expulsions, maintained peace among the comrades, decided disputes that might arise among them. It was the tribunal before which all accusations made by comrades against comrades had to be tried. The Christians were not less suspicious of state courts than Socialists are now. Their social views also were in sharp contrast with those of the state judges. A Christian would have considered it a sin to appear before a state judge to seek his rights, particularly in a case involving litigation with a comrade. Thus the germ of a special judicial power was planted, a power always claimed by the Church over its adherents, as opposed to the state courts. Of course, in this matter also, the original character of Church law was later completely distorted, for, in the beginnings of the Christian congregation, it signified the abolition of all class justice, the trial of the accused by his peers.

In the First Epistle of Paul to the Corinthians (vi, 1-4), we read:

"Dare any of you, having a matter against another, go to law before the unjust, and not before the saints (*meaning the comrades*)? Do ye not know that the saints shall judge the world? and if the world shall be judged by you, are ye unworthy to judge the smallest matters? Know ye not that we shall judge angels? how much more things that pertain to this life? If then ye have judgments of things pertaining to this life, set them to judge who are least esteemed in the Church."

The maintenance of discipline and peace in the congregation at first had as little form and as little connection with any definite office or any definite authority as had the propaganda itself.

But the economic factor required regulation even at an early stage, the more since the congregation was not a mere propaganda organization, but from the very start also a mutual aid association.

According to the Acts of the Apostles, the need was soon felt in the Jerusalem congregation of intrusting certain comrades with the collection and distribution of members' gifts, particularly the serving of meals at table. *Diakoneo* (διακονέω) means to serve, particularly at table. Obviously this was at first the chief task of the *deacons*, as the common meal was the chief function of primitive Christian communism.

We read in the Acts of the Apostles:

"And in those days, when the number of the disciples was multiplied, there arose a murmuring of the Grecians against the Hebrews, because their widows were neglected in the daily ministration (παρεθεωροῦντο ἐν τῇ διακονίᾳ). Then the twelve (*apostles, then actually only eleven, if we are to take the accounts in the Gospels at their face value*) called the multitude of the disciples unto them and said: It is not reason that we should leave the word of God and serve tables. Wherefore, brethren, look ye out among you seven men of honest report, full of the Holy Ghost and wisdom, whom we may appoint over this business" (vi, 1-3).

The report informs us that this suggestion was carried out, which seems quite plausible, as it is in the nature of the case.

The apostles were therefore relieved of their service as waiters in the dining-hall, which they had originally been obliged to perform in addition to propaganda, and which became burdensome to them with the increase of the congregation. But the newly appointed waiters (deacons) also necessarily had to divide their tasks. Service at table and other serving and cleansing operations were quite a different matter from the collection and administration of members' dues. The latter involved a position of trust of the highest order, particularly in a large congregation with increased income. This post required a considerable measure of honesty, business knowledge, and kindliness, coupled with severity.

An administrator was therefore appointed over the deacons.

The appointment of such an administrator was inevitable. Every organization having property or income must have such an administrator. In the brotherhoods and societies of Asia Minor, the administrative and financial officials bore the title of *Epimeletes* or *Episkopos* (ἐπίσκοπος, observer, overseer). The same name was also applied in the government of cities to certain administrative officials. Hatch, who traces this evolution in detail, and describes it in a book to which we owe much information on this subject,[7] quotes a Roman Jurist Charisius as follows: "Episcopi (bishops) are those who supervise the bread and other purchasable things, serving for the daily sustenance of the city population" (*episcopi, qui praesunt pani et caeteris venalibus rebus quae civitatum populis at quotidianum victum usui sunt*).

The city bishop therefore was an administrative official particularly concerned with the proper feeding of the population. It was natural to give the same title to the administrator of the Christian "people's house".

We have already read of the common treasury of the congregation, mentioned by Tertullian. We learn from the First Apology of Justin the Martyr (born about 100 A.D.) that the administration of this treasury was assigned to a special trustee. Tertullian says:

"The wealthy and willing may give at their discretion of their possessions, the gifts being collected and deposited with the overseer; the latter supports therewith the orphans and widows, those in distress because of illness or other reason, prisoners and strangers in the city, and takes care of all the needy in general." Much labor, much responsibility, but also much power was thus placed in the hands of the bishop.

---

[7] Edwin Hatch, *The Organization of the Early Christian Churches*, eight lectures delivered before the university of Oxford, in the year 1880. London, 1882, p. 38. Kautsky quotes a German translation and commentary by Adolf Harnack (Giessen, 1883).—TRANSLATOR.

In the beginnings of the congregation the office of the bishop as well as that of his aides and other functionaries of the congregation, was an honorary office, discharged without compensation in addition to each official's regular trade.

"The bishops and presbyters of those early days kept banks, practised medicine, wrought as silversmiths, tended sheep, or sold their goods in open market. . . . The chief existing enactments of early local councils on the point are that bishops are not to huckster their goods from market to market, nor are they to use their position to buy cheaper and sell dearer than other people." [8]

But as a congregation grew, it became impossible to discharge its numerous economic functions as an avocation. The bishop was made an employee of the congregation and received a salary in payment.

But this rendered permanent his tenure of office. The congregation had the right to remove him if he did not fulfill its requirements, but it is evident that some reluctance would be felt in depriving of his position a man who had been taken away from his calling. On the other hand, the administration of the congregation's business required a certain degree of skill and an acquaintance with the conditions of the congregation, which could be acquired only by long activity in office. It was therefore necessary, in order to facilitate the discharge of the congregation's business, to avoid any unnecessary change in the office of bishop.

But the longer the bishop remained in office, the more his prestige and power necessarily increased, if he was equal to the demands of his office.

He did not remain the only permanent official of the congregation. The office of the deacons also could not permanently be held as an avocation. The deacons also were paid, like the bishop, from the treasury of the congregation, but were his subordinates. The bishop, who would have to work with them, was for this reason consulted in their appointment. Thus the bishop had the privilege of distributing jobs in the congregation, which necessarily increased his influence.

As the congregation increased, it became impossible for it to

[8] Hatch, *op. cit.*, pp. 151, 152.

look after matters of its own discipline. Not only the numbers of the members increased, but also the varieties of their occupations. While at first all constituted a single family, in which everyone was acquainted with all the other comrades, all being completely united with each other in thought and feeling, thus composing an élite of self-sacrificing enthusiasts, this condition gradually changed with the increase of the congregation. The most varied elements gained admission, elements from different classes and regions, often strange and without understanding for each other, sometimes even hostile to each other—such as slaves and slave-owners—also elements that were not impelled by enthusiasm, but by crafty calculation, to take advantage of the credulity and generosity of the comrades. In addition, there were differences of views—all this necessarily produced disputes of all kinds, disputes that often could not be decided by a simple discussion in the gathering of the congregation, but required rather long investigations of the actual facts.

Therefore a committee, the committee of elders, or presbyters, was intrusted with the task of maintaining discipline in the congregation and settling disputes arising within it, reporting to the congregation on the expulsion of unworthy members, perhaps also on the admission of new members, whose admission this committee celebrated by the initiating ceremony, baptism.

The bishop, who was precisely informed on all congregational matters, was the chairman of this committee. He thus obtained an influence over the moral policing and jurisdiction of the congregation. Where the presbyters (the word *priest* is derived from *presbyter*), by reason of the increasing size of the congregation, became its permanent paid officials, they were placed immediately under the jurisdiction of the guardian of the congregation's treasury, the bishop, as were also the deacons.

In a large city, the congregation might easily become so large as to require more than one building to house its gatherings. It was then divided into districts; in each district gathering, a deacon had to wait upon the members, while a presbyter was delegated by the bishop to conduct the gathering and represent the bishop. The case in the suburbs and villages was similar. Where these lay close to a congregation like that of Rome or Alexandria, the influence of the latter was overwhelming, and the neighboring congregations fell directly under the influence of the great city and its bishop, who sent out his deacons and presbyters to them.

Thus there was gradually formed a congregational bureaucracy headed by the bishop, which became more and more independent and powerful. One had to have the greatest prestige in the congregation to be elected to a position that was so much sought after. Once the position had been gained, it conferred so much power on the incumbent that any bishop with a little intelligence and ability could impose his will more and more, particularly in personal matters, the more since his tendencies had from the first coincided with those of the majority of his congregation.

The result was that he acquired authority not only over persons who discharged functions in the administration of the congregation, but also over such as were concerned with propaganda and theory.

We have seen how the apostles were forced aside in the Second Century by the prophets. But both, apostles and prophets, probably came into frequent conflict with the bishop, who would not hesitate on such occasions to let them feel his financial and moral power. He probably found no difficulty in forbidding apostles and prophets and even teachers to sojourn in the congregation as soon as they displayed tendencies that did not please him. And this probably occurred very frequently in the case of apostles and prophets.

The bishops, in other words, the holders of the cash, were of course not chosen by preference from the unworldly enthusiasts, but from among sober, businesslike, practical men. These men knew the value of money, and therefore also the utility of having many wealthy communicants. It is natural to suppose that it was these men who represented the opportunistic revisionism in the Christian congregation, that they strove to attenuate the hatred against the rich man in the congregation, to weaken the teachings of the congregation to an extent that would cause the wealthy to feel more at home in it.

The wealthy of that day were also the cultured. The act of adapting the congregation to the requirements of the rich and cultured meant a weakening of the influence of the apostles and prophets and a reducing of their tendencies to absurdity, as well as of the tendencies of those who fought the wealthy through mere cussedness. But this effect was also produced on those who fought them with an enthusiastic and profound hatred, the more since they had given their entire property to the congregation, while they were still wealthy, in order to realize their high communistic ideal.

In the struggle between rigorism and opportunism, the latter was victorious; in other words, the bishops were victorious over the apostles and prophets, whose liberty of motion, whose very right to live, perceptibly decreased in the congregation. Officials of the congregation displaced them more and more. Since at first every member had had the right to take the floor in the gathering of the congregation and to engage in propaganda activities, an official of the congregation might also display such activity, which they probably did on a large scale. It is clear that members who stood out from the nameless mass as well-known speakers had a better chance to be elected to office in the congregation than entirely unknown members. On the other hand, those elected probably also were required to carry on propaganda work in addition to their administrative and judicial activities. Many administrative officials probably were more active in the former function than in the work that was theirs originally, since the growth of the congregation created new positions which relieved the others. Thus the deacons were enabled in many cases to devote more attention to propaganda work, if their functions in large congregations were taken charge of by special hospitals, orphan asylums, poor houses, inns for members from other towns.

On the other hand, it became necessary, precisely because of the growth of the congregation and its economic functions, to give its officials some training in preparation for their office. It would now have been too costly and dangerous to permit every man to acquire wisdom only by his actual experiences. The new supply of congregational officials was trained in the house of the bishop and there made acquainted with the duties of Church offices. Where the officials had also to conduct propaganda in addition to their official business, it was natural to train them for this job also in the house of the bishop, to instruct them in the teachings of the congregation.

Thus the bishop became the center not only of the economic, but also of the propaganda activity of the congregation, ideology being once more obliged to bend the knee to economic conditions.

There was now developed an official doctrine, recognized and disseminated by the congregational bureaucracy, which applied repressive measures more and more to all doctrines with which it did not agree.

This does not mean that the official doctrine was always hostile to intelligent opinion.

The tendencies opposed by the bishops were those of the original proletarian communism, hostile to state and property. In accordance with the ignorance of the lower classes of the population, their credulity, the incompatibility of their hopes with reality, it was precisely these tendencies that were associated with a special faith in miracles and with an exalted mental state. Much as was accomplished by the official Church in this field, the sects which it persecuted in the first few centuries far exceeded it in their insane exaggerations.

The sympathy with the oppressed, the aversion to all oppression, must not mislead us into regarding every opposition to the official Church, every form of heresy, as certain to represent a higher mental state.

The formulation of an official doctrine of the Church was also facilitated by certain other circumstances.

We are but poorly informed as to the doctrines taught in the early beginnings of the Christian congregation. To judge by mere indications, they were not very extensive, and of very simple nature. Surely we may not assume that they already contained everything later represented as the teaching of Jesus in the Gospels.

While we may perhaps go so far as to admit the probability that Jesus lived and was crucified, probably because of an attempted insurrection, there is practically nothing else that can be said about him. What is reported as his teaching has so little evidence to support it, is so contradictory and so little original, so full of commonplace moral maxims then current in the mouths of many, that not the slightest trace can be assigned with certainty to the actual teachings of Jesus. Concerning these we know nothing.

On the other hand, we have all the more right to imagine the beginnings of the Christian congregations as similar to those of socialistic organizations, to which they present many other similarities. A glance at these beginnings never reveals to us an overpowering personality whose doctrine becomes the rule for the later history of the movement, but always a chaotic germ, an uncertain, instinctive seeking and groping of numerous proletarians, none perceptibly more prominent than the others, all moved forward on the whole by the same tendencies, but often displaying the most striking individual deviations. Such a picture is, for instance, presented by the beginnings of the proletarian socialistic movement in the 'thirties and 'forties of the Nineteenth Century. Thus, the League of the Righteous, the later League of Communists, was already an institution of some age before Marx and Engels gave it a definite theoretical basis in the *Communist Manifesto*. And this League itself was only the continuation of earlier proletarian tendencies in France and England. Had it not been for Marx and Engels, its teachings would have continued to remain in the stage of ferment for a long time. The two authors of the *Communist Manifesto* were only enabled to secure their dominant and determining position by virtue of their mastery of the science of their times.

We have nothing to show—on the contrary, it is absolutely impossible—that a truly cultured person presided over the cradle of Christianity. It is expressly reported of Jesus that he did not surpass his comrades, plain proletarians, in education. Paul does not refer to his superior knowledge, but to his martyr's death, and his resurrection. This death made a profound impression on the Christians.

The apostles and prophets are not repeating definite doctrines handed down to them by others, but speak just as the spirit moves them. They express the most varied views; the early congregations are filled with bickering and dispute.

Paul writes to the Corinthians:

"Now in this that I declare unto you, I praise one, that you come together not for the better, but for the worse. For first of all, when ye come together in the church, I hear that there be divisions (σχίσματα) among you; and I partly believe it. For there must be also heresies among you, that they which are approved (δόκιμοι) may be made manifest among you" (I Corinthians xi, 17-19).

This need for various tendencies, heresies (Paul uses the word αἱρέσεις) in the congregation was later by no means recognized by the official Church. In the Second Century this vague seeking and groping comes to an end. The congregation has a history behind it, and in the course of this history various doctrines of faith have come out victorious, gaining recognition among the great mass of the congregation. Furthermore, educated persons now enter the congregation; on the one hand, they put the history and doctrines of the movement, transmitted to them by word of mouth, into written form, thus preserving them against further changes; on the other hand, they elevate the congregation's teachings, quite simple as they find them, to the level of the science of their time, which is still quite low, fill these teachings with their philosophy, thus making them palatable to the cultured also, and fortify them against the objections of pagan criticism.

He who would now become a teacher in the Christian congregation had to possess a certain amount of knowledge. The apostles and prophets, who had merely fumed about the sinfulness of the world and predicted its early collapse, could no longer compete with them.

Thus the unhappy apostles and prophets were restricted and

oppressed from all quarters. Their petty business soon had to succumb to the immense mechanism of the Christian bureaucracy; they disappeared. But the teachers were deprived of their freedom and made subordinate to the bishop. Soon no one dared open his mouth in the gathering of the congregation, the Church,[9] without previous permission from the bishop; i.e., no one outside of the congregation's bureaucracy, which was managed by the bishop, in other words, the clergy,[10] which was becoming more and more distinct from the mass of members, the laymen,[11] and assuming a superior position. The metaphor of the shepherd and his flock becomes popular, and the flock means a flock of such docile sheep that they permit themselves to be driven and shorn without resistance. The supreme shepherd is the bishop.

The international character of the movement also contributed to an increase in the power of the bishop. It had formerly been the apostles who had maintained the international cohesion of the various congregations, by their constant traveling among them. But as the apostles were relegated to the background, it became the more important to find other means of cementing and uniting the congregations. If disputes should arise, where a common action or common regulation were required in any matter, congresses of delegates from the congregations would meet, provincial congresses, and even imperial congresses, beginning with the Second Century.

At first these gatherings served only for discussion and mutual agreement. They could not pass resolutions that were binding. Each individual congregation felt itself to be supreme. Cyprian, in the first half of the Third Century, proclaimed the absolute independence of the congregation. But it is clear that the majority from the first must have swayed the congregation. Gradually this superiority attained binding power, the resolutions of the majority became a law for all the congregations represented, they

[9] *Ecclesia, ἐκκλησία*, originally means a *gathering of the people.*
[10] *Kleros* (*κλῆρος*), the bequest, the property of God, the people of God, those chosen by God.
[11] From *laos* (*λᾶος*), the people.

all resolved themselves into a single united body. All that was lost by the individual congregation in its freedom of action was now gained in the strength of the movement as a whole.

Thus the Catholic Church was created.[12] Congregations that refused to comply with the decisions of the congresses (synods, councils) were driven out of the Catholic Church organization, being excluded by the central body. But an individual who was expelled from his congregation, could no longer find admittance to other congregations. He was expelled from all the congregations. And the effects of expulsion or excommunication were now far more severe.

The right to expel members who opposed the purposes of the organization will surely not be denied to the Church while it was a specific party or organization existing by the side of many other parties or organizations within the state, pursuing a specific aim. It could not have attained this aim if it had renounced the right to expel anyone opposing its goal.

But things were different when the Church had become an organization embracing the entire state, the whole of European society, of which the nations constituted only the various parts. Expulsion from the Church now was equivalent to expulsion from human society; it might amount to a sentence of death.

The right to exclude members who do not recognize the objects of the organization is necessary for the formation and successful operation of definite parties in the state, for an active and fruitful political life therefore, for a healthy political development; but it becomes a means of preventing party formations, for rendering impossible all political life and political development, if, instead of being utilized by various parties in the state, it becomes a function of the state itself, or of an organization of state-wide proportions. But it is pure nonsense to demand from the various parties, for all the members of an organization, the same freedom of opinion that every democratic party must demand from the state. A party tolerating all possible opinions in its ranks ceases

---

[12] *Catholic*, from *holos* (ὅλος), complete, full, and from the preposition *kata* (κατα) meaning *downward, concerning, belonging to. Katholikos* means *pertaining to the whole;* the Catholic Church therefore is the Church as a *whole.*

to be a party. But the state, when it prosecutes certain views, itself becomes a party. Democracy must demand not that parties cease to be parties, but that the state cease to be a party.

No objection may be made from a democratic standpoint to excommunications by the Church, while the Church remains merely one of several parties. He who does not believe in the doctrines of the Church, who will not comply with its rules, has no place in the Church. Democracy has no right to demand tolerance of the Church—while the Church contents itself to remain a party among many other parties, unless the state takes sides with the Church or identifies itself with it. Then a democracy of the Church policy must be introduced, not a demand for the toleration of unbelievers in the Church, which would be only a weak half-measure.

But while no objection could be raised from the democratic standpoint to the Church's right of excommunication *per se,* before it became a state Church, much might already be said against the manner in which this right was applied. For it was no longer the great mass of the members, but the bureaucracy, by whom excommunication was applied. The more damage could thus be done to the individual, the more did the power of the ecclesiastical bureaucracy and of its head, the bishop, grow.

The latter's power increased also by virtue of the fact that he was the delegate of his congregation at ecclesiastical congresses. The bishop's power therefore begins simultaneously with the Councils, and these were gatherings of bishops from the very start.

The prestige and authority enjoyed by the bishop because of his administration of the congregation's funds and his appointing and governing the entire administrative, judicial, propaganda, and learned apparatus of the congregational bureaucracy, was not supplemented by the authority held by the whole, the *Catholic Church,* as opposed to the part, the congregation. The bishop approached the congregation with all the authority of the Church behind him. As the organization of the entire Church became more rigid, the congregations became more powerless as opposed to the bishops, at least in cases where the latter represented the tendencies of the majority of his colleagues. "This association of the bishops entirely took away the rights of the laity." [13]

The bishops were not wrong in asserting that their authority came from the apostles, and in considering themselves as their successors. The bishops, like the apostles before them, were the international and unifying element among all the congregations and it is precisely this fact that gave them much of their influence and power over individual congregations.

Even the last remnant of the original democracy of the congregation now soon disappeared, namely, the right to elect the officials that were needed. With the increase of the independence and power of the bishop and his adherents among the congregation, it became easier for him to persuade the latter to elect persons suitable to him. It was actually the bishop who filled these offices. But in the election of the bishop himself, candidates proposed by the clergy had the best prospects from the start, owing to the clergy's power in the congregation. Finally it came to pass that only the clergy elected the bishop, the mass of members of the congregation retaining only the right to approve or reject this election. But even this gradually became a mere formality. The congregation was finally degraded to a mere claque, who, when the elected bishop was presented by the clergy, were obliged to greet him with jubilant applause.

This meant the final destruction of the democratic organization of the congregation, by confirming the absolute power of the clergy, and completing its transformation from a humble "servant of the servants of God" to their absolute master.

It was natural that the property of the congregation now should actually become the property of its administrators, of course not their personal property, but that of the bureaucracy as a body. The property of the Church ceased to be a congregational prop-

---

[13] Harnack, *The Expansion of Christianity in the First Three Centuries*, London and New York, vol. ii, p. 59. As an example of the great power attained by the bishop over his congregation, Harnack cites the incident of a Bishop Trophimus. When the latter was converted to paganism in a period of persecution, the greater part of his congregation went with him. "But when he returned to the fold and did penance, the others followed him again, none of whom would have come back to the Church if Trophimus had not led them."

erty of the members. It became the property of the clergy. This transformation found powerful support in, and was accelerated by, the state recognition of Christianity in the beginning of the Fourth Century. But, on the other hand, the recognition of the Catholic Church by the emperors was only a consequence of the progress made by the power of the bureaucracy and of the bishop's absolute power within the bureaucracy.

As long as the Church was a democratic organization, it was absolutely opposed to the imperial despotism in the Roman Empire. On the other hand, the bureaucracy of bishops, which absolutely ruled and exploited the people, was a very good instrument for imperial despotism. Furthermore, the latter could not ignore the Church, but had to come to terms with it, as otherwise the Church might have grown over its head.

The clergy had become a power that every ruler of the Empire had to reckon with. Among the various pretenders to the throne before the civil wars in the beginning of the Fourth Century, *Constantine,* who had made an alliance with the ecclesiastical clergy, was the victorious one.

The bishop now became the master, ruling the empire by the side of the emperors. The emperors often presided in the Councils of Bishops, but in exchange they placed the state authority at the disposal of the bishops for carrying out the decisions of the councils and the excommunications.

Simultaneously, the Church now attained the rights of a legal personage capable of holding and inheriting property (321 A.D.). Its proverbial appetite was thus enormously stimulated, church property grew apace. But the exploitation practiced by the Church also increased.

Thus the organization of a proletarian, subversive communism gave rise to the most faithful support of despotism and exploitation, a source of new despotism, of new exploitation.

The victorious Christian congregation was at every point the precise opposite of that congregation which had been founded three centuries before by poor Galilean fishermen and peasants and Jerusalem proletarians. The crucified Messiah became the firmest prop of that debased and infamous society whose complete destruction the messianic congregation had expected him to accomplish.

e. The Monastery

The Catholic Church, particularly as it had been recognized by the state, transformed the tendencies of the original messianic congregation into their precise opposite; but this was not done by peaceful means, without resistance and struggle. The social conditions that brought about the democratic communism of the primitive Christians continued to exist, in fact, became more aggravating and tormenting as the Empire dissolved.

We have seen that voices protesting against the new conception had made themselves heard from the very start. But when the innovation had become the dominant and official attitude of the Church, not tolerating other views among the congregation, new democratic and communistic sects again and again arose by the side of the Catholic Church. Thus, for example, at the time when this Church was recognized by Constantine, the sect of the Circumcelliones became widespread in Northern Africa, ecstatic mendicants who pushed to the extreme the struggle of the Donatist Sect against the State Church and the state itself, preaching hostility to all the wealthy and powerful. As in Galilee at the time of Christ, so in Northern Africa in the Fourth Century, the peasant population rose in desperation against its oppressors, and the banditry practiced by numerous bands shows the manner in which their protest expressed itself. As had formerly been the case with the Zealots, and perhaps also with the first adherents of Jesus, the Circumcelliones now set for these bands the goal of liberation and freedom from all oppression. With extreme audacity they gave battle even to the imperial troops, who sought, hand in hand with Catholic clergymen, to put down the insurrection, which lasted several decades.

But this effort failed, as did every other effort to introduce communism into the Church again by peaceful or violent means. They all were defeated by the same causes which had finally transmuted the primitive communism into its opposite, causes which continued to exist side by side with the stimulus producing such efforts. While this stimulus was increased by the rising distress, it must not be forgotten that the Church's resources were also increasing, enabling the Church to shield an increasingly large portion of the proletariat from the worst temptations by means of its charitable institutions, thus making the proletariat dependent on the clergy, and corrupting it and stifling all enthusiasm and all higher ideals within it.

When the Church became a State Church, a tool of despotism and exploitation more powerful and more gigantic than any that had yet appeared in history, the doom of all communistic tendencies within it seemed finally sealed. And yet these tendencies were to draw new strength precisely from the State Church.

Up to the time of its recognition by the state, the spread of the Christian congregations had as a rule been limited to the great cities; only in these could they maintain themselves in periods of persecution. In the provinces, where it is easier to observe each individual, secret organizations may maintain themselves only when they enjoy the support of the entire population, as, for example, in the case of the Irish secret bodies in the last few centuries, in opposition to the English yoke. A minority opposition movement in society has always encountered the greatest difficulties in the provinces, and this applies also to the Christian movement in the first three centuries.

The obstacles to its spread in the provinces disappeared when Christianity ceased to be an opposition movement and was recognized by the state. From this time on nothing stood in the way of the organization of Christian congregations in the provinces. For three centuries Christianity—like Judaism—had been almost exclusively a city religion. Now for the first time it became a religion of the peasants also.

Together with Christianity, its communistic tendencies invaded the provinces, finding different and far more favorable conditions than in the city, as we have already seen in our discussion of Essenism. The latter immediately awoke to new life in a Christian form, as soon as the possibility of open communistic organizations was offered in the provinces, which indicates how strong was the want it fulfilled. Precisely at the time when Christianity was recognized by the state, in the beginning of the Fourth Century, the first monasteries were established in Egypt, soon followed by others in many parts of the Empire.

This form of communism was soon not only not opposed by the ecclesiastical and national authorities, but even favored by them, as the communistic experiments in America in the first half of the Nineteenth Century were similarly not unsympathetic to the governments of France and England. They could not fail to gain by having the restless communistic agitators of their large cities seclude themselves from the world, to devote themselves to a peaceful cultivation of cabbages in the wilderness.

Unlike the communistic experiments of the Owenites, Fourierists and Cabetists in America, the experiments of the Egyptian peasant Anthony and his disciples met with the most brilliant success, as did also the peasant communistic colonies in the United States in the Eighteenth and Nineteenth Centuries, which were very similar to the Egyptian movement. Many persons would like to ascribe their success to their religious enthusiasm, lacking in the adherents of modern Utopias; no communism without religion. But the same religious enthusiasm that had inspired the monks in the monasteries had also inspired the Christians of the large cities in the first centuries, and yet their communistic experiments had been neither thorough nor of long duration.

The cause of success in the one case and failure in the other is not to be found in religion, but in their material circumstances.

As contrasted with the communistic experiments of the primitive Christianity of the large cities, the monasteries, as well as the communistic colonies in the wilderness, have the advantage that agriculture requires a combination of the farm and the family, and large-scale agriculture had not only become possible, but had already attained a high stage of development in the "*oikos* system" of the large landed proprietors. This large-scale operation of the *oikos* system had, however, been based on slavery. Slavery set the limits for its productivity and for its existence too. The cessation of the supply of slaves caused the large farms of the large landowners to disappear. The monasteries took them up again and continued them; in fact, could develop them to a higher point, as the monasteries replaced slave labor by that of their own free members. In view of the general disintegration of society, the monasteries finally became the only places in the decaying empire in which the last remnants of ancient technology were preserved through the storms of the migration period and even perfected in many points.

Aside from the influences of the Orient, particularly of the Arabs, the monasteries were the points from which civilization in Europe again started to grow during the Middle Ages.

The coöperative mode of production of the monastery was excellently adapted to the conditions of rural production toward the end of the ancient period and in the early Middle Ages; this explains its success. In the cities, on the other hand, the conditions of production were opposed to coöperative labor, and communism could exist only in the form of a mere communism of consumption, but it is the mode of production, not the mode of distribution or consumption, which determines in the last analysis the character of social relations. It was only in the country, in the monasteries, that the community of consumption originally desired by Christianity obtained a permanent basis in the community of production. On this basis, the brotherhoods of the Essenes had flourished for several centuries, being finally destroyed by the sudden annihilation of the Jewish community, and not as a result of internal causes. It is on a community of production that the great structure of the Christian monastery arose, enduring to the present day.

But why have the colonies of modern Utopian communism been failures? Their basis was not unlike that of monastic communism, but the mode of production has completely changed since then. In place of the isolated single industries of antiquity, developing an individualism in labor, and rendering the coöperation of urban workers very difficult, inspiring them with an anarchistic attitude toward production, we now find immense plants in urban industry in which each worker constitutes only a cog operating together with countless other cogs. The habits of work in coöperation, of discipline in labor, of a subordination of the individual to the requirements of the whole, in the modern instance replaces the anarchistic attitude of the individual worker. But only in production; consumption is a different matter.

The conditions of life were formerly so simple and uniform for the mass of the population, that there resulted a uniformity of consumption and of needs, making a permanent community of consumption by no means intolerable.

The modern mode of production, which throws all classes and nations together, gathers all the products of the entire world into the great commercial centers, produces new products unceasingly, tirelessly creating not only new means of satisfying needs, but also creating the needs, thus establishes in the mass of the population a great variety of personal inclinations and desires, an "individualism" that could formerly be found only in the wealthy and aristocratic classes. In other words, many modes of consumption, taking the word in the broadest sense of "enjoying" material things. The crudest, most material means of consumption, foods, beverages, clothing, are of course, in many instances, subject to standardization in the modern mode of production. But it is of the essence of this mode of production not to limit even the consumption of the masses to such substances, but to create among the workers also a corresponding demand for more articles of culture, educational, artistic, sporting, and other articles, these needs differentiating themselves more and more and finding varying expression in each individual. Thus the individualism of enjoyment, formerly the privilege of the wealthy and cultured, is spread among the working classes also, first in the large cities, thence gradually permeating the remainder of the population. Although the modern worker is obliged to make great concessions to discipline in his coöperation with his fellow workers, and recognizes such concessions as necessary, he nevertheless emphatically resists all attempts to govern his consumption, his enjoyment. In this field he is becoming more and more an individualist, or if you like, anarchistic. The reader will now understand how the modern city proletarian must feel in a small communistic colony in the wilderness, which cannot be more than a large agricultural establishment with subsidiary industrial operations. As we have already stated, industry and the household have always been related in this branch of production. This was an advantage for Christian communism, which began with a community of consumption. In the monastic institutions in the provinces, this communism was therefore obliged to unite with a communism of production, which gave it great power of resistance and development.

Modern Utopian communism, beginning with a community in production, and finding a very solid basis in this community, was forced, on the other hand, by the close relation between consumption and production, in its small settlements, to add a communism of consumption to the communism of production, the former affecting the latter as red cloth does a bull, producing eternal bickering of the most repulsive sort, on petty provocations.

Only elements of the population that had remained untouched by modern capitalism, unworldly peasants, could still found communistic colonies in the Nineteenth Century within the area of modern civilization. Their religion has no bearing on their success, except to the extent that religious enthusiasm as a social phenomenon, not as an individual idiosyncrasy, is now found only in the most backward strata of the population.

Communism of production can be executed in modern large-scale industrial populations only at such an advanced stage that a very far-reaching individualism of consumption—in the widest sense of the word—may be united with it. It was a communism of production that met with failure in the non-religious communistic colonies of the Nineteenth Century; for capitalism has been successfully practising such communism for some time. It was communism in the standardization of personal consumption, so contrary to modern habits, that failed.

In ancient times, and also in the Middle Ages, there was no trace among the masses of the people of an individualization of wants. Thus, monastic communism encountered no such obstacle, and could flourish the more as its mode of production excelled that commonly prevalent, in accordance with its own economic superiority. Rufinus (345-410) who founded a monastery himself on the Mount of Olives near Jerusalem, in 377 A.D., maintains that almost as many persons lived in the monasteries in the country districts of Egypt as in the cities. After due allowance for an exaggerated pious imagination, there is no doubt this statement was based on a number of monks and nuns that must have appeared extraordinary.

Thus the monastic system gave a new lease of life to the communistic enthusiasm in Christianity, since the latter here found an expression that was not obliged to appear as an heretical opposition to the dominant ecclesiastical bureaucracy, but might very well come to terms with the latter.

But this form of Christian communism could also not become the universal form of society, but was limited to certain strata. Therefore the new communism also necessarily again and again turned into its opposite, which was the more likely, the greater its economic superiority. The latter factor was most likely to transform its participants into an aristocracy, superior to the remainder of the population, and finally dominating and exploiting it.

The monastic communism could not become the universal form of society if only for the reason that its conduct of a common household, on which it was based, necessarily rejected marriage, as the Essenes had done before, and as the religious communistic colonies in North America did later (in the Nineteenth Century). The prosperity of the common household required only the renunciation of individual marriage; a sort of community marriage would have been quite compatible with it, as is also shown by a number of the colonies referred to. But this relation between the sexes too sharply contradicted the general social feeling of the later Middle Ages to be generally recognized and publicly practiced. In general, this period was characterized by a down-in-the-dumps feeling which made abstinence from all enjoyment, asceticism, a more natural solution, besides which it surrounded with a peculiar halo those who practised such abstinence. But the practice of celibacy doomed monasticism in advance to remain limited to a minority. This minority might at times increase considerably, as the above quoted passage from Rufinus shows, but even Rufinus's obvious exaggeration does not dare represent

the monastic population as a majority. And the monastic enthusiasm of the Egyptians in Rufinus's day soon abated.

As monastic communism became firm and durable, the wealth
of the monastery necessarily increased. The monastic industries
soon furnished the best products and the cheapest, since the common household rendered the cost of production quite low. Like
the *oikos* system of the great landed proprietors, the monasteries
produced themselves almost everything they needed in foodstuffs
and raw materials. The workers showed far more zeal than had
the slaves of the great landed proprietor, for they were members
themselves, receiving the entire product of their labor. Besides,
each monastery included so many workers that it might select
for each of its industries those workers best fitted for it, thus
introducing a far-reaching division of labor. Finally, the monastery, as contrasted with the individual, was eternal. Inventions
and business secrets which might easily be lost with the death of
the inventor and his family, became the enterprise of many members in the monastery, being transmitted by them to their successors. Besides, the monastery, being an eternal personage, was
not beset with the destructive danger of dissipating its patrimony
by inheritance. Its accumulations of property were never divided
in the form of bequests.

Thus the wealth of each monastery grew, also the wealth of
combinations of monasteries under a single head and under uniform regulations, the so-called orders of monks. But no sooner
did a monastery become rich and powerful, than the same process
took place in it that has recurred in many other communistic
organizations since then, embracing but a portion of society, as
may still be observed in productive coöperative organizations now
in existence. The owners of the means of production now find it
easier to have others work for them than to work themselves, if
they can find the necessary workers: penniless wage laborers,
slaves, or serfs.

While the monastic system in its beginnings imparted new life
to the communistic enthusiasm in Christianity, it nevertheless
finally took the same path that the clergy of the Church had taken

before it. Like the clergy, it became an organization for exploitation and domination.

To be sure, this controlling organization did not always consent to be a mere blind tool of the rulers of the Church, the bishops. Economically independent of them, rivaling them in wealth, with an international organization like theirs, the monasteries were able to oppose the bishops when no one else would have dared do so.

They thus occasionally aided in somewhat attenuating the despotism of the bishops, but even this clemency was destined ultimately to turn into its opposite.

After the division of the Church into an Eastern and a Western Church, the emperor became the liege-lord of the bishops in the former. In the latter there was no state authority that could have controlled the entire realm of the Church. Therefore it was the Bishop of Rome who first obtained precedence over the other bishops in the Western Church, thanks to the importance of his diocese. This precedence in the course of centuries developed more and more into a domination over the other bishops. As the absolute monarchy of modern times developed out of the class struggle between the feudal nobility and the bourgeoisie, so the absolute monarchy of the Pope developed out of the class struggle with the aristocracy of bishops and monks, the owners of the large monastic industries. With the consolidation of the Papacy, the ascending curve of the Church's development reaches its culmination. All later evolutions in state and society involve defeats for the Church; the development is now against the Church and the Church against all development; it becomes an out-and-out reactionary, anti-social institution.

Even after its transformation into the opposite of its early stage, after becoming an organization of domination and exploitation, the Church still succeeded for a time in achieving great things. But with the end of the Crusades, the Church had no further function to discharge for the human race. Its contribution, after it had become the state religion, consisted in rescuing and developing the remnants of ancient civilization as it found them. But when a new mode of production, far superior to the ancient, developed on the basis of the system that had been rescued and perfected by the Church, when capitalism was the result and an all-embracing communism of production arose, the Catholic Church could be nothing more than an obstacle to social progress. Born from communism, it is now among the bitterest enemies of modern communism.

Will not this communism in turn develop the same dialectic process as the Christian communism and also become a new mechanism for exploitation and domination? This question is the last one requiring our attention.

VI. CHRISTIANITY AND SOCIALISM

THE famous introduction written by Engels in March, 1895, for the new edition of Marx's *Class Struggles in France from 1848 to 1850* closes with the following words:

"Now almost sixteen hundred years ago, there was at work in the Roman Empire a dangerous revolutionary party. It undermined religion and all the foundations of the State; it denied pointblank that the emperor's will was the highest law; it was without a fatherland, international; it spread out over the entire realm from Gaul to Asia, and even beyond the borders of the Empire. It had long worked underground and in secrecy, but had, for some time, felt strong enough to come out openly in the light of day. This revolutionary party, known under the name of Christians, also had a strong representation in the army; entire legions were composed of Christians. When they were commanded to attend the sacrificial ceremonies of the Pagan established church, there to serve as a guard of honor, the revolutionary soldiers went so far in their insolence as to fasten special symbols—crosses—on their helmets. The customary disciplinary barrack measures of their officers proved fruitless. The emperor, Diocletian, could no longer quietly look on and see how order, obedience and discipline were undermined in his army. He promulgated an anti-Socialist—beg pardon—an anti-Christian law. The meetings of the revolutionaries were prohibited, their meeting places were closed or even demolished, the Christian symbols, crosses, etc., were forbidden as in Saxony they forbid red pocket handkerchiefs. The Christians were declared unfit to hold office in the State, they could not even become corporals. Inasmuch as at that time they did not have judges well drilled as to the 'reputation of a person', such as Herr Köller's anti-Socialist law presupposes, the Christians were simply forbidden to seek their rights in a court of law. But this exceptional law, too, remained ineffective. In defiance, the Christians tore it from the walls, yea, it is said that at Nicomedia they fired the emperor's palace over his head. Then the latter revenged himself by means of a great persecution of Christians in 303 A.D. This was the last persecution of its kind. It was so effective that, seventeen years later, the army was composed largely of Christians, and that the next autocratic ruler of the entire Roman Empire, Constantine, called 'the Great' by the clericals, proclaimed Christianity as the religion of the State." [1]

He who knows his Engels and compares these last lines of Engels's "political testament" with the views Engels expressed throughout his life, cannot have any doubts as to the intentions behind this humorous comparison. Engels wanted to point out the irresistible and elemental nature of the progress of our movement, which he said owed its inevitability particularly to the increase of its adherents in the army, so that it would soon be able to force even the most powerful autocrat to yield.

This narration is interesting chiefly as an expression of the healthy optimism which Engels retained up to his death.

But the passage also has been interpreted differently, since it is preceded by statements to the effect that the party at present flourishes best when pursuing legal methods. Certain persons have maintained that Engels in his "political testament" denies his entire life-work and finally represents the revolutionary standpoint, which he has defended for two generations, as an error. These persons inferred that Engels had now recognized Marx's doctrine—to the effect that force is the midwife of every new form of society—as no longer tenable. In drawing a comparison between Christianity and Socialism, interpreters of this stamp did not place the emphasis on the *irresistible and elemental* nature of the advance, but on Constantine's *voluntary* proclamation of Christianity as the state religion; the latter was brought to victory without any *violent convulsions* in the state, by *peaceful* means alone, through the *friendly assistance of the government.*

These persons imagine that Socialism will also conquer thus.

[1] Karl Marx, *Class Struggles in France, 1848-1850,* with an *Introduction* by Frederick Engels, translated by Henry Kuhn, New York: 1924, pp. 29, 30.

Immediately after the death of Engels this hope indeed seemed about to be fulfilled, as M. Waldeck-Rousseau came out as a new Constantine in France and appointed a Bishop of the new Christians, M. Millerand, as his Minister.

He who knows Engels and judges him without bias, will know that it never even entered Engels's mind to abjure his revolutionary ideas, that the final passage of his introduction cannot therefore be interpreted in the sense indicated above. But it must be admitted that the passage is not very clear. Persons who do not know Engels, who imagine that he was assailed immediately before his death by sudden doubts as to the utility of his entire life-work, may interpret this passage, standing alone, as indicating that Christianity's path to victory is a pattern for the journey that Socialism has still to make.

If this had really been Engels's opinion, no worse judgment could have been spoken on Socialism; it would have been equivalent to a prophecy not of approaching triumph, but of a complete defeat of the great goal proposed by Socialism.

It is characteristic that the persons who thus utilize this passage overlook all the great and profound elements in Engels, but greet with enthusiasm such sentences as—if they really contained what is alleged to be in them—would be entirely erroneous.

We have seen that Christianity did not attain victory until it had been transformed into the precise opposite of its original character; that the victory of Christianity was not the victory of the proletariat, but of the clergy which was exploiting and dominating the proletariat; that Christianity was not victorious as a subversive force, but as a conservative force, as a new prop of suppression and exploitation; that it not only did not eliminate the imperial power, slavery, the poverty of the masses, and the concentration of wealth in a few hands, but perpetuated these conditions. The Christian *organization*, the Church, attained victory by *surrendering* its original aims and defending their opposite.

Indeed, if the victory of Socialism is to be achieved in the same way as that of Christianity, this would be a good reason for renouncing, not revolution, but the Social-Democracy; no severer accusation could be raised against the Social-Democracy, from the proletarian standpoint, and the attacks made by the anarchists against the Social-Democracy would be only too well justified. Indeed, the attempt by bourgeois and socialistic elements at a socialistic ministerial function in France, which aimed to imitate the Christian method of rendering Christianity a state institution in the old days—and applied, strangely enough, in this instance, to combat the State Church—has had no other effect than to strengthen the semi-anarchistic, anti-socialistic syndicalism.

But fortunately the parallel between Christianity and Socialism is completely out of place in this connection. Christianity, to be sure, is in its origin a movement of the poor, like Socialism, and both therefore have many elements in common, as we have had occasion to point out.

Engels also referred to this similarity in an article entitled "On the History of Primitive Christianity," in *Die Neue Zeit*,[2] written shortly before his death, and indicating how profoundly Engels was interested in this subject at that time, how natural it therefore was for him to write the parallel found in his introduction to the *Class Struggles in France*. This article says:

"The history of primitive Christianity presents remarkable coincidences with the modern workers' movement. Like the latter, Christianity was originally a movement of the oppressed; it first appeared as a religion of slaves and freedmen, of the poor, the outcasts, of the peoples subjected or dispersed by Rome. Both Christianity and Socialism preach an approaching redemption from servitude and misery; Christianity assigns this redemption to a future life in Heaven after death; Socialism would attain it in this world by a transformation of society. Both are hunted and persecuted, their adherents outlawed, subjected to special legislation, represented, in the one case, as enemies of the human race, in the other, as enemies of the nation, religion, the family, of the social order. And in spite of all persecutions, in some cases even aided to victory by such persecutions, both

[2] Vol. xiii, No. 1, p. 4 *ff.*, September, 1894 (*Zur Geschichte des Urchristentums*).

advance irresistibly.   Three centuries after its beginning, Christianity is the recognized state religion of the Roman Empire, and in barely sixty years Socialism has conquered a place that renders its victory absolutely certain."

This parallel is correct on the whole, with a few limitations of course; Christianity can hardly be called a religion of the slaves; it did nothing for them.   On the other hand, the liberation from misery proclaimed by Christianity was at first quite material, to be realized on this earth, not in Heaven.   This latter circumstance, however, increases the similarity with the modern workers' movement.   Engels continues:

"The parallel between these two historical phenomena becomes apparent even in the Middle Ages, in the first insurrections of oppressed peasants, and particularly of urban plebeians. . . . The communists of the French Revolution, as well as Weitling and his adherents, make references to primitive Christianity long before Ernest Renan said: 'If you would form an idea of the first Christian congregations drop in at the local section of the International Workers' Association.'

"The French litterateur who wrote the ecclesiastical novel *Les Origines du Christianisme,* a plagiarism of German Bible criticism unparalleled for its audacity—was himself not aware how much truth these words contained.   I should like to see any old 'international' who would read, let us say, the so-called Second Epistle to the Corinthians, without feeling the opening of old wounds at least in a certain sense."

Engels then goes into greater detail in comparing primitive Christianity and the International, but he does not trace the later development of either Christianity or the workers' movement. The dialectic collapse of the former does not receive his attention, and yet, if Engels had pursued this subject, he would have discovered traces of similar transformations in the modern workers' movement.   Like Christianity, this movement is obliged to create permanent organs in the course of its growth, a sort of professional bureaucracy in the party, as well as in the unions, without which it cannot function, which are a necessity for it, which must continue to grow, and obtain more and more important duties.

This bureaucracy—which must be taken in the broad sense as including not only the administrative officials, but also editors and parliamentary delegates—will not this bureaucracy in the course of things become a new aristocracy, like the clergy headed by the bishop? Will it not become an aristocracy dominating and exploiting the working masses and finally attaining the power to deal with the state authorities on equal terms, thus being tempted not to overthrow them but join them?

This final outcome would be certain if the parallel were perfect. But fortunately this is not the case. In spite of the numerous similarities between Christianity and the modern workers' movement, there are also fundamental differences.

Particularly, the proletariat today is quite different from the proletariat of early Christianity. The traditional view of a free proletariat consisting of beggars only is probably exaggerated; the slaves were not the only workers. But it is true that slave labor also corrupted the free working proletarians, most of whom worked in their own homes. A laboring proletarian's ideal then strove, as did that of the beggar, to realize an existence without labor at the expense of the rich, who were expected to squeeze the necessary quantity of products out of the slaves.

Furthermore, Christianity in the first three centuries was exclusively an urban movement, but the city proletarians at that time had but little significance in the composition of society, whose productive basis was almost entirely that of antiquity, combined with quite important industrial operations.

As a result of all this, the chief bearers of the Christian movement, the free urban proletarians, workers and idlers, did not feel that society was living on them; they all strove to live on society without giving any return. Work played no part in their vision of the future state.

It was therefore of course natural that in spite of all the class hatred against the rich, the effort to gain their favor and their generosity becomes apparent again and again, and the inclination of the ecclesiastical bureaucracy to favor the rich members in the mass of the congregation encountered as little resistance as did the arrogance of this bureaucracy itself.

The economic and moral decay of the proletariat in the Roman Empire was further increased by the general decline of all society, which was becoming poorer and more desperate, while its productive forces were declining more and more. Thus hopelessness and despair seized all classes, crippled their initiative, caused all to expect salvation only at the hands of extraordinary and supernatural powers, made them helpless victims of any clever impostor, or of any energetic, self-confident adventurer, caused them to relinquish as hopeless any independent resistance to any of the dominant powers.

How different is the modern proletariat! It is a proletariat of labor, and it knows that all society rests upon its shoulders. And the capitalistic mode of production is shifting the center of gravity in production more and more from the provinces to the industrial centers, in which mental and political life are most active. The workers of these centers, the most energetic and intelligent of all, now become the elements controlling the destinies of society.

Simultaneously, the dominant mode of production enhances the productive forces enormously and thus increases the claims made on society by the workers, also increasing their power to put through these claims. Hopefulness, confidence, self-consciousness, inspire them, as they once inspired the rising bourgeoisie, giving it the power to break the chains of the feudal, ecclesiastical, bureaucratic domination and exploitation, and drawing the necessary strength from the great growth of capital.

The origin of Christianity coincides with a collapse of democracy. The three centuries of its development previous to its recognition are characterized by a constant decline of all remnants of autonomy, and also by a progressive disintegration of the productive forces.

The modern workers' movement originates in an immense victory of democracy, namely, the great French Revolution. The century that has elapsed since then, with all its changes and fluctuations, nevertheless presents a steady advance of democracy, a veritably fabulous increase in the productive forces, and not only a greater expansion, but also a greater independence and clarity on the part of the proletariat.

One has only to examine this contrast to become aware that the development of Socialism cannot possibly deviate from its course as did that of Christianity; we need not fear that it will develop a new class of rulers and exploiters from its ranks, sharing their booty with the old tyrants.

While the fighting ability and the fighting spirit of the proletariat progressively decreased in the Roman Empire, these qualities are being strengthened in modern society; the class oppositions are becoming perceptibly more acute, and this alone must frustrate all attempts to induce the proletariat to relinquish its struggle because its champions have been favored. Any such attempts have hitherto led to the isolation of the person making them, who has been deserted by the proletariat in spite of his former services to them. But not only the proletariat and the political and social environment in which it moves are entirely different today from the conditions of the primitive Christian era; present-day communism and the conditions of its realization are quite different from the conditions of ancient communism.

The *struggle* for communism, the *need* for communism, today originate from the same source, namely *poverty*, and so long as Socialism is only a Socialism of the feelings, only an expression of this want, it will occasionally express itself even in the modern workers' movement in tendencies resembling those of the time of primitive Christianity. The slightest understanding of the economic conditions of present-day communism will at once recognize how different it is from the primitive Christian communism.

The concentration of wealth in a few hands, which in the Roman Empire proceeded hand in hand with a constant decrease in the productive forces—for which decrease it was partly responsible—this same concentration has today become the basis for an enormous increase in productive forces. While the distribution of wealth then did not injure the productivity of society in the slightest degree, but rather favored it, it would be equivalent to a complete crippling of production today. Modern communism can no longer think of an equal distribution of wealth; its object is rather to secure the greatest possible increase in the productivity of labor and a more equitable distribution of the annual products of labor by pushing the concentration of wealth to the highest point, transforming it from the private monopoly of a few capitalist groups into a state monopoly.

But modern communism, if it would satisfy the needs of the new man created by modern methods of production, must also fully preserve individualism of consumption. This individualism does not involve an isolation of individuals from each other when consuming; it may even take the form of a social consumption, of social activity; the individualism of enjoyment is not equivalent to an abolition of large enterprises in the production of articles of consumption, nor to a displacement of the machine by hand labor, as many æsthetic Socialists may dream. But the individualism of consumption requires *liberty* in the choice of enjoyments, also liberty in the choice of the society in which the consumer consumes.

But the mass of the urban population in primitive Christian days knew no forms of social production; large enterprises with free workers can hardly be said to have existed in urban industry. But they are well acquainted with social forms of consumption, particulary common meals, often provided by the congregation or the state.

Thus the primitive Christian communism was a communism of *distribution* of wealth and standardization of *consumption;* modern communism means *concentration* of wealth and *concentration* of *production.*

The primitive Christian communism did not need to be extended over all of society in order to be brought about. Its execution could begin within a limited area, in fact, it might, within those limits, assume permanent forms; indeed, the latter were of a nature that precluded their becoming a universal form of society.

Therefore primitive Christian communism necessarily became a new form of aristocracy, and it was obliged to accomplish this inner dialectic even within society as it then was. It could not abolish classes, but only add a new form of domination to society.

But modern communism, in view of the immense expansion of the means of production, the social character of the mode of production, the far-reaching concentration of the most important objects of wealth, has not the slightest chance of being brought about on any smaller scale than that of society as a whole. All attempts to realize communism in the petty establishments of socialistic colonies or productive coöperatives within society as it is, have been failures. Communism may not be produced by the formation of little organizations within capitalist society, which would gradually absorb that society as they expand, but only by the attainment of a power sufficient to control and transform the whole of social life. This power is the *state power*. The conquest of political power by the proletariat is the first condition of the realization of modern communism.

Until the proletariat reaches this stage, there can be no thought of socialistic production, or of the latter's effecting contradictions in its development that will transform sense into nonsense and benefactions into torments.[3] But even after the modern proletariat has conquered the political power, social production will not come into being at once as a finished whole, but economic development will suddenly take a new turn, no longer in the direction of an accentuation of capitalism but toward the development of a social production. When will the latter have advanced to the point where contradictions and abuses will appear in it, destined to develop the new society in another direction now unknown and absolutely obscure? This condition cannot be outlined at present and need not be dwelt on here.

As far as we can trace the modern socialistic movement, it is impossible for it to produce phenomena that will show any similarity with those of Christianity as a state religion. But it is also true that the manner in which Christianity attained its victory cannot in any way serve as a pattern for the modern movement of proletarian ambitions.

The victory of the leaders of the proletariat will surely not be as easy as that of the good bishops of the Fourth Century.

But we may maintain not only that Socialism will not develop

---

[3] Vernunft wird Unsinn, Wohltat Plage;
Weh dir. dass du ein Enkel bist!—Goethe's *Faust*.

any internal contradictions in the period preceding this victory, that will be comparable with those attending the last phases of Christianity, but also that no such contradictions will materialize in the period in which the predictable consequences of this victory are developed.

For capitalism has developed the conditions for placing society on an entirely new basis, completely different from all of the bases on which society has stood since class distinctions first arose. While no new revolutionary class or party—even those that went much further than Christianity in the form recognized by Constantine, even when they actually would abolish existing class distinctions—has ever been able to abolish all classes, but has always substituted new class distinctions for the old ones, we now have the material conditions for an elimination of all class distinctions. The modern proletariat is moved by its class interest to utilize these conditions in the direction of this abolition, for it is now the lowest class, while in the days of Christianity the slaves were lower than the proletariat.

Class differences and class oppositions ought by no means to be confused with the distinctions brought about between the various callings, by a division of labor. The contrast between classes is the result of three causes: private property in the means of production, in the manipulation of weapons, in science. Certain technical and social conditions produce the differentiation between those who possess the means of production and those who do not; later, they produce the distinction between those who are trained in the use of arms and those who are defenseless; finally comes the distinction between those well versed in science and those who are ignorant.

The capitalistic mode of production creates the necessary conditions for abolishing all these oppositions. It not only works toward an abolition of private property in the means of production, but by its wealth of productive forces it also abolishes the necessity of limiting military training and knowledge to certain strata. This necessity had been created as soon as military training and science had attain a rather high stage, enabling those who had free time and material means exceeding the needs of life, to acquire weapons and knowledge and to apply both successfully.

While the productivity of labor remained small and yielded but a slight surplus, not everyone was able to gain sufficient time and means to keep abreast of the military knowledge or the general science of his day. In fact, the surplus of many individuals was required to enable a single individual to make a perfect performance in the military or learned field.

This could not be obtained except by the exploitation of many by a few. The increased intelligence and military ability of the few enabled them to oppress and exploit the defenseless ignorant mass. On the other hand, precisely the oppression and exploitation of the mass became the means of increasing the military skill and the knowledge of the ruling classes.

Nations that were able to remain free from exploitation and oppression remained ignorant and often defenseless, as opposed to better armed and better informed neighbors. In the struggle for existence, the nations of exploiters and oppressors therefore defeated those who retained their aboriginal communism and their aboriginal democracy.

The capitalistic mode of production has so infinitely perfected the productivity of labor, that this cause for class differences no longer exists. The latter are no longer maintained as a social necessity, but merely as a result of a traditional alignment of forces, with the result that they will cease when this alignment is no longer effective.

The capitalistic mode of production itself, owing to the great surpluses created by it, has enabled the various nations to resort to a *universal military service*, thus eliminating the aristocracy of warriors. But capitalism is itself bringing all the nations of the world market into such close and permanent relations with each other that world peace becomes more and more an urgent necessity, war of any kind a piece of ruthless folly. If the capitalistic mode of production and the economic hostility between the various nations can be overcome, the state of eternal peace now desired by the great masses of humanity will become a reality. The universal peace realized by imperial despotism for the nations around the Mediterranean in the Second Century of the Christian era—the only advantage which that despotism conferred on these nations—will be realized in the Twentieth Century for the nations of the world by Socialism.

The entire basis of the opposition between the classes of warriors and non-warriors will then disappear.

But the bases of the contrast between educated and uneducated will also disappear. Only, now, the capitalistic mode of production has immensely cheapened the tools of knowledge by cheap printing, making them accessible to the masses. Simultaneously it produces an increasing demand for intellectuals, which it trains in its schools in great numbers, pushing them back into the proletariat, however, when they become more numerous. Capitalism has thus created the technical possibility for an immense shortening of the working day, and a number of classes of workers have already gained certain advantages in this direction, with more time for educational activities.

With the victory of the proletariat these germs will at once be fully developed, making a splendid reality of the possibilities of a general education of the masses that are afforded by the capitalistic mode of production.

The period of the rise of Christianity is a period of the saddest intellectual decline, of the flourishing of an absurd ignorance, of the most stupid superstition; the period of the rise of Socialism is a period of the most striking progress in the natural sciences and a speedy acquisition of knowledge by the classes under the influence of the Social-Democracy.

The class opposition arising from military training has already lost its basis; the class contrast arising from private property in the means of production will also lose its basis as soon as the political rule of the proletariat produces its effects, and the consequences of this rule will soon become evident in a decrease in the distinction between educated and uneducated, which may disappear within a single generation.

The last causes for class distinctions and class oppositions will then have ceased.

Socialism must therefore not only attain power by entirely different means than did Christianity, but it must produce entirely different effects. It must forever eliminate all class rule.

INDEX

INDEX

A

Acts of the Apostles, 341, 343, 344
Acts of the Apostle Paul, 137, 350, 351, 377, 382, 384-387, 393, 394
Æneid (Virgil), 127
Africa, 90, *see also* Carthage, Egypt, Alexandria, Memphis
Agrippa, King of Judea, 248, 249, 402
Agrippina, Roman empress, 122
Albinus, Roman governor, 303, 304
Alexander of Abonuteichos, 141, 142
Alexander· Severus, Roman emperor, 325
Alexander the Great, 142, 143, 242, 246, 250, 251, 274
Alexandria, Egypt, 124, 247, 249, 250, 251, 288, 297, 315, 316
Alkinoos, king in the Odyssey, 52
Allegories of the Law (Philo), 121
Amelius, 141
Amos, Hebrew prophet, 219
Ananias, deceiver, 331, 332, 343
Angels, 179-181
Anthony, Saint, 451
Antinoos, Greek youth, 127, 128
Antioch, ancient capital, 249, 288, 299
Anti-Semitism, 390, 391
Antonius, triumvir, 70, 113, 124
Antwerp, Belgium, 98, 199
Anubis, Egyptian god, 132
Apion of Alexandria, Jew-baiter, 141, 268, 269, 276, 315
Apis, Egyptian god, 175
Apollo, Greek god, 126
Apollonius of Tyana, 135, 136, 165, 175
Appian, historian, 54, 112, 113
Arabia, 90, 192, 194-197
Aramaic language, 258, *see also* Kaddish prayer
Areus, Alexandrian Stoic, 124
Aristophanes, 153, 154
Arnuphis, Egyptian magician, 138
Artaxerxes, Persian king, 279, 280, 287
Artisans in ancient times, 47-50, 67
Asiani company, bankers, 106
Asidæans, 282, *see also* Revelation

B

Asklepiades of Mendes, 131
Assembly of citizens, Roman, 93-95, 97
Assyria, 198, 213, 216, 220, 221, 222
Astronomy, 8, 129, *see also* Sciences
Atia, mother of Augustus, 131, 132
Augustine, Saint, 331
Augustus, Roman emperor, 81, 85, 109, 113, 124, 126-128, 131, 132, 150, 163, 164, 252, 253, 285, 361

Baal, Phœnician god, 200
Babylon, city, 98, 192, 198, 209, 213, 225, 230, 231, 234, 241, 242, 246, 288, 289
Babylonian Exile, 187, 235, 237-239, 241, 242
Bagaudi, insurrections of the, 83
Banking, in ancient times, 105, 106, *see also* Bishop, Hatch
Baptism, 264
Barabbas, murderer, 400, 403
Barnabas, 343, 385
Bauer, Bruno, 7, 32, 33, 40, 120, 125, 365, 385, 397
Bebel, August, 367
Bedouin tribes, 196, 210, 213, 298
Berlin, Germany, 87, 367, 399
Bethlehem, 361
Bishop, rise of the, 433-449
Breakfasts, Caesar's public, 109
Brutus, *see* Junius Brutus
Buddha, 176

C

Cabetists, experiments of, 451
Caesar, Julius, 80, 102, 103, 105, 106, 109, 111-113, 127, 158, 168, 249-252, 318, 319, 381
Caius Cassius, 160
Caligula, Roman emperor, 81, 125, 128, 267-270
Callistus, Roman Christian, 157, 166, 167, 352, 413
Canaan, 210, 211, 212-217, 233
Canus Julius, 125

THE END